Snow, Forest, Silence

Snow, Forest, Silence

The Finnish Tradition of Semiotics

Edited by Eero Tarasti

Assistant Editors
Paul Forsell
Richard Littlefield

Acta Semiotica Fennica VII

Indiana University Press, Bloomington
International Semiotics Institute at Imatra
1999

ACTA SEMIOTICA FENNICA
VII

Editor
Eero Tarasti

Assistant Editors
Paul Forsell
Richard Littlefield

Editorial Board

Honorary Members:
Juri Lotman †
Thomas A. Sebeok

Pertti Ahonen
Henry Broms
Jacques Fontanille
André Helbo
Marja-Liisa Honkasalo
Altti Kuusamo
Ilkka Niiniluoto

Oscar Parland †
Pekka Pesonen
Veikko Rantala
Hannu Riikonen
Kari Salosaari
Sinikka Tuohimaa
Vilmos Voigt

Indiana University Press
International Semiotics Institute
Imatra • Bloomington

This book is a publication of

Indiana University Press
601 North Morton Street
Bloomington, IN 47404-3797 USA

http://www.indiana.edu/~iupress

Telephone orders 800-842-6796
Fax orders 812-855-7931
E-mail orders iuporder@indiana.edu

Copyright 1999 by The International Semiotics Institute & Contributors

All rights reserved

Printed by Hakapaino, Helsinki 1999

ISBN 0-253-21320-7 (paperback)

1 2 3 4 5 04 03 02 01 00 99

Contents

Foreword by *Eero Tarasti* 11

GENERALITIES

Thomas A. Sebeok
   My 'Short Happy Life' in Finno-Ugric studies 16

Vilmos Voigt
   Sketch of a Finno-Ugric semiotic 26

Henri Broms
   Metaphysical contemplations – Finland and eastern thought 32

Henri Broms
   Swedish-speaking Finns between East and West 34

Thorsten Botz-Bornstein
   A mediator between Russia and the West:
   V. Sesemann as a philosopher and semiotician 41

FROM PHILOSOPHY TO CULTURE

Pauli Pylkkö
   Ontological nihilism, or, the meaning of
   the so-called Finnish passive construction 54

Kristian Bankov
   Text and intelligence 67

Heikki Kirjavainen
   Peirce, Rantala, and theological semiotics 81

Matthieu Guillot
   La neige et le silence 95

Eero Tarasti
   Finland among the paradigms of national anthems 108

Anti Randviir
   Invasion as an object of semiotics:
   Representing invasion – creating invasion 126

Niilo Kauppi
   Cultural arbitrariness and linguistic bias 136

Maarja Pärl Lõhmus
   Approaches to media semiotics: Journalism in social context 146

Viktor Shibanov
   Ethnofuturism in Udmurtia 154

SIGNS IN HUMAN BEHAVIOR

Heikki Majava
   Ethnic identity in the light of an ancient myth: Psychoanalytic
   and semiotic interpretations of the Finnish Kullervo-legend 162

Tuomo Jämsä
  Signs and meanings in education 175

Hannu Lauerma
  Inside out – from verbal imagery and
  inner voice to verbal hallucinations 192

ARTS I: MUSIC

Erkki Pekkilä
  Ethnomusicology and media reality 202

Anne Sivuoja-Gunaratnam
  Music as narrative discourse 211

Eero Tarasti
  Jean Sibelius as an icon of the Finns and others:
  An essay in post-colonial analysis 221

ARTS II: THEATER AND CINEMA

Ilkka Niiniluoto
  Film and reality 248

Henry Bacon
  Actors as characters, characters as actors in audiovisual fiction 262

Kari Salosaari
  The signs of the player: A solution 274

ARTS III: LITERATURE AND VERBAL SIGNS

Harri Veivo
    Problems of reference in description 290

Hannu Riikonen
    The lure of etymology in the poetry and prose
    of Pentti Saarikoski 303

Sinikka Tuohimaa
    Rebellious words: *Avant-garde* literature and theories
    from Formalism to Post-structuralism 314

Pirjo Kukkonen
    The Kanteletar as poetic text and discourse
    in the semiotics of culture 336

Immo Pekkarinen
    The poetic legacy of the eighties: In the home of human
    voices and touches 357

Erja Hannula
    Signs between 372

ARTS IV: GASTRONOMY

Eero Tarasti
    On culinemes, gastrophemes, and other signs of cooking 386

Contributors 404

Foreword

It has been said that science is universal, never national. This may be especially true of semiotics, "the language of international scholarship". Yet even semiotics flourishes in places that have their own unique spirit – a *genius loci* that influences the make-up and the quality of the scientific practices that take place there. Globally, it appears that semiotics is becoming more and more localized, to the degree that the semiotic approach as such is no longer a new Parisian fashion as it was in the 1960s and 70s, nor a strictly language-based research paradigm as in the early years of formalism and linguistics, nor a unified international movement of any kind. So it is natural that semiotics in such Northern areas as Finland and its neighbouring countries, or in racial terms, among the Fenno-Ugrians, has its own special "flavor" which distinguishes it from all similar enterprises in other parts of the world. Finnish semiotics of course forms part of the European scene, but it has always been open as well to developments and modifications coming from Russia and the United States. We may further assume that Finnish semiotics is no longer relatively unknown among specialists, thanks to various international symposia held regularly for some years now in Imatra and Helsinki.

We can in fact say that by now very few internationally known semioticians have *not* visited Imatra. There the International Semiotics Institute (ISI) was founded in 1988 by an international 40-member collegium to promote the "dissemination of knowledge and international mobility of students and scholars". Since then the Institute has organized scores of international symposia, seminars, and summer schools in cooperation with the Semiotic Society of Finland, The Nordic Association for Semiotics, and Toronto University's Victoria College. A little later the ISI created the international publishing series *Acta Semiotica Fennica*, in which this volume is appearing and which sometimes is distributed world-wide by Indiana University Press.

But why focus on semiotics just in Finland? Why a Finnish tradition of semiotics? Is the topic particularly worthy of such a heavy volume as this one? In *The Semiotic Sphere*, a book edited and published in 1986 by Jean Umiker-Sebeok and Thomas A. Sebeok which presented a semiotic map of the world, I wrote this about Finland: "It is hardly possible to speak yet of a Finnish school of semiotics, although conditions for the development of such a movement already exist". I must frankly admit that over ten years later, in spite of the tremendously rapid growth of semiotic studies in Finland, both in quantity and quality, I believe that a Finnish "school" of semiotics still does not yet exist, if by "school" we mean a single prevailing theoretical paradigm, a unified terminology, and an axiomatic methodology. Rather, it is more appropriate to speak about a semiotic *tradition* in Finland, though not in the pejorative sense which the composer and conductor Gustav Mahler once gave it: "*Tradition ist Schlamperei*". Tradition in our case indicates the existence of a certain community with a mutual understanding of the aims and intentions of its members, a certain society that supports the efforts of its individuals. Though we have doubts, as voiced above, about the continued existence of any one, "Great Society" in semiotics, to use the term coined by the great contemporary of Charles Sanders Peirce, Josiah Royce, then the growth and strength of smaller "societies", like that of semioticians in Finland, is a self-evident fact.

The articles in this anthology, while featuring Finnish writers, pertain not only to Finland but also reflect the international situation in which "grand narratives" no longer prevail, neither in society at large nor in semiotics. For today semiotics is made up largely of a multiplicity of smaller projects that utilize rather freely the tools offered by various schools or classics of semiotics. The emphasis in this book is therefore empirical and eclectic, with topics ranging from explicitly national issues to "universal" subjects such as the signs of media, cinema, actors, gastronomy, mental illness, language, and other fields.

Moreover, *tradition* indicates a history, and so a good deal of the articles deal with the origins of what could be called "Fenno-Ugric" semiotics. If we ask why semiotics has taken so strong a hold in Finland, one answer must be because Finland's own semiotics has such strong historical ties with international semiotic movements and paradigms. Yet who in the United States knows that Thomas A. Sebeok began his career as an anthropologist studying the culture of the Mari and

Tcheremiss peoples in Siberia, two Fenno-Ugric tribes? Who realizes that the great Lithuanian philosopher whom A. J. Greimas highly esteemed, Vassilij Seseman, was half Finnish? Who is aware of the fact that Finnish folklorists Antti Aarne and the brothers Krohn profoundly influenced the Russian formalists, Vladimir Propp among others, and thus helped to found all modern narratological research? If in the 1980s the annual meetings of the Semiotic Society of America always included a session on unknown pioneers of semiotics, this anthology continues that line.

But with a major difference: the tradition we are talking about here is a living and constantly changing reality. Finnish semiotics stays in such close contact with general developments in this science that the topics of this anthology are in a way representative of all that flies the banner of semiotics of our time. There is a saying in France and Italy that *La sagesse vient du nord,* "wisdom comes from the North". Whether or not this is true in semiotics is not for us to judge, but we should at least note that many scholars in that geographical area have devoted the major part of their energies to promoting this science. It was fashionable in the 1970s to say, "Semiotics is dead". Now, on the threshold of a new millennium, we find that we perhaps have something worthy to transmit to future scholars of meaning and communication: an intellectual heritage whose real consequences and achievements may be fully realized only in the next century.

Eero Tarasti
Helsinki, December 8, 1998

GENERALITIES

Thomas A. Sebeok

My 'Short Happy Life' in Finno-Ugric studies

My twenty years or so in Finno-Ugric (FU) studies, as reflected in my list of publications, began in 1942 and, except for a few oddments, appear to have come to an end in 1962. In later years, I did issue, responding to special requests – seldom for original work but rather for scattered reminiscences about this portion of my early academic life – some pertinent reports. Thus, in a pedagogical vein rather than intending to contribute to scholarship, I wrote in 1969 on "The Study of Finnish in the United States," and in 1992(c) on "Uralic Studies and English for Hungarians at Indiana University." More generally, in my retirement address to my colleagues at a festive convention on March 22, 1991, informally looking over my half-century academic career, I included a synoptic account of my "Finno-Ugric years" at Indiana University (1992b).

In the Fall of 1993, I was a Visiting Professor at the University of Helsinki, also lecturing at the Universities of Tampere, Turku, and Vaasa, as well as to various Finnish learned societies, including the Suomen Kirjallisuuden Seura. After my talk to this group one afternoon, a lady approached me from the audience introducing herself as having come from Ioshkar-Ola, the capital of the Mari (Cheremis) Republic in Russia, and as being a native speaker of the Cheremis language. Since, from the second half of the 1940s into the early 1960s, I had conducted an intensive study of this language and culture, then finally publishing two additional books on Cheremis subjects as recently as the 1970s (1974, 1978), she allowed that my name was well-known among her people. However, because I had published nothing more about them lately, the conclusion had been reached in Mari-land that I must have died two decades before. Determined to prove the contrary to her people, she, Dr. Lidia Tojdobekova (whom I have met with several times since), insisted on taping a lengthy "live" interview with me for transmission to and deposit in Ioshkar-Ola's archives.

Any narrative of my activities as an FU practitioner has necessarily two aspects: a private one and a public one. The latter is bound to be the more interesting, but makes little sense without the former to illuminate it. So I will begin with some personal background.

My 'Short Happy Life' in Finno-Ugric studies

In my beginning years at The University of Chicago, I had every intention of becoming a biologist, viz., a geneticist. Not to belabor my academic trajectory here, the outbreak of World War II in 1939 inexorably impelled me toward linguistics instead. My eminent professor, Leonard Bloomfield, advised me to build upon my native knowledge of Hungarian but to expand upon that base by learning as much as possible about Finnish and the other accessible languages of the family to which both of the aforementioned belonged. This was sensible advice, except for what soon loomed an insuperable quandary: none of the FU languages were taught, programmatically or otherwise, at Chicago or, as far as I could ascertain, anywhere else in the Americas. Not long before Professor Bloomfield left Chicago for Yale, he somehow found the time to read with me and critique a just-published *Outline of Hungarian Grammar*, but it soon became obvious that, were I to expand my glottal horizons in the directions he counseled, I had to fall back on my own resources and devices. The theoretically obvious option of continuing my studies somewhere in Europe was blocked by the inaccessibility of all regions, even Swedish Lappland, where FU populations were indigenous.

In 1941, I too left Chicago for the East Coast, to continue my formal studies at Princeton University, supplemented by semi-formal but demanding studies with Roman Jakobson at Columbia University and vicinity. I was also appointed civilian chief of the War Department's Hungarian and Finnish desks at one of its New York City offices, and was, moreover, busily engaged in other kinds of war work. However, before the war ended in 1945, I was able to publish, besides more than a dozen papers on FU topics, two hefty pedagogically oriented books plus a monograph constituting my doctoral dissertation. My first book, which ran to about 500 printed pages, was titled *Spoken Hungarian* (1945a), and was enhanced by twenty-five 12-inch vinylite recordings, as well as a separate *Guide's Manual*. My second book, of about the same size, was titled *Spoken Finnish* (1947a); comparable recordings accompanied it. On the bilingual recordings for my Hungarian book, the English voice was that of the American linguist, Henry Lee Smith, Jr. (d. 1972), the Hungarian my own; to the contrary, on those to go with my Finnish book, while I spoke the English parts the native voice was that of His Excellency, the Ambassador of Finland to Washington, Mr. Jutila.

In a special study I was invited to prepare at the time for the *Modern Language Journal* (1945b), I described the pedagogical and other uses to which the materials on which these twin manuals were based had been put to train a large numbers of armed personnel as well as, after the war, Foreign Service Officers of the U.S. Department of State; the books eventually became available for civilian uses in a somewhat different, commercial version and both may still be in print.

Thomas A. Sebeok

During my residency in Princeton, I frequently commuted to meet with Jakobson and to attend various lectures and colloquia he offered at several institutions in New York, including a semester he spent leading an advanced evening seminar at Columbia devoted entirely to the typology of case systems. Since case constitutes a pivotal grammatical category in several FU languages, he asked me to prepare detailed accounts of relevant materials for a series of class presentations and discerning discussion. In this way, the idea for a dissertation topic came to me, namely, to conduct an inquiry into the shape of the case system in the FU proto-language as reconstructed by a comparison of the case systems of extant daughter languages.

Jakobson urged me to establish contact with John Lotz, who was at the time Director of the Hungarian Institute (1936–1957) at the University of Stockholm. I wrote to Lotz immediately and he responded promptly. Massive correspondence and thoroughgoing exchange of ideas between us ensued, in spite of wartime delays and interruptions. "Lotz asked to see my dissertation, then offered to publish a portion of it, edited by himself. I accepted his assistance with gratitude, but asked to see my proofs. These never reached me, however, for, as we learned afterward, the ship bringing them [from Sweden] was torpedoed. The monograph was therefore published in the raw [1946] and I received my authors' copies only some two years after the war" (1989:235).

In the Spring of 1945, I received a Ph.D. from Princeton University's Department of Oriental Languages and Civilizations, with probably the first dissertation on a FU topic awarded to anyone by any North American institution; and, the following year, I joined the peacetime faculty of Indiana University. Even before the war in the Pacific drew to a close, I proposed to Herman B Wells, this institution's "visionary and international-minded President, that we immediately commence building, solidly and with an eye to permanence, upon the resources that had serendipitously accumulated here during those years. He strongly supported all such endeavors, which ultimately flowered into an amazing diversity of research, teaching, and publication schemes" (1992b:115), among which I shall concentrate here only on developments that bear directly on FU studies.

By now, it was amply clear to me that no one, anywhere in this country, could receive anything approaching adequate professional training in the full extent and depth of FU studies. I therefore resolved to proceed along two tracks simultaneously, one *personal*, the other *institutional*.

To realize my *personal* goal, I initiated conversations with the American-Scandinavian Foundation, and presented a coherent plan which would enable me to visit Sweden and Finland for three or four months in 1947 in order to:

(1) Spend as much time as was necessary to get a feel for the shape of the field, over-all, from John Lotz, who, by dint of his assignment to the University

of Stockholm since 1936, was at its sole neutral epicenter throughout the war years;

(2) Get acquainted with as many FU specialists in the Nordic countries, or, as it turned out in practice, mostly in Finland;

(3) Conduct a Summer's worth of all-out but as yet preliminary field-work among one of the FU groups of the region (I chose to settle in a Lapp speech community in Outakoski, on the Finnish shore of the Teno River across from Norway); and to

(4) Determine, in consultation with Lotz and others, to which of the extant dozen or so FU language-and-culture configurations I could most productively devote my own research energies in the decade or more ahead. For various reasons, I settled on the Cheremis (Mari), pursuing my intensive studies initially with Paavo Siro in Helsinki, thereafter moving on for some months to what turned out to be a remarkable one-on-one learning experience with the controversial but surely greatest living specialist of those times, Ödön Beke, in Budapest. (See further below.)

The American-Scandinavian Foundation approved all the facets of my application, enabling me to obtain some of the training post-doctorally that I was unable to get in my graduate years. This, however, was the lesser, personal part of my strategy, which would have been relatively worthless without the institutional part of the scheme.

To prepare the ground locally, I first submitted an internal proposal to President Wells, calling for the creation of a curricular Program in Uralic and Altaic Studies. This entity, which was rapidly approved by the Board of Trustees, grew organically out of my wartime duties and experiences.

(The term "Uralic" is a well-established linguistic concept which comprehends all of the Finno-Ugric languages plus several languages spoken in Siberia, together called Samoyedic; on the other hand, "Altaic" is a much looser areal concept. This logical incongruity notwithstanding, these two concepts are sometimes combined mainly for institutional convenience, as they were, by mutual agreement with Lotz, at both Columbia University and ourselves.)

Now armed with the authority of the Chairmanship of this new academic unit, I turned for assistance to The Rockefeller Foundation. "Fortunately," as I had reported elsewhere (1992b:7), "I had befriended an exceptionally farsighted officer..., Mr. Stevens, who most bountifully financed the launching of a sound academic program in this arcane field, then and again today uniquely featured at Indiana University, with a multi-year donation which enabled me to invite a series of senior visiting professors from Scandinavia and Finland to help give it a durable shape." The first of these visiting scholars, Björn Collinder was a Swede, and two who succeeded him, Asbjörn Nesheim and Knut Bergsland (both Lapp specialists) were Norwegians; the rest were prominent Finns: Paavo Ravila, Lauri Posti, Aimo Turunen, Osmo Ikola, and Valentin Kiparsky (a Slavists). Most of them taught in our Program for about a year, usually taking a vigorous role in building up basic resources, mainly our Library holdings. The Rockefeller Foundation and the University both provided liberal funding for stockpiling books and other research materials, which enabled me to purchase large private libraries and special collections on sale, notably, in Finland. To cite just a single example, rich materials from the heritage of Professor Yrjö Wichmann were transferred here wholesale. There were so many books available at the time that Wichmann's Hungarian widow, Julia, having wearied of preparing catalogues, preferred to sell them to me by weight – so many kilos of printed matter for a price she chose to set.

To veer from the main story-line, I should mention here that, in 1960, I inaugurated, and became the Editor for nine years of, a unique *Uralic and Altaic Series*. By 1969, when I retired as the Editor, one hundred numbered volumes had appeared, with Vol. 67 alone, however, consisting of 21 separate tomes. Contributors of Hungarian provenance – living and dead – included, *inter alia*, Péter Hajdú, Kálmán Keresztes, Béla Kálmán, Károly Rédei, Gyula Décsy, János Gulya, Stephen Erdély, Ioannes Sylvester Pannonius, Vilmos Diószegi, János Eckman, János Zsilka, Edith Vértes, László Szabó, Ferenc Kiefer, Stephen Foltinyi, György Lakó, Lajos Tamás, Erzsébet Beöthy, László Arany, Joannes Sajnovics, Sámuel Gyarmathy, Denis Sinor, Klára Magdics, Szenciensis Albertus Molnár, besides John Lotz and myself. Among the Finnish contributors were: Alexander Castrén, Lauri Hakulinen, Valter Tauli, Meri Lehtinen, Toivo Vuerela, Paavo Ravila, Elli Köngäs, and Jaako Ahokas. And among the Estonian contributors were: Ants Oras, Felix Oinas, Alo Raun, Ilse Lehiste, Paul Ariste, and George Kurman. There were also Russian, Ukrainian, Latvian, German, Swedish, French, Turkish, Mongolian, and Chinese authors, to say nothing of the dozen or more native Americans. The series enjoyed an immense domestic and world-wide popularity, with scores of volumes going out of print or achieving multiple editions. A long time afterwards, when I spent some time in Ulan Bator, I found these many volumes in the library of the Mongolian Academy of Sciences; but I was truly astonished, although not displeased, to be widely introduced by my hosts as the Editor of the series!

Returning to Paavo Ravila: he was an admirable linguistic technician, a warm human being, and a visionary organizer who returned to Finland to eventually serve as the Chancellor of the University of Helsinki. While he was at Indiana University, I proposed to him the establishment of a permanent, rotating Chair for Finnish Studies within the frame of our of Uralic and Altaic Program. Indeed, such a Chair was created, even financed, on Ravila's initiative, largely by the

Finnish government, but these fruitful arrangements were some years afterwards abrogated because of destructive internal political machinations of a later administration.

The Visiting Professors – especially the Finns, who generously shared with me facets of their vast collective scholarly expertise as well as their individual friendship – contributed to my education in varying degree. Via this unconventional route – since (to paraphrase the Russian proverb) the mountain could not come to Mahomet, a throng of Mahomets graciously came to the mountain, such having been the only practical avenue open to me in those times – I gradually secured my footing in the FU field at large. At the same time, however, I was busy forging a particular specialty on and of my own, to wit, in studies of the language and culture of a particular FU population situated mainly in the Mari Republic of the Soviet Union, better known to Western scholarship as the Cheremis. In this endeavor – having been coached as to the basics by my Finnish tutor, Siro, and thereafter guided far beyond by my Hungarian mentor Beke (see above) – I henceforth came to increasingly rely on the services of a native speaker, Ivan Jevsky.

Jevsky had fortuitously landed in the United States in February 1952. It soon became possible for me to secure the necessary funding for importing him to and supporting him in Bloomington, and to formally embark upon what became known as the Cheremis Project (under circumstances described elsewhere, e.g., in 1956:7). The attendant intensive researches, which concluded in 1963, were funded by a substantial grant from Indiana University, with additional aid, to name only some of the major contributors, from the U.S. the Department of State, Department of the Air Force, Office of Education, the Arctic, Desert, Tropic Information Center of the Research Studies Institute, located at Maxwell Air Force Base, the National Science Foundation, the American Philosophical Society, the American Council of Learned Societies, the Social Science Research Council, the John Simon Guggenheim Memorial Foundation, the Wenner-Gren Foundation for Anthropological Research, and the Newberry Library. I enumerate these in some detail to attest that, in the decades whereof I write, many U.S. funding agencies – Federal, State, and private – were concerned with the national development of not just FU studies in general but such specialized branches of it as Cheremis studies.

A deserter from the Red Army to a German camp from which he was in due course "liberated" by advancing American forces, a semi-literate barber by trade, Jevsky was the first member of his culture and the first speaker of his language ever to have come to this Continent; beside his native Cheremis, Jevsky spoke only some Tatar and a little Russian. Although, by and large, he cooperated with my team of assistants and students cheerfully enough, he complained with some regularity that "work with the head is almost unbearably fatiguing as opposed to work with hand." He seemed relieved to finally be allowed to revert to his tonsorial slog at the conclusion of our dedicated undertaking.

Some half a dozen students participated in the Cheremis project, three of them (one a Finn, Eeva K. Minn) earning their doctorates with dissertations on relevant topics. In 1952, I launched and edited a mini-series, *Studies in Cheremis*, in which eleven volumes, by members of the faculty or advanced graduate students at Indiana University, appeared before the series petered out 26 years afterwards (for a list, see 1978:5). I should also mention that, in the course of some half a dozen professional trips to the Soviet Union in the 1950s and 1960s, I managed to purchase hundreds of books published in the Mari Republic, anything from grade school textbooks to technical training manuals to novels and poetry to transcribed folklore texts of various genres, etc. I eventually donated this unique stockpile to the Indiana University Libraries, along with my entire FU collection, which included not only hundreds of grammars, dictionaries, and the like, but complete bound runs of practically every journal series, both Hungarian and Finnish, in the field, plus many items from Soviet times and well before.

It would be erroneous to conclude from the foregoing account that FU studies constituted my exclusive academic preoccupation during the twenty years covered here. In addition to a host of articles having to do with the Cheremis and other FU groups and their languages, I wrote, as early as 1951, several papers eventuating from parallel investigations of a language spoken by the Aymará, a large community of Indians in Bolivia. Among the latter, I compiled a sizeable collection of materials for a modern dictionary (1951). And, as far back as the mid–1940s, I had conducted extensive field work, under the auspices of the Cranbook Academy, among the Winnebago, a Siouan population in the Green Bay area of Wisconsin (see, e.g., 1947b).

By the mid–1950s, I was also, and remained for more than a decade to come, thickly involved in collaborative work, under the auspices of the Social Science Research Council, with several colleagues in psychology and linguistics (1954) – but this is not the place to recount these attendant experiences. Furthermore, during the 1950s and 1960s, I became engaged in problems of stylistics, along with Lotz, Jakobson, I.A. Richards, and a host of others, including several prominent psychologists (1960). This aspect of my work is particularly relevant here because it served as one bridge – although I was not explicitly aware of it being so at the time – between my fading efforts in the FU field on the one hand and my fumbling entry into the domain of general semiotics on the other. Let me briefly describe one such Janus-like project, which resulted in a major – although, for FU studies, a highly unconventional – book: the *Concordance and Thesaurus of Cheremis Poetic Language,* which became simultaneously the eighth in the Studies in Cheremis series (1961).

As a part of the Cheremis project over-all, I had assembled a rather large corpus of about 1,200 folksong texts, which I began to analyze off and on throughout 1958–59, while I was in residence at the Department of Anthropology of the University of Arizona and a Fellow of the John Simon Guggenheim Memorial Foundation. Then, for 1960–61, I was unexpectedly appointed a Fellow of the Center for Advanced Study in the Behavioral Sciences, with absolutely no restrictions as to my activities there. In consquence of this total freedom, my year's stay at the Center had a momentous, if unforeseen, effect on the remainder of my scholarly career. While, on the one hand, I saw this as a singular opportunity to strike out in a wholly novel research direction – to examine how animals communicate – I also felt bound to finish up, albeit in an innovative way, the analysis of the corpus of folksong texts I had been working on for the past few years.

As to the latter, I was fortunate to be accompanied to the Center by one of my "Postdocs," the late V. J. Zeps, supported by two consecutive grants I obtained for him from the National Science Foundation for "Computer Research in Psycholinguistics." Zeps was a member of my team which had worked with Ivan Jevsky, but his true talents and inspired enthusiasms lay in computational linguistics, these at the dawn of the era – almost forty years ago – when such predilections and preoccupations became the rage. Zeps was a quintessential hacker *au pied de la lettre,* who conceived and implemented our programs. Based on an empirical exploration of large quantities of Cheremis verse and other such devices in the light of considerations of problems of poetic language in the widest sense, this investigation was, for its time, a pioneering effort in the automatic compilation of concordances and related scholarly tools with a then-state-of-the-art IBM 650 electronic data processing system, equipped with four magnetic tape units, three index accumlators, and a host of separate peripheral equipment. While the over-all design of and prose passages in the resulting book (finished on New Year's Eve in 1960) were mine, Zeps accomplished most of the computational work, thus becoming its junior author. Perhaps not surprisingly, this particular work of ours was greeted with complete silence by all FU media – who, after all, would have been competent to review it?

Over a decade, I faithfully attended international congresses of FU studies, for instance, in Helsinki (1965), Tallinn (1970), and Budapest (1975); in due course, I was even elected to represent the United States on the world-wide body that was responsible for organizing them. At each of these conventions I gave a paper on some traditional topic, most often on a Cheremis theme. However, at the Budapest congress I decided to tackle a seemingly unfamiliar subject: in my presentation I argued that since human beings communicate amongst each other by both verbal and non-verbal means – indeed, according to some scholars (notably John Lotz), most messages by far are transmitted non-verbally – it would be instructive to scrutinize the non-verbal behavior of each extant FU population and to juxtapose this with their corresponding verbal behavior as well as to compare every system with every other. There was of course nothing radical about this research proposal, which was implemented with rich multiple inflections by ancient orators and actors (Hamlet: "Suit the action to the word, the word to the action"); which in "the systematic use of gesture speech" so assiduously explored Garrick Mallery among North American Indian tribes in the 1880s; which David Efron, the Argentinian PhD of Franz Boas, famously carried out in the 1930s in his exemplary comparison of facial expressions and body movements among Italian and Jewish immigrants in New York City; and by countless others (1991:27–32). Notwithstanding a highly respectable pedigree for probes of this sort, the reception for my Budapest overtures of over two decades ago was so uncompromisingly frosty that I knew, for me, a change of venue became henceforth mandatory.

My paramount preoccupation at the Center for Advanced Study started out with a youthfully naive premise. As I have noted elsewhere, I always considered myself a biologist *manqué* – a student who, frustrated by World War II, had missed his true vocation. So, having been told by Ralph Tyler, the Center's Director, to spend my time during my residence doing what I liked, I mistakenly imagined that I could, in a single year, "catch up" with developments in the life sciences over the past twenty years. Soon I was so overburdened that I had to strictly confine my readings to a narrow segment of biology. The wedge of this pie I settled on was ethology, the biological study of behavior, which led me straight to a review of the literature on animal communication.

Readings in this domain led me to formulate the following abduction: the attentive, empirically founded, study of communication systems in the other animals will clarify fundamental questions about the evolution of language in hominids. By way of a series of publications since then (periodically collected, e.g., in 1972, 1980, 1990), I satisfied myself that this hypothesis has been *falsified*. Nonetheless, this literature, supplemented by my own observations of animals in the wild and in captivity, led me, through multifarious fascinating detours and occasional blind alleys, to develop what I regard as my principal contribution to general semiotics, the field which I (and now many others) call Biosemiotics (1992a). That, however, is a convoluted story that would carry us far beyond – in Ernest Hemingway's evocative 1936 attribution to Francis Macomber – my "short happy life."

My 'Short Happy Life' in Finno-Ugric studies

Selected references

1945a Spoken Hungarian. New York: Henry Holt.
1945b Linguist, Informant and Units. *Modern Language Journal* 29.376–381.
1946   *Finnish and Hungarian Case Systems: Their Form and Function.* Stockholm: Acta Instituti Hungarici Universitatis Holmiensis, Series B, Linguistica 3.
1947a *Spoken Finnish.* New York: Henry Holt.
1947b Two Winnebago Texts. *International Journal of American Linguistics* 13:167–170.
1950   The Meaning of "Ural-Altaic." *Lingua* 2:124–139.
1951   Materials for an Aymará Dictionary, Journal de la Société des Américanistes 40:89–151.
1954   *Psycholinguistics: A Survey of Theory and Research Problems.* Supplement to the *Journal of Abnormal and Social Psychology* 49:4.2. [With C.E. Osgood, et al.]
1956   *The Supernatural: Studies in Cheremis 2.* Viking Fund Publications in Anthropology No. 22. New York: Wenner-Gren Foundation for Anthropological Research. [With Frances J. Ingemann.]
1960   *Style in Language.* New York: John Wiley. [Ed. and co-author.]
1961   *Concordance and Thesaurus of Cheremis Poetic Language: Studies in Cheremis 8.* 'S-Gravenhage:Mouton & Co. [With Valdis J. Zeps.]
1962   Sources for a Mari Chrestomathy. *Ural-Altaische Jahrbücher* 34:26–40.
1969   The Study of Finnish in the United States. In: *The Finns in North America: A Social Symposium* 170–174. East Lansing: Michigan State University Press (for Suomi College).
1972   *Perspectives in Zoosemiotics.* The Hague: Mouton.
1974   *Structure and Texture: Selected Essays in Cheremis Verbal Art.* The Hague: Mouton.
1978   *Cheremis Literary Reader With Glossary: Studies in Cheremis 10.* Louvain: Editions Peters.
1980   *Speaking of Apes: A Critical Anthology of Two-Way Communication with Man.* New York: Plenum Press. [With Jean Umiker-Sebeok, et al.]
1989   John Lotz: A Personal Memoir; & Parasitic Formations and Kindred Semiotic Sets: Notes on the Legacy of John Lotz. In: *The Sign & Its Masters* 2 231–252. Lanham: University Press of America.
1990   *Essays in Zoosemiotics.* Toronto: Toronto Semiotic Circle.
1991   *American Signatures: Semiotic Inquiry and Method.* London: University of Oklahoma Press.
1992a *Biosemiotics.* Berlin: Mouton de Gruyter. [With Jean-Umiker Sebeok, et al.]
1992b Into the Rose-Garden. *Ural-Altaische Jahrbücher* 64: 1–12.
1992c Uralic Studies and English for Hungarians at Indiana University: A Personal View. *Hungarian Studies* 7:1/2:149–152.

Vilmos Voigt

Sketch of a Finno-Ugric semiotic

Within the domain of Finno-Ugric studies, semiotics has appeared only during the past few decades as a special field of research. Important works taking a semiotic point of view have been published in linguistics, literary studies, musicology, art history, cultural analysis, psychology, folklore and sociology, and so on. Detecting the signs in different Finno-Ugric cultures became a fashionable topic. The international acceptance of Finnish, Hungarian, and Estonian semiotics has been overwhelming. But we know relatively little about the semiotics among other Finno-Ugric peoples. Historical-research surveys have appeared relatively frequently; but until recently there was no attempt to summarize the scope and prospects of "Finno-Ugric semiotics". About thirty years ago Thomas A. Sebeok in a lecture before a Helsinki University audience spoke on the necessity of collecting data of non-verbal behaviour among the Finno-Ugric peoples, including their sign systems. But this lecture remained unpublished, and without direct results.

If we want to give a short sketch of Finno-Ugric semiotics, the following main topics should be presented:

1. Finno-Ugric background of native semiotic terms

Hungarian *jel/jegy*, the basic term in semiotics, occurs in historical manuscripts from 1416/1224 on. It means "sign", and medieval sources contain verbs or derivatives from it in their scholarly references. For example, in a Dominican codex, *Sermones Dominicales* (1456–1470), we read the following, quite explicit Latin gloss: "Et hoc vobis i.e. signatum vel pro signo *Jel* signum", where the correct and erudite Latin terms deserve the most attention. It is a well known fact that in the *Magyar Encyclopaedia* by János Apáczai Csere (1653) we could trace a highly developed classification and terminology of signs in Hungarian. The most striking feature is that the words used in Hungarian for semiosis are not from the common European (Graeco-Latin) vocabulary, but refer to older strata in the language. Hungarian (TESZ II: 270) and Finno-Ugric etymological dictionaries

(UEW I: 2, 91) agree that *jel/jegy* can be derived from the Finno-Ugric **jälke*, "footprint", and thus belong to the vocabulary of an ancient culture of hunters (see my summary article, Voigt 1990). In other Finno-Ugric languages we do not find such old words used today as semiotic terms. Finnish *merkki* or Estonian *märgi (süsteemi)* are recently coined forms with a non Finno-Ugric background. In other Finno-Ugric languages the analogous terms are quite new ones, too.

2. Semantic development and recent status of terms denoting the "scientific study of signs" from a Finno-Ugric perspective

Following the development and terminology of international semiotics, *semiootika* has been invented recently, as a term from the 1960s which originated from Russian terminology at the same time. Somewhat later Finnish *semiotiikka* appeared, following the main international semiotic trends and terms. This term is from the Anglo-German-Russian tradition (not from the French), and does not represent (with some exceptions) the form *sémiologie*, despite the very close contacts of Finnish semioticians with the French schools.

Somewhat earlier, Hungarian *szemiotika* was used as a scholarly term. It came directly from Russian (more precisely, from early works of the Moscow-Tartu school) but had an international frame of reference, and with some regard to older usage. The Hungarian equivalent, *jeltudomány*, is understandable, but it does not exist in everyday use. The Hungarian term finally belongs to the American (Peircean) tradition, but coloured with Russian intermediary reasoning. In other Finno-Ugric languages we could not find a special term for semiotics or for the study of signs in general usage that is not a direct translation from Russian. In sum, in the Finno-Ugric languages, *semiotika* and not the *sémiologie* form became the generally accepted term.

It is an important task to describe the semantic development of the terms for "semiotics" in all Finno-Ugric languages, with special emphasis on their origin and differences. Unfortunately, no such summarizing attempts exist.

3. Recent "schools", "trends", and "circles" in Finno-Ugric semiotics, and their research history

From the mid-sixties on in Estonia the Tartu-Moscow School has been in operation, initiated by Yury Lotman in Tartu. Other Soviet scholars (from outside Estonia) played a major role, yet an Estonian ambiance has always surrounded activities of the School. Recent summaries of the history of that school give the first glimpse into the history of Estonian semiotics, too (see my review, "In memoriam of 'Lotmanosphere' "; Voigt 1995).

In Hungary only some years later, around 1968, structural studies in linguistics and literature, plus the search for models in folklore, mass communication, and cultural phenomena were grouped into a special circle that drew upon semiotic terminology and concepts. Informal (but not persecuted) groups, projects, conferences, and publications also embraced terms and methods of semiotics. Since then semiotics in Hungary has thrived and has gained a positive international response. On the other hand, there is no "Hungarian school" of semiotics. Hungarian semioticians have worked in Yugoslavia, Romania, and Czechoslovakia, and we have kept regular contact with Hungarian semioticians living in the United States, France, Italy, and so on.(The only introduction to semiotics in Hungary is still my old booklet, *Bevezetés a szemiotikába* Budapest, 1977; an updated version is in preparation.)

After a few predecessors, Eero Tarasti started the Finnish Semiotic Society in 1979. The first group of Finnish semioticians came out of late French structuralism and also had contacts with the Tartu school. The membership of that society and the scope of its interests grew fast, and by now Finnish semiotics is the best organised nation-wide trend in Europe, having gained all possible international acceptance. Later, between 1985–1988, the International Semiotics Institute (in Imatra) became a well-known forum, and in recent years it has been organizing an international summer school of semiotics. The Finnish Semiotic Society and the International Semiotics Institute maintain extensive contacts with Estonian, Soviet, Nordic, American, French, and other schools. Semiotics in Finland is many faceted: semiotics of music, literature and theatre, film and art, semiotics of culture and personality. Symposia very often deal with the characteristics of Finnish people and culture. It is interesting to observe in Finland the gap that exists between semioticians who follow very contemporary themes and models (marketing, information theory, politics), and traditional scholars (as e.g., linguists), who do not use the vocabulary and ideas of semiotics.

The best introduction to current Finnish semiotics is the famous interdisciplinary journal *Synteesi*, in publication since 1982; Eero Tarasti's book *Johdatusta semiotiikkaan* (1990); and a collection of the Finnish Semiotic Society newsletters for the years 1979–1991, edited by Tarasti and entitled *Merkkien kronikka* (Imatra, 1991). My remarks on Finnish semiotics can seen in my reviews of the aforementioned books in the journal *Semiotica* (1995).

The success of Finnish semiotics can be contrasted with other Finno-Ugric cultures, Estonia and Hungary excluded, which seem to have no particular semiotical school or trend – at least at this time and according to our current information.

At the Finno-Ugric congresses in both Debrecen (1990) and Jyväskylä (1995), Komi ethnographers and mythologists declined the usage of semiotic terms and concepts. As N. Konakov wrote at the 1992 Imatra ISI meeting, Komi (Zyrian) semiotics considers the works by A. Sidorov (from 1924 on), L. Gribova (from 1968 on), V. Semenov, N. Chesnokova, and D. Nesanelis as its predecessors. In September 1991, the third all-republic meeting, "Death as a Phenomenon of Culture – Komi Seminar of Culture", was held in Syktyvkar. At the Eleventh Annual Meeting of the Semiotic Society of Finland (Imatra, 13–19 July 1992) a session on the "Semiotics of Nature and Culture of the Komi Zyrians" was organized by Jouko Seppänen and Nikolai Konakov, consisting of four papers and an introduction in which Konakov declared their affiliation with the Tartu school. In the papers presented the terminology of semiotics occurs very rarely, thus giving the reviewers no possibility for further comment. The descriptive papers by N. D. Konakov, P. F. Limerov, O. Uljaschov, and V. Sharapov were published in the collection of essays, *On the Borderlines of Semiosis* (Tarasti 1993: 121–146).

Finally, one wonders whether in the lost manuscript by Gerd Kuzebaj (1898–1937) from 1922–25, on Udmurtian ornaments we could not see another (Udmurt) forerunner of Finno-Ugric ethnosemiotics.

(I do not list here the "foreign" scholars, who as early as from the nineteenth century have described signs used among the Finno-Ugric peoples, but without using properly semiotic terminology. It should also be mentioned that during the 1950s Thomas A. Sebeok utilised structural analysis to describe the genres of Cheremis folklore.)

4. Future tasks and perspectives

From the 1960s to the 1990s was the "new golden age" of semiotics in Europe, America, and elsewhere. Today its institutions are stable, even though most of the pioneer semioticians have died. Now we are witnessing the "silver age" of international semiotics, as new centres and schools appear, while others (e.g., from France) disappear. The Tartu-Moscow school in its original form no longer exists. Hungarian semiotics remains as loose a formation as ever, and Finnish semiotics has become one of the leading groups in the whole world. Hopefully the coming years will bring fresh new semiotic impulses from other Finno-Ugric peoples as well.

International cooperation among Finno-Ugric semioticians is not a new phenomenon. They have known of each other's work, and for many years Finnish and Hungarian semioticians, as well as Finnish and Estonian semioticians, have regularly held joint meetings. In May 1997 the Nineteenth Finnish-Hungarian semiotic symposium was held in Budapest. (About the previous meetings there are some reports, collected into a small private publication called *Valami más Proceedings of the Finno-Hungarian Semiotic Symposia 1985–95 Helsinki – Budapest*, edited by Henri Broms (1995), a second volume of which appeared in 1997.)

For future tasks and perspectives we should suggest first of all a better exchange of information. Perhaps the International Semiotics Institute in Imatra could regularly collect and disseminate information on Finno-Ugric semiotics. Along with bi- or tri-lateral symposia, there could be a multinational Finno-Ugric semiotic symposium, too. Existing journals or other series of publications could edit special issues devoted to Finno-Ugric semiotics. International congresses of Finno-Ugrists would offer excellent opportunities for the organisation of special sessions devoted to signs and sign systems.

Though to complete a "Handbook of Finno-Ugric Semiotics" seems today to be a difficult task, we might hope to have one in the not too distant future. If one could develop a good framework for it, and if we could get good experts for writing the chapters from most of the Finno-Ugric peoples, then perhaps for the next Finno-Ugrists Congress a handbook could prove to be a possible project.

International semiotics has not realized until now the existence of Finno-Ugric semiotics. The best handbook of the recent history of semiotics is *The Semiotic Sphere*, edited by Thomas A. Sebeok and Jean Umiker-Sebeok, and it contains articles arranged according to countries. Eero Tarasti wrote on Finland, and myself on Hungary. The chapter "Semiotics in the U. S. S. R." was written by an American Slavist, Stephen Rudy, who described mainly the Moscow-Tartu school, even mentioned the fact that it includes non-Russian participants. The chapters were written more than twelve years ago, thus a new, updated version would be welcome that takes into account other Finno-Ugric peoples. And, of course, as its authors, we should need productive semioticians from several Finno-Ugric peoples.

In closing let me say that it is a very optimistic achievement that between 26–28 November 1998 in Germany (!), Berlin, and Frankfurt there will take place the next Finnish-Hungarian Semiotic Symposium on the semiotics of culture. And, following my official suggestion, the next International Congress of Finno-Ugric Studies (Congressus Nonus Internationalis Fenno-Ugristarum Tartu, 7–13 August 2000) will feature a special symposium on Finno-Ugric semiotics.

Good prospects, finally!

Literature

Broms, Henri (ed.) (1995). *Valami más Proceedings of the Finno-Hungarian Semiotic Symposia 1985–95 Helsinki – Budapest*. Helsinki: n.p.
– (ed.) (1997). *Valami egészen más Proceedings of the Finno-Hungarian Semiotic Symposia 1996–97*. Vol. 2. Helsinki: n.p.

Sebeok, Thomas A. and Umiker-Sebeok, Jean (eds.) (1986). *The Semiotic Sphere*. New York: Plenum Press.
Tarasti, Eero (1990). *Johdatusta semiotiikkaan* [Introduction to semiotics]. Helsinki: Gaudeamus.
– (1991). *Merkkien kronikka* [Chronicle of signs]. Imatra, Finland: International Semiotics Institute.
– (1993) (ed.). *On the Borderlines of Semiosis*. (= Acta Semiotica Fennica II.) Imatra, Finland: International Semiotics Institute.
TESZ (A magyar nyelv történeti-etimológiai szótára) (1970). Vol. II. Editor-in-Chief L. Benkó. Budapest: Akadémiai Kiadó.
UEW (Uralisches Etymologisches Wörterbuch) (1992). Vol. I. Editor-in-Chief K. Rédei. Budapest: Akadémiai Kiadó.
Voigt, Vilmos (1977). *Bevezetés a szemiotikába* Budapest: Gondolat.
– (1990). Auf den Spuren einer uralischen (Vor) Semiotik Specimina. *Sibirica* 3: 241–250.
– (1995). "In memoriam of 'Lotmanosphere' ". *Semiotica* 105(3–4): 191–206.

Henri Broms

Metaphysical contemplations – Finland and eastern thought

European nations show their different natures in their reactions to economic recession. Many Finnish journalists who are busy watching premonitions of destruction keep one eye on Germany at the same time. They share the old Germany-belief: "Ille faciet" – Germany will do it, Germany will pull us out!

Two years ago in Munich I was looking at a picture book about the German economic miracle. There was a picture of the remains of the Herder Bookshop in totally destroyed Munich. The old shopkeeper had stripped off his tie and rolled up his sleeves, and the whole family had begun to collect bricks and to build a new house and shop, bnck by brick. This is what you do when you focus all your attention on the job in hand.

Is the German working method unshakeably logical? Another view of Germany: a field within a city, a wide and empty area, yet with traffc lights in the middle. In France I had learnt that traffc lights were more or less symbolic, to be obeyed when it was sensible. But the Germans stood stolidly waiting for the light to change. I started crossing the road against the red light. Someone immediately shouted "Schweinhund" ('filthy swine') at me.

The West Germans were filled with this unshakable logic when they opened their arms to East Germany. "Sure we can put her back on her feet," it was thought. According to the Frankfurter Allgemeine and Helmut Kohl's speeches, the beginning of 1991 was to see East Germany's miraculous rise.

To Finns the recession came as a complete surprise, with the effect of an unexpected punch that stops a heavyweight boxer. Now we wait and wonder what is going to happen, while the daily press goes on moaning. The French are complete fatalists. The recession gets amazingly little coverage in Le Figaro. The Frenchman remains bon vivant, eats well, moves swiftly and elegantly in his social circles.

Are these national differences real or have I only been telling funny stories?

Certainly there are differences, and – as the Romantics believed – they may lie in the language. Professor Andre Laurent of INSEAD has studied the differences between management styles. He calls Americans, Germans and the English low-context nations. This means that they do not allow any side issues, trivialities, to interfere with what they are doing; they concentrate on what is right under their noses. These people take everything literally and do not go for interpretation: a man is expected to mean what he says. They deal with one issue at a time.

High-context nations – the French, the Italians, the Middle East and Asian people – are quite different. They take regulations symbolically, "interpreting" even traffic lights. A Frenchman's café is his world. There everyone gets service, at least a little, at the same time. But at an Arab bank simultaneous service, carrying on with many things at the same time, reaches its maximum efficiency. "Here's your receipt; now what was your problem? give it to me; you take this money..."

I suspect Finland also to be a high-context country where people are concerned with side issues and read between lines. The Russians did manage to easternize Estonia and energetic East Germany, but did they also discover the Eastern element in us Finns? At least we are masters at reading between lines (cf. the Treaty of Friendship, Co-operation and Mutual Assistance), just as we are experts in the "Russian business practices" (a day on the booze).

Maybe even Stalin will some day be presented as a great Asian prophet. He byzantinized and orientalized large parts of Europe, filled them with readers between lines and listeners to special signals, made them into high-context areas ruled by rumour, centres of sloth and Oblomovism. Milan Kundera in his much debated article "The Tragedy of Central Europe" (*New York Review of Books*, April 26, 1984) says that "The old Central-Eastern Europe with Habsburg culture does not exist any more. The area was engulfed with Soviet obscupant practises, that have left a mark on them."

Are we too inside that oriental magic circle? Or did the potent German influence of the "jaeger" movement[1] (and the centuries-old Swedish influence) manage to westernize us? Were the 20's and 30's a period of great Spenglerian initiation rites during which Finland developed a western, Faustian ego, whose existence we would ultimately prove to ourselves in the wars?

Note

1. Finnish youngsters were trained in Germany in 1915–1918, and played an important role in the birth of independent Finland.

Henri Broms

Swedish-speaking Finns between East and West

Reflections on Oscar Parland's "Tieto ja eläytyminen. Esseitä ja muistelmia" (Reason and Empathy. Essays and Reminiscences). Helsinki: WSOY, 1991

The latest book by Oscar Parland, psychiatrist, author and semiotician, is probably his principal work in non-fiction. It is a collection of essays, from someone who has previously been known as a Swedish-language novelist (*Metamorphoses* 1945; *The Enchanted Way* 1953, Engl. translation; *The Year of the Bull* 1962, Engl. translation). The book is subtitled "Essays and Reminiscences", although "essay" is perhaps not the best word to describe it. Essay-writing is sometimes associated with some sort of witty, intellectual column-writing, but this book carries a heavier weight.

Since we are dealing with a semiotician (Oscar Parland's contribution to the development of Finnish semiotics is well known), we could attempt an analysis of the book based on two different communication methods, as defined by Lotman. One form of communication is to convey factual information to the audience; the other is the method employed by art, communication through internal meditation, food for the soul and inspiration. Both of these sides, a scientist searching for facts and an inspiring artist, are present in this book.

Vasilius Sesemann[1]

Parland's book contains a great deal of information that is entirely new to many Finnish readers. We thought we knew the history of our philosophy, but Parland brings on stage an important Finnish philosopher whose name was totally strange to me. This person is Oscar Parland's uncle, Vasilius Sesemann.

Oscar Parland has given a few lectures on him for the Finnish Semiotics Society. We just did not know before that Finland, too, had a Gulag philosopher – and among the first generation of formalists, which might be of special interest to semioticians. It is typical of the mystery around Sesemann's person that we cannot read his principal work because it was written in Lithuanian! There have been attemps to have it translated, but so far no translator with a sufficient proficiency in Lithuanian has been found.

After the Russian civil war, in 1921, Vasilius Sesemann followed the Parland family and moved to Helsinki, to Kilo. He was a professional philosopher, to whom Finland offered nothing, not even a docentship as an academic form of charity. His degree from St. Petersburg was misinterpreted by the Department of Philosophy at the University of Helsinki, so he moved to Lithuania in 1923 and became a professor of philosophy. In 1950 he was sent to the Gulag Archipelago, and these brutal events are described in the book with an impact which could best be described as monumental.

In 1950, a young member of the MVD, the Lithuanian Secret Police (where do all these Quislings come from?) enters Sesemann's study. A quiet but intense discussion goes on for a couple hours behind locked doors, and Mrs. Sesemann thinks that her husband is examining some students in there – but no. When the door opens this philosopher, not even a Soviet but a Finnish citizen, leaves for Siberia for a long stretch of time, 15 years.

I for one did not know we were so close to the East that – horrible though it sounds – we too have our share of this new form of stoicism, Gulag literature! It is Gulag literature that lends Estonians and Russians that nearly saint-like glow which hardly any Westem writer can hope for. This may sound cynical but is not meant to be so. See for example how the new Estonian journal Akadeemia deals with their own Gulag literature.This theme has placed Solzhenitsyn in the class of people possessing special knowledge, that is moral philosophers, where indeed Sesemann also belongs. Sesemann's Siberian quotations are samples of an astounding Finnish literature.

> When I think of the past I would like to associate it with you, my dear; from you I do not only want support for my memory but also a harmony of souls for the moments when vivid pictures of the past are revived. How nice it would be if we could relive all the most important moments of our life together, have them running like a film in front of our eyes! Wouldn't it? (Vasilius Sesemann, writing to his wife from the prison camp.)

Sesemann's theories as introduced by Parland bear witness to the existence of two kinds of knowledge, rational and intuitive. Parland associates these categories of knowledge with the influence of Sesemann's teachers N.O. Lossky, Husserl and Bergson.

Indeed, the theory of two knowledges was typical of the formalists, Sesemann's contemporaries. Polivanov referred to the existence of two different languages and believed that research should be done on mumbling, soliloquy, somniloquy and child language. Jakobson further clarihed the notion of two different languages, carefully defining the synchronic and diachronic functions of language (for example in his *Poetics and Linguistics*). In his Freudianism, Bakhtin discusses the existence of two different consciousnesses, official and unoffcial (the subconscious).

Up against Communism, the formalists had to reject the notion of art as symbolic knowledge. Since Sesemann knew some important formalists well, at least Zhirmunsky, he probably observed Russian theorists carefully even after the revolution.

> According to Sesemann, only "Wissen" – understanding through experience – and not "Erkenntnis", understanding based on reason, changes us internally and expands our self- knowledge, enriching it with new experiential material which we can really absorb. This is an age-old psychological fact, known to religions, philosophies and Oriental doctrines, and for instance modern psychoanalysis and Zen Buddhism also make use of it. This is the reason why an artistic performance is so overwhelmingly more effective than a scientific report. This is also the basis of Socrates' famous maxim: "Know yourself!." (Oscar Parland on Sesemann s thinking.)

Henry Parland

This leads us to the other central character in the book, Oscar Parland's author-brother Henry, who died young. Sesemann personally contributed to the establishment of formalism, the glory of Russian philosophy. He also introduced his nephew to formalistic ideas so effectively that young Henry became a genuine formalist, too.

Later Stalin expelled the formalists, who emigrated to Prague en masse and went on working on their theories at about the same time as Henry Parland. Later they contributed to the emergence of New Criticism, semiotics and structuralism in the West. But for the emigration of these philosophers we might have come to know Henry Parland as the first formalist of all Western countries.

The book reveals many new features about Henry Parland, once again astonishing the reader with the precocity of this young man. Charlotte Bühler sometimes used the term *Kurzleben*, 'short life', which seems precisely to apply to Henry Parland.After a bohemian period in Helsinki he was sent to his uncle in Lithuania to calm down. With his extraordinary assimilative talent he understood the Russian formalists his uncle introduced to him. For example, Henry Parland's film essays show that he also saw the long-range potential of formalism, including the semiotic notion of two cultures.

We may ask ourselves: how was it possible for this precocious boy to comprehend the basic doctrine of a new scientific school which remained a closed book to contemporary professional scholars in Finland? Henry Parland was able to perceive formalism as if it had been a new explanation of the world. He sensed how adequately formalism explained the century of technology, including all sectors of its culture. He realized (as in particular his film essays indicate) that this was a cultural explanation. (Formalism went beyond its own time, reaching over the generation of great French structuralists of the 50's to the present surge of American semiotics.)

Oscar Parland's book depicts Henry's year in Lithuania in a new light. Henry's revelries are amusingly commented on: "Without a sign of repentance, which our parents expected, Henry defiantly continued his maniac pub-crawling until the very day of his departure, if possible with an ever-increasing intensity... He claimed that some kind of 'spinning and engulfing' philosophy cancelled every purpose of existence and gave him the right to live his life as a farce." This comment on brother Henry also gives us a taste of the humour contained in Oscar Parland's book.

Ontology and methodology of internationalism?

I believe that we need the methods of mythological research in order to grasp the greatest merit of the book, its internationalism.

What kind of international emotional environment does the book reflect? There are so many different forms of internationalism. The first thing that catches the reader's attention is the multilingualness of the Parland family. But the Parlands are international in other senses as well.

The reader immediately becomes conscious of the strong but intangible feeling of internationalism in the book.There is a semiotic notion which might help us to explain this feeling, namely, AlttiKuusamo's notion of homotypia and heterotypia. Some writers clearly represent just one nationality to the very core. Traditional Finnish literature is largely written by authors of this type, for example Sillanpää (cf. Aarne Laurila's article in LEIF 3/91). Our tradition of folk life description represents homotypia, similarity, although varied within itself.

Other writers are capable of passing on messages from foreign cultures to their own, otherwise monolingual culture, which in itself is an entire coherent world.

What this second kind of writer does is to match two worlds without any common denominator, joining two elements that would generally not be expected to match. This is heterotypia, a phenomenon which may underlie the international atmosphere that Parland's book breathes. Knowing foreign languages is not always enough for promoting internationalization within a culture: apart from languages you also need heterotypia, sensitivity to the originality of an alien culture.

Foreign languages are mastered by many, but who could have brought Russian cultural influences and phenomena closer to Finns than Parland did?

This is a very bad time for predictions, but there is one prophesy that still has some credibility. Let us accept here a pinch of Spengler's and Friedell's cultural mythology, which alone can reveal the symbols of cultures, the underlying powers! Friedell, Spengler and Rilke held that light would come from the Orient. To some extent this belief has come true in the samizdat literature and science of Russian and East European dictatorships. There is meditation tried by severe hardships, and there is a new, internally moral man. We are not referring to Solzhenitsyn alone but also to Havel and Göncz.

But there also exists a more easily conceivable easternness, which is generally associated with St. Petersburg and the Karelian Isthmus, and a closely related cultural tradition which easily absorbs international and modern influences. The works of all the Parlands, especially the book under review, seem to carry on that particular tradition. Both the author himself with his new psychoanalytical ideas, and likewise his brother Henry as a pre-semiotician, are responsible for the modernistic features.

These elements of difference and foreign culture explain why Parland's book brings a different, St. Petersburgian world – albeit in a fennicized form – into our own, otherwise "different" world. The book is about Finnish citizens, although at times you might find this hard to believe.

Topical questions currently and repeatedly asked at seminars are: what is Eastern Europe? What instrument is it going to play in the European symphony orchestra? We might answer: moral values, hardened in the fight against the gulags, internationalism and universalism, hardened in the same fight.

The discord between East European nations may well continue. But Edith Södergran and the Parland brothers have succeeded in combining three cultures (Russian, Finnish, Swedish-speaking Finnish) in a higher understanding, which rises above journalistic and political conflicts.

Turn to the West: on the virtues of Swedish-speaking Finns

Let us now forget about the easternness of Parland's book for a while and look at a cultural phenomenon which was very well expressed by an art exhibition entitled Nordic Light; some time ago it toured all international centres.

This Nordic light is present in Parland's book as a typical element of the Swedish-language culture in Finland. A critic reviewing Christer Kihlman's *Den blå modern* (Blue Mother) claimed that one of the characters possessed "the best features of Swedish-speaking Finns, a capability of reasonable thinking and a consciousness of the limits of good taste". These features have their reasons far back in time, and they have to do with a myth fundamental to culture, in the same way as the feature of easternness mentioned above.

Swedish-speaking Finns are imbued with two or three major cultural influences. One of these, the Gustavian tradition, is effective in their culture but non-existent in Finnish literature focusing on folk life. Gustavus III (late 18th century) was a strong ruler, almost a genius, who was capable of forcing changes in his country. Inspired by the French Enlightenment, he demanded reason of writers as well as others, and he established an Academy in support of his demand. The motto of the Academy was Smak och Snille (Taste and genius).

As author Johan Henrik Kellgren, one of the King's closest men, put it, whatever you say you must say it with clarity and avoid unnecessary pathos. Romanticism soon rejected these ideas, but they lived longer among Swedish-speaking Finns, thanks to Runeberg and Topelius. Critics still claim to see this rationalism for instance in Christer Kihlman's and Jörn Donner's work (modern Swedish-writing authors and cosmopolitans).

Oscar Parland's book also illustrates this combination of Gustavian rationalism and man's demonic powers. In his attitude there is also a touch of aristocracy which comes from the confidence in one's ability to deal rationally with all disparity in one's heritage.

Nationalism versus internationalism

Thus there are a number of perfectly real phenomena which connect this eastern area to the West. Only languages keep it apart, and so do the more or less silly nationalisms of different countries.

But languages are no obstacle to Parland. In the beginning of his book he describes the multilingualness of his home in an interesting way. The family spoke German and Russian at home, he learnt Swedish at school and Finnish at work. Most of the book was in fact written in Finnish.

> When I was a fresh school-leaver in the early 30's, I used to say: "I am an Englishman who was born in Russia, whose mother tongue is German, who went to a Swedish-language school and is a Finnish citizen." (Oscar Parland)

Now that national feelings are being roused again I am tempted to ask what the role of nationalism will be in an era otherwise marked by internationalism. A national ideology is generally believed to be bound to the national language, the voice of the people, in a mystic and irrational way. In the case of the Parlands no such language-bound nationalism is needed for achieving a profound outcome. The whole notion of a national ideology is something unexplained that remains outside science.

In the case of the Parlands, then, language has not been an omnipotent factor. On the contrary, multilingualness has made them into voices of internationalism and humanism. This is a very valuable talent, in these days of nationalist outbursts.

This conflict between internationalism and nationalism is probably an eternal and unsolvable paradox, a Janus face of which we see the side we currently want to see. In his books – in this latest one, too – Oscar Parland finds a third angle from which to view the paradox, a tertium comparationis.

Humanism already characterized Parland's early novel *Metamorphoses*, where many characters appear to be acting under some superior laws, in a manner reminiscent of Thomas Mann. Similarly, in this new book there is some superior level of benevolent tolerance or acceptance from which all the incredible events are viewed: the Gulag, or pieces of handwork made by mental patients, which, interpreted as works of art, are claimed to reflect the general objectives of modern art and, in terms of content, to represent a scientific worldview.

Professor Sesemann's descriptions of Soviet life, "von dieser Hölle", are said to express a stoic calmness and acceptance of the finality of his fate. What could he have done?

> The alienation and pessimism that are manifest in our contemporary culture may at least partly arise from our loss of faith in the traditional personified view of the world. It is difficult for modern man to accept a scientific worldview with all its consequences. In our perplexity we try to mythologize our reality with new kinds of superstitions and heresies, science fiction, political and social ideologies, etc. Mostly, however, these appear to be superficial and banal if compared with the profundity of traditional worldviews – especially in an ethical sense. (Oscar Parland).

Note

1. For more information on Sesemann, see the following article by Thorsten Botz-Bornstein – *Editor's Note*.

Thorsten Botz-Bornstein

A mediator between Russia and the West: V. Sesemann as a philosopher and semiotician

The Finnish-Lithuanian philosopher Vassilij (or Wilhelm) [or Vasilius, see p. 34 – *Editor's Note*]) Sesemann might share the fate of many multilingual and multicultural authors who have decided to publish in more than one language. Being always inaccessible to the "other half" of their readers, being unclassifiable in terms of national culture, and remaining thus always somehow "exotic" in every country, they seem not to be predestined for overwhelming success. If the author has, as in the case of Sesemann, also had considerable problems with the Soviet regime, ending up at the peak of his career in a Siberian labour camp, one has some reason to suppose that some valuable thoughts might never have had the chance to meet the appreciation of a larger public.

As a historical figure Sesemann is a fascinating character, because of his two-sided background. Though raised in Viborg and St. Petersburg in a traditional German-Lutheran home, Sesemann maintained throughout his lifetime a remarkable interest in Russian culture, including a fascination with Russian Orthodox catholicism. Given his Germanic background, the motives for his decision to write a large part of his work in Russian appear especially obscure. The same is true of Sesemann's engagement in the so-called "Eurasian Movement" (in which his first wife played a militant role); it gives rise to much speculation about a possible link between these activities and his academic philosophical works.

Thus, given the relative obscurity of some facts of Sesemann's life, the historical person Vassilij Sesemann cannot and will not be the subject of the present work. The subject of our examination will rather be some of Sesemann's ideas, which appear quite unique within the Soviet environment of his time, and which suggest comparisons with some ideas produced by the Bakhtin circle and with those of some representatives, such as Yuri Lotman, of a later generation of Russian formalists.

Still, in spite of Sesemann's obvious originality, his real strength does not seem to consist *mainly* in the production of spectacular views on certain philosophical subjects; it consists rather in the capacity to produce very careful and solid analyses of difficult philosophical problems. Some of his writings manifest a profound treatment of several questions that, especially in the first three decades of this century, went back and forth between Germany and Russia, among which are these: the idea of *empathy* as a model for philosophical *Erkenntnis*, the ambiguity of "form" in aesthetics, the danger of materialism and positivism to the tradition of European thought, and, linked to this, the question of the subject in psychology.

Apart from this, because of his intellectual preferences, Sesemann represents a perhaps unique link between German Neo-kantism and the Russian formalist tradition because he constantly focuses on themes that are common (and also given to criticism) in both of them.

A study of Sesemann's thought is thus not only of historical interest. Sesemann's ideas, very much like those of Bakhtin, are still dynamic today; and, because of new components which he introduced into the discussion of the phenomenon of form, his ideas hold interest also for contemporary treatments of "structuralist" topics in their largest senses.

Vassilij Sesemann was born in Viborg in 1884. His father was a doctor of German origin (cf. Schweizer 1993: 29ff), and his mother was the daughter of a Baltic-German priest from Livland. Sesemann's family moved to St. Petersburg where the young Sesemann went to the German Katharinen-Schule (which had been founded by one of his ancestors) and where he, according to his long-time friend Victor Zhirmunsky, received a thoroughly classical education.

From 1905 to 1909 Sesemann studied at the historical-philosophical faculty of the University of St. Petersburg, from which he received qualifications in philosophy and philology. Among his teachers were N. O. Lossky, who exercised considerable influence on him. Sesemann finally became a candidate at the philosophical institute. From 1909 to 1911 he went to study in Marburg under Hermann Cohen and Paul Natorp. During that time he founded his lifelong friendship with Nicolai Hartmann. Later he went to Berlin.

Back in St. Petersburg he taught philosophy and classical languages at a high school. At the outbreak of World War I he fought on the Russian side as a volunteer (from 1914 to 1915). From 1915 to 1917 he taught philosophy as a *Privatdozent* of the University of St. Petersburg, and from 1918 to 1919 at the Viatka Pedagogical Institute. He received a docentship in Saratov where he was working (together with Zhirmunsky) until 1921. Being a Finnish citizen, the animosities between Finland and Russia forced him to move to Finland. Unable to find work there, he went to teach for two years at the Russian Institute in Berlin until he received a professor's position at the new University of Kaunas in Lithuania.

He stayed there (moving in 1940, together with the university, to Vilnius), writing a large number of works which testify to a broad intellectual horizon. His wife and sons living in Paris, he maintained, through his regular visits, direct contact with European intellectual life (being also well acquainted with Parisian immigrant circles). He also frequently visited Leningrad and Moscow in order to keep up with Russia's newest intellectual developments.

The campaign against formalism, which started officially in 1946, put an end to all this. In 1950, at the age of 66, Sesemann was arrested by the secret police and sent to a Siberian camp. He was set free in 1958 under the Kruschev regime. His Finnish citizenship was withdrawn, and he became a Soviet citizen, regaining his former position at Vilnius University. He died in 1963.

Sesemann wrote as much in Russian as he did in German, and at a later stage of his life he also wrote and taught in Lithuanian. Certainly, the inaccessibility of his Lithuanian writings makes any appreciation of the entirety of his work very difficult. It is particularly regrettable that the *Estetika*, a posthumously published collection of his essays and lectures on aesthetics, is, though generally considered one of his most important works, only available in Lithuanian.

Nonetheless, it is possible to extract some of Sesemann's main philosophical tendencies by concentrating only on his Russian and German works. These tendencies, which were created within a uniquely Baltic ambiance (which has traditionally been determined by a strong tension between Russian and Germanic culture), often manifest an ambiguous character. Sesemann's critical relationship with Neokantism, for example, made him react in a particular way not only to Russian formalism but also – and this *together with* the Russian formalists – to Russian intuitivism and related movements.

In any case, Sesemann can be seen as a mirror that reflects the confusing situation into which, in the first three decades of our century, were inscribed even the most basic philosophical concepts in Europe (a confusion which becomes *very* obvious as soon as we stretch our horizon from Russian Futurism to Heidegger's *Being and Time*), all by finding an admirable way to structure the chaotic situation to some extent. Sesemann's philosophy establishes a link between the standard Formalist problem of the "dynamization of the structure" and appreciation of an outspokenly Heideggerian concept of Being; and in this way it has a genuinely European flavour of "comprehensiveness".

Nicolas O. Lossky, in his *История русской философии* [*History of Russian Philosophy*] (1991: 405ff) dedicates three pages to Sesemann and integrates him into the group of those Russian philosophers [the Russian original is omitted here and in other quotations – *Editor's Note*] [who kept contact with German post-Kantian philosophy] (p. 405). Among those were also the representatives of transcendental-logical idealism, especially S. Hessen who, together with F. Stepun and B. Jakovenko, founded a Russian branch of the international journal *Logos*. Sesemann is thus acting within a group of young Russian philosophers who insist on their clearly Western orientation, and among whom number also G. Gurvitch, G. Lanz, V. Savalsky, N. Boldyrev and, last but not least, Gustav Shpet.

However, though Sesemann might, for several reasons, superficially be classified as a Russian transcendental idealist (especially because of his connection with his teacher Lossky), in reality Sesemann's relationship with idealism is as ambiguous as is his relationship with realism. That his concern for particularly formal questions of linguistics and aesthetics cause some people to view him even as a precursor of modern semiotics (cf. Parland 1991: 85) makes his case rather complex.

To put it briefly, Sesemann's philosophy comes close to what he himself preferred to call "gnoseological idealism", a self-definition of philosophical thought (to which Nicolai Hartmann probably would have subscribed), which tries, all by remaining relatively close to the neo-Kantian tradition, to revive metaphysics through a reevaluation of the metaphysical tradition of *ontology* instead of insisting on the *subjectivist* component of metaphysics only. By doing so, Sesemann (and Hartmann) manage in a consistent way to resist any leanings toward positivism. Apart from Hartmann, Max Scheler in Germany and Lossky in Russia held to very similar philosophical lines.

Initial access to Sesemann's "gnoseological idealism" can be gained by an analysis of the discourse held by several important philosophers of his time on a central philosophical problem in the theory of understanding. At stake, as suggested already, is the option for either idealism or realism (or a possible reconciliation between them). Directly linked to this issue are the definitions of subjectivism and objectivism, respectively.

Put most simply: idealism submits the object to the subject, whereas objectivism intends to submit the subject to the object. Possibly the most notable tendency in post-Kantian thought is that philosophy has been, in general, all too quickly ready to abandonin spite of the constant attempts of a relatively long-lasting neo-Kantian tradition to point to the existence of an "interplay" between objectivist and subjectivist thinkingany doubts which could have prevented it from falling into total subjectivism. An extreme example of this is positivism. As mentioned, Neokantism, the philosophy of Scheler, and also Lossky's intuitivism can be considered as world-wide pre-Heideggerian movements which were trying to push positivism back in order to produce more ontological views in philosophy.

V. Sesemann as a philosopher and semiotician

Formalism and Neokantism

Sesemann's simultaneous preoccupation with Neokantism and Russian formalism, all by being linked to Lossky's school of St. Petersburg intuitivism, seems to make of Sesemann a quite unique testimony of the philosophical discussions that dominated Europe before the second world war. In a rather early text Искусство и культура [к проблеме эстетика] [*Art and Culture: The Problem of Aesthetics*] (1927), Sesemann regrets an [estrangement of aesthetics from concrete, living art] (p. 185). Sesemann certainly has in mind, when formulating his regrets, the pre-positivist and idealist aesthetics of Lipps and others, and he points to what appears to him as an alternative:

> The work of Wölfflin and his followers on the one hand, and the school of the Russian formalists on the other, represents not only a valuable contribution to the theory of painting, but they also have a purely philosophical significance, indicating to aesthetics the direction in which it should seek its original object (ibid: 185).

In subsequent elucidations concerning his idea of aesthetics, as well as in those reflections which he presents through the other branches of his philosophy, Sesemann points, again and again, the danger of subjectivist theories of knowledge whose only declared aim would be to produce "objective knowledge". What would be lost through these procedures is, so Sesemann explains, the "thing".

Sesemann thus distinguishes between the '*предметный*' ["thingly"] and the *об'ективный* [objective] components of an aesthetical phenomenon. Interestingly, the (objectivist) suggestions of the Russian formalists are recognized as logical and consistent reactions that were produced within a difficult situation. Still, on the ground of some of their observations, Sesemann is able to take his considerations further, in order to reveal some essential deficiencies in their thoughts as well.

Sesemann speaks of the *общая предметная основа* [common-thingly basis] of all aesthetic being. This foundation, if it exists, could not be represented by art itself; however, it should not be looked for in an abstraction *from* art either. Sesemann's view on the problematical relationship between subjectivism and objectivism manifests itself through the following reflection:

> What is thus their [aesthetic beings'] common thingly basis? At first glance, this question seems to allow one or two answers: if this basis can not be discovered in art itself, in its works, then one has to look for it outside of art, and this means: either in the aesthetic subject itself (creating or perceiving), or in those meanings and ideas which are embodied in the artistic image. Aesthetics tried both of these paths, but they both led to a hopeless dead end. Neither the one nor the other conception managed to trace the thingly (objective) unity of art. Both the subjective-psychological and the

objective-idealist theory overlooked that which is most essential in aesthetic expression. ... (Ibid: 186)

The "thingly" unity of art can be apprehended neither by subjective-psychological, nor by objective-idealistic (rationalistic) conceptions of aesthetics. Both of these 'ложных тенденций [false tendencies] can be overcome only if aesthetics

> rejects purely systematic constructions and obtains more profound insights into the thingly element out of which flows and in which is realized artistic expression in the different arts (ibid: 186)

As an alternative Sesemann points to research into the phenomenon of "structural form", which he understands in a way slightly different from that of the formalists: the "structure" should be seen as a living "rhythm" that exists inside the work of art and that constantly determines its nature. This would be, in Sesemann's view, the "most intimate task of aesthetics, not approaching art from the outside but directed exclusively by its inner rhythm" (ibid).

Note that Sesemann points to the wholeness of the work of art whose structure can only be seized from the inside. The influence of Lossky's organic philosophy (as well as Russian formalist thought) is evident here. However, Sesemann's search for the *inner form* is, in a clear way, not restricted to the localization of psychological quantities, which would be existent in the mind of the contemplating subject, nor does he try to seize the work *through* these very structures, as an objective, systematized phenomenon.

Sesemann might adhere to a structuralist-formal alternative in aesthetics, but his idea of the structure itself seems to be dependent on Lossky's idea of the "organical whole" on the one hand, and on neo-Kantian ambitions to dynamize static logical systems (no matter if these logical systems are founded on objectivism or subjectivism).

Still, Sesemann's apparent seduction by formalist theory should not, in spite of the interesting aspects and possibilities for reflection which it offers, be overestimated. In the end, Sesemann's philosophical aim was never to find a *system*, but a *thing*: a living phenomenon that is neither purely subjective nor purely objective. And his relationship with formalism is determined by this conviction.

In this context it is important to mention one point that dominates Sesemann's writings, and which is closely linked to the subjects mentioned above: the relationship between material and form. Though the importance of this topic for formalist thought is evident, Sesemann uses it within a relatively large context. He incorporates it, for example, into a lengthy discussion on rationality and irrationality in the domain of the philosophy of knowledge.

V. Sesemann as a philosopher and semiotician

Sesemann also makes, in the aforementioned article, some characteristic and original points in regard to anti-objectivist philosophy in general and its relationship with Russian formalism. His main criticism of formalism is that the reduction of material to "dead" matter, a reduction which enables the subjective mind to arrange matters in any way it desires them to be arranged, does not only contradict the character of material as "things", but it also introduces, in Sesemann's view, a basically wrong definition of the notion of structure. About the formalist urge to establish "structures" he writes:

> The composition is the ... formal moment as all ... those factors which are obliged to the very nature of the felt material. The structural form is not imprinted by the artist on the material on which he works ... but materializes and reveals only those aesthetic possibilities ... which are rooted in [the material's] own nature. Only on the basis of such a notion of form can an objective aesthetics be created as a doctrine of the thingly structure of the aesthetical phenomenon. The notion of 'device', as it is used by the school of the formalists, which is for them a substitute for form – in spite of all the methodological convenience it offers – from a philosophical point of view cannot be considered sound. Form understood only as a device of artistic expression takes on a subjective-intentional character, and seems to exist without any relation to the material itself. (Ibid: 187)

Few quotations could better characterize better Sesemann's relationship with formalism. As one of the first persons who integrated the critique of formalism into a more comprehensive, general philosophical discourse, Sesemann points to their weakest points, and finally predict the poor destiny which Futurism and formalism would meet. Sesemann admits the following:

> ... the formalists are absolutely right in insisting that poetics, for example, should above all flow out of linguistics, and that for this reason every chapter of the science of language should correspond to a distinct chapter of theoretical poetics. As a matter of fact, in the sound structure of the word, in the rhythm and in intonations of living speech, in its grammatical and syntactical structures, and finally in its semantic aspects (i.e. in its figurativeness, logical meaning and emotional tension) are found the formal elements, or devices, which are used by poetic language. (Ibid: 187-188)

Sesemann's formalism (if we can call it that) is an aesthetical one, and it is interesting to locate this aesthetic formalism even in those domains (like that of psychology) which are quite removed from aesthetics. A sense of the wide spectrum which these thoughts actually do have, can be derived from the following remark by Sesemann:

> Indeed the reality ascribed to the structural form is an aesthetic reality which not only does not overlap with physical or psychological reality, but which requires for its construction an absolutely distinct orientation of the consciousness (ibid: 188).

The special orientation of the consciousness which is asked for here is founded on the aspired overcoming of the subjective-psychological *and* the objective-idealistic (rationalistic) elements in the theory of knowledge in general. Finally, these two kinds of unacceptable abstractions, the subjectivist and the objectivist, are–and this is important–traced back to one and the same root; to the philosophy of *Einfühlung*. Sesemann asks: "Is the distinction between the felt-*formal* and the thingly-semantic moments not dissolved within the limits of the aesthetic form?" (ibid: 190). In the end, he urges us to recognize that "in poetry the opposition between the felt-phenomenal and the thingly-semantic becomes more complicated" (ibid: 192).

This kind of anti-formalist criticism is as profound as it is penetrating. All by philosophizing on the ground of what only a solid theory of knowledge can provide, Sesemann seems to be (together with Croce) among the first aestheticians to recognize the nonsensical character of the Futurist notion of "transrational speech", a notion that dominated Europe at that time, being characteristic of the cultural climate. However, the Futurist 'заумный язык' is, so we learn from Sesemann, nonsensical not in a logical, but in an aesthetical way. It *must* be nonsensical because it tries to "feel" the structure of artistic composition in a pure way; and this means that it tries to "feel" art as if it were "nothing". Sesemann concludes that "transrational speech", as language devoid of all thingly meaning, is a pure fiction" (ibid: 192). An art which expresses nothing but itself does not express anything. However, "feeling" should be the feeling of something. Structuralist empathy thus represents a kind of objectivist subjectivism which will one day make Futurism run out of contents.

We can conclude that Sesemann did certainly adhere to a general spirit which was present in formalist thought as far as it represented a way to define a philosophical position that was opposed to positivism. Yet, generally speaking, Sesemann's notion of "aesthetic form" should better be defined as that of a self-critical, "historically open" formalism. In this sense, Sesemann seems to be willing to evaluate the formalist idea of form when writing that the aesthetic form "as an expression independent of its thingly meaning is able to provide, in the domain of aesthetics, a philosophical foundation for formalism, and together with this explicate the inner link between art and the rest of culture" (ibid: 195).

Sesemann sides with Croce when claiming that any "transformation of the motive into a pure device is the first symptom of a weakening of expressive tension.... [I]t degrades into a simple play of aesthetical hedonism" (ibid: 196). It should be said in defense of the formalists that "hedonism" was certainly one of the last things they would have been likely to become addicted to. Yet it is not only Croce who would have supported Sesemann's attempts to depict Futurism as a basically playful kind of hedonism. A statement almost identical with that of Sesemann is made by a philosopher whose overall resemblance to Sesemann should have become clear in the preceding pages: Bakhtin.

V. Sesemann as a philosopher and semiotician

The statement in question can be found in Bakhtin's *The Problem of Contents, Material, and Form in Verbal Art*; it reads as follows: "Any feeling, deprived of those things which gives its object meaning, gets reduced to a merely factual state of the psyche, to an isolated and extracultural state. And therefore form expresses a feeling which relates to nothing, then such a feeling becomes simply a state of psychophysical organism, a state free of any intention that opens the closed circle of bare psychic givenness. It becomes simply pleasure which, in the final analysis, can be explained and understood only in purely hedonistic terms (Bakhtin 1990: 264)."

Also, Bakhtin's main ambition was to overcome "romantic" individualist subjectivism (which he saw, perhaps by simplifying things slightly, embodied in the tradition of Herder's and Humboldt's linguistics, and also in modern branches of psychologizing linguistic philosophy), *and at the same time* of abstract objectivism, whose overcoming he tried to effectuate through very pointed criticisms of, for example, Leibniz's *grammatica universalis*, the Geneva School's distinction of *langue* and *parole*, and also the Russian formalists' juxtaposition of content and form.

This means that also for Bakhtin and his circle language could be neither an abstract form nor a direct "materialization" of a mysterious psycho-physical energy. And in this sense his thoughts overlap with those of Sesemann, who approached the same subjects whilst coming from the heart of German post-Kantian philosophy.

Even on a more general level, however, Sesemann shares with Bakhtin a quite common view on that philosophical notion which was of particular interest to Bakhtin and which we now draw into the present considerations: the notion of style. Sesemann defines style as a quantity which has an inner link with the 'жизненной установкой' ([structure of life], *op. cit.*, p. 198) and which is thus dynamical because it is determined by real life. In this sense, for Sesemann as well as for Bakhtin, aesthetic form and artistic expression are engendered neither through "inner life" only, nor do they depend on life's "objective structures"; they must be seen as a communication which an individual, creative mind entertains with the "things" that he finds in his exterior environment.

A question asked by Sesemann, which refers to a problem that flows directly out of this constellation of things, illustrates very well this parallelism. Sesemann says, "the basic question remains unclear: what was it in particular which opened the artist's eyes to the aesthetical unity of just these forms?" (ibid: 197). An interplay of subjective judgement and exterior influence, an act of *choice* which would, as Lotman has insisted so often, subsist even within the "final" and readily determined structure: these are the only quantities which represent the ground for the creation of the aesthetic form. Finally, in the words of Voloshinov (Bakhtin) the same problem is described like this: "Individual choice has no meaning. *Only that which has aquired social value can enter the world of ideology, take shape, and establish itself there*" (Voloshinov 1973: 22).

Quite often it appears as if Sesemann has been laying the "metaphysical ground" for some of those questions which were also central for Bakhtin and his circle. Looking at one of Voloshinov's suggestions, made at the beginning of *Freudianism* (1973), we note an immediate connection between Voloshinov and Sesemann (a connection which can also be interpreted in the context of certain reflections on the philosophical justification of "scientific psychology", as far as it was present in Germany at that time). Voloshinov asks: "which of the two kinds of apprehensions – internal-subjective or external-objective – ought to form the basis for a scientific psychology? Or might not some particular combination of the data of both serve that purpose?" (1973: 19). It is this question, which is also central to a large part of Bakhtinian philosophy, that Sesemann seems to have linked to the discussion of objectivism and subjectivism as it taking place in Germany at that time and of which Theodor Lipps's conception of psychology as a "philosophy made scientific" represents a cornerstone.

In his later writings Sesemann elaborates, among other things, an aesthetics of Being which produces unconventional ideas of time (as a concrete, dynamic phenomenon), of contingency (as a constitutive part of Being), and of structure, which is seen as unformalizable in an either subjective or objective way. It might be apt to say that Sesemann's entire philosophical work culminates in a new aesthetics of that domain within which all these factors play an equally prominent role in regard to their respective theoretization: it culminates in a new *logic of dream* (see Sesemann 1931).

The dynamical aspect of all timely actions in which logical rationality would be present in, as Sesemann says, a "more relaxed" (*gelockert*) way, is also relevant for subjective Being. Among all the devices which Sesemann suggested concerning the prevention of an undue objectivization of the subjective, there is one which appears as both remarkably Heideggerian and Bakhtinian at the same time. Subjective, psychic Being should, so Sesemann declares, always be defined as a *Mitbewusstsein* (co-consciousness) which cannot be logically formalized. This means that subjective life should be seen as appearing only *through* a social aspect of non-determination; and only through this aspect does subjectiveness receive a timely character:

> *Eine Sonderstellung nimmt das eigentlich subjektive (psychische) Sein ein. Seine ursprüngliche Seinsweise (soweit sie einsichtig wird) ist die des Mitbewusstseins. Das Mitbewusstsein liegt aber noch diesseits aller Gegenständlichkeit. Als Mitbewusstes ist das psychische Sein daher ein Vorgegenständliches. Da aber logische Bestimmtheit an Gegenständlichkeit gebunden ist, so steht das psychische Sein als solches in keiner direkten Beziehung zu den logischen Gesetzen.*

[The *subjective* (psychic) Being occupies an exceptional position. Its original way of Being (as far as it is recognizable) is that of *co-consciousness*. But co-consciousness exists even beyond all objectiveness. Psychic being is therefore, as the co-conscious, pre-objective. However, because logical determination is linked to objectiveness, psychic Being maintains no direct relationship with the laws of logic.] (Ibid: 216)

The existence of a certain "logic of the psychic", of the subjective and of dream is explained, paradoxically (and not so far from what has been suggested by Lacan), through a "pre-objective" link with what can be located *outside of the individual consciousness*. The myth of individual *subjectiveness*, as far as it neglects its own state of Being-in-the World, thus creates an unreflected idea of *objectiveness* that it claims, subsequently, to be valid within the domain of the subjective. The estrangement (*Entfremdung*, cf. 202) of man from the world is to a very large extent effectuated through such an abstraction from the (co-conscious) concrete, subjective contents of psychic life; and it always functions – though in a hidden way – through scientific objectification.

References

Bakhtin, Mikhail (1990). *Art and Answerability*. Austin: University of Texas Press.
Lossky, N.O. (1991). *История пусской философии.*. Moscow: Высшая школа.
Parland, Oscar (1991). *Kunskap och inlevelse*. Esbo: Schildt.
Schweizer, Robert (1993). *Die Wiborger Deutschen*. Helsinki: Veröffentlichungen der Stiftung zur Förderung deutscher Kultur.
Sesemann, Vassilij (1927). Искусство и кульытыра (к проблеме эстеики). *Версты*. (Paris) 2, 185–204.
– (1931). *Die logischen Gesetze und das Sein* (*Eranus* III) Kaunas: Metai.
Voloshinov, Valentin N. (1973). *Marxism and the Philosophy of Language*. New York, London and Ann Arbor: Seminar Press.
– (1976). *Freudianism: A Marxist Critique*. New York: Academic Press.

FROM PHILOSOPHY
TO CULTURE

Pauli Pylkkö

Ontological nihilism, or, the meaning of the so-called Finnish passive construction

The dogma of reification and its semantic variants

One dogma that prevails in linguistic and logical studies of language dictates that, in order to be able to carry meaning, the language experience must be reified into structures and objects. One version of this dogma is expressed as the claim that every language must have an ontology. This dogma is often so compelling that it even may be difficult for us to imagine how any language could be meaningful without an ontology, that is, without object-like words that refer to other, non-linguistic objects. In what follows, we mean by *ontology* of a language the most elementary entities that are used to give meaning to the expressions of the language and that, in all normal cases, the language can be used to speak about. It is often thought that the meaning of every expression of a language should be definable or characterizable in terms of an ontology. For example, in the standard semantics of a first-order language, the semantic primitives are the individuals of the universe of discourse, and the nonlogical constant symbols and variables of the language receive their meaning by referring to the individuals. In this and similar cases, we can say that the ontology of a language is given when the individuals whose properties and relations the language can speak about are determined.

When first-order languages are used to analyze the logical structure of natural languages, it is tempting to correlate the proper names of natural language with non-logical, individual, and constant symbols of the first-order languages and to say that natural languages also have a universe of discourse in relation to which words receive their meaning. For example, it is often suggested that in natural language proper names refer to persons, ships, places, towns, animals, and so on, and that these things comprise a part of a universe of discourse that contains all sorts of macrophysical objects. Then the variables of the language are said to "range" over these objects. In this case, the ontology of natural language would contain, at least, some macrophysical objects.

Ontological nihilism

The proper names of natural languages, however, need not be analyzed according to the direct analogy provided by the nonlogical, individual, and constant symbols of first-order languages; and if this analogy is adopted, it is not necessary to place macrophysical objects into the universe of discourse. In linguistic and logical studies of natural language, the characterization of *individuality*, what is taken to be an individual (entity, object, thing) can be given in many different ways. The characterization may be either semantic, or it may reside more on the ontological side and resort either to physical theories or to commonsense views. Within semantics, individuality can be either intensional or extensional. The primitives of the theory can be all manner of things such as sense data, elementary physical objects or properties, behavioral invariances, and so on.

In what follows, no sharp distinction is made between semantics and ontology; nor is such a contrast vital to the following argument. We don't think that the *dogma of reification* – that meaning always requires the reification of experience into structures and objects in order to arise – can be challenged with the help of a full-fledged semantic or semiotic theory that claims to be free of all ontological constraints and commitments. One might suggest, for example, that a semantic theory need not specify its ontology, and therefore that meaning is, in principle, independent of ontology. But this is not a particularly convincing view. A semantic theory seems not to be *so* independent of ontological implications. By fixing the elementary semantic units, we determine both a kind of minimal ontology, namely, the ontology of the semantical units themselves, and, at the same time, a set of *possible* ontologies.

Similarly, if we adopt the syntax/semantics (or signifier/signified) contrast, as most semanticists do, already the syntax requires a minimal ontology which comprises, for example, typographical signs and the concatenation function. Hardly anyone wants to do, say, model theory *without* syntax. Usually the discussion focuses on such problems as whether or not syntax can express everything that we want to express, not whether there exists a syntax in the first place (see Pylkkö 1997a). For example, Gödel's famous "incompleteness results" begin with the assumption that there is a recursively enumerable syntax of the first-order language in which one attempts to formalize the arithmetic truth. The idea is that all arithmetic truths cannot be derived or generated by syntactic methods alone. In other words, there is no way to generate mechanically all arithmetic truths as syntactic objects from any finite set of axioms. But Gödel's demonstration wouldn't make much sense if there did not exist a well-defined syntax to begin with. And if we have the syntax, we have, minimally, the ontology of syntactic objects.

Similarly, it is more natural to say that every semantic theory provides and outlines, if not a definite ontology, at least a set of possible ontologies. Even model-theoretical semantics requires a set of models at the outset. In what follows, the central issue is not whether there exists semantically independent entities that require or refer to no ontology, but, rather, *whether or not there is meaning outside of the reification or objectivization of human experience*. Hence what is said of the smallest or most primitive entities that provide meaning to the expressions of a language, could just as well be said of any stable or identity-preserving primitive *semantic* units. Thus, there is a sense in which semantics and ontology are never perfectly separate: semantics, say the standard model-theory for first-order languages, is *ontology-driven*, that is, biased toward *some* ontology.

Most semantical theories put some constraints upon what is ontologically possible. So, whether you think of models as semantic or ontological entities doesn't always make a big difference. Without weakening the argument, we could call the set of the smallest semantic units an *ontology* as well. What kinds of things the ontology actually comprises doesn't matter either. It can comprise abstract objects such as sets, or concrete things such as physical objects; it can comprise phenomenal things such as sense data; or cognitive structures such as languages of thought, and so on. In one way or another, ontology enters the scene, either by a conscious decision of the semanticist or semiotician, or unwittingly, by the tacitly reifying or objectivizing nature of the theoretical attitude itself. What matters is whether the elements of which an ontology consists possess an identity, separability, and individuality of their own, and whether language, in order to be meaningful, necessarily needs an ontology in this sense.

Ontological relativity and ontological nihilism

Ontological relativity doesn't question the dogma of reification. *Ontological relativity* means that, given a language, the ontology is not predetermined by any natural or logical necessity. The ontology of our basic vocabulary can vary, depending on what our language, beliefs, world-view, cultural background, and so on, happen to be. For example, different historical phases of one language can resort to different ontologies, and revolutions in our basic world-view can alter our ontology, too. Occasionally, we may even choose our primitive individuals just as we like, and interpret our basic vocabulary according to our various interests and goals, though in some areas of language such liberties are extremely difficult to attain.

But if two languages differ radically with respect to their ontology, translation from one language into another becomes difficult or even impossible, as Quine has taught us (1969). In other words, even the most accurate translation, which retains behavioral, perceptual and social invariants, may fail to mediate ontological differences and, therefore, may fall short of preserving meaning-identities, too.

Ontological nihilism

In principle, ontological variety doesn't seem to imply untranslatability. We could imagine a metalanguage in which ontological differences could be described and which would serve as a foundation for translations between languages with differing ontologies. It could be suggested, for instance, that something similar happens when we switch from particle object-language to wave object-language within a proper metalanguage of quantum theory. But it is far from obvious that there exists an ordered way to do the translation. For example, it is not obvious that, within quantum theory, a metalanguage is available in which both of the object-languages can be described and which has a model or consistent interpretation.

The existence of a universal metalanguage in which different ontologies can be described is a semantic credo or agenda rather than a fact or a naturalistically tenable position. The first problem that anyone who believes in a universal metalanguage has to address is why the problem of ontological relativity wouldn't concern the metalanguage itself. If two physicists or philosophers disagree about which metalanguage should be chosen, who settles the issue? Thus, if there are several metalanguages with competing ontologies, we re-encounter the problem of translation. We have just moved the problem to a higher level.

There seems to be no way to stop this regression. Most certainly sense data, physical particles, (energies, waves, or other physical predicates), behavioral invariances, social games, or anything similar, are unable to do that. Therefore, if there are languages, or even fragments of languages, which have no ontology at all, then prospects for intertranslations become even more gloomy: a language without ontology, if possible in the first place, would carry meanings that are too unique, local, historically and culturally specific to allow any seriously meaning-preserving translations to be established. Though one of the main reasons semanticists adopt the dogma of reification (or the ontological dogma) is that only a common ontology secures a possibility of reliable translations, it hasn't yet been shown that the utterances or expressions of a language that lacks ontology must lack meaning altogether. Such utterances and expressions may be, or may have been, experientially influential in a special natural and cultural environment, even if the language never produced an ontology, and even if the language remained untranslatable.

Neither do pragmatic views of meaning usually question the dogma of reification. Linguistic pragmatism doesn't necessarily imply ontological relativity, let alone *ontological nihilism*, that is, the destruction of ontology. If meaning arises when language is used in proper action, say, in some rule-governed game situations, it is still possible that games in different pragmatic contexts share a necessary meaning invariance or structure that can impose a common ontology upon different languages. Or, there may exist some *a priori* or pre-empirical gaming structures which determine the set of all possible ontologies for the speaker.

Those who advocate the pragmatic approach to the problem of meaning, however, often tend to assume that different historical and social contexts produce different ontologies. For example, it is often suggested that different historical and social circumstances encourage speakers to parse the world into different conceptual slices according to the various purposes which speech is intended to serve. But this is a version of ontological relativity, not yet a violation of the dogma of reification (the ontological dogma). Among other things, pragmatic theories seem to require the minimal ontology of rational agents, and rationality, however minimal, requires its own residual ontology. A pragmatist who accepts ontological relativity can still believe that it is human action and its universal rationality that ultimately provide the foundation for translations between languages.

Thus, ontological relativists, too, seem to assume that every language necessarily has an ontology, though they admit that languages may have different ontologies, or that the ontology of one language may vary as a function of the beliefs (or culture) of the speakers. Ontological relativists may also believe that meaning-preserving translations are impossible and that meaning is always undermined by an indeterminacy that cannot be overcome. Nevertheless, they do not usually question the dogma of reification (or, the ontological dogma). Typically, they think that a first-order language can be interpreted in many ontologically different ways. But now the question is whether a language can be interpreted, in some interesting sense of *interpretation*, altogether *without* an ontology.

Keenan and Faltz on ontology

It is understandable that Keenan and Faltz's semantics (1985) complies with the dogma because, as their *Criterion of Logical Adequacy* requires, their theory is intended to represent the logical entailment relations of natural language (1985: 2). Yet it is characteristic of their semantics that the proper names of natural languages are not analyzed as individual terms that are standard, first-order, nonlogical, and constant. Therefore regular individuals such as persons, ships, and dogs, which we denote by natural proper names, are not semantic primitives in their semantics. It is well known that, in the Montague school to which Keenan and Faltz's theory belongs, the denotations of proper nouns are handled as sets of properties. For example, the denotation of *John* is the set of all John's properties.

This kind of semantics still has an ontology, though in some cases the primitives of the semantics cannot be directly denoted in the language itself. In order to avoid the situation where the semantic primitives of a language cannot be denoted in the language itself, Keenan and Faltz decided to eliminate the regular universe of discourse altogether and replace it by a new ontology, *property algebra P* (1985: 30). The advantage of this property-ontology is that the elements of *P*, namely properties, can be denoted by common nouns, and the semantic primitives are denotationally accessible. We could thus say that the ontology of Keenan and Faltz consists of properties (1985: especially 52 and 53).

Keenan and Faltz on the passive construction

An intrinsic tension is built into Keenan and Faltz's (1985), as well as Keenan's (1985), analysis of passive constructions. The authors begin with what they call the *basic passive*, which has no agent-phrase and which is said to be the most widespread passive construction in the world's languages (Keenan and Faltz 1985: 203). For example, *John was slapped* represents the basic passive in English. But when the authors move to logical analysis, they claim that the basic passive is, in the end, elliptical in its meaning, and that the agent lies hidden in the underlying logical form. For example, they suggest that the meaning of *John was slapped* is actually *someone slapped John*. One gets the impression that empirical reasons have forced Keenan and Faltz to concede that the agentless passive is the basic one, but, at the same time, they are still unwilling to accept this in their logical analysis.

According to Keenan and Faltz (1985: 203), a passive predicate like *was slapped* results from a transitive verb *slap* through a valence-affecting operation. In categorical grammars, expressions of category X/Y (say, verb phrase, S/N) combine with expressions of category Y (say, noun phrases, N) to produce expressions of category X (sentences, S). Then a set of possible denotations is associated with each category, and, for example, the denotations of verb phrases is seen as a function from the denotations of noun phrases into the denotations of sentences (typically truth values).

The analysis can be extended to the structure of verb phrases. For example, the form of *was slapped* is understood as an intransitive value of a valence-reducing, morpho-syntactic function f which takes transitive verbs as arguments. If p_2 represents the transitive form, *slap*, then the passive form is derived from p_2 by prefixing $f(p_2)$, that is *slapped*, with an auxiliary verb, *was*. Then it holds that *aux* $f(p_2) = $ *was slapped* $= p_1$.

Keenan and Faltz's basic passive is not so basic after all. It is derived from a transitive form that is even more basic. This accords with the semantic analysis of a passive phrase that paraphrases *John was slapped* as *someone slapped John*. But, at the same time, it obscures the sense in which their basic passive is "basic" after all. Semantically speaking the meaning, M, of the passive, *pass*, is a function from the denotations of the category of transitive verbs, P_2, into the denotations of the category of intransitive verbs, P_I, such that $M\ (pass)(slap)(John) = (slap\ (John))\ (Exist\ y)$, where y range over persons. The right side transforms eventually into *for some person y it holds that y slapped John* (for more details, see Keenan and Faltz 1985: 204).

Some properties of Finnish passive-like expressions

The Finnish passive is vaguely collective in meaning, but it is not obvious at all that a Finnish native speaker understands passive expressions in a way that presupposes a reference to missing or implied persons. In traditional grammatical terms, the so-called Finnish passive construction is formed by the addition of a special morphological suffix, *-aan* (or *-ään*), directly to the root of a verb. For example, from the root *ole-* (*be-*) we get the passive form *ollaan*, and from the root *koke-*(*experience-*) the passive form *koetaan*. (We skip all the intriguing details of the morpho-syntax, which is much more complicated than the respective English one.) The result is itself an independent sentence-like unit with a complete meaning of its own, which in written language is often separated by periods from the rest of the text. In other words, the passive-like "meaning unit", even if it has only one word, is by no means elliptical. Yet, intuitively speaking, it doesn't always refer to or hint at an omitted person or subject. It is strongly impersonal.

A Finnish passive-like expression can be enriched by the addition, for example, of a modifying phrase that tells us where or how the passive being, experiencing, or doing happens. For example, *ollaan erällä* says, by and large, that the peculiar way or mode of being, which is expressed by *ollaan*, takes place in the wilderness, and the way or mode of being comprises hunting, fishing, and other such activities. Yet it doesn't necessarily bear connotations of any definite means-end activity, that is, doing something with a specific intentional goal in mind. Because of its errant or nomadic connotations, the meaning of *erällä* suggests that the mode of being to which it is attributed is contrasted with the regular domestic way of life, say, that of an agricultural community.

No English translation can quite capture the crux of the meaning which the Finnish passive-like utterance suggests. This is especially so with *ollaan*, because the English *be-*, like many other Indo-European counterparts, cannot be passivized. It would be misleading to translate *ollaan* by *one is* (or *there is one who is*); or *koetaan* by *one experiences*, let alone by *it is experienced* or *there is someone who experiences*. The Finnish passive-like expression doesn't and cannot refer to some *one* who does the being or experiencing; neither is it necessary to assume that there is someone to whom the act of experiencing is directed. In other words, the meaning of the Finnish passive-like utterance doesn't refer, not even tacitly, to an agent who is supposed to be the hidden initiator of the passivized activity; neither is it necessary to assume that there is an object or a person toward which or toward whom the activity is directed. Yet the Finnish passive is almost always used in the human context. In spite of this, there is no hidden subject-predicate structure underlying its meaning. Syntactically speaking, there are no obligatory variables or valences which have to be attached to the verbal root. In grammatical terms, agent is impossible but patient is permissible.

It seems that the understanding of these passive-like expressions doesn't necessarily require reference to any individuals (or set of individuals). This holds both for logical and grammatical individuals, as well as for intentional agents. At the same time, we can say that when we are in the mode of *ollaan* or *koetaan* we are not there alone. Or, it would not be quite natural to use *ollaan* for a solitary mode of being. Therefore the proper understanding of these expressions requires that there exists a mode of being which is preindividually human and collective, and that the speaker has experiential access to that mode of being (cf. Pylkkö 1995; also Pylkkö 1997b, especially Chapter 8). The preindividual collectivity is experiential, that is, it is an experience of being together, such that the one (sic) who experiences the togetherness is neither an individual nor a set of individuals. In the English description of these expressions we are almost always forced to use the metaphysically loaded vocabulary of such words as "one", "there is", and "it" or even "we".

It seems as if the preindividual meaning can be understood only in terms of some primitive, nonsubjective experience, that is, in terms of an experience that in some sense precedes the emergence of individual subjectivity (cf. Pylkkö 1997b). One aspect of the emergence of subjectivity is the ability to discern experiential centers among the amorphous and preindividual collective experience, recognize these centers as separate individuals, and, simultaneously, experience oneself as a separate individual, too. This process of articulation is possible only if the experience of which we are here speaking has also been organized into a conceptual form. For example, the conceptualization would require that the subject represents the environment and itself by such concepts as object, person, and I. At the same time, the subject would understand itself as a goal-directed agent. Contrary to this articulation, *ollaan* and *koetaan* still carry with them ingredients of the originally aconceptual and asubjective mode of being, and therefore they hint at a meaning that precedes all conceptualizations and the emergence of subjectivity.

Of course, it is possible to passivize Finnish transitive verbs, too. Even *koetaan* (but not *ollaan*) can take a semantical object toward which the experiencing is directed: *kärsimyksiä koetaan* – suffering is being experienced; or *verkot koetaan* – the fishing nets are "experienced"; the meaning being that it (sic) is found out whether there actually are any fishes entangled in the net under the water's surface. Passivization, however, is not an operation restricted only to transitive verbs. All normal man-related intransitive verbs take the passive form: *nukutaan* (*nuku-* = sleep-); *rakastutaan* (*rakastu-* = fall- in love); *pyörrytään* (*pyörty-* = become-unconscious); *pudotaan* (*puto-* = fall- down), and so on.

A look at the history of the Finnish passive

It is widely believed that the Finnish passive is not a particularly old formation (Hakulinen 1979: 243) and that it didn't emerge until the Baltic-Finnish period (Early Proto-Finnish). This hypothesis is undermined, however, by the fact that Lapp and Hungarian also have a similar passive construction, and the period when these languages were in contact with Finnish dates back to much earlier times than those of the Baltic-Finnish period (ibid.). But even if the common origin hypothesis is abandoned, it is possible to assume that the passive constructions of these three languages evolved in parallel, though without mutual contact, originating from analogous structural ingredients (perhaps the causative or reflexive) and expressive needs. These structural ingredients themselves may share a common origin and thus be very old.

The Finnish passive and its history is somewhat obscured by the overwhelming effect of unification which the analogy to Indo-European languages imposes upon the Finnish language and the study of it. The urge to find the underlying personal inflection structure, or a causative or reflexive meaning, seems to originate from the hope to establish an analogy between the so-called Finnish passive construction and the allegedly respective Indo-European construction. This holds also for Tuomikoski (1971) who has suggested that the Finnish passive represents the fourth person. The fourth person is, however, still a person. Tuomikoski pays no attention to the possibility that there might occur strongly nonpersonal or impersonal verbal meanings in language, not only in the grammatical sense of the word *person*, but also in the sense which relates the word *person* to an intentional subject. Strongly impersonal meanings originate from the human experience which precedes the appearance of the subject. In a similar vein, many Finnish utterances, for example, certain word derivations with verbal suffixes (such as -*stu-*, -*sty-*, -*tu-*, -*ty-*, -*utu-*, -*yty-*), which suggest that the subject's or agent's power to initiate and control its own action is weakened or undermined, are analyzed as reflexive structures. The reason for this misinterpretation is, most probably, that such meanings in which the power and autonomy of the subject is undermined are rare, marginalized, or nonexistent in the culturally dominant Indo-European languages.

How to apply Keenan and Faltz to the Finnish passive

Keenan and Faltz generalize their analysis of the passive to cover such cases where it is in a sentence form, p_0 (1985: 212–216). In this case the passive is derived from the intransitive form p_1. They apply their rules to the Latin word *curritur* (allegedly p_0 which is supposed to mean something like *running is being done*), which is derived from p_1 *currit* (*runs*). The semantical analysis ends with the following equation: *M (pass)(currit) = currit (Exist y) = for some individual y it holds that y runs*.

The analysis is convincing in many respects, at least as long as we accept the dogma of reification (or, the ontological dogma). But if a similar analysis is applied to Finnish intransitive passive utterances, the meaning becomes necessarily ontologized and a central part of the intuitive meaning is lost. *Ollaan* ends ups meaning the same as *for some individual it holds that it is*. Here existence appears both as a quantifier and predicate, which may indicate that, because existence appears already as a predicate in natural languages, such forms as passive should not be analyzed as if their underlying logical structures, too, were hidden existential quantifiers.

More importantly, Keenan and Faltz's analysis of passive constructions necessarily envisions the passive as a hidden predication that deals with individual agents and patients as if they were logical subjects. Of course the authors concede that in some languages the surface form doesn't always reveal the full logical structure. But nevertheless, their analysis is bound to impose an ontology of individuality upon all experience of language: what we speak of consists necessarily of identity-preserving, separate objects, and we, the speakers, appear in the form of language as logical subjects. If language doesn't show this immediately, it is because we are considering its surface. The proper meaning lies under the surface.

This necessary ontologization conforms with the *Criterion of Logical Adequacy* which they have adopted. But it seems that in the case of the Finnish passive, the logical adequacy is bound to conflict with the explanatory adequacy. The alleged surface syntax of the so-called Finnish passive construction doesn't provide any hints whatsoever that we should derive the passive form from an underlying p_1 form. Valence reduction isn't essential in the Finnish passive. Perhaps it is just the other way round: the preindividual mode of being and doing is, in some sense, *primary*, and the personal mode of being and doing is *derivative*. In addition, it may also be the case that the requirement of logical adequacy is in conflict with experiential adequacy, especially if Finnish native speakers do not always experience a hidden logical subject or an agent in such passive forms as *ollaan*.

Contrary to the Finnish passive, the Latin p_0 form possesses a complete personal inflection system the output of which always carries a reference to an absent patient of the activity. For example, the suffix *-tur* in *curritur* refers to the absent patient (the third person singular) of the running activity, which in certain idioms can be present in the "surface" form of language, too. Keenan and Faltz's analysis doesn't reflect this meaning. Instead, they introduce a hidden logical subject as an agent for the running activity.

But contrary to the Latin passive, no signs of a hidden personal inflection system can be discerned in the so-called Finnish passive construction. Moreover, Finnish passive-like expressions indicate neither gender nor number. The scarcity of the syntax conforms with the native intuition that the meaning of the Finnish passive is more unstructured and amorphous than the allegedly corresponding Indo-European form. If this is so, it is understandable that Keenan and Faltz's analysis doesn't give us adequate explanatory or experiential results, and this holds for the syntax as well as for the semantics. The main reason for this inadequacy is that the meaning of the Finnish passive is related to such a primitive and primordial asubjective experience that it defies all analysis which is carried out according to ontological or ontology-driven notions.

This critique is "transcendental" with respect to the paradigm (of model-theoretical semantics) within which Keenan and Faltz work. Yet it is far from obvious that some other semantic theory within the same paradigm could do better than that of Keenan and Faltz. On the contrary: by being convincing, their analysis reveals the boundaries of the very paradigm. It is, perhaps, the best way to ontologize the passive expressions in the world's languages.

Adequacy

It seems plausible that the meaning of the Finnish passive cannot be understood adequately in *any* theoretical framework which accepts the dogma of reification, that is, which presupposes that meaning must be reified in order to arise, or that meaning must always be explained in terms of an ontology. This, of course, cannot be shown here. But, for example, what Keenan and Faltz call the *Criterion of Logical Adequacy* seems to require a strong ontological commitment, which in their case is the property-ontology. The property-ontology is just one example of those ontologies that satisfy the classical conditions of individuation and separability. These conditions are accepted, for example, by many Western common-sense thinking habits, by classical physics, and classical logic. Of course, the set of objects that is accepted as real by a common sense that is oriented by modern Western technology, is not the same set as Keenan and Faltz's property-ontology. But it is the commitment to the same underlying conditions of individuation and separability that prevents us from understanding adequately what Finnish passive-like utterances mean.

It is always possible to build an ontology/semantics upon the Finnish passive-like language and thus illuminate its meaning from a grammatical and logical angle. This happens, for example, when we suggest that *ollaan* should be translated as *one is, we are, there exists, there exists more than one person*, or something similar. Regardless of how the quantifier is understood, how weak or strong it is supposed to be, such a build-up doesn't cover all varieties and dimensions of the meaning of *ollaan*, and, perhaps, not even its original and central meaning. This seems to suggest that an ontological, grammatical, and logical structure can be imposed upon almost any area of natural language, and language which is seen in the light of the imposition can be used for many metaphysical purposes, including those of logical entailment. But this cannot force us to concede that language primarily or primordially is a mechanism for logical entailment, that there is no language outside of the context of entailment, or that those areas upon which the logical structure is imposed carry no meaning other than what the logical analysis allegedly reveals.

The question is, How important or relevant is that "other meaning"? A legion of good reasons exists for ignoring or suppressing such other meanings. These reasons include political ideals that aim to reduce differences in cultural meaning and by doing so lay the foundations for global intercultural communication. It is not surprising that the standard scientific attitude, for example, that which makes itself manifest in grammar and logic, tends to overemphasize the universal aspects of meaning and thus obviously works for the purpose of political and cultural unification. We can see a repercussion of this attitude also in Keenan and Faltz's analysis of the passive in the world's languages: they do choose the most widely-used passive form as the most basic one but posit, at the same time, an even more fundamental, underlying logical structure. Is it just by chance that this underlying structure also happens to be the Indo-European structure?

But, in spite of all the good reasons to ignore the uniqueness and variety of meaning, and the good intentions behind doing so, we may ask if this good-willed suppression is really naturalistically acceptable. In other words, does it eventually give us a credible picture of what language actually is, or, at least, of what it used to be before global unification became too overwhelming? I think the answer is, No. It is possible that language is a basically aconceptual and asubjective experience which is originally unique and local but which, in certain social circumstances and in pursuit of certain political and economic "ideals", can be seen as if it were a medium of communication, for example, an entailment-preserving mechanism for the communication of propositions.

Words or utterances that lack a logical or grammatical structure are not always elliptical. They can be full of complete asubjective and local meaning. In order to arise, meaning doesn't necessarily require a reference to (or existence of) objects or individuals, let alone elementary or atomic objects or individuals. Those conditions under which the reification of experience or an ontology is imposed upon natural language are always, to some extent, counterfactual in nature, sometimes violently so. It is only by ignoring the local uniqueness and variation — ambiguities, amorphisms, fluctuations, contradictions, deviations, irrelevancies, marginalities, perversions, or whatever you want to call them — that natural language can be made to look like a useful medium for the communication of concepts, ideas, and propositions.

References

Hakulinen, Lauri (1979). *Suomen kielen rakenne ja kehitys* [The Structure and Development of the Finnish Language]. Helsinki: Otava.

Keenan, Edward (1985). Passive in the world's languages. In: *Language Typology and Syntactic Description, Volume 1: Clause Structure*. Timothy Shopen (ed.). 243–281. Cambridge: Cambridge University Press.

Keenan, Edward and Faltz, Leonard (1985). *Boolean Semantics for Natural Language*. Dordrecht: Reidal.

Pylkkö, Pauli (1995). Indeterminacy and experience. In: *Current Trends in Connectionism*. Lars Niklasson and Mikael Bodén (eds.). 321–329. Hillsdale, New Jersey: Lawrence Erlbaum.

– (1997a). Eliminative holism as a solution to Bohr's puzzle with two languages. In: *Brain, Mind and Physics*. Paavo Pylkkänen, Pauli Pylkkö, and Antti Hautamäki (eds.). Amsterdam: IOS-Press. [Forthcoming]

– (1997b). *The Aconceptual Mind: Heideggerian Themes in Holistic Naturalism*. Amsterdam: John Benjamins. [Forthcoming]

Quine, Willard van Orman (1969). *Ontological Relativity and Other Essays*. New York: Columbia University Press.

Tuomikoski, R. (1971). Persoona, tekijä ja henkilö. *Virittäjä: Kotikielen Seuran Aikakauslehti* 75: 146–151. Helsinki.

Kristian Bankov

Text and intelligence

In the spirit of deconstruction let us take Umberto Eco's phrase – "we are dwarfs on the shoulders of giants" (1979: 49)[1] – and try to understand what it means. To begin reducing the universe of possible meanings for this phrase we look first at its context (or better, co-text). They are the last words of a chapter dedicated entirely to Peirce, entitled "Peirce: The semiosic foundations of textual cooperation". The aim of the chapter is to prove that in Peirce's system, and based on the concept of interpretation, one can find all the essential ideas for a unified semiotics that conciliates "the semiotics of the code and the semiotics of the texts and discourses" (ibid.).

Our textual competence might lead us to think that Eco's statement about dwarfs and giants is metaphorical, and we could attempt to interpret it as such, hoping not to violate any limits of interpreting that figure (Eco 1990: 152–174). When Eco says "We" it is reasonable to infer that he, as an interpreter of Peirce's work, belongs to that category of contemporary thinkers (or theoreticians) who interpret the work of other thinkers, especially important philosophers from the past. The phrase tells us literally that these kinds of contemporary thinkers are "dwarfs on the shoulders of giants", which we could interpret as saying that they are somehow inferior to the philosophers of the past. Of course, neither Eco nor we intend the use of the word "dwarfs", in its denotation of inferiority, as referring to real individuals of such physical status. Rather, this metaphor is inspired by the world of fiction, and thus the "vehicle" (Richards 1936) of that metaphor is itself metaphorical. Let us now try to see what kind of inferiority Eco's metaphor attributes to contemporary thinkers.

The topic of the chapter by Eco could be paraphrased as the "systematisation of Peircean semiotic thought". Since the phrase in question is a kind of conclusion for the whole chapter, it is legitimate to see the inferiority in question as an intellectual or theoretical one. A less metaphorical expression for interpreting that metaphor might sound like this: "My colleagues and I, in our theoretical work, are inferior to the important philosophers of the past, on the basis of whose theories we are now making ours." This idea is not an unusual one, and we find something very similar in Bergson: "Vous trouverez parfois, chez le meilleur disciple d'un grand maître, une exposition plus systématique de la doctrine et aussi l'apparence d'une clarté supérieure. C'est justement parce qu'il a suivi jusqu'au bout, avec sa logique plus abstraite et plus simple, les idées dominantes du système." (1895: 370)

Now that we have a satisfying interpretation of Eco's phrase, we proceed by reflecting on the fact that, in saying essentially the same thing, Eco uses metaphor and Bergson uses clear concepts. This is quite strange indeed, because Eco never uses figurative speech in defining his main notions, or at least it is never his only means of doing so. By contrast, Bergson dedicates many pages to criticising the use of rigid concepts in philosophy at the expense of figures (see especially Bergson 1903). The most probable reason for this "paradox" is that the use of figures seems a very obvious idea to Bergson, whereas Eco finds it quite difficult to fit with the rest of his doctrine. Also, Eco finishes his chapter with that phrase unelaborated, but Bergson goes on to give an explanation: "Mais il faut remonter à l'œuvre du maître pour entrer en communication avec sa logique personelle et profonde, modelée sur le réel, souple comme la vie, et capable, comme la nature, de présenter des éléments toujours nouveaux à notre pensée qui voudrait vainement en épuiser l'analyse" (1895: 370). Bergson's writings are full of such reflections, which form one of the main topics of his later work (cf. Bergson 1932).

Of course one need not perform a thorough analysis to see how difficult it is in semiotic terms to say that someone's work is theoretically inferior to that of another. A simple historical view could solve this problem. One of the main weapons of modern (understood as after Peirce and Saussure) and post-modern thought is that kind of analysis which searches for "the truth" not in the intentions of the subject (its subjectivity), but in something external to it, something objective in which the subject participates. It is said that this approach originates with Nietzsche, but Marx, Freud, and Heidegger are also quite fashionable in modern and post-modern thought. With structuralism, which ontologises some methodological artifices of linguistics (cf. Eco 1968), we had the science of the non-existent subject. The "author" became *persona non grata* in literature and generally in semiotics. His death was celebrated by Barthes, and his corpus of work became the subject of some sadistic deconstructive practices. There is no creation, but only the reproduction of what is objectively immanent to the structures or simply the derivation of their absence. The individual no longer speaks but is instead spoken *by* language and other sign systems. In this epistemological system, authorities do not exist, for they are "logically" inadmissible. There are no giants, only dwarfs.

The 1970s witnessed the "rediscovery of the subject" and a turn towards pragmatics, but we had to wait until 1979 for Eco's metaphor, which appeared in a book – and this is not pure chance – dedicated precisely to the problem of interpretation. But in 1979 was semiotics, as a pragmatics of the text, yet ready to speak about theoretical dwarfs and giants? In other words, was this metaphor merely decorating something that is said in the text in a "scientific" way, or is this is a cognitive metaphor? (Cf. Eco 1984: 99–103.) Can we find in *Lector in Fabula* a semiotic or pragmatic explanation of the assertion that Eco, as interpreter of Peirce, is a dwarf and the latter is a giant? No, we cannot.

On the one hand, Eco at a certain place specifies that his main interest lies in narratives, and the Peircean text is not of that kind. On the other hand, when Eco speaks in general for all types of communication he leaves us a trace from which to infer such an explanation by using the theoretical tools placed at our disposal in his book. But Eco speaks neither metaphorically nor theoretically about narrative giants and dwarfs, even though it is quite easy to attribute those labels to thousands of authors and readers.

What is this trace? We find it on page 53: "This obvious condition of the existence of the texts collides with another, no less obvious pragmatic law, which, even if it could remain covered for such a long time in the history of communication, is [no longer hidden] today. The law could be easily formulated in a slogan: *the competence of the addressee is not necessarily the same as the competence of the addresser.*" (Eco's italics) Eco speaks about pragmatic law, which posits a difference between author and reader, and this is quite an encouraging beginning for our research. For the difference between the dwarfs and the giants could be sought in their different competencies. And, indeed, a great part of the book is dedicated to the concept of competence. Eco calls it "encyclopedic competence", and this is one of the most significant notions of his model.

Space limitations hinder us from making a detailed examination of Eco's model, but we can easily verify if he is theoretically inferior to Peirce as concerns their relative encyclopedic competence. And the obvious answer is "no". Eco knows more than Peirce; he owns a bigger portion of the encyclopedia; he has read more books than Peirce (although the latter is also a "champion" of the encyclopedia); he has a hundred more years of history to draw upon; and he has studied a major part of what Peirce's writings. From the purely quantitative point of view (which this model encourages), Eco's encyclopedic competence surpasses that of Peirce.

What, then, makes Eco consider himself a dwarf on the shoulders of a giant? and to such a degree that he precedes his metaphor with the phrase, "It is well known". He says something similar about the pragmatic law ("which, even if it could remain covered for such a long time in the history of communication, it is no longer so today."). But in the whole chapter he cites no other author who shares his view (and this is may be the only chapter in which Eco does not quote some contemporary theoretician). In *Les limites de l'interprétation* (1990) we find no further explanations as to who is dwarf and who giant in the Reader-Author relation.

It turns out that Eco's metaphor remains quite isolated from mainstream semiotic thought, although the years of orthodox structuralism have come and gone. On the one hand, Eco as Reader incessantly demonstrates his respectful appreciation for authorities; but on the other, as a semiotician he cannot provide a satisfactory explanation of the obvious pragmatic law, because of the very nature of the semiotic approach.

We can try to indicate the complexity of this problem. Indeed, if we accept that the competence of the reader differs from that of the author, and if we also accept that it is not only a question of encyclopedic knowledge but of something more fundamental, then this pragmatic law could become a time-bomb that threatens many of the certainties of the semiotics of interpretation. Because it means that the difference between reader and reader is also not merely encyclopedic.

One of the many places where we find Eco as a reader of Aristotle is in *Semiotics and the Philosophy of Language*, in the chapter dedicated to metaphor (1984: 87–129). There, after a short but significant introduction on the importance of that argument, Eco states: "Not least of the contradictions encountered in a *metaphorology* is that, of the thousands and thousand of pages written about the metaphor, few add anything of substance to the first two or three fundamental concepts, stated by Aristotle" (p. 88). This implicit "giant-dwarfs" statement spurs us in turn to become readers of Aristotle, and to begin our inquiry into the non-encyclopedic differences between authors and readers with some of the philosopher's words concerning metaphor: "It is a great thing, indeed, to make a proper use of these poetical forms, as also of compounds and strange words. But the greatest thing by far is to be a master of metaphor. It is the one thing that cannot be learnt from others; and it is also a sign of genius, since a good metaphor implies an intuitive perception of the similarity in dissimilars [sic]." (*Poetics*: 1459a 4–11.) Here we see a very explicit expression of the pragmatic law, with the addition of something very substantial: the thing that makes the difference cannot be learned. And the objection that Aristotle speaks "only" about metaphor is not very well-grounded, because we now know that the very constitution of natural languages is metaphorical. Much has been written on this subject, but it will suffice to mention only work by Richards (1936) and Ricœur (1975) to give us some idea of the metaphoricity of language and of the importance of Aristotle's statement. Indeed, Richards, interpreting Aristotle, says: "A <command of metaphor> – a command of the interpretation of metaphors – can go deeper still into the control of the world that we make for ourselves to live in" (1936: 135; see also, Lakoff 1980).

Text and intelligence

This important statement leads us to see things in a new light. We, as users of language, differ from each other, and each person has his own ability to manipulate language, an ability that cannot be learned. This means we also differ in our abilities to interpret texts, which, we repeat, is not a question of the quantity of one's knowledge. The sense of the text is not immanent to the language. We need intersubjective conventions in order to determine the meaning of written signs. And in the text there is not only the content (or rules for its production), but also the ability of the author to deal with signs. The reader perceives this ability, in addition to the encyclopedic "charge" of the text, which we shall see is not merely a question of writing style.

Richards issues the following warning: "Our skill with metaphor, with thought, is one thing – prodigious and inexplicable; our reflective awareness of that skill is quite another thing – very incomplete, distorted, fallacious, over-simplifying" (1936: 116; also cited in Ricœur 1975: 106). When we state that the sense of the text is immanent to the language and to the encyclopedia we are also stating that skill is immanent to them. But skill, in the immanence hypothesis, becomes something very sterile, if anyone considers it at all; at best, something is said about "savoir-faire" or "pouvoir-être". The problem of skill is also ideological. We saw above that twentieth-century thought exposes subjectivity; and modern aesthetics, with pretensions to scientific status,[2] opposes itself to nineteenth-century aesthetics based on the idea of genius.[3] The situation calls to mind Lenin's attack on scientists and philosophers who, "in the light of radical changes in the field of physics, mistook the crisis of erroneous conceptions regarding matter for the disappearance of matter itself."[4] If romantic aesthetics had an erroneous or exaggerated notion of the Author's skills, this need not mean that those skills do not exist. But unfortunately, in contrast to physical matter (which seems not to have disappeared) the geniuses disappeared when the new epistemological frame came and "scientifically" excluded the possibility of their existence. Now there are only Dwarfs. But if the geniuses have disappeared, this is not true of the particular metaphorical (linguistic) skill of authors and readers, and we can proceed by trying to understand better this "radical" pragmatic law.

As we have said before, with the exception of twentieth-century thought, the idea that individuals have different competencies is quite traditional, and pragmatics only rediscovers something obvious. When Socrates (Plato) discusses with Theaetetus the nature of knowledge he puts things in these terms:

> *Socrates*: Please assume, then, for the sake of argument, that there is in our souls a block of wax, in one case larger, in another smaller, in one case the wax is purer, in another more impure and harder, in some cases softer, and in some of proper quality.
>
> *Theaetetus*: I assume all that.

Socrates: Let us, then, say that this is the gift of Memory, the mother of the Muses...
(*Theaetetus*, 191 D).

Kant speaks about Transcendental judgement in very similar terms:

> If understanding be considered the faculty of rules, judgement will be the faculty that *subsumes* under rules, the faculty that distinguishes whether something stands under a given rule or not [...] the understanding is capable of being instructed and qualified by rules, whereas judgement, again, is but a special talent that may indeed be exercised but not taught. Judgement, in point of fact, constitutes what is specific in so-called *mother-wit*, the want of which cannot be supplied by any scowling. (Kant 1881: 245; his italics)

The idea of innate faculties is quite important for Descartes, and we find it also in Bergson, who reflects on the problem of the relation between built-in and acquired faculties:

> Mais il est rare que la nature produise spontanément une âme affranchie et maîtresse d'elle même, une âme accordée à l'unisson de la vie. L'éducation doit intervenir le plus souvent, non pas tant pour imprimer un élan que pour écarter les obstacles, plutôt aussi pour lever un voile que pour apporter la lumiére. (Op. cit.: 366)

The question that arises from Bergson's point is somewhat broad, but nevertheless provides the concluding topic of the present paper: Are innate intellectual properties important for the interpretation of texts, or does everything depend on acquired and culturally determined faculties (the encyclopedia)?

We shall later give our opinion on that problem (which is implicit in the giants-dwarfs relation) in philosophic and semiotic terms. But "for the sake of argument" we begin with a very important example, borrowed from psychology. This example is IQ tests. Theories of IQ are contemporary with semiotics (Binet is more or less a contemporary of Peirce and Saussure), and they deal with tests, whereas semiotics deals with texts. Considering the obvious fact that IQ tests are texts, it is reasonable to search for some of their common traits regarding the process of interpretation. IQ tests have their model reader, which is quite universal, yet they are also intended to be interpreted differently from the way one interprets narratives. They measure a pragmatic ability of their readers, the same one – competence – required for actualising the sense of the text. Indeed, intelligence is considered generally to be the faculty (ability) of the individual to take advantage of the environment; but environment in semiotic terms is nothing than cultural units, text, or semiosphere. Being "condemned to sense", our actions are always interpretative processes, where "interpretation" stands for adaptation in psychological terms. Although our every practical action is culturally determined, thus semiotically analysable, the theory is developed mainly on narrative texts, which supposedly do not have a referent, at least in the real world. In the same way, IQ tests (on which is based the corresponding theory) do not refer to any concrete act of adaptation, but measure the potential adaptability of the individual.

It seems that all texts are IQ tests, with different degrees of complication and degrees of objective measurability of the interpretative results. IQ tests have a "correct" solution, and nobody speaks about their being interpreted. Why, then, should we speak about detective stories in terms of interpretation, when their mechanism is the same as that of IQ tests? Do they not challenge the reader's intelligence, which is constrained to compete with the detective's (author's)? Surely an objective scale of measurement could be constructed by which to determine how well readers solve detective stories, or how well they read many other types of "closed" texts (cf. Eco 1962, 1975, 1979, 1990). But the point is that in the majority of these texts the author does everything possible to insure that the readers do not have to overexert their intelligence. Eco calls "textual strategy" the author's inscribing within the text a model Reader that most resembles the empirical readers he writes for (Eco 1979). To create this kind of "insurance" is one of the hardest tasks of the textual strategy. The Author has double the work, and presupposing the reader's encyclopedia is only part of it. The whole positive conception of knowledge goes in this direction. The "scientist" works with his mind for the other members of the scientific community. Once a discovery is made, he communicates it in the way that requires the right portion of encyclopedia and *nothing else* from his readers. Verifiability means that he has to ensure the possibility of everyone reproducing his experiment. For his communication he can count only on what is common convention, on what he *is sure* is possessed by the others. He cannot count on the fact that each member of the community will have sufficient intelligence to deduce from the results the validity of the discovery (except for cases such as Coulomb's egg, which doesn't require scientific communication in order for the community to understand it).

The fact that scientific texts are not made the same as IQ tests is quite positive and could be considered a great achievement of the Western culture. But this is only the ideal case, the limit situation. Real scientists are as much readers as authors of texts, and for them it proves convenient that, when they read, there are established standards which guarantee their understanding the text. So the focus of their activity (the use of their intelligence) is to work on the bases of their specialisation and to communicate the results if they make progress toward the solution of an existing problem. They gain time in their readings which they use afterwards to write according to the norms. The advantage is obvious – one writes and many read. One loses time in order to write well, and thousands take advantage of the effort.

All this stresses the fact that the dominant mode of thinking and communicating is constituted in a way that masks one's individual responsibility in the process. It took semiotics many years to realise that the competence of the reader usually differs from that of the author. But the model of encyclopedic competence is only the first step in this direction. The communicative competence of the individual has many different dimensions, and quantitative knowledge is only one of them.[5] All of those competencies take part in the pragmatic law mentioned above, and pragmatics has to work in this direction.

If we develop further the analogy between IQ tests and text we soon reach very undesirable conclusions. Discourse about the human faculties has passed from the philosophy of the nineteenth century to the psychology of the twentieth. While some of the most important philosophers of our own century were busy trying to "clarify" their discipline and render it as a perfect dictionary (thereby rendering a service to all future philosophers), psychology was reducing intelligence to a matter of genes and neurons. Intelligence became something immanent. Both sides of the so-called "IQ controversy" agree on that point. The "geneticists" explain IQ differences as a kind of genetic fact. From there, the road to racism was a short one, leading to great controversy. The progressive side of the controversy sees the differences among mental faculties as immanent to the cultural environment (the encyclopedia). Of course, real debates on this issue begin by all sides accepting the fact that both innate and environmental factors determine IQ, but the question is the weight of each type. More and more scientific proofs were necessary to defend one or the other viewpoint. Intelligence was reduced more and more to such objectively measurable elements as the speed of bio-electronic impulses or the elaboration of sense data in the short-term memory. But the growing illusion is that "this is the truth", because it is scientifically provable. Richards' warned that "Our skill with metaphor, with thought, is one thing – prodigious and inexplicable; our reflective awareness of that skill is quite another thing – very incomplete, distorted, fallacious, over-simplifying." (1936: 116). Such a statement might be insulting to the experimental psychologists of today. But those same psychologists would find it difficult to explain scientifically the existence of a "giant-dwarf" relation between Peirce's and Eco's theories. Somewhere in his work Bergson suggests that the brain is only the organ of thought, a kind of muscle, but that the mind is something else(where). Maybe the most simple conception of intelligence coincides with the objective and "physical" strength of that muscle, but this is certainly an oversimplification.

We have seen that, on one hand, pragmatics could learn something from psychology, such as the notion of communicative competence. But on the other hand, the way psychology goes about dealing with some problems is dangerously reductive. We might even say that, where psychology leaves off, interesting things begin.

Text and intelligence

We have spoken thus far only about closed texts, but the real tests of intelligence come from open texts. Or better, they are the tests of real intelligence. We cannot say what is real intelligence, just as we cannot say what is the right interpretation of open texts, but we can make some valid hypotheses on its limits.

As the hermeneutic tradition suggests, texts constitute the self of the reader, and there is an "achèvement de l'intelligence du texte dans une intelligence de soi" (Ricœur 1970: 195). This intelligence differs from that of the psychologist, and it is this intelligence that interests us. So the text is on one hand a measure (or challenge) to the intelligence of the reader, but on the other it is also a lesson (or example) of intelligence. Kant's ideas on that matter are very clear and help us to clarify what we mean. In the same chapter that we quoted above, after writing that judgement cannot be learned, Kant nevertheless leaves some possibilities for its modification:

> A physician, therefore, a judge, or a statesman may have in his head many fine pathological, jurisprudential, or political rules – may have them in his head to such a degree, as to be actually a profound teacher of them, and yet he shall easily blunder in the application of them; either he wants natural judgement (not understanding as a faculty of rules), and, though he can very well understand the universal *in abstracto*, he is unable to decide of the particular *in concreto* as a case in point; or because it may be also, <u>he has not been sufficiently exercised in examples or inured to actual practice</u>, for the formation of such a judgement. For this, in that reference, is precisely the <u>one sole great use of examples: they sharpen the judgement</u>. (Kant 1881: 246; his italics; my underlining)

In this way Kant suggests that generally this special ability cannot be learned, but it can be "sharpened" by examples.

Somewhere François Truffaut says that every good movie is a lesson of cinema and a lesson of life. We can say after reading Kant's considerations that each good text is a portion of the encyclopedia and is also a lesson (example) of intelligence. Intelligence from this point of view is the general competence to manage knowledge, not to possess it.[6] To have a portion of the encyclopedia is to possess the signs and the *rules* (Eco's very word; 1979: 23) for their use in a given culture. But special competence is the ability to subsume "reality" under these rules, to know when one sign or rule is more adequate than another. The point is a subtle one. The encyclopedia gives us ready-made solutions for standard (according to statistical constancy) situations or frames. But always we need a superior instance in order to decide the case *in concreto* for the rule *in abstracto*. Generally speaking, sense transcends the encyclopedia (or the text). There is something external to the text and the encyclopedia which is part of the actualised sense. This is the author's example of intelligence, this silent instruction, which goes together with the noisy word, the sign, the structural games.

The author never dies! Ricœur somewhere says about the structural anthropology of Lévi-Strauss, that it is a kind of "kantism without a transcendental subject". Similarly, artificial intelligence would be "encyclopedism without a transcendental subject". One can program many rules (frames) into the robot's "mind", and then add more sophisticated, interactive rules for how to use the previous rules, and so on, and so on. But always there will be a necessary, superior instance to make the decision. Kant is "merciless" on this point:

> ... for let the schooling amply offer, or even cram, a limited understanding with rules borrowed from another; still, the ability rightly to apply them must be the pupil's own. No rule whatever that may be supplied him with this intention would, in default of natural gift, be safe from misuse. (Ibid.)

Perhaps to have artificial intelligence we shall have to wait until IBM produces some "gifted" computer. Until then let us respect the transcendence of the subject.

In order to give our version of the "giant-dwarfs" relation we have to assume some concepts, proposed by Ricœur (1975), reintroducing metaphor as an example of the creative use of language and of the mind in general. Above all it is necessary to specify what the text is. Ricœur writes:

> Par texte [...] j'entends, par priorité, la production du discours comme une œuvre. Avec l'œuvre, comme le mot l'indique, de nouvelles catégories entrent dans le champ de discours, essentiellement des catégories pratiques, des catégories de la production et du travail. (1975: 277)

This dimension of the text is very important for our research. The text is always a product of concrete linguistic and intellectual work. This view helps us to enlarge the prospects for pragmatic analysis. The usual pragmatic approach always focuses on the effects of speech on the understanding of the text or of the circumstances. Those are all synchronic views. Even Eco's detailed analysis of textual cooperation deals with the different phases of the achievement of sense, and not on the linguistic work necessary for it – as in those films where the director shows us in 30 seconds how a few men built a house, making us see only the results of the work and not the work itself. It is strange that, in semiotics and in structuralism, Marxist thought is quite popular, but almost everybody considers the text as something independent of its author, thereby taking the side of textual fetishists.[7] We agree that the text could mean something different from what the author intended and could be the arena of some objective structural relations, but the text will always be also an example of linguistic work. For, unlike industrial products, texts are unique.

The second important assumption is that the text always refers to something. The text is an utterance (*énonciation*), an instance of discourse. Ricœur dedicates a whole chapter to this problem (1975), arguing mainly with the orthodox structuralist dictum that literature has no referent. Eco's position is more flexible, and he introduces the concept of cultural unit (cf. Eco 1975). But if we assume that language is work, we have to assume also that the reference is always something *conquered* by means of intellectual effort. We cannot neglect the fact that each utterance (or instance of discourse) is produced in a unique moment and that we have to work at it each time. Otherwise, we would behave like a robot, which expects the situation to offer the exact stimulus to coincide with the frame that has been programmed into its "mind". On our own, we have to apply each time the *abstract* system of rules (encyclopedia) to the *concrete* situation. This holds true always – in everyday communication, as well as in the most abstract philosophical theory. The utterance is always work and the exercise of the capacity of the author. Those people who live by ready-made phrases (frames) and use the common encyclopedia as their only "reference guide" are usually called "stupid" (those who don't use it at all are called "crazy").

We shall let Ricœur himself introduce the third notion, which is "ontological vehemence":

> Le premier mouvement – naïf, non critique – est celui de la *véhémence* ontologique. Je ne le renierai pas, je le médiatiserai seulement. Sans lui, le moment critique serait infirme. Dire « cela est » , tel est le moment de la *croyance, l'ontological commitment* qui donne sa force « illocutionnaire » à l'affirmation. Nulle part cette véhémence d'affirmation n'est mieux attestée que dans l'expérience poétique. Selon une de ses dimensions, au moins, cette expérience exprime le moment extatique du langage – le language hors de soi; elle semble ainsi attester que c'est le désir du discours de s'effacer, de mourir, aux confins de l'être dit. La philosophie peut-elle prendre en compte la non- philosophie de l'extase? Et à quel prix? (1975: 313; Ricœur's italics)

The answer to this question is positive, and the last chapter of the book is dedicated to "Métaphore et discours philosophique".

Now we see that to affirm something is a very, very hard task. Above all one must *dare* to make this affirmation, to have this vehemence, in some way to attack the "non-said". And this is the first moment of that speculation which Aristotle defines simply as the capacity to see similarity in apparently different things. Bergson calls this faculty "intuition". After this ecstatic moment the real linguistic work begins – the speculation, the use of the encyclopedia. But we saw that here the author needs what Kant calls transcendental judgement (but we can call it transcendental intelligence or competence), which is necessary in order to introduce this state "out of language" inside it. (We cannot accept that the limits of our world are the limits of our language. The limits of our world are the limits of this ontological vehemence, this offensive semiotic power, which individuals possess in different degrees.)

We can at last answer the "giants-dwarfs" question. In our view, Eco says that "we are dwarfs on the shoulders of giants" because the difference between him and Peirce turns on their ontological vehemence. Peirce dares to say things that it would be impossible to say today, and this is not because they are untrue. The ambition of his philosophical enterprise is incommensurable with today's standards and not because it is "bigger" in terms of the encyclopedia. After a hundred years of modern thought and the "professionalisation" of philosophy, it is very easy to say that Plato and Aristotle are saying obviously wrong things. But let us think in terms of intellectual work and ontological vehemence. According to Aristotle "being is what is said in many ways", and his enormous ontological vehemence brought him to risk saying what being really is. Following him, the whole philosophical tradition continued to speak about being.[8] But not anymore. Today we cannot discuss being, but only what is said about being. We are living in the intertext, which is a kind of simulacrum of being. The ontological vehemence of past times is now *onto-textual* vehemence. Each assertion is a compilation of explicit or implicit citations. And nobody believes anything that is not said in this way. We no longer search for similarities between apparently different things, but for similarities between apparently different authors and texts. We end by quoting Bergson, who captures this situation well (1895: 367):

> Peut-être avez vous remarqué, devant nos monuments et dans nos musées, des étrangers qui tiennent à la main un livre ouvert, un livre où ils trouvent décrites, sans doute, les merveilles qui les environnent. Absorbés dans cette lecture, ne semblent-il pas oublier pour elle parfois, les belles choses qu'ils étaient venus voir? C'est ainsi que beaucoup d'entre nous voyagent à travers l'existence, les yeux fixés sur des formules qu'ils lisent, dans une espèce de guide intérieur, négligeant de regarder la vie pour se régler simplement sur ce qu'on en dit, et pensant d'ordinaire à des mots plutôt qu'à des choses.

Notes

1. All references are to the Italian edition of the book, and the translations are my own. The English edition doesn't contain the parts that interest us. Also, during the writing of this paper we had not yet learned of the origins of that metaphor. We thought it was Eco's invention. From Prof. Ugo Volli we later learned that this is only a citation of very well known aphorism, the story of which has formed the object of an entire book by Robert Merton called *On the Shoulders of Giants*. In a sense we are glad not to have read this book before completing the present paper, because in that case we should not have been able to use an inquiry into the meaning of metaphor as a rhetorical tool for our argument. Eco himself gives us justification for doing that, as found in his *Les limites de l'interprétation* (1990: 152) where he cites Henry (1983: 9): « L'interprète idéal d'une métaphore devrait toujours se placer du point de vue de celui qui l'entend pour la première fois ».
2. According to Richard Rorty (1982: 139–159), literary criticism tries to problematize the orthodox scientific model. Here we put them both under the same denominator of "scientificity" because the former derives from the Saussurian turn in the science of language, being the exploration of its extreme consequences.
3. This opposition between old and new models could be very well explained by Lotman as a dialogue between semiospheres. This dialogue is based on the relation

of opposition, which is constitutive for the sense of modern discourse. Only the non-old is acceptable.
4. Lenin, quoted in Ponzio (1993: 29–30).
5. See Ricci-Bitti (1983). According to the author communicative competence, besides semiotic competence, (seen as the sum of linguistic and paralinguistic competencies), also involves pragmatic and performative competence. These two competencies do not concern the contents of our knowledge, but the capacity to apply it in a concrete situation. More interesting to us are the considerations of Kjolseth (1972), quoted by Ricci-Bitti. Kjolseth divides communicative competence into background knowledge, foreground knowledge, emergent grounds, and *transcendent* grounds.
6. Plato can helps us explain what we mean. In the following passage there is a clear distinction between the intellectual work necessary for acquisition of the encyclopedia and its use:
   Socrates: Once more, then, just as a while ago we contrived some sort of a waxen figment in the soul, so now let us make in each soul an aviary stocked with all sorts of birds, some in flocks apart from the rest, others in small groups, and some solitary, flying hither and thither among them all.
   Theaetetus: Consider it done. What next?
   Socrates: We must assume that while we are children this receptacle is empty, and we must understand that the birds represent the varieties of knowledge.
   {...}Socrates: Continuing, then, our comparison with the acquisition and hunting of the pigeons, we shall say that the hunting is of two kinds, one before the acquisition for the sake of possessing, the other carried on by the possessor for the sake of taking and holding in his hands what he had acquired long before.
   (Plato, Theaetetus, tr. Harold Fowler, 197 D, 198 D)
7. A very important exception is represented by the Italian philosopher of language, Ferruccio Rossi-Landi. He introduces the idea of linguistic work in *Il linguaggio come lavoro e come mercato* (1992). We are indebted to him for many ideas, but his approach is quite (anti)ideological and is focused always on the social side of the problem and not on the individual, which interests us here.
8. Important philosophical texts have ontological vehemence inscribed within them – and not only philosophical texts, but all those that have contributed to our common encyclopedia. Also we can propose a distinction between this type of text and the great majority of other texts. For the latter kind of text, the litmus tests of interpretation, proposed by Eco (1979, 1990), are universally valid, as are Newton's laws of space and time. But the former texts are like those objects that move with the speed of light. As examples of interpretation or structural analysis, semioticians rarely give philosophical texts; and when they do, their analyses of them are very partial and reductive. The problem is that, in many cases, interpretation is something more for the reader than mere understanding. The reader is "illuminated", he is infected with the author's ontological vehemence, and his intelligence is "sharpened" by that of the writer. Such readings could generate a new philosophical doctrine or other types of thought exercises. And this absolutely will not be any *use* of those texts. But in saying what it is, I would be obliged to use notions from the nineteenth century.

References

Aristotle (1926). *Poetics*. Trans. Ingram Bywater. Cambridge, Mass. ; London : Harvard University Press.

Bergson, Henri (1895). "Le bon sens et les études classiques". In: *Henri Bergson. Mélanges: Textes publiés et annotés par André Robinet*. 360–372. Paris: P.U.F.
– (1903). "Introduction à la métaphysique". *Revue de Métaphysique et morale* 29(1): 1–36.
– (1932). *Les deux sources de la morale et de la religion*. Paris: Félix.
Eco, Umberto (1962).*Opera aperta. Forma e indeterminazione nelle poetiche contemporanee*. Milano: Bonpiani. In French: *L'œuvre ouverte*. Paris: Seuil, 1965.
– (1968). *La struttura assente*. Milano: Bonpiani. In French: *La structure absente*. Paris: Mercure, 1972.
– (1975). *Trattato di semiotica generale*. Milano: Bonpiani. In English: *A Theory of Semiotics*, Bloomington: Indiana University Press, 1976.
– (1979). *Lector in fabula*. Milano: Bonpiani. In English: *The Role of the Reader*. London: Hutchinson, 1981.
– (1984). *Semiotica e filosofia del linguaggio*. Turin: Einaudi. In English: *Semiotics and the Philosophy of Language*. London: Macmillan, 1985.
– (1990). *I limiti dell'interpretazione*. Milano: Bonpiani. In French: *Les limites de l'interprétation*. Trans. Myriem Bouzaher. Paris: Grasset, 1992.
Kant, Immanuel (1881). *Critique of Pure Reason*. Trans. James Hutchison. Sterling and London: Simpkin, Marshal, and Co.
Kjolseth, Rolf (1971). *Zur Soziologie der Sprache : ausgewählte Beiträge vom Weltkongress der Soziologie*. Opladen: Westdeutscher Verlag.
Lakoff, George (1980). *Metaphors We Live By*. Chicago: University of Chicago Press.
Merton, Robert K. (1965). *On the Shoulders of Giants*. Toronto and Ontario: Collier-Macmillan Canada.
Plato (1987). *Theaetetus*. Trans. Harold Fowler. .Harmondsworth: Penguin Books.
Ponzio, Augusto (1993). *Signs, Dialogue and Ideology*. Philadelphia: J. B. Amsterdam.
Ricci-Bitti, Pio E. and Zani, Bruna (1983). *La comunicazione come processo sociale* [*Communication as a Social Process*]. Bologna: Mulino.
Richards, Ivor Armstrong (1936). *The Philosophy of Rhetoric*. New York: Oxford University Press.
Ricœur, Paul (1970). "Qu'est-ce qu'un texte?" In *Hermeneutik und Dialektik*. Vol II. 181–200. Tübingen: Mohr.
– (1975). *La métaphore vive*. Paris: Seuil; In English: *The rule of metaphor: multi-disciplinary studies of the creation of meaning in language*. London: Routledge and Kegan Paul, 1986.
Rorty, Richard (1982). *Consequences of Pragmatism*. Minneapolis: University of Minnesota Press.
Rossi-Landi, Ferruccio (1992/1968). *Il linguaggio come lavoro e come mercato*. Milano: Bonpiani (first edition: 1968). In English: *Language as Work and Trade*. South Hadley, Mass.: Bergin & Garvey, 1983.

Heikki Kirjavainen

Peirce, Rantala, and theological semiotics

1. Introduction

Theology is sometimes understood as a part of religion, as an extension of religious thinking, but one can also view it as an enterprise that is conceptually independent of religion. In the latter case, theology is not based on religion but takes religious concepts as its object of study. Theology, in its academic and scientific sense, has to be comprehended in this way. Seeing theology as not bound to religion proper is compatible with that philosophy of religion which takes the clarification of religious language as its main focus. In this sense theology is clearly a second-order activity. Since both semantics and semiotics deal with problems of meaning, particularly questions of linguistic meaning, these two ventures seem to come very close to the aforementioned way of seeing the main tasks of philosophy of religion to lie in its linguistic turn. Yet when looking at the boundless ocean of different types of signs and symbols, both linguistic and non-linguistic, which we face in the area of theological research, we can easily see the need for a sufficiently strong metalevel theory that would contrive all the various situations that carry meanings. My concern is not with semantics as such a meta-theory, but with semiotics. Therefore, I am trying to advance some points that purport to answer whether semiotics can offer such a strong metalevel theory. In the same breath I want to express my hesitancy to approach such a theory, because it inevitably implies serious philosophical difficulties. Of course we face similar difficulties in semantics, too.

2. The problem of the universal theory of meaning

Let us look at efforts developed as the most extensive theoretical approaches to the analysis of meaning in semantics and in semiotics. In semantics this kind of approach is found in so-called Model Theory, i.e., possible-worlds semantics; in semiotics a similar status has been given to structuralist and post-structuralist approaches, as well as to those methods developed on the basis of Charles Peirce's theory of signs. Yet both semantic and semiotic approaches have their own faults.

In my view, semiotic theories, especially, suffer from grave defects precisely due to their extensiveness; that is to say, in casting too broad a net these theories cannot do justice to all the nuances by which signs can mean something. But though still somewhat wary, I have become a little more optimistic in certain respects, namely, in attaching positive possibilities to the systematic progress of semiotics. I want to express my present view in a somewhat parabolic way. In its most generalized, metalevel form, semiotics corresponds to the drawing of "auxiliary figures" in geometry in order to solve certain geometrical problems, only in this case the problems concern meaning. That no general theory exists of how to draw such auxiliary figures, can be understood as the basic restriction to systematizating any philosophical method, semiotics included. It follows that, among other things, it is difficult to separate semiotic activity from semiotic theorizing or, in other words, to distinguish between doing semiotics and speaking about the determination of semiotic meaning. Put yet another way, it is precisely the distinction between first- and second-order analysis that becomes problematic.

The lack of systematization does not afflict semantic model theory. On the contrary, systematization can be completely carried out on the propositional level. Rather, model theory does not seem to be much help in determining *lexical* meanings in natural language. Even this flaw can be greatly amelioriated within model theory, but I will not go into that. Instead, in the following I put forth some reasons for my slight optimism concerning the possiblity of systematizing semiotics. I go on to say something about the relationship between semiotics and semantics. And finally, I try to illustrate how we might apply semiotic approaches to the study of religious language, or "do" a theology of religious concepts.

3. The Chinese Room Argument

Perhaps the reader will recall John Searle's Chinese Room Argument. But to be safe, I will briefly review its main content. Let us consider a person who is competent in Finnish but no other language. He has been placed in a room with an input hole on one wall and an output hole on the other. Signs will be given to him through the input hole. Moreover, he has been supplied with complete precepts in Finnish of how to deal with each sign. He acts according to the precepts and transfers the results out through the output hole. He receives Chinese characters, and transfers out correct English writing. In this case, the person has translated Chinese into English without understanding anything from the text. Nevertheless, he has succeeded because the precepts in Finnish were flawless and he has followed them correctly. The person has performed a task that is done nowadays by advanced translation computers. Searle's main point is that those computers do not, and never will, really understand anything of what they are doing. They simply process the marks according to the rules. Searle's argument has triggered lively discussion within cognitive science and among researchers of artificial intelligence. Instead of going into that, however, I will try to say in what sense the argument can be taken as a starting point for the exploration of problems in theological semiotics and semantics.

The argument is purported to prove that such intentional matters as understanding and intending cannot be explained even by the perfect following of rules and precepts governing such issues. Consequently, if we conceive the rules of sign manipulation as the syntax of these signs, then understanding cannot be exhausted by syntax. What we need is semantics, that is, something that links the signs with the things they represent, and this is to happen in such a way that our person in the Chinese room becomes conscious of what the signs signify or mean. Somebody would immediately say that what we need is a new syntax: a set of directions that say how the Chinese marks are translated into Finnish, which is the language understood by the person in the room. But does this free us from the problem?

4. Eco and Peirce

In his article "On truth: A fiction", Umberto Eco tries to answer this question by starting from the idea that the meaning relation is not one between an expression and the world but a relation between two expressions. How do we know, asks Eco, that a sign signifies something? He gives the example of a philosopher conversing with a very sophisticated computer to find out if the machine really understands what it says. Typically the computer is called Charles Sanders Personal. The model used by Eco presupposes that CSP entails a hierarchical series of "dictionaries". A semantic relation is supposed to obtain between an expression in one dictionary and another expression in a different dictionary. The philosopher asks, for example, if CSP knows what the expression "salt" means. CSP replies that one of his dictionaries says that "salt" means "sodium chloride". Our philosopher tries to ask further if CSP knows what "sodium chloride" means, and CSP answers again, saying that it will check the matter in a more advanced dictionary of chemistry, which is part of his hierarchical dictionary system. And so the process continues indefinitely. Of course the problem our philosopher faces is this: is it possible that, if the process of leafing through dictionaries continues long enough, we will arrive at the point where it will be unnecessary to ask if CSP really understands something? In other words, could we in principle, with the help of purely syntactic tools, settle the semantic relation between the expression "salt" and that stuff in reality which "salt" signifies, and do this in such a way that we can state that we understand the meaning of this expression? The situation corresponds to that of the occupant of the Chinese room, who has no opportunity to set up the meaning relations of the expressions (marks) other than by looking in books in order to see what marks certain other marks represent. The optical correspondence-relation between signs serves as the basis of semantic relation.

The idea behind Eco's theory is interesting, though he leaves it undeveloped. We could think, as Peirce did, that the real world, too, is a kind of dictionary; the reality we live in is, in the last analysis, the reality of marks, signs, and symbols. The immediate relation between a mark and something in the world produces the ground of meaning. This is the starting point for Peirce's "indexes" and "icons" (not for "symbols") as well as for Barthes's "signification". But to think in this way presupposes, at the same time, that the relation between a mark and its meaning is a union consisting of strong ontological ties.

There remain two serious problems, however, if we think of the world as a kind of "dictionary", that is, that the things we face in the world are essentially signs. For one thing, since the dictionary model is in principle a syntactic one, we could maintain that it simply lacks semantics. This is to say that we do not really know what is the ground for meaning in different "dictionaries", including the "world-dictionary". Therefore, epistemic support as the ground for semantics easily becomes an option. Secondly, if we say that the "world-dictionary" is a different one, in the sense that it includes semantics, then we still have to demonstrate how it does this and for what purposes we would any longer need the other "dictionaries". Let us see how we might proceed with these questions.

5. Meaning in semiotics

In the area of systematizing semiotics, Charles Sanders Peirce must be esteemed a very important thinker. The main lines of Peirce's theory of signs are well known, at least among semioticians, and I will not rehearse them here, even though my procedure draws stimulus from his theory. What I instead want to do is examine certain of Roland Barthes's post-structuralist ideas, and especially Veikko Rantala's suggestions which, in my view, provide good means for understanding Barthes's ideas. We can start from a statement repeated a thousand times by semioticians, that just anything can be a sign: a word, a sentence, a gesture, a mien, a piece of art, scientific theory, a certain way of behavior, a traffic sign, a reindeer track, a symptom of an illness, or a natural phenomenon. So it seems very natural to say, as does Peirce, that meaning relations are often very diverse. Only some signs are conventional, such as vocal and written marks. It is essential to conventional signs that their meaning or content be independent of the sign itself. In a certain sense, however, the mark cannot be separated from its content, according to Barthes and other post-structuralists. The idea is that signs, in their proper role, are not conventional symbols at all but instead bear, as it were, all possible meanings in themselves as their properties. This idea can be taken as the ontological and metaphysical background presupposition of most semiotic thinking. Indeed, signs in this sense are units composed of an external mark (*signifiant*) and its content (*signifié*). Since everything in the world is marks, which metaphysically are meanings at the same time, the semioticists are narrowing the metaphysical thoughts of German Idealists: reality is essentially a network of ideal entities; we swim in an ocean of meanings, and this ocean is itself the basic reality.

Semioticians call the relationship between a mark and its content a signification relation (*signification*). For example, because Barthes leans toward an idealism of the type mentioned above, we have to take the signification relation as a kind of ontological one. But we also have to remember that the relation in question can settle itself in many different ways. This feature brings us back to Peirce, who labelled the multiple signification relation *interpretant*. When he defines the sign as something "which represents something in some respect", we can interpret this definition either conventionally or ontologically. We can assume that the meaning relation of a sign is settled either "naturally", as it were, or by cultural environment. In other words, the *interpretant*, the factor that settles meaning, is either something given by nature or in any case distinguishable by some sort of external analysis – and that external analysis is semiotics. Or alternatively, the *interpretant* is more or less intentionally installed and is distinguishable by internal analysis. This kind of conceptual analysis is semantics. Consequently, semiotics *à la* Peirce is very flexible; it may include potentially a similar metalevel of meaning determination as does semantics. On the other hand, its flexibility may lead to a confusing mixture.

6. Functional meaning

What features in semiotics, and correspondingly in semantics, can be connected to Peirce's flexibility? On the semantic side the solutions pursued by Eco correspond partly to so-called game-theoretical semantics. According to it, the semantics of a central part of expressions can be given if we substitute the arbitrary "dictionaries" for different moves and rules of games by which we deal with the external world. This would mean, as applied to the Chinese Room Argument, that the person in the room, who is competent only in Finnish, would be given a "dictionary" that would tell which marks in Finnish correspond to which marks in Chinese. Or, to put the matter in game-theoretical form, he would be given instructions as to what kind of practice-rules govern how the marks are anchored to the world. Let us imagine, however, that our person is not only competent in Finnish, in the sense that he knows perfectly the Finnish vocabulary and grammar, but also that he has lived his whole life in the Chinese room, so that the only semantic games he has learnt and can really play are ones such as "that is a window", "this is a wall", "this is a room", and the like. But to things outside the Chinese room he cannot refer directly by any semantic practice, only indirectly. Nevertheless, it is often thought that to grasp a lexical meaning is something like looking at the "dictionary" when it is available, pointing to the wall or touch it, and so on. The flaw here is that meanings cannot be grasped always (if at all) by referring directly (e.g., through observation or some other epistemic means) to the things we are acquainted with; they are instead grasped by our reliance on the different practices and ways with the help of which we try to speak of things. To put the matter more technically, even a "natural" meaning does not combine only the values of meaning-determining functions, but also the functions themselves. The situation could be illustrated as follows:

(1)   a means b ≡ the syntactic-functional correlate of a is b

It is easy to understand that in this case we cannot separate successfully the "natural" from the conventional. If this inseparability or mixture is typical in semiotics, then semiotic theories cannot be explicated as metalevel theories.

7. "All meaning is connotative"

Ever since the Middle Ages the distinction between proper (absolute) and connotative meaning has been vital to semantic discussions. For instance, Ockham defined an absolute term by saying that it signifies the individual (or individualized property) which the term stands for in a proposition. The significations of connotative terms are sets of individuals in respect to their qualities or to other individuals. According to this, all indirectly referring relations, the relations which the term can "call to mind", are connotative. We could try to use Ockham's distinction to explicate the semiotic theory of meaning. We start with a somewhat provocative thesis and say that, in semiotic meaning-theory, every meaning relation is at the same time both direct (absolute) and connotative.

I will try to sharpen this thesis by utilizing Veikko Rantala's interpretation of Barthes's thought. We symbolize Barthes's signification relation in the following way:

(2)   (sa | sé).

The formulation says that every sign is composed of an outer part "sa" and a content part "sé". Barthes calls this ontologically inseparable pair a "denotative system". The ontology of a sign, therefore, presupposes in the denotative sense the above-mentioned ontological linkage between the outer part of the sign and its content. This is the direct meaning of the sign. But how does what Peirce called the "interpretant" fit into this picture? A possible answer would be this: Every denotative system is interpreted by such an interpretant, which determines the system "naturally". In this way we get a connotative sign:

(3) (sa | sé) | sé'

where sé' is now the context causing an indirect, or connotative, meaning. Since there can be a countless number of contexts we can generalize the situation by maintaining, as semioticians have done, that anything can be the sign of anything. In other words:

(4) (sa | sé) | sé' ... [sé'', sé''' , sé'''' , ...].

We can take (4) as summarizing two typical doctrines in semiotics: for one, that a sign entails an ontological connection to its signification or meaning; secondly, that anything can be a sign, i.e., that all meaning is connotative. How might we get from this semiotic situation to the semantic one? This question brings us back to the end of section 5, above. We can ask, Does Peirce's thought support the possibility of metalevel semiotic theorizing?

8. Semantics – the possibility of metalanguage

Veikko Ranatala states that we could reverse the order in the formulae above so that we could capture signs that speak about other signs explicitly, for example, a sign that speaks about the connotative sign (sa | sé) | sé':

(5) SÉ| [(sa | sé) | sé'].

What kind of a sign is this? Since SÉ now speaks about another sign, namely, [(sa | sé) | sé'], it is obviously a sign in *metalanguage*. Hopefully we are beginning to realize by now that semantics and semiotics are, in the end, two sides of the same coin. In fact, semantics amounts to having definable meaning relations. This kind of definable meaning relation, in the systematic sense, cannot exist in any way other than with the help of a metalanguage. In other words, in order to define a meaning (or a truth, for that matter) we must have an instrumentality which, by being on a different level, is in that sense independent of the signs or terms to be defined – be this instrumentality a natural language, an illustrative implementation, or some formal, set theoretical, or game theoretical tool that can be used to describe the meaning relations under consideration.

An additional remark is necessary. The definition occurring in the metalanguage can be fulfilled in various ways. In order to express adequately the connotative contexts which the meaning relations defined in the metalanguage speak about and which we want to consider, it is important that our metalinguistic tools be rich enough to account for any arbitrary situation. This requires much from them. The tools must be able to express with satisfactory clearness how far the meaning of a certain sign or term can "slide", as it were, and still remain in the same "crib". To remain in the area of the same crib can be imagined as the possibility of using the same variable, that is, the same sign or word, without any reinterpretation. As far as this is possible we are staying within the same conceptual form. This is an important point because the systematic study of semantics is precisely the study of what particular meaning relations can be presented within the same form, i.e., within the same logical, conceptual, or even syntactical conditions. This procedure is in fact the only systematic way to penetrate into the relation between language and reality. We need it in order to see to what extent we really swim in the ocean of meanings, that is to say, how much reality is in fact given to us through language, and how able we are to, as it were, "subtract" the distortion of language from reality.

Setting up the metalinguistic sign is in no way problematic in itself. The problem lurks in semantics: how could we set up the metalinguistic signs in such a way that the settings match the logical and conceptual form which a certain context and network of connotations presuppose? Precisely this is the main task in systematic semantics and, at the same time, its main difficulty. There are opposing views about whether the task can be carried out and how it might be done (see Kusch 1989). The demand of carrying out this task leads to the deepest questions in semantics. For example, what is the real import of Gödel's incompleteness proof? Or what is, in the last analysis, the status of Wittgensteinian "language games"? And so on. I cannot touch those problems here, but must hasten to my stated objective.

9. Theological study of religious language – semantics or semiotics?

Thus far I have presented some rather abstract ideas that may have prompted the reader to ask, When do we get to the point? What have those abstract ideas to do with theology? These questions are justified and I have to answer them. I am trying to be a little more specific in my exploration by introducing some examples of how a semiotic and semantic point of view could work in theological study. But let me first summarize the steps we have taken thus far:

(i) Anything can be a sign of anything else – [semiotics].
(ii) All meaning is connotative; connotations are ontological relations – [semiotics].
(iii) All meaning can be specified syntactically – [Eco].

(iv) There is no explicit semantics – [Wittgenstein: Language and Logic as Universal Medium, not as reinterpretable Calculus].
(v) There is no semantically transparent religious or theological language – [An analogy to the Chinese Room argument plus (1) – (3)].
(vi) Signs in the semiotic sense are *implicitly* intentional; by setting up meanings through connotations the "interpretant" can be any context or circumstance; in semantics the "interpretant" is made *explicit* or "visible" by defining the meaning, determined by the connotative network, in the metalanguage.

I mentioned earlier the situation where the occupant of the Chinese room would have only very unsatisfactory semantic games at his disposal. Such a case comes quite near the situation in religious language. Consequently, the user of religious language is in fact quite close to the person of the Chinese room. He "speaks" a language the vocabulary of which contains terms such as "God", "Holy Spirit", "Trinity", and the like. He masters the syntax of this language with the help of various "dictionaries", practices and games, but the semantics of this specific language is not clear or transparent. It is tempting for him to say (as followers of Eco and Wittgenstein do) that the semantics of religious language is nothing other than the correlates of the "dictionary" meanings or of the practices involved. In other words, he suggests that it is impossible to *define* the meanings of religious terms and propositions in any way other than by *showing* the factors or games (or "deep grammar", for that matter) that express the meanings as their correlates.

If we take theological study as being mainly a second-order activity that concerns religious language, it is obvious that we cannot easily find situations where we could set up the semantic relation directly. This is apparent, for example, when we try to describe the divine reality. Nevertheless, it does not follow that theological semantics is doomed to remain theoretically impotent. Despite the similarity between the situation of the Chinese room and religious language, certain systematic tools are available for a semantics of the latter. Let us ask, How could, say, a Finnish-speaking roomer, with the help of often meager or otherwise non-standard semantic games plus certain specific "dictionaries", reach the position where the syntactically available signs begin to become interpreted as referring to something in reality? The argument would go as follows:

(I) However syntactically correct, religious language is usually semantically non-transparent because its terms lack "natural" direct reference, which means that the meanings of religious expressions are always connotative or functional correlates.
(II) Since we cannot put our finger on an exact boundary between the connotation and reality, or between the function and its correlate, semantics in general and the

semantics of religious language in particular cannot be defined ("said"), only expressed ("shown"). Therefore, the semantics of religious language is transcendent or inexpressible.

(III) On the other hand, semantics, in general, can be infinitely defined (i.e., given truth conditions) on the basis of the distinction between first-order and metalevel activity. Semantics is not transcendent but transcendental.

(IV) Furthermore, semantics and semiotics are two sides of the same coin; therefore,

(V) semantics (with its systematic metalevel tools) is the explicating ("saying") side and semiotics (starting from the network of connotations) is the implicit ("showing") side of the same coin.

(VI) Consequently, the semantics of religious language is infinitely definable.

10. Starting points for the collaboration of semiotics and semantics in theology

Taking a semiotic-interpretative perspective on religious speech, how do we understand the presence of Christ in the Holy Communion? Allegedly bread, wine, words of consecration, and contextual liturgical actions would compose the Barthesian denotative system. We could express it by structure (4), above. But then we would ask, How can all these be signs of the presence of Christ (in the semiotic Barthesian sense)? How is it possible that one connotation is inevitably connected with another connotation? Perhaps a further example will help us to find a way for both semiotic and semantic ways of looking at the matter.

In J. J .R. Tolkien's book, *The Lord of the Rings*, the wizard Gandalf, using his secret skills, lights a fire under very rainy and stormy circumstances. He says to his companions that, if there are any spies or guards in the neighbourhood, his way of lighting the fire would be in those circumstances a sure sign that "Gandalf is here". Can we say similarly that those denotative signs connected to the Holy Communion are sure signs that "Christ is present"? The answer is naturally positive, if the sentence "Christ is present" is true when the Communion takes place. In the same way, Gandalf's typical magical tricks contributed to his presence, if the sentence "Gandalf is here" is true. Certain forms of Christianity hold that Christ is present in the Holy Communion. What is tempting in this situation, however, is to say, like Eco, that what we mean by "the presence of Christ" is a functional correlate of the Communion Game, not anything observable at all. From the point of view of semantics, this means that we may be able to describe the game or model that implies this statement, but we cannot point out any observable difference between the situation where somebody denies the presence of Christ and the situation where some other person admits it. The two opposing models are not based on two different observational facts. Although the meaning of the expression "Christ is present in the Holy Communion" cannot be worked out in our empirical world by reliance on any semantic setting other than certain pragmatic criteria, it does not follow that this expression lacks a realistic meaning. Somebody might succeed in fooling us by doing exactly the same tricks as Gandalf, in which case the sentence "Gandalf is here" would not be true. But it would not follow that the sentence "Gandalf is here" has no realistic meaning. (I will return to this issue in the next section.)

Here, of course, lie the origins of theological confusion and schools. Just as there would be schools quarrelling about what traits of a "lighting game" would be enough to reveal that the sentence "Gandalf is here" is true, there are schools debating what characteristics the Communion Game must have in order to satisfy the demand of the presence of Christ. The debate naturally concerns the functional correlate of the Communion Game, not anything specified on the basis of independent observation. This kind of debating is actually the material of academic theological research. We wonder whether there is anything an explicit semantic analysis can do as a tool of theological research, for example, in the example at stake? I would maintain that it can reveal what kind of confusion of conceptual or semantic conditions might be involved in the thinking of a particular school.

At the outset I spoke of "auxiliary figures", which have to be understood in the transcendental sense. By using the method of auxiliary figures we can map, step by step, the conceptual models for different starting points to religious language (e.g., for different epistemic arguments). Because in semiotics nothing in principle restricts the use of "auxiliary figures", correspondingly, in this situation anything can be an interpretant of anything else. The semiotic approach demands only that we map all contexts that might set up the interpretant. The semiotic way of exploring, e.g., the theological notion of grace would be, then, to examine different interpretants for certain practical purposes, for example, by asking whether they in some way improve the self-understanding of the people.

The semantic contribution to this would be the systematic analysis of interpretants on the metalevel. Through the systematization of conceptual ties between different interpretants (games) we continuously specify, so to speak, the whole meaning of "grace" and step by step approximate the limit correlate of the term "grace", which, at the same time, would coincide with the ontological reality of grace. By defining continuously these mappings on the metalevel, we approach the limit situation where all possible mappings (for a certain language) are defined. This situation is identical to metaphysical reality. The opening of eyes in this change of point of view lurks in transcendentality: in realizing that we can get closer to the reality, not only by *a posteriori* methods, but by specifying continuously our conceptual, *a priori* tools. The practices or "dictionaries" linked with religious language can be used as step by step approximations for setting up the *real* semantic relations as the limit values of the approximation.

11. Semantics and epistemology

Let us now take a biblical word as a sign; for example, the word "grace". We start from Barthes' denotative system (2). Of course, there are countless contexts that could give a connotative meaning to this word, be it the Lutheran context, a classificatory context, the context of some author, (e.g., the one in Simone Weil's book, *Grace and Gravity*), and so on. Furthermore, some context, say that of psychoanalysis, could be such that there would be almost nothing left of the original meaning of "grace" if we were to define its meaning in metalanguage. Let us leave aside how this would happen formally. The core of the matter is that, if we explicate the meaning of the word in metalanguage, some contexts will destroy the original meaning. There is nothing miraculous in this, as long as business proceeds on the syntactic level by merely changing the vocabulary according to some "grammar". But the situation becomes quite fascinating if we look at it from the point of view of genuine semantics. In that case we are not simply labelling the term "grace" for another meaning, namely, the psychoanalytic one. Instead we are trying to define, by relying on a certain game, practice or whatever contextual matter, the very conceptual model which we have to postulate as a general form in order to specify the psychoanalytic meaning for that word. Defining this practice in metalanguage amounts to doing explicit semantics; in other words, we create a model that equates with the specification of consistency conditions for a set of possible states of affairs. On the other hand, if we let the game or practice be as it is, we do implicit semantics by only "showing" the syntactical rules (grammar) of "grace" in the psychoanalytic context. Instead of trying to do explicit semantics we may make efforts to "say" explicitly how signs, first semiotically apprehended perhaps, are restricted or transgressive in their meanings and how their connotations change.

Let us apply the procedure described above to the word "grace" as it is used in the Lutheran context. This would mean here not only that precisely the Lutheran context would be reflected in the proper way as contributing to the meaning of "grace", but also that we could somehow grasp the real thing referred to by "grace". We face a problem here: what kind of semantic reflection could perform both of those tasks? For one thing, we perhaps could map the game or practice to a certain extent through the texts of the Lutheran tradition. But this is not the end of the problem. Lutheran theology implies that the Lutheran way of understanding grace is the right and authentic one. Behind this claim, however, we see the basic semantic problem to be entangled with an epistemological one. Obviously the problem is the one that I said bothers all religious language, namely, that representative relations in religious language are functional. This is to say that the meanings and references of religious expressions (whatever they are as things in themselves) are ontological correlates of religious experiences and emotions, often endowed with mythical or metaphorical form. They reflect certain ways of speaking about reality or of relating to it. The semantic games that assign meanings to religious terms are usually connected precisely with such experiences and emotions. Although the games, and the practices linked with them, reveal some explicable rules, the rules belong more or less to the "surface grammar" (implicit semantics) than to the "deep grammar" (explicit semantics). They are, for instance, not so complete that we could solve the problem of whether Lutheran "grace" has a properly New Testament meaning or not. Instructions in the Chinese room are unsatisfactory.

In such a case what we need are the means, in modeltheoretic terms, to grasp the ontologically correct reference of the term "grace" in all possible worlds compatible with the factual use of this word in the Lutheran context, and compare this reference to the corresponding New Testament reference. However, this grasping happens to be epistemically blocked since we do not simply know what would set up the basic New Testament meaning without relying, at the outset, on different competing interpretations, that is, competing ways of grasping. Here many thinkers take a fatal step by saying that if only we had epistemic access to an independent basic New Testament meaning, we could compare between all the other interpretations to see whether or not they deviate from the original one.

This being the case, theologians and philosophers have tried to find any support – historical, doctrinal or philosophical, anything conceivable as epistemic evidence – for their suggestions as to what the original semantic set-up would be. The aim has been to grasp the rule which helps to identify the basic theological meaning of the term "grace" in reality. Yet the major flaw in such an aim has been due precisely to its reliance on epistemic means. Consequently, the intended solution to the problem of the semantics of this piece of religious language has been that one tries to look for an epistemological argument. It follows that semantics would be based on epistemology. The correct order, however, is precisely the opposite: it is not only that we can approach reality externally by means of epistemic empirical tools or by introducing ever new arbitrary meaning relations, but that we can also approximate things in themselves internally, depending on how distinctive our semantic tools (concepts) are. The interplay between epistemology and semantics enters the picture in that there is no fixed Archimedean point from which we should start our approach.

This opens up the following opportunity. On the metalevel we can always try to set up the semantic rule that explicates the interpretant in such a way that it takes care of all contextual factors. This presupposes, however, that we can at least to some extent specify the possible states of affairs that are compatible with those contextual factors, that is, which are *accessible alternatives* to the actual circumstances. In doing this specification we learn, at the same time, what the meaning of a certain religious or theological term demands of the actual world. The meanings of religious terms may have, for example, deviating ontological implications, in which case we can easily see in what sense something is to be held real or unreal. A certain theological school may consider that the sentence "Christ is present in the Communion" is real only if it is ontologically implied that Christ is substantially identical with the bread. Another theological school holds that this implication is not necessary; yet the sentence itself is interpreted realistically. It seems to me that, in this way, we can overcome the hopeless attempt to ground religious statements on epistemological argument, and we can also overcome the hopelessly arbitrary business of semiotics in desystematizing the meaning relations in religious language.

References

Barthes, Roland (1972). *Elements of Semiology*. London: Cape.
Eco, Umberto (1986). On truth: A fiction. *Versus* 44/45: 41–59.
Kusch, Martin (1989). *Language as Calculus vs. Language as Universal Medium: A Study in Husserl, Heidegger and Gadamer*. Synthese Library, Vol. 207. Boston and London: Dordrecht.
Peirce, Charles Sanders (1932). *Collected Papers of Charles S. Peirce*. Vol. II. Cambridge, Mass.: Harvard University Press.
Rantala, Veikko (1994). Merkitys semiotiikassa [Meaning in semiotics]. *Merkitys: Filosofisia tutkimuksia Tampereen yliopistosta* 45: 161–175.

Matthieu Guillot

La neige et le silence

Bien qu'elle prolonge et tente de préciser certains points engagés sur la même problématique lors de travaux précédents (Guillot 1994–95)[1], cette étude trop brève ne prétend pas à l'exhaustivité. Nous cherchons néanmoins à nous y interroger sur les raisons profondes qui rendent la neige naturellement ou automatiquement inséparable de l'idée de silence, idée qui, incontestablement, apparaît toujours comme une évidence lorsqu'on parle de la neige, mais comme une évidence telle, justement, que l'on s'abstient finalement d'en chercher l'origine première. Pourquoi faut-il en effet que la neige, dans son évocation ou sa représentation, soit continuellement associée à cette véritable logique du silence ? On se proposera ici de passer en quelque sorte "derrière" l' "évidente façade" de la neige, d'une part afin de démonter ses mécanismes psychologiques, d'autre part afin de dégager les liens qui l'unissent comme son ombre au silence, son *éternelle escorte* (ce qui nous permettra momentanément de nous en extirper quelque peu). Avant toute chose un rappel s'impose pour ouvrir ce sujet : dans la très remarquable étude que Gilbert Durand, disciple de Bachelard, lui a consacré en la faisant figurer parmi les « obstacles qui émerveillent l'esprit », la neige est considérée comme « l'éternelle présence d'une matière, au même titre que la terre, l'air, l'eau ou le feu » (Durand 1953: 638 et 616) – assertion que ne démentirait certainement pas le sémioticien dans l'optique spécifique de la culture finnoise.

Mise en situation : paysage de neige

Si l'on y pense, qu'y-a-t-il de plus définitivement, mais aussi de plus désespérément silencieux qu'une large étendue de paysage, toute de neige recouverte ? Quoi de plus merveilleux, mais en même temps de plus oppressant que de voir le Blanc prendre possession de toute chose, transfigurant *sans un bruit* le plus petit élément de la nature qui frissonnait encore, et figeant celle-ci dans une immobilité absolue ? Quoi de plus mystérieux, finalement, que ces vastes espaces immaculés se confondant presque avec le ciel hivernal qui semble les rejoindre, là-bas loin à l'horizon ? S'il émane bien de la neige une indiscutable "consistance", une insondable "épaisseur" que par commodité nous nommons volontiers mystère, il n'est pas moins étrange de constater à quel point cette neige et ce "mystère" engendré sont susceptibles de nous procurer la sensation d'un indéfinissable malaise, un malaise a priori inexplicable, tout à fait comparable (en guise d'exemple) à celui qu'éprouve le narrateur de la *Maison Usher* à la vue du singulier bâtiment. Or si E. A. Poe assure qu'un tel malaise a bien « la puissance de nous affecter de cette sorte », il admet que « l'analyse de cette puissance gît dans des considérations où nous perdrions pied ». Ne nous arrive-t-il pas en effet de ressentir confusément une certaine gêne face à une immensité de neige ? Que la neige nous fasse peur *en ses débauches blanches*, selon le vers de Boris Pasternak[2]? Il faudrait alors nous demander, pour paraphraser ici Poe : qu'est-ce donc, – arrêtons-nous pour y penser –, qu'est-ce donc ce je ne sais quoi qui nous tracasse ainsi en contemplant la neige ? Si l'on veut tenter de répondre à cela, il n'est guère d'autre solution que de se plonger par l'imaginaire dans une atmosphère hivernale intégralement blanche, de retrouver ce *pur désert* (selon Valéry) que constitue le paysage blanc afin de pénétrer au cœur de la neige. En somme, il nous revient nécessairement d'interroger cette « douce neige qui a pris la forme d'une dure assise sans signification » (Gunnar Ekelöf), en la considérant d'abord dans son état de matière, c'est-à-dire, selon G. Durand, d' « obstacle qui arrête et étonne la pensée » (Durand 1953: 617).

Présence et esthésie

S'il paraît évident et donc peu contestable dans un premier temps qu'un champ de neige « représente l'extériorité pure, la spatialité radicale » et que « son indifférenciation, sa monotonie et sa blancheur manifestent l'absolue nudité de la substance », pour reprendre ici une remarque de J.-P. Sartre lui-même (Sartre 1943: 670), l'observateur ou le sujet sensible ne peut cependant s'empêcher de dépasser aussitôt ce stade du raisonné – et du raisonnable – pour tendre vers un regard plus intérieurement, plus intimement orienté. Car s'il est parfois vrai pour lui que « la présence silencieuse des choses est une invitation au recueillement » (Rassam 1980: 62), elle est aussi et surtout incitation et prétexte, au travers de la neige, à questionner sans l'audace "scientifique" cette présence muette mais insistante qui lui fait face. Ainsi, lorsque Sartre finit par estimer dans ses démonstrations que « le sens secret de la neige [...] est un sens ontologique », qui serait à chercher dans sa qualité de liquidité secrète (Sartre 1943: 692 et 691), on ne peut qu'approuver entièrement G. Durand voyant une absurdité dans ce genre de considérations, déjà trop éloignées du réel immédiat, car la neige, assurément, « ne se laisse pas classer et mépriser en tant que simple eau gelée », insiste-t-il. Bien au contraire selon lui, elle est indéniablement et définitivement « hostile à toute confusion possible avec la trivialité de l'eau ». C'est d'ailleurs pourquoi il n'a pas hésité à voir en elle ce qu'il a nommé « un obstacle épistémologique » (Durand 1953: 617 et 629).

Si donc nous voulons avec lui « recueillir le silence neigeux à l'état pur » (Durand: 618) – tel est bien ici le sens de notre démarche –, il nous faut nous efforcer de maintenir la réflexion au niveau esthésique de la présence sensible effective, et ce en retrouvant la démarche de Bachelard qui avait ainsi très bien compris que « la connaissance poétique du monde précède [...] la connaissance raisonnable des objets », que « le monde est beau avant d'être vrai » et « admiré avant d'être vérifié » (Bachelard 1943: 192). Il revient donc à l'observateur de demeurer attentif à la *présence* de l'espace enneigé et réceptif à son *atmosphère*, prise au sens de "qualité émotionnelle" et "degrés de présence" tels que Pierre Kaufmann a pu les cerner : dans ses analyses en effet, cette atmosphère correspond à « la qualité émotionnelle en tant qu'elle est inhérente à la totalité d'un champ d'expérience, et non pas à un objet déterminé », montrant par exemple que pour le sujet, « le paysage, à l'instant qui précède l'orage, est "lourd de menaces" » (Kaufmann 1967: 224). D'où le fait pour l'auteur qu'il soit « légitime de parler à la lettre de l'espace comme d'une atmosphère émotionnelle » (ibid.: 228). De la sorte l'observateur, sujet ému, vérifiera pleinement la remarque de Max Picard selon laquelle « le silence est là comme un monde » (Picard 1954: 10), et qui replacée dans le contexte singulier de la neige, revêt soudain toute son importance.

Le silence partagé entre écoute et vision

A priori, l'on ne discuterait point l'idée selon laquelle le silence serait exclusivement lié à la sphère de l'audible. De par sa nature en effet, la réalité familière que nous nommons silence renvoie bien d'abord à l'univers des sons. Mais tout en y renvoyant d'office, elle ne saurait se limiter pour autant à ce seul cadre, même si elle y trouve évidemment sa pleine autonomie. Au contact de l'expérience visuelle en effet, et plus précisément au sens notamment conféré par P. Kaufmann à l'expérience émotionnelle, qui serait d'après lui « habilitée à développer sa propre phénoménologie » (Kaufmann 1967: 19), nous posons ici l'hypothèse selon laquelle il serait pertinent d'évoquer l'existence de véritables "apparitions du silence". Pourquoi ? C'est que l'expérience de la neige semble bien enseigner avec insistance à l'œil qu'il peut lui aussi recueillir l'impression de silence, en percevoir le halo (ou "rayonnement de silence") à la façon d'un halo de lumière. Avec la neige et la singularité de son apparaître sensible, l'observateur va donc prétendre ramener le silence dans le champ visuel et l'inclure comme phénomène visible à part entière, parce qu'il ne fait aucun doute pour lui qu'un tel silence lui "saute aux yeux". A travers la neige, en d'autres termes, le silence *manifeste* sa présence au sens fort de ce mot, il se concrétise, se corporalise. Pour l'observateur en résumé, il se *montre*, se présente au regard en revêtant une apparence (Guillot 1994: 143). C'est dire que l'articulation entre les deux ordres sensoriels – auditif—>visuel – s'opère d'elle-même, bien qu'il nous reste encore à comprendre comment l'un se répercute dans l'autre, en abordant poétiquement (au sens bachelardien) la neige : pour G. Durand justement, « c'est par l'œil et par l'oreille à la fois qu'elle entre dans la conscience poétique » (Durand 1953: 617).

Ecoute et silence

Face à un univers uniformément blanc de neige, telle une plaine enneigée qui s'étendrait devant lui à perte de vue, l'observateur tendant l'oreille n'y décèle pas le moindre signe de vie ni le moindre son, même s'il tente d'écouter « ce qu'on entend lorsque rien ne se fait entendre » (Valéry).[3] Le monde blanc est immédiatement perçu par lui comme un monde de l'absence (les premières neiges étant « les neiges de l'absence », écrit Saint-John Perse[4]), où l'espace sonore est déserté, mais aussi comme un monde pétrifié, assoupi dans un interminable sommeil blanc : pour le dire avec Karin Boye, « la terre est paralysée et le ciel, aveugle, la vie déserte gît ».[5] De cette fixité inhabituelle se dégage en premier lieu le silence, un silence « épais, comme le brouillard du matin. Epais et immobile » ; un silence qui envahit l'espace et le sature « comme un gaz pesant et irrespirable » (pour emprunter à Vercors).[6] Silence "feutré", silence de "chape" sont aussi les expressions phoniques témoignant de la densité d'un tel silence. Qu'en résulte-t-il pour l'observateur, sinon une certaine forme d'angoisse face à ce silence « pensif et solennel » (Pasternak) ? « C'est un tel silence tout autour qu'il me faut crier. C'est un tel silence tout autour que mon cri ne s'entend pas », répond Ekelöf, parce qu'alors même « la parole des hommes est recouverte par la neige du silence », comme l'observait Picard (Picard 1954: 87), en expliquant plus loin : « Quand le silence dans la nature est si dense que les choses n'y paraissent que des condensations plus fortes encore du silence, alors il semble que l'homme cesse de posséder la parole », qu'il va « se dissoudre dans ce silence et de ne devenir qu'une partie du silence de la nature » (ibid.: 110).

Mais d'où vient ou de quoi ce silence illimité résulte-t-il réellement ? Tiendrait-il simplement d'une modification de l'atmosphère, c'est-à-dire d'une pression atmosphérique particulière, d'une certaine qualité de "magnétisme" atmosphérique ? L'hypothèse peut se vérifier. Ainsi, dans ses commentaires aux écrits de Nietzsche touchant au ciel d'hiver et à son silence, Bachelard a pu relever avec une grande finesse une « synthèse substantielle de l'air, du froid et du silence », en déduisant que « par l'air et le froid, c'est le silence qui est aspiré, c'est le silence qui est *intégré* à notre être même », et qu'en certaines situations particulières (les hauteurs), « le silence a besoin de l'offensivité du froid » (Bachelard 1943: 160–161). Cette vérité sera d'ailleurs recensée par le compositeur canadien R. Murray Schafer dans ses nombreuses catégories de paysage sonore, soulignant que « la géographie et le climat donnent sa tonalité propre au paysage sonore d'une région. [...] Les sons dépendent alors de la température » : on peut par exemple distinguer que « dans la neige fraîche et poudreuse, les patins des traîneaux eux-mêmes oublient leur crissement traditionnels » (Schafer 1979: 38–39). Néanmoins, nous sommes presque inévitablement tentés de ne voir dans le silence de neige qu'un « silence muet » qui, explique Joseph Rassam, « ne communique rien » mais « isole et déconcerte » parce qu' « on ne sait pas d'où il vient » (Rassam 1980: 107). Continuons donc à préciser davantage.

Est-ce que le silence s'installe seulement parce qu'en recouvrant toutes choses en hiver et en les empêchant ainsi de bruire, la neige absorbe les sons ? Pour Durand plus précisément, « l'expérience sonore de la neige est liée à un processus tactile et kinésique : c'est la mollesse, la lenteur, la douceur de la neige qui contient son silence. [...] C'est pour cela que la neige est si souvent comparée à du coton, à quelque chose qui amortit et étouffe » (Durand 1953: 617–618). En fait, tout se passe comme si la neige, en se déposant partout sur le sol, baillonnait les voix murmurantes de la nature et y faisait soudain régner un silence sans partage. En effet, la neige fait taire les bruits les plus familiers, et son silence nous gêne ou même nous insupporte tant nos oreilles en ressentent la lourdeur, en devinent l'envergure imposante. La densité du silence nival se révèle alors impressionnante, à tel point que celui-ci en devient proprement *assourdissant* : dans la neige nous devenons *sourds de silence* (Pasternak), parce que celui-ci est un « rien immense aux oreilles », selon le mot de Valéry. La cause et l'effet se renversent, le silence étant tellement *envahissant* qu'il en dépasse son propre seuil a-phonique pour déborder, empiéter sur le sonore. Pour l'observateur, il semble alors non seulement que « le vide se repose » (Edith Södergran)[7], mais aussi bien plus que « seul, le grand silence écoute » (Oskar Milosz)[8] – renversement sémantique proprement hallucinant qui autorise une sorte de mise en abyme de l'audibilité (ce n'est plus le sujet ému qui écoute, mais le silence "en personne" qui opère un retour sur lui-même!). La neige se montre donc réellement *lourde* de silence – au sens où Mikel Dufrenne juge que « le silence est [...] lourd d'audible comme l'invisible est lourd de visible »[9], c'est-à-dire que le silence est « ce bruit fin qui est continu » (Valéry).

Pour bien cerner sa capacité à *faire silence* dans tous les registres sensoriels, il nous faut maintenant évoquer ce que Durand appelle cette « fonction de la défaite et du néant que possède la neige », puisque celle-ci « ne défait pas que les sons, mais encore les couleurs et leur audace luxuriante », se montrant ainsi capable de produire « un silence qui entre en nous par tous les sens », preuve pour lui de la réalité de « ce silence renforcé que l'on peut appeler un méta-silence » (Durand 1953: 622 et 621).

Matthieu Guillot

Silence de la blancheur

Si la neige est d'abord associée au silence, elle l'est également à la lumière en raison de son extrême et absolue blancheur – « blancheur "étincelante", "immaculée", "infinie" » précise Durand (1953: 618). Mais l'un n'allant pas sans l'autre, nous sommes ici de fait en présence d'une véritable trilogie blanc-lumière-silence, le blanc devenant « l'équivalent plastique du silence » (ibid.: 619). Comment ce phénomène se concrétise-t-il ? Pour l'observateur, il y a évidemment négation d'un environnement familier de couleurs dans ce blanc qui n'en finit plus. L'impact d'un espace complètement uniforme, vierge de toute autre présence chromatique, marque nécessairement une absence, un manque, d'où l'impression de vide laissée par cette blancheur « triomphante et envahissante » (Durand), Vladimir Jankélévitch allant même jusqu'à estimer à propos des neiges éternelles que « dans cette blanche solitude des sommets *la nudité-limite ne se distingue plus du néant* » (Janlélévitch 1960/78: 14 ; je souligne). Dans la théorie picturale de Kandinsky, le blanc « apparaît comme le symbole d'un monde d'où toutes les couleurs, en tant que propriétés matérielles et substances, auraient disparu ». Pour le peintre russe le blanc relevait d'un monde insonore, d' « un néant d'avant le commencement. C'est peut-être ainsi que sonnait la terre aux jours blancs de l'ère glaciaire », ajoutera-t-il à titre de comparaison.[10] Et de même que le silence est absence de sonorité sensible, la blancheur peut bien elle aussi apparaître comme une absence de couleur, jusqu'à représenter une absence *en soi*, tel « le monde blanc de l'absence d'objets » cher à Malevitch. Incontestablement, la beauté innommable de la blancheur de la neige laisse l'observateur ou l'analyste sans voix : « Quand un alchimiste parle d'un précipité *blanc comme la neige*, déjà il admire, déjà il vénère », remarquait Bachelard, et si la poésie énonce un vers tel que *la neige belle comme la neige*, alors « le cercle de beauté substantielle, de l'intimité de beauté, se ferme » (Bachelard 1948: 47–48). Jankélévitch (ibid.: 14–15) a aussi montré que le pur, le lisse sont des sortes de surfaces transparentes contre lesquelles le verbe et la pensée glissent et ne peuvent s'accrocher, et littéralement « où les mots n'ont plus prise » (Saint-John Perse).

Mais s'il est du moins évident que « la lumière [...] elle-même, en elle-même, ne peut pas être vue », comme l'a montré Jankélévitch (ibid.: 15), la phénoménologie va jusqu'à s'interroger sur le point de savoir si la blancheur même est bien *vue*, M. Dufrenne estimant ainsi que « les peintres nous apprennent à en douter, et l'on pourrait montrer qu'elle-même n'est pas perçue sans le secours de l'imagination ».[11] Une problématique semblable se pose d'ailleurs quant au lien unissant la neige à sa température : R. Chambon précise sur cette question que si « la froideur de la neige n'est pas "vue" [...] au sens strict, proprement sensoriel du terme », c'est qu'elle est « attachée au visible » par le concept d'association, qui « peut indiquer génétiquement l'origine du lien : il a fallu que, dans le passé, les deux "contenus d'expérience" ([...] l'impression thermique et la blanche étendue de neige) se soient "soudés", pour que le retour de l'un fasse percevoir l'autre » (Chambon 1974: 239). C'est bien ainsi que le silence de la neige s'"attache" également au visible.

En vérité, et c'est là le paradoxe, *il n'y a rien à voir* face à une blanche étendue de neige : en se déposant sur le sol et en le recouvrant, la neige déstructure le paysage, en gomme les arêtes vives, masquant les terres sous un voile blanc. La configuration végétale disparue, l'observateur se voit alors privé de la notion élémentaire d'orientation. Avec un espace toujours identique parce que sans marques distinctives, et l'éblouissement aidant dû à la surconcentration de blanc, le regard ne parvient plus à "accrocher" – tout est rigoureusement *identique* – ce qui ne l'empêche pourtant pas de s'émerveiller malgré lui devant ce vide ou ce néant qu'est le paysage recouvert d'une impassible blancheur : ce « Blanc comme venu de nulle part. Qui sait même s'il est blanc », constate Ekelöf. Regarder une neige étale revient finalement à regarder un ciel pur : le regard s'y perd, fasciné ; il s'y enfonce, s'abandonnant totalement à l'emprise du blanc[12] : « en regardant attentivement la neige je décompose sa "blancheur" apparente qui se résout en un monde de reflets et de transparences », rapporte Merleau-Ponty.[13] Si donc la neige est silence visible, c'est qu'elle est avant tout lumière, c'est qu'elle est silence *par l'intermédiaire* de la lumière, pure au point d'en devenir aveuglante : « Mais la neige trop blanche me lacère les yeux », dit ainsi un vers d'Ossip Mandelstam. Dès lors, la neige se confond avec la lumière même, celle qui « apparaît comme l'intérieur du silence [...], comme l'accomplissement du silence » (Picard 1954: 108) ; c'est la raison pour laquelle « nous en arrivons à dire qu'*un silence est blanc* ou qu'*une clarté est silencieuse* », conclue Durand (1953: 620 ; je souligne). Le silence neigeux englobe donc aussi bien le canal auditif que le canal visuel. Pour l'observateur, seule subsiste dans l'atmosphère la présence tenace de ce silence : « Dans l'hiver, le silence est là comme quelque chose de visible : la neige est silence, silence devenu visible », écrivait Picard (1954: 87). La neige serait donc bien en ce sens un « absolu de vide et de silence » (Durand 1953: 621).

Neige et mort

Cependant, cette neige nous entraine parfois aussi vers l'image négative de la mort à travers la métaphore du blanc linceul. On sait par exemple que le *Lit de neige* de Paul Celan n'est rien d'autre qu'un affreux lit de mort, et Michel Guiomar, qui pense que « les images de pureté et de linceul » attachées à la neige relèvent d'une « symbolique immédiate et trop facile » (Guiomar 1988: 340), a commenté plusieurs œuvres liées à la symbolique du Seuil et de l'Au-delà dans le cadre général d'une esthétique de la mort (1988: 340–346). Dans un tout autre registre, André Malraux, relatant son séjour chez le général De Gaulle à Colombey en décembre 1969, mentionne la neige à plusieurs reprises en en faisant un élément pathétique doué d'une symbolique tragique, relié à un ensemble complexe de réflexions sur l'histoire, la destinée humaine, le déclin de la France et la disparition prochaine du Général. Et parce qu'elle est liée au contexte de sa rencontre avec lui, la neige prend dans l'esprit de l'auteur un relief tout particulier, se rapportant autant à de sombres pressentiments qu'à des pensées désespérées sur les tragédies du passé. La « neige des siècles », « cette neige qui reviendra inépuisablement sur la terre »[14] devient alors une neige quasi "métaphysique" qui semble inviter à une méditation sur le Temps et l'Existence. C'est une neige qu'on devine surtout comme emblème d'une fin.

On retrouve une perception assez comparable dans le poème *Neige* d'Artur Lundkvist, où domine la vision traumatisante et tourmentée d'une neige qui n'en finit pas de s'étendre et de se renouveler. Une neige oppressante qui gagne sur le monde, si intensément présente qu'elle semble avoir été là *de tout temps et en tous lieux*. En outre, l'inlassable répétition du mot *neige* traduit aussi ce sentiment d'immense lassitude face à la matière blanche, interminable et infinie, qu'il faut subir, encore et toujours. Deux vers résument bien l'ensemble de l'idée : « neige sur notre visage dans le monde [...] Neige sur le monde qui hiberne ». Le monde blanc est ici celui de l'engloutissement définitif. Par ailleurs, la neige est souvent associée à l'entrée dans un sommeil : la nature ne ressemble plus qu'à un espace statufié « où somnolent les neiges comme mortes » (Pasternak).[15] La neige renferme ce phénomène d'extinction qui "anesthésie" (Ekelöf y voit « la neige éternelle de la fatigue »), rend le monde léthargique et pesant, qui ralentit considérablement la marche, qui entrave, empêche le mouvement, et s'avère capable de paralyser la volonté ou la pensée, jusqu'à provoquer l'anéantissement de la raison. Mais ce sommeil est aussi lié à l'engourdissement par le froid, à la température qui se fait menaçante pour l'homme, qui risque s'il n'y prend garde de traverser cette phase de "transition" qui le conduira très doucement de la vie à la mort. Tel est ce que Tarjei Vesaas a minutieusement décrit dans une scène de son merveilleux *Palais de glace*, celle de la mort d'Unn au cœur du "palais" précisément, c'est-à-dire de cette cascade pétrifiée par le gel qui n'est que silences et blancheurs. Ici, le blanc rejoint réellement l'idée de mort via celle d'une forme d'absolu.

Mais sans doute est-ce encore l'intuition poétique la plus apte à résumer le mieux ce rapport étroit entre mort et neige, quand Pierre Reverdy évoque « des neiges perdues dans les cimetières ».[16] Et si le thème du cimetière enfoui sous la neige fut fréquemment traité en peinture par deux importantes figures de l'art romantique allemand, Caspar David Friedrich et Carl Gustav Carus, c'est que leur attitude se manifestait chez eux dans une perspective purement religieuse. Silence de neige, silence de mort : une matière froide et inerte ne correspond-elle pas à la représentation d'un corps sans vie ? Une des réponses possibles figure dans un petit opuscule dédié à la neige : « Tout est mort. Non : tout dort. Non : tout vit d'une vie alentie, profonde » – d'où le judicieux qualificatif imaginé par l'auteur : « la mortneige, la neigevie ».[17] Mais là encore il serait nécessaire, pour mieux affiner cette problématique de la réception, de reprendre les analyses chez Kaufmann, notamment lorsque l'auteur s'interroge de savoir « sur quelle dimension différencier le sinistre ou le paisible, l'oppressant ou le radieux – et toutes les nuances de l'atmosphère » (Kaufmann 1967: 224).

Floconnement et silence

Non seulement la neige est silencieuse en son étalement, non seulement elle "observe le silence", mais son état vertical nous affecte tout autant, car selon la juste remarque de J. Favez-Boutonnier, « c'est jusqu'au fond de notre âme que les flocons de neige mettent leur silencieuse pureté » (Chambon 1974: 269). Ce qui frappe en effet avec « la neige soigneusement partout qui descend » (E. E. Cummings), c'est qu'elle tombe tout autour de nous, sur nous, nous recouvre : nous sommes en contact direct avec la matière, nous la sentons, la touchons, mais *aucun son n'en parvient*, d'où la présence irréelle ou immatérielle du phénomène. Max Picard offre une vision des choses encore plus "silencieuse" lorsqu'il écrit que les flocons de neige « tombent ensemble sur la terre qui est déjà blanche dans le silence : le silence rencontre le silence » (Picard 1954: 87). Mais bien que le flocon soit « élément semi-aérien », comme l'a très bien relevé Durand (1953: 629), la neige, comme son silence, « pèse de toute sa paix » (Saint-Exupéry)[18] sur la terre.

Pour le sujet ému, le trouble naît dès l'avènement de la neige virevoltant dans les airs ; car il ne peut s'imposer à l'esprit que c'est là simple péripétie météorologique. Même la conscience lucide se fie d'abord au regard, qui enregistre malgré lui l'émerveillement intense suscité par le floconnement. Par conséquent, l'homme sous les flocons de neige se sent quitter la logique des conditions climatiques par trop "terrestres" ou "terre à terre" pour saisir l'instant sublime de la venue d'un autre monde. Et de même que nous choisissons d'ignorer Sartre insistant sur l'importance de la liquidité pour mieux cerner la neige, il nous faut éloigner et oublier la thématique développée par M. Guiomar lorsqu'il montre qu'il existe dans la littérature « un fantasme plus profond qui suppose l'équivalence paradoxale de la chute de neige et de la pluie de sang » (Guiomar 1988: 340). Non : ici vraiment, l'expression impersonnelle "il neige" revient à dire sans détour qu' "il neige du silence", qu' "il *tombe* du silence", ou même que " *le silence neige* ". L'image de la « pluie de silence » employée par Picard (1954: 10) dans un autre contexte conviendrait bien encore.

Mais y a-t-il véritablement mouvement dans la chute des flocons ? L'observateur attentif assiste plutôt à un effet de paralysie lié au phénomène optique lui-même ; cette impression de "sur-place" ne lui donne que l'illusion d'un "mouvement", qui se rapproche plus en définitive de l'immobilité par son aspect répétitif ainsi que par le blocage du devenir. « D'ailleurs ne dirait-on pas que les flocons planent, et remontent même, sans jamais tomber ? », s'interroge Durand à ce propos (1953: 629). Ce n'est qu'un « vain mouvement [qui] piétine », remarquait très justement Jankélévitch à propos de la pièce pour piano de Claude Debussy, *The snow is dancing* : certes « les flocons tourbillonnent en tous sens : mais la danse de la neige est immobile » (Jankélévitch 1976: 127 et 131). Telle est ce que nous montre la partition aux premières mesures, un peu à la manière d'une "musique pour les yeux" de la Renaissance italienne (exemple 1) :

Exemple 1. Debussy, The snow is dancing, mesures 1–9.

C'est aussi cette vision des flocons en musique que nous offre le passage d'une œuvre de Morton Feldman, *Three voices* (1982) pour trois voix féminines, composée sur un poème de Frank O'Hara : lorsque la première phrase – « who'd have thought – that snow falls » – est chantée, le second vers devient « snow that falls » par l'interversion progressive des trois mots, répétés ad libitum par une figure chromatique descendante. Et c'est bien finalement le non-mouvement des flocons, leur "perpetuum immobile", qui leur confère leur "magnifique insignifiance", selon la belle expression de Cummings.

Neige et infinitude

Mais la neige est-elle pour autant un "ailleurs" ? Cette question paraîtra peut-être absurde aux Finnois qui la côtoient au plus près puisqu'elle fait partie durant de longs mois de leur univers quotidien, l'expression *la neige de l'oubli* ("unohduksen lumi") témoignant du reste pour eux des premières neiges hivernales qui viennent effacer la moisissure et la pourriture de l'automne pluvieux et humide.[19] Et quand bien même elle serait un "Ailleurs", présence ou signe de celui-ci, la neige est bel et bien là, encombrante, contraignante. Elle devient alors plaisir par la nécessité de surmonter les contraintes premières : pour celui qui vit avec la neige et qui *vit la neige*, il faut composer avec elle, non qu'elle constitue un obstacle permanent, mais qu'elle devienne utile et utilisable. Il lui faut donc l'apprivoiser, la domestiquer, ultime stade de la familiarité entre l'homme et la neige. Dans cette perspective, la neige ne représente pas un Ailleurs, mais bien une *réalité maxima*, tangible, englobant l'univers quotidien et conditionnant les gestes les plus simples et les plus courants. Dans son mode paradoxal de réception, elle oscille ainsi entre l'émerveillement premier et la banalité du quotidien. Pourtant, a montré Sartre, même si elle est utilisée pour glisser, pour que je sois porté par elle, « la neige demeure impénétrable et hors d'atteinte ; en un sens, l'action du skieur ne fait que développer ses *puissances* » (Sartre 1943: 674).

La neige est bien, selon les termes de Durand, « la grande transformatrice » (Durand: 626) qui opère une métamorphose radicale sur les choses (et les êtres ?), les transfigure à tel point parfois que nous ne reconnaissons plus rien : la terre devient un « neigeux nullepart » (Cummings). Car cette transfiguration opérée par la neige sur le monde est parfois telle, que nous ne pouvons à la rigueur plus affirmer vivre dans *le même monde* : le monde blanc marquerait alors pratiquement *l'advenue d'un autre monde* sur la terre. Du moins, la neige semble s'interposer entre le monde et nous, elle l'éloigne et nous en sépare ; en cela, on peut la considérer en tant que "matière d'interposition" qui, par sa masse dominatrice qu'elle impose, réduit le monde à une désolante et parfaite *monotonie* (Guillot 1994: 146). La blancheur qui repose sur Terre n'est pas cependant de nature terrestre *stricto sensu* : la neige en effet « se place [...] vers les au-delà et les en-deçà du monde terrestre » ; mais plus encore, ajoute Durand – et l'on atteint là peut-être le comble de son aspect paradoxal –, « non seulement elle serait anti-terre mais encore "avant-terre", matière primordiale » (Durand: 633 et 636), tel ce blanc que Kandinsky comparait à la glace terrestre de l'avant-monde.

D'après Durand, l'infinitude est donc « le sens profond de la blancheur désertique et de la négation des couleurs familières » (Durand: 624). Infinitude... et neige, *Äärettömyyttä ja lunta* : c'est justement par ces mots qu'Eeva-Liisa Manner achève un de ses poèmes, et il n'y a là sans doute pas de hasard. Nul doute non plus que devant un paysage de neige, ou sous une neige qui tombe en lents et lourds flocons, nous nous trouvions projetés vers un ailleurs, mais un ailleurs bien peu aisément définissable tant il apparaît décidément insaisissable et impénétrable. En vérité, tout en la neige semble relever du paradoxe : son silence muet qui contraste singulièrement avec les cris de joie des enfants à sa venue, la lumière fabuleuse qu'elle dégage mais aussi l'apparence de linceul qu'elle revêt pour certains, la fascination qu'elle exerce mais aussi la peur qu'elle inspire, son caractère "familier" mais néanmoins comme "venu d'ailleurs". Car il ne demeure toujours qu'une prégnante étrangeté dans cet univers qui perturbe et dérange, où seule subsiste la présence tenace du silence, qui « occupe l'espace entre le ciel et la terre » (Picard 1954: 87).

Nous en arrivons de la sorte au point d'aboutissement qu'est le silence des sens chez l'observateur : aveugles et sourds, ainsi sommes-nous dans la neige éblouissante de lumière et assourdissante de silence. Et alors que dans l'optique d'une logique plus "géographique", un pays ou un espace enneigé serait dénommé un *no sound's land*, le silence de la neige représenterait quant à lui une forme topographique du silence, la neige elle-même devenant un toponyme du silence.

Notes

1. Nous tenons à exprimer notre profonde gratitude au Professeur Tarasti pour avoir rendu possible la traduction finnoise de l'un de ces textes (voir nos références).
2. Boris Pasternak, « La tempête », in *Ma sœur la vie*.
3. Paul Valéry, « Poésie perdue » : *l'ouïe*.
4. Saint-John Perse, « Neiges », in *Eloges*.
5. Karin Boye, « Dédicace », in *Pour l'amour de l'arbre*.
6. Vercors, *Le silence de la mer*, Paris, Editions de Minuit, 1942, p. 17 et 48.
7. Edith Södergran, « Printemps nordique », in *Dikter* (1916).
8. Oskar Milosz, « Dans un pays d'enfance ».
9. Mikel Dufrenne, *L'œil et l'oreille*, Montréal, L'Hexagone, 1987, p. 90.
10. Wassily Kandinsky, *Du spirituel dans l'art*.
11. M. Dufrenne, *Phénoménologie de l'expérience esthétique*, Paris, P.U.F., 1953, tome II, p. 437.
12. La comparaison avec un ciel parfaitement bleu appelle cependant la remarque suivante : une étendue terrestre blanche de neige qui se détache sur fond de ciel bleu ne possède évidemment pas la même force que lorsqu'elle se confond avec un ciel d'une teinte semblable à elle, un ciel bouché qui ferme par le haut l'espace comme un couvercle, favorisant chez l'observateur l'impression d'un complet enfermement. Il n'y a plus dans ce cas ni ciel ni terre. Inversement, l'ouverture d'un sol neigeux sur le ciel bleu permet une éclatante bichromie ; la blancheur de la neige se

métamorphose, et la confrontation blanc/bleu vire, sinon à la fusion, du moins à une sorte d'échange (ciel—>neige/neige—>ciel) qui annule l'effet propre à chacun. En outre l'emprise du blanc cède du terrain, il n'est plus aussi implacable dans sa domination. Ce qui entraîne parallèlement la régression du silence et l'avènement d'une certaine "sonorité" avec le bleu azur. Pour de plus fines analyses sur le ciel bleu, voir Bachelard (1943).

13. Maurice Merleau-Ponty, *Phénoménologie de la perception*, Paris, Gallimard, 1945, p. 244.
14. André Malraux, *Les chênes qu'on abat*, Paris, Gallimard, 1971, p. 21 et 60.
15. B. Pasternak, « La tempête ».
16. Pierre Reverdy, « Remords », in *Flaques de verre*.
17. Suzy Morel, *Célébration de la neige*, Ed. Robert Morel, 1968 (sans pages).
18. Antoine de Saint-Exupéry, *Vol de nuit*.
19. Nous sommes très reconnaissant à Madame Marjatta Ecare (Helsinki) de nous avoir fourni cette information.

Bibliographie

Bachelard, Gaston (1943). *L'air et les songes. Essai sur l'imagination du mouvement.* Paris: J. Corti.
– (1948). *La terre et les rêveries du repos.* Paris: J. Corti.
Chambon, Roger (1974). *Le Monde comme perception et réalité.* Paris: J. Vrin.
Cummings, Edward Estlin (1979). *58 + 58 poèmes.* Paris: C. Bourgois (trad. fr.).
– (1983). *95 poèmes.* Paris: Flammarion/textes (trad. fr.).
Durand, Gilbert (1953). Psychanalyse de la neige. *Mercure de France* 1080, 615–639.
Ekelöf, Gunnar (1988). *Une nuit à l'horizon.* Paris: Gallimard.
Guillot, Matthieu (1994). La neige silencieuse, de la vision à l'écoute. Université de Tours : *Cahiers du CIREM* 32-33-34, 143–148.
– (1995). Lumi ja hiljaisuus. Helsingin yliopisto : *Synteesi* 1/1995, 79–88. Trad. de : Neige et silence. *Revue d'Esthétique* 28, 1995-96, 91–100, Paris: J.-M. Place.
Guiomar, Michel (1988). *Principes d'une esthétique de la mort.* Paris: J. Corti (2e éd.).
Jankélévitch, Vladimir (1960/78). *Le pur et l'impur.* Paris: Flammarion/Champs (2e éd.).
– (1976). *Debussy et le mystère de l'instant.* Paris: Plon.
Kaufmann, Pierre (1967). *L'expérience émotionnelle de l'espace.* Paris: J. Vrin.
Picard, Max (1954). *Le monde du silence.* Paris: P.U.F. (trad. fr.).
Rassam, Joseph (1980). *Le silence comme introduction à la métaphysique.* Publications de l'Université de Toulouse-Le Mirail, série A, tome 44.
Sartre, Jean-Paul (1943). *L'Etre et le Néant. Essai d'ontologie phénoménologique.* Paris: Gallimard.
Schafer, Murray R. (1979). *Le paysage sonore.* Paris: J.-C. Lattès (trad. fr.).

Eero Tarasti

Finland among the paradigms of national anthems

One thing that makes music unique among the arts is that no great composers can come into being until musical life reaches a certain maturity and degree of organization. Literary talents and geniuses in painting can emerge directly out of folk art, but great symphonies and operas cannot be created until symphonic orchestras, conservatories, choirs, and also enlightened audiences exist to ensure their performance. None of these could be found in Finland before the German violinist, conductor, and composer Fredrik Pacius, born in Hamburg and trained in Kassel, arrived in Helsinki in 1835.

Those who take on the responsibility of founding the musical life of a region usually must abandon their own creative activities in order to perform the many mundane tasks which the organizing of performances demands. Pacius was no exception to this rule. He had to put together his orchestra and choirs *ex nihilo* in order to perform such master works as Handel's *Messiah* and Louis Spohr's oratorio *Die letzten Dinge*. Thus his position differed little from that of Hector Berlioz who at the same time in Paris, a city with centuries of active musical life behind it, had to collect musicians whenever he wanted any of his gigantic symphonic works to be performed.

Though Pacius brought music from Germany, no one in Finland considered him a musical "colonizer" of that nation. When at the beginning of the nineteenth century the "canon" of German music expanded into peripheral regions of Europe, it was seen as exporting musical grammar to these countries. Using this grammar, or *langue* (to use Saussure's term), Jean Sibelius and others could then create a genuinely national art. Pacius, however, should not be judged with the horizons of the subsequent period of national romanticism, but rather starting from the *Zeitgeist* of his own time: the age of *Biedermeier*.

Biedermeier was a nickname designating a kind of continuation of the solemn and joyless empire style. *Biedermeier* was always the art of a closely-knit *bourgeois* community and therefore fitted particularly well in Finland. The *Biedermeier* era has been characterized pejoratively as the age of the *bourgeoisie*. In 1847 Ludwig Pfau wrote a poem, *Der gute Bürger*, which he later renamed *Herr Bied-*

ermeier. Mitglied der besitzenden und gebildeten Klasse. In the poem Mr. Biedermeier appears in a fairly sarcastic context:

Schau, dort spaziert Herr Biedermeier
Und seine Frau, den Sohn am Arm;
Sein Tritt ist sachte wie auf Eier,
Sein Wahlspruch: Weder kalt noch warm!
Das ist ein Bürger hochgeachtet,
er geistlich spricht und weltlich trachtet;
Er wohnt in jenem schönen Haus
Und – leiht seine Geld auf Wucher aus.

The last phrase, "And lends his money to a profiteer", serves as the ironic refrain to all the verses (quoted in Geismeier 1979: 15).

In art history *Biedermeier* meant a harmless *bourgeois* idyll and a kind of lamentable style of stylelessness. Music along with theater and poetry was particularly favoured during this period in which the purpose of art was to provide social entertainment, as E. T. A. Hoffman stated through his protagonist Kapellmeister Kreisler. Art was meant to give man respite from his more serious, salaried work in the service of the state, and nothing was better at doing this than music, which "*... einen wunderbaren Reiz verursacht bei dem man des Denkens ganz überhoben ist*" [yields the wonderful joy that one is completely freed from thinking] (ibid.: 86).

Bourgeois homes and societies replaced the royal courts as performing venues. There most of the music played was written for relatively small performing forces of piano trios and quartets, solo voices and duets, plus piano arrangements of operas as well as operettas and "singing-plays" (*Singspiele*). The so-called singing academies and *Liedertafeln* founded in Berlin prompted a huge amount of music to be written for male choir. Music festivals took place, and people gathered casually to sing in schools, universities, churches, and theaters. Concerts were held in gardens, and their programs displayed a motley mix of symphonies, overtures, dances, marches, and opera scenes. General taste favored comedy: statistics show that from 1815–1830 at the Berliner Schausspielhaus, 56 tragedies and 292 comedies were performed. Yet the center of *Biedermeier* was the Vienna of Metternich, where on one side *Ruh und Ordnung* prevailed, but on the other the rebellious mind smoldered in the student societies, or *Burschenschaft*, and *Schubertiades* took pride of place in social life. Carl Dahlhaus reduces the music principles of *Biedermeier* to three essential points: social life, educational task, and representation of *bourgeois* values (1989: 168–170). All these manifested in a purely musical expression that Dahlhaus describes as the undeniable *Biedermeier* tone (however, without analyzing it more carefully).

None of this was known in Finland before Fredrik Pacius was nominated as music teacher of the University of Helsinki. Everything about the man and his music bespoke *Biedermeier* as we have just described it. Pacius had received thorough training in violin from Louis Spohr, whom Dahlhaus mentions as a typical *Biedermeier* in music. The Spohr school was the very antithesis of Paganini's championing of virtuosity, and it emphasized a singing violin tone and the expression of the inner qualities of music. Throughout his life Pacius idolized Spohr, and this probably helped to nurture in Pacius a kind of obstinate independence. It also partly explains why Pacius left for a country such as Finland, which had never been tempting to eminent foreign musicians. Indeed, Busoni came to Finland fifty years after Pacius but only in order to get his first permanent job, whereas Pacius had no similar reason to move there. Pacius had in fact been nominated as a court musician in Stockholm where he had served for five years before deciding to apply for the post of music teacher at Helsinki University. It is not surprising that Pacius got the position, given his high level of his musicianship, as demonstrated by the E-flat Major Overture that he wrote at the age of seventeen.

Pacius's father tried to teach his son such courtly manners as gracious politeness and obeisance to those of higher station. But such behaviour did not suit Fritz, who wrote the following to his father:

> I cannot penetrate to the company of the noble and grovel at their feet, like Mr. P. Whom you consider the most charming man in the world, but who in my eyes is the most unbearable. [Such a person] crawls and wags his tail as soon as his interests are concerned but who treads down some poor drummer or some other modest man of the chapel greeting him with respect....

Dr. Michael Wittman (Berlin) believes that the Freemasonry ideas of Spohr may have taken root in Pacius. This might explain why he did not like living in Stockholm but traveled on to Finland – certainly a very exotic country to a German – and remained here for the rest of his life. The price to be paid was a longing for Germany, efforts to return home, and the depression caused by homesickness. He must have been something of an adventurer since when he arrived in February in 1834 he had to travel on the ice from Stockholm to Helsinki.

What happened in Helsinki is a part of Finnish music history. Pacius's enviable task was to serve as the mythical founder-hero of Finnish music. He had to build everything out of nothing: he organized the first large-scale orchestral concerts, performed masterworks of music (such as Spohr's oratorio, mentioned above), founded choral singing, and wrote the first Finnish opera *The Hunt of King Charles*. In addition to all this he composed the Finnish national anthem, *The Song of Our Country* (*Maamme-laulu*).

In the following I focus on the Finnish national anthem as belonging to two main kinds of paradigm. I first examine it in the context of other national anthems of Europe, then as compared to competing versions based on the same text by the Finnish-Swedish poet, Johan Ludvig Runeberg (1804–1877).

How are national anthems born?

Some scholars are convinced that words, not music, are the essential ingredient of national anthems. One argument supporting this view would be that national anthems are sometimes based on "wandering melodies"; that is, the same tune may serve various purposes and accompany different words. A good example of a wandering melody is the British national anthem, *God Save the King*, whose composer is not known but which originates from the turn of the sixteenth into the seventeenth century. In Germany the same melody was known as a folk song. It became the national anthem of the Prussians with the words *Heil Dir in Siegerkranz*. The same tune was also offered to Switzerland and Austria as their national songs. It is a catchy melody, mostly scalar and easily sung. It occurs as early as in Telemann and Dvorák. Beethoven also thought highly of the melody and wrote variations on it. On Joseph Haydn it made a deep enough impact during his London trip that he decided to write a corresponding tune for Austria, thus creating his famous Emperor hymn (Nettl 1952: 53).

While one would assume that every nation wants to distinguish itself from other nations by all possible signs, it is ironic to note that music can in fact unite different nations. Music knows no ideological boundaries nor can it in itself serve a specific religious belief or idea. This fact is well illustrated by the story of the French national anthem, *La Marseillaise*, which captain Rouget de l'Isle wrote in one night in Strassburg after a dinner party on 24 April 1792. The lyrics of the song expressed opposition to the attacking armies of Prussia and Austria, and at that time it went by the name of *Chant de guerre pour l'armée du Rhin*. The tyrants attacked in the lyrics of this song were German princes and not at all the Bourbons of France. When the song was later christened *Marseillaise* in homage to volunteers from Marseille who were serving in the army, it became acceptable to the revolutionaries in Paris. Paradoxically, the poet-composer then abruptly renounced such use of the song, was cast into prison, and barely avoided the guillotine (Eyck 1995: 40–41).

In contrast to the situation above, where one melody represents several countries, many nations typically have several competing hymns. The English have in addition to *God Save the King* the tune *Rule Britannia* which at one time depicted the actual status of the British Empire. It, too, had a great effect on many composers. Beethoven used it and Wagner wrote an overture on it, saying that its first eight bars were the purest musical manifestation of the British race (Nettl 1952: 50–51). When in the mid-nineteenth century discussions were held in Finland about what song would be elevated to the status of a national anthem, the statesman J. V. Snellman criticized Runeberg's poem *Vårt land* (*Our Country*) and suggested that *Rule Britannia* be used as the model (Klinge 1982: 166). Although Snellman probably had the words of *Rule Brittania* in mind more than the music, even quoting the melody would not have been impossible if one considers the eclectic practices by which national anthems are selected.

In Finland the *Maamme-laulu* had several contemporaries: Karl Collan's *Mun muistuu mieleheni* (a song depicting the Savo, a southeast region in Finland), Bernard Henrik Crusell's *Hell dig du höga nord*, and Jaakko Juteini's *Eläköön Armias, Rakkahin Ruhtinas* (*Long Live You Dear, Merciful Sovereign*), which was addressed to the Russian emperors, of course, and sung to the tune of *God Save the King*. Later came Pacius's own choral song, *Suomis sång*, and the hymn of farewell from his opera, *The Hunt of King Charles*, and later still, Sibelius's *Finlandia*.

In most countries the choice of a national anthem from among competing pieces of music has been settled in favor of some hymn from a particular occasion that constitutes a mythical event in the history of the nation, such that the society has emotionally identified with the chosen tune. In the semiotic sense such an occasion serves as the indexical catalyst of a certain kind of behaviour. And it is for such extraordinary situations that hymns exist, either for unusually solemn festivals or for moments of extreme danger and distress. Like myths, such occasions strengthen people's social roots and unite them, with the aid of music, to their physiologico-biological essence, as Lévi-Strauss has stated (1971: 587). A typical example – and a frequent topic for novels and movies – is the birth of the *Marseillaise* on that tumultuous night in Strasbourg when the words "*patrie, aux armes, libre*" were on everyone's lips, thus prompting Rouget de l'Isle to create his work. The composer himself later described this event: he had taken his violin and at the first stroke of the bow found the right tune; the words burst forth from the melody, and the melody from the words.

Similar is the birth of the Norwegian national anthem, with words by Björnstjern Björnsson, entitled *Ja vi elsker detta land* (*Yes, I Love This Country*) and also called *Sang for Norge* (*Song for Norway*). The music was composed by Björnsson's cousin Rikard Nordraak and was first performed on the national holiday of Norway, 17 May 1864. On that rainy day Björnsson made one of his famous speeches to a crowd gathered at the Slotplats in front of the King's Residence in Christiania. He referred in his talk to freedom and progress, and to the flag and song symbolizing those *desiderata*. In the evening the crowd convened in the auditorium of the university and the choir performed *Sang for Norge*. At once the old hymn written in 1820 was forgotten.

Those events in Norway are analogous to the ones in Finland because there, too, a momentous event gave birth to the national anthem. Finnish students celebrated the coming of spring on the day of Flora on May 13, and traveled in procession from the cathedral to the field of the Kum Star a little outside the town. For the celebration of 1848 a song was commissioned from Fredrik Pacius, and the Finnish aesthetician and best known orator of the time, Fredrik Cygnaeus, gave a speech (whose content is unfortunately not known). The hymn itself was not sung for the first time at the field of Kum Star but was performed, accompanied by military band, on the so-called "long bridge".

It is further characteristic of national anthems that they are usually always composed, although their author may remain unknown or may even be subjected to accusations of plagiarism. In 1797, for example, Joseph Haydn wrote his *Kaiserlied*, which became the symbol of Austrian patriotism and was later sung in Germany to the words *Deutschland, Deutschland über alles*; yet he was called a plagiarist when in 1837 the rumor circulated that his tune was in fact written by the Italian opera composer Nicola Antonio Zingarelli. The truth, however, was as follows: Haydn's song was naturally printed in all languages of the Austrian-Hungarian empire, Italian included. Zingarelli had merely discovered this translation and used the tune in one of his own works. Another scholar tried to prove that Haydn's theme was in fact a Croatian folk song that Haydn had borrowed. But even though an entire book was written in defense of Haydn, the question of authorship is irrelevant. Most melodies are reminiscent of each other, and furthermore, national hymns always serve as functional music.

The hymn by Pacius shared the same destiny as Haydn's tune. *Maamme-laulu* was printed in Stockholm and translated into German as the musical appendix to a collection of poetry entitled *The Stories of Field Sergeant Ståhl* and published in 1852; written by J. L. Runeberg, the collection praises the heroism of Finnish soldiers in the war of 1809 between Swedes and Russians. The book met with success in Germany and as early as 1854 a new edition of it came out. The melody soon appeared in Germany in a collection of (German) melodies as a (German) folk song with the words *Wohl auf in Gottes schöne Welt*; there it received the title *Volksweise* and was arranged for four-part female choir. The melody appeared also in Stuttgart in the collection by Immanuel Faisst, *Liederbuch des deutschen Sängerbundes*, now with the new words, *Es zog die freude wohlgemuth*. An amusing incident took place when Pacius, during his stay in Hamburg in 1878, made a tour to the neighboring village of Eppendorf where he heard in a local restaurant a men's choir singing his melody with German words. When he asked if anyone there could name the composer, nobody knew the answer. Pacius then revealed himself as the composer of the song and was celebrated with much enthusiasm. Upon his return to Finland, Pacius arranged his melody for male choir using both the original and the German words. Its cover bore the title, "The

Finnish National Anthem" along with the words, "Often performed in Germany without knowledge of who is the composer".

But the matter was not yet settled. In 1933 the Finnish choral conductor and music historian Heikki Klemetti published an article called "The Origin of *Maamme-laulu*" in the music magazine *Suomen musiikkilehti*. He was convinced that Pacius had used as his model a German *Burschenschaft* song that mocks the Pope: *Der Papst lebt herrlich in der Welt*. Klemetti first proves that the tune existed before Pacius's melody, then after comparing the tunes note by note he states: "The melody of *Maamme-laulu* has obviously been built upon the Pope song, such that it absolutely evokes a conscious quotation.... [This is not] a mere accident, for there are too many notes in common between the Pope song and Pacius's melody" (Klemetti 1933: 160). Unfortunately later music scholars did not confirm Klemetti's view, but it has survived as a funny anecdote – and such stories have always been told about national anthems.

Music Example 1. The Pope Song and Maamme-laulu in the "paradigmatic" analysis by Heikki Klemetti.

More significantly, Klemetti performed nothing other than a paradigmatic analysis of the type later so well-known in musical semiotics through Nicolas

Finland among the paradigms of national anthems

Ruwet and Jean-Jacques Nattiez (see Nattiez 1976). We might here reconsider the paradigmatic method from a new point of view, namely, that there exist always two paradigms: the inner and the outer. This view can be applied to the case of Finland's national anthem in the following way.

(1) In the first place we can proceed as in a normal paradigmatic analysis, that is, by identifying similar motifs, or "theme-actors", within the musical text itself, as in the chart above.

2) Second, Pacius's melody belongs to series of other alternative melodies competing with it for the status of national anthem:

(a) These are melodies in Pacius's own output:

Music Example 2 a. Fredrik Pacius: *Maamme-laulu*, the national anthem of Finland and Estonia (Helsingfors 1848).

Eero Tarasti

Music Example 2 b. Fr. Pacius: Suomis sång, to the poem by E. v. Qvanten (Andersson 1937: 2).

Finland among the paradigms of national anthems

Music Example 2 c. Hymn to Finland, by Fredrik Pacius, from the end of his opera "The Hunt of King Charles" (Andersson 1937: 108).

(b) Or Pacius's melody can be compared to other composers' melodies for the same poem by Runeberg:

Music Example 3 a. J. L. Runeberg's own tune for Maamme-laulu, arranged by Robert Kajanus.

Music Example 3 b. A. G. Ingelius's melody for Maamme-laulu.

Music Example 3 c. J. A. Josephson's melody for Maamme-laulu.

(3) Lastly, we encounter the broadest paradigm, that of other national anthems in Europe:

Music Example 4 a. Germany, Deutschland, Deutschland über alles. (Joseph Haydn.)

Finland among the paradigms of national anthems

Music Example 4 b. England, God Save the Queen. (Henry Carey.)

Music Example 4 c. France, Marseillaise. (Rouget de Lisle.)

In these cases we are only following Lévi-Strauss's original method of discovering transformational systems in order to determine the meaning of a myth, which we apply here to a musical work. In these paradigmatic changes, however, the essential question one must ask is, Who is the subject to whom these transformations make sense? This subject can also be a collective entity if one conceives of transformations in historical processes in the Hegelian sense: there must be a subject who carries them. Lévi-Strauss omitted the subject, but without it no series of transformations could even take place since there would be no entity to determine the pertinence of the paradigmatic categories. Lévi-Strauss thought that the subject of what we might call the "inner paradigm" does not see the "outer paradigm" surrounding it. This view also comes close to Alfred Schütz's theory of the subjective and objective sense of action. The observer-sociologist catches the objective, external sense, which is the same as joining the phenomenon to the "outer paradigm", as for instance is the case in the class structure of a society. Moreover, both inner and outer paradigms can be either synchronic or diachronic. They both presuppose from the subject a so-called "transcendental act": the realization of diachrony implies the comprehension of history, because the transformations take place as series in time; the synchrony is in turn based upon what Rudolph Carnap called *Ähnlichkeitserinnerung*, iconicity. These relationships are not abstract, however, but are motivated by the consciousness of the subject. Thus we repeat, the fault in the Ruwet-Nattiez paradigmatic method lies in its trying to reduce the inner paradigm to the outer one and to search for criteria of pertinence there.

These methodological reflections can be seen in the background of our study of national anthems. Even here we have to deal with various kinds of subjects, from the "actors" in the musical text itself to the composer, other composers, and other tunes to which it can be compared. (This would be one way to "semiotize" further the whole issue with a more extensive and complex layering of theoretical concepts.)

One may further ask whether national anthems reflect in any way the nation they are supposed to serve. There are different opinions about this. F. Gunther Eyck in his book *The Voice of Nations: European National Anthems and Their Authors* is of the opinion that they do not: "Only in a few instances did the melodies act as true indicators of a national identity. Music by definition is transnational, and tunes are interchangeable" (Eyck 1995: xiv). In this study, however, Finland has curiously enough been omitted from consideration.

Paul Nettl in his book *National Anthems* takes an opposing standpoint: "There are not many anthems which do not correspond somehow to the national characteristics of the people which they represent. That is why an analysis of the musical and psychological character of national anthems is interesting not only from the point of view of the historian of music but also from that of the student of ethnology" (Nettl 1952: 51).

National anthems also often escape conscious political regulation. Many efforts have been made to modify, criticize, or change certain anthems into new ones, but most often without success. National anthems are bound to the collective memory of a nation, to a country's living semiosphere that always follows its own laws. Thus very seldom has one been able to create a national hymn by an arranged competition whose winner has not been the "real" winner.

European national anthems can be classified into at least five categories: (1) hymns of the *Ancien régime* (Holland, England, Denmark), which emphasize the continuity and stability of the government; (2) hymns of resistance (*Marseillaise*, and the *Dabrowski Mazurka* of Poland); (3) hymns of independence (the

Hungarian *Himnusz* and the Norwegian anthem); (4) hymns of unification (the German anthem and Italy's *Inno di Mameli*; and (5) hymns of contentment (Sweden's, among others). This classification by Eyck (1995) is somewhat unsatisfactory, however, because it is based completely on the purely social-historical-political function of the hymn and does not account for other criteria. Doubtless the Pacius version of the Finnish *Maamme-laulu* would belong to the fifth category as regards both the words and the melody, whereas other musical versions of *Maamme-laulu* try to make it "our *Marseillaise*", to use Matti Klinge's expression.

Variants of Maamme-laulu

With what kind of melodies did Pacius's version have to compete? Were there really any alternatives? In this case the musical criteria are decisive for answering these questions since the text remains the same. The sources for comparison come from Alfhild Forslin's work *Runeberg i musiken* (1958), and for copies of the melodies I am indebted to the archives of the Sibelius Museum at the Åbo Academy in Turku.

As Matti Klinge pointed out in his 1982 book, *Suomen sinivalkoiset värit* (*The Blue-White Colors of Finland*), the poet Runeberg had intended from the beginning to have his poem set to music. One of the first versions was by August Engelberg, published in 1846 for mixed choir and orchestra. Engelberg, a composer living in Turku (1817–1850), wrote a septet on the theme "War and Peace" and also a treatise on fugue. He ended up drowning himself in the river Aura. Engelberg's musical version of the poem features a solemnity arising from the dotted rhythms, unexpected register shifts, wide leaps and otherwise lively melodic characteristics. Yet it sounds more like a choral scene from a *Singspiel* than a catchy hymn to be sung collectively, and it was quickly forgotten.

Fredrik August Ehrström (1801–1850), a well-known lied composer in the genuine *Biedermeier* style, published his version as the musical appendix to the second edition of the *Stories of Field Sergeant Ståhl* in 1847, and even before that in the *Fosterländskt Album III*. As the oldest printed musical setting of the *Maamme-laulu*, it was first performed at the annual festival of the Osthrobotnian student's club on 9 November 1846. The performance went by without much notice, and the occasion did not turn Ehrström's setting into a national anthem. It was criticized for its tempo indication of *andante*, and the music writer Axel Gabriel Ingelius thought it more an Italian gondolier's song than a Finnish patriotic tune. In spite of the tempo indication of *andante animoso* it sounds more like a march, more like "our *Marseillaise*" or a resistance hymn than a lyrical independence song. Also, a bit manneristic is the twice repeated cadence on scale degree II. As such it has a certain vividness:

Music Example 5. *The setting by Fredrik August Ehrström (1847).*

From Fredrik Eimele (1804–1871) we also have an undated musical setting of the poem. This composer, who was born in Finland but moved to Sweden in 1837, has left us a rather solemn piece that contains more than the normal amount of chromaticism. The plagal cadence at the end can be heard as a kind of Nordic color.

Runeberg's own musical "composition" for his *Maamme-laulu* (*Vårt land*) deserves special mention. Runeberg had asked the teacher of singing at the Borgå Lyceum, Carl Frans Blom, to transcribe and arrange for quartet the melody he had invented for his poem. Under Blom's direction this song was performed at the 500th anniversary celebration on 3 December 1846. Runeberg's version was later performed fairly often, mostly as a curiosity, but also as arranged by Robert Kajanus for the 90th anniversary celebration of the *Akademiska Sångföreningen* (Academic Singing Association) held in 1930.

Runeberg's melody is one of the most successful and singable in our material. It is based on a stable scale passage and features (perhaps a little monotonously) a repeated dotted figure. Unexpected is the syncopated half note in the fourth measure, which is, however, followed by an overly strong cadence on tonic that brings the melody to perhaps too strong a stop. The next section is also somewhat monotonous, but the ending is better, containing more varied harmonies than even in Blom's arrangement. In Kajanus's version the suspended seconds create expressivity, and drama is provided by the diminished seventh chord on the aforementioned syncopated half-note.

Also noteworthy are compositions by Axel Gabriel Ingelius (1822–1868), who set the tune to a graceful *siciliano* rhythm, Hampus Wetterling, the German Heinrich Wächter, Reinhold Böning, and Bror Bendt Broms.

Swedish composers, too, were inspired by Runeberg's poem. Among them was Adolf Fredrik Lindblad (1801–1878), whose song collection on the *Stories of Field Sergeant Stål* appeared in 1856 in four booklets. His *Vårt land* doubtless counts among the best of the musical settings of the poem. In fact, it is in my view the only one whose quality and professionality approaches that of the version by Pacius. But could the *Vårt land* composed by a Swede ever become the national anthem of Finland?

Another Swedish version, written by J. A. Josephson (1818–1880), was printed as the appendix to the second edition of the *Stories of Field Sergeant Stål*. Later it appeared in numerous Swedish collections of songs for quartet. Josephson had been the music director at Uppsala University since 1849, hence in the same position as Pacius in Helsinki. Josephson's tune became very popular in Sweden but not in Finland, according to some because it could not be comfortably sung in unison. Still, Josephson's melody has its own value. The sequence in the consequent of the first period is impressive. But the sudden shift in bar 10 to the lowered seventh sounds somewhat forced and causes a too complicated modulation.

Against this background the merits of Pacius's hymn become obvious. Although the up-beat at the beginning is difficult to perform in collective singing, the tune is melodically varied and reflects the contours of the poem without implying any minor-mode harmony. One can thus with purely musical criteria explain why precisely this setting of Runeberg's poem won the competition. (Why it was victorious over entirely other texts and tunes is another matter, which requires one to account for many other reasons concerning the words and social-historical aspects.) Notice especially the fanfares at the end of the melody, which seem to turn the lyrical quality of the tune toward a *Marseillaise* type of song.

Though the beauty of the foregoing hymn is undeniable, perhaps Pacius's best choral song by strictly musical criteria is the *Suomis sång* which he wrote a year later. Its minor-mode atmosphere has been interpreted in the light of the composer's fate, the death of his mother, and the like. But the dawning national style can also be heard in passages where melody and harmony iconically portray various traits of Finnishness. It has been said that Pacius sighed after hearing his own piece, marveling over how he had ever been able to write anything so beautiful. The song was performed at multiple festivities and thus had many chances to become accepted as the national hymn.[1] It was heard for the first time when Emperor Alexander II visited Helsinki on Easter in 1856.

The image of Finland in *Suomis sång* differs from Runeberg's view. The poem by Emil von Qvanten (1827–1903) emphasizes the melancholy of Finland's nature. It would have offered another type of object for with which the Finns could have identified.

Pacius's vocal output includes several congenial places in which momentarily he already transgresses the framework of *Biedermeier*, which was sometimes even better and more genuinely and Germanically represented by his son-in-law, Karl Collan. In Pacius's last work, the opera *Lorelei*, he was amazingly enough not able to find any fresh melodies, as melodious as its tonal language is in other respects. There he instead returns to the early romanticism of his youth; it is pure *Biedermeier* although it is a tragedy.

From the point of view of postcolonial music history Pacius illustrates a composer who steps out of his role as a dominant: he was a German who became a Finn. He was lucky to have made the right choice, achieving full recognition from his new fatherland. It is much more difficult to travel the other direction – from the position of dominated to being accepted by the dominant – as the case of Jean Sibelius subsequently showed.

Note

1. Concerning occasions for music-making, see my essay on Ville Vallgren in this anthology; pp. 388–404.

References

Andersson, Otto (ed.) (1937). *Fredrik Pacius' Manskvartetter*. (=Acta Musica. Källskrifter och studier utgivna av musikvetenskapliga seminariet vid Åbo Akademi. 1.) Åbo: Åbo Akademi.
– (1938). *Den unge Pacius och musiklivet i Helsingfors på 1830-talet* [Young Pacius and the Musical Life in Helsinki in the 1830s]. Helsingfors: Holger Schildts Förlag.
Dahlhaus, Carl (1989). Nineteenth-Century Music. Berkeley, CA: University of California Press.
Elmgren-Heinonen, Tuomi (1959). *Laulu Suomen soi ... Fredrik Pacius ja hänen aikansa* [Finland's Song Sounds ... Fredrik Pacius and His Time]. Helsinki: Fazer.
Eyck, F. Gunther (1995). *The Voice of Nations: European National Anthems and Their Authors*. Westport, Connecticut, London: Greenwood Press.
Forslin, Alfhild (1958). *Runeberg i musiken* [Runeberg in music]. (= Skrifter utgifna av Svenska Litteratursällskapet i Finland 367.) Helsingfors. Svenska Litteratursällskapet i Finland.
Geismeier, Willi (1979). *Biedermeier. Das bild vom Biedermeier. Zeit und Kultur des Biedermeier. Kunst und kunstleben des Biedermeier.* Leipzig: VEB E.A. Seemann Verlag.
Klemetti, Heikki (1933). Maamme-laulun alkuperä [The Origin of *Maamme-laulu*], *Suomen musiikkilehti* 8: 159–161.

Klinge, Matti (1982). *Suomen sinivalkoiset värit* [The Blue-White Colors of Finland]. Helsinki: Otava.
Lévi-Strauss, Claude (1971). *Mythologiques IV: L'homme nu.* Paris: Plon.
Nattiez, Jean-Jacques (1976). *Fondements d'une sémiologie de la musique.* Paris: Gallimard.
Nettl, Paul (1952). *National Anthems.* New York: Storm Publishers.
Rosas, John (ed.) (1959). *Körsånger av Fredrik Pacius* [*Choral Songs by Fredrik Pacius*] (= Acta Musica. Källskrifter och studier utgivna av Musikvetenskapliga Seminariet vid Åbo Akademi III.) Turku: Åbo Akademi.
Salmenhaara, Erkki (1998). "Maamme-laulu kansallisena symbolina" [Maamme-laulu as a National Symbol], in: *Siltoja ja synteesejä. Esseitä semiotiikasta, kulttuurista ja taiteesta* [Bridges and Synthesis. Essays on Semiotics, Culture, and Art] (=Festschrift to Eero Tarasti), Irma Vierimaa, Kari Kilpeläinen, Anne Sivuoja-Gunaratnam (eds.), pp. 193–207. Helsinki: Gaudeamus.
Voigt, Vilmos (1998). "Nykyajan kansallishymnit" [National anthems of our time], in: *Siltoja ja synteesejä. Esseitä semiotiikasta, kulttuurista ja taiteesta* [see Salmenhaara 1998], pp. 184–192.

Anti Randviir

Invasion as an object of semiotics: Representing invasion – creating invasion

This article draws together two seemingly different fields by means of their semiotic interrelationships. Art has long been one of the most favored subjects of semiotic analysis. Invasion, on the other hand, has met with little interest from semioticians – although both terms refer to phenomena that originate in the same vague prehistoric era. This one-sided focus may be explained by the fact that there exists a general, common understanding of topics that belong to cultural discourse, the structure of which seldom reserves space for "barbarian" or non-cultural phenomena. There is no doubt that invasion, as a common-sense term pointing at a certain event in the "outer world", relates primarily to the brutal realm of atrocity. Nevertheless, in what follows I present an alternative view, according to which invasion refers mainly to a thoroughly semiotic phenomenon of cultural dynamics that turns an event "out there" into a meaningful unit of semiosphere.

Let us limit our theme by looking at some "officially accepted" meanings of "invasion". The *Dictionary of English Language and Culture* describes invasion as "An act of invading, especially in war when the enemy spreads into and tries to control a country, city, etc." *Webster's Encyclopedic Unabridged Dictionary of the English Language* defines "invasion" as follows:

> the act or an instance of invading or entering as an enemy, especially by an army;
> the entrance or advent of anything troublesome or harmful, as disease.
> entrance as if to take possession or overrun;
> infringement by intrusion: *invasion of privacy.*

All of these definitions have one thing in common: they all render "invasion" as an act of brute physical force. If this is so, how can one compose a theme focused on art and yet accentuating invasion? How can one correlate the sphere of the "most cultural" with the field of the "barbaric"? Before answering these questions, we first analyze the semiotic aspects of invasion. After that, we examine the following types of invasion: invasion of space, invasion of time, and invasion of subjects or discourse and/or topics belonging to the cultural discourse.

The semiotic nature and mechanism of invasion

Another common thread in the above definitions is that they all feature two parties or actantial subjects: invader and invaded. Also, each of those definitions interprets invasion from the viewpoint of the invaded party. This one-sided perspective leaves little possibility for interpreting invasion as a semiotic phenomenon, in the sense of determining how it circulates as a meaningful unit in sociocultural discourse.

It is precisely the differentiation of viewpoints – into invader and invaded – that helps us to see the communicational aspect of invasion. When approaching the topic from another point of view, namely, from the side of the society that does the invading, the relation between the sphere of the cultural *oikumene* and the nature of the act of invasion becomes more transparent. Namely, invasion is first of all an ideological act. It is an activation and actualization of an ideological discursive mechanism which has the function of *explaining* the invasion (as a brutal act of force). An explanation, of course, is necessary to maintain equilibrium in *Weltanschauung*, and therefore any explanation can be carried out by using the most "cultural" terms and explanatory strategies. And the other way round: any invasion inevitably needs explanation, or more correctly, justification, because otherwise the ideological system that binds society together would appear too incongruent with events in the "physical realm", which have to be explained in terms of a coherent world-view as dictated by a certain ideology. In other words, invasion needs explaining in order for it to be transferred out of the realm of pure physical force, so as to be accepted and supported by the members of the society that does the invading.

We can further infer that the above definitions of "invasion", aided by the notion of "force", are tightly connected to the core of the "cultural". This connection can of course be rationalized from the standpoint of the invading society. On such a view, invasion is no longer a negative notion, but is a device by which (1) to actualize the cognitive map of the ideal *oikumenic*; i.e., to transfer an idealized mental construct of the *oikumene* by means of an invasion into physical reality, in order to supply the signification system with the empirical substrate that is necessary for its functioning. Second, (2) invasion is a pragmatic device by which to spread the territorial expression of the *oikumenic* for the purpose of "cultivating" surrounding areas.

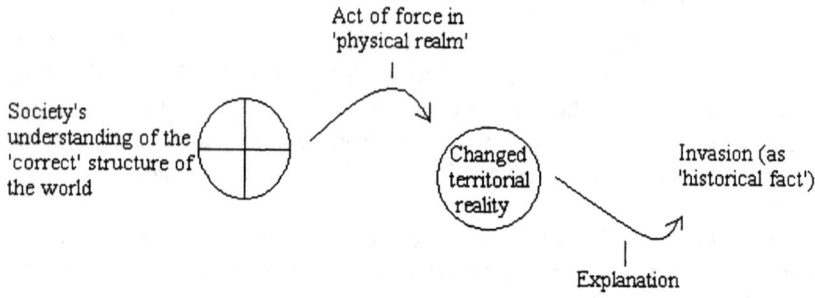

Figure 1. The relation of "invasion" as an act of force and "invasion" as a discursive term.

Thus, instead of considering invasion as a negative phenomenon in relation to the *cultural*, we can also understand invasion as a tool by which to spread the *cultural*, in which case it is no longer an independent entity. Rather, invasion obtains meaning and status in its relation to the *cultural*. This situation is shown schematically in Figure 2:

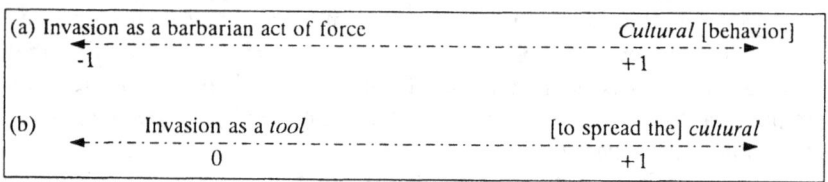

Figure 2. The position of invasion on the axis of the "cultural": (a) as an act of force, (b) as a functional phenomenon semioticized by the cultural.

To talk about invasion as a tool for spreading culture – from the analytic point of view – gives it a neutral status. But from the phenomenological point of view of a cultural insider, it may already occur as a positive fact.

Explaining an act of force

We mentioned above the role of art in connecting the two seemingly opposing spheres of the "cultural" and the "barbarian". Here we go on to a point of more semiotic interest. As we have said, invasion is never anything other than a brutal act of force, if it is not legitimated by an evaluative establishment. The latter may be a chronicle or other kind of message belonging to the genre of "official document". The document helps to place the act of invasion in its "proper" position in the catalogue of "historical facts". The document can do this because it is enunciated by a center of power that directs how members of a given society are to make sense of a given act of force.

Thus, even though invasion is basically a forceful act pertaining to the field of economy and politics, it is ideological in its semiotic mechanism. From this it follows that invasion has to be presented through evaluative filters. Consequently, such ideological presentation of an historical fact – or rather, the *construction* of an historical fact – is actually a *re*-presentation. (Differentiating between presentation and representation is not an aim of the current paper. For the sake of convenience, we here relate "presentation" to the communicative genre that claims and pursues objectivity and reliability, whereas re-presentation makes no such claims.) So we have found one more characteristic by which to measure enunciations describing invasion: the axis of "officiality". I therefore propose to connect the opposition *presentation / representation* with that of *document / work of art*. This helps us to move from distinguishing between terms belonging to analytic discourse (presentation / representation) to a phenomenological opposition between two different categories of artifacts that gain their definitive status (as either document or work of art) in the act of social discourse.

To make certain heuristic distinctions we must ask, How does one differentiate between the (official) "document" and the "work of art"? And what is the semiotic status of each? Having already mentioned the ideological dimension of both invasion and the depiction of it, we now refer to Paul Ricœur's (1986) distinction between the "ideological" and the "utopian". For Ricœur, "ideological" as a term refers to the domain characterized as being related to "others", whereas the "utopian" refers to the realm of sameness, of being one's "own" or relating to oneself. Thus we again come to the opposition of own / alien, but in the following it has no other function than as an instrumental opposition.

Invasion of space

Here we illustrate what has been said thus far. To do so, let us consider eras of extensive invasions, namely, times of territorial discoveries. This does not mean just the Age of Discovery, which was itself followed by intense invasive practices. We should also bear in mind examples from different time periods that share similar semiotic features of invasion (see Figure 3).

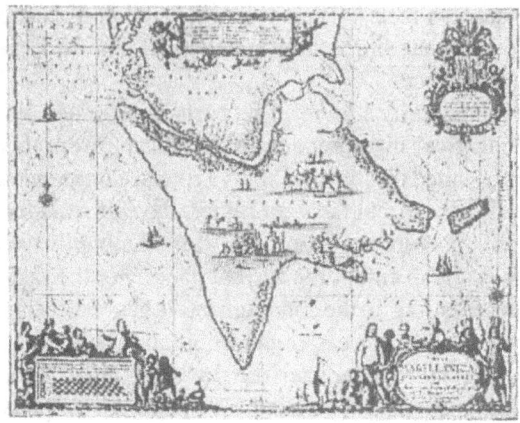

Figure 3. Representations of discovered and/or invaded lands, using society's conception of the "cultural" to explain the need for invasion. (J. Jansson, "Magellanica", from Novus Atlas, 1658.)

Here we find texts that are intended as "documents", more exactly, as cartographic documents. Semiotically, these maps exhibit three major areas of interest. (1) They depict territorial invasion (an event in the physical realm). (2) As documents, they interpret invasion, showing the need for it by means of representations (e.g., the depiction of savages fighting leads the spectator to understand the need to settle such a tumultuous land). (3) In performing such an interpretation, the maps make explicit the authorized understanding of the "cultural".

It is commonly said nowadays that such maps also share features of artworks. Going even further, we can "panchronically" say that they were to a great extent composed as artworks. The point I want to draw attention to, is that what differentiates the artwork from the documentary is the role of interpretation in the former. This is not to say that documents do not call for interpretation. Artwork, however, is composed with the distinct awareness that it is to be interpreted. In other words, the difference between the document and the artwork lies in their ambition: a "document" is intended to describe a state of affairs, whereas an "artwork" is created as an interpretive composition. The relevant interpretive praxis is, of course, carried out through the filters of the cultural. This is done implicitly, and often explicitly as well (e.g., by framing a map with depictions of human figures set on opposite edges, placed there according to racial principles such as same / alien; European / savage).

Nevertheless, "a document is a document is a document". It therefore makes its primary impact in how it both reflects and composes a social world-view. In other words, to document something is to enact and/or establish a *Weltanschauung*. And when talking about art and invasion, we can see the importance of such maps. They are documents that share features of an artwork, and they also serve as evaluative filters that explain events of forceful invasion.

Conceptual invasion

Having viewed the above maps as in a sense both belonging to representative discourse, we now draw examples from "official reality". Hopefully, the following type of invasion will also illustrate the close connection between spatial (or territorial) and conceptual invasion, which is the immanent relation between a referential substrate and a conceptual designate. The invasion of topics of cultural discourse, surely, is also an intrinsic aspect of both the invasion of space and of time.

Here I would like to make brief reference to a common maneuver of invasive praxis. This is the tradition of renaming cities (since the city is the major entity of cultural space) that nearly always accompanies the practice of invasion. We can exemplify the case with several renamings of Tartu. First, the long-official tradition places the origin of this city in the year 1030, the date officially recorded in Russian chronicles, and the settlement is referred to by the name of Jurjev. Because it is known that archeological evidence fixes the origin of this town as early as the second or third millennium BC, we can add another crucial term to our discourse; namely, "conceptual re-documentation". This last is necessary in order to (1) make the brutal act of force fit the features of "positive invasion" (to give the impression that the Russians founded the city and thus cultivated the area), and (2) to organize the (social) cognitive map of the given "cultural space" (i.e., to subject an Estonian town to Russian cultural domination).

The renaming of cities as a way to re-organize a society's cognitive map of its cultural space (and almost all invaders do this) shows that invasion does not necessarily have to have physical force at all. Attempts to control individuals' cognitive maps of their "meaningful territory" – which is an inevitable part and aim of any invasion – is widely practiced even today. Take, for example, the city of Kingissepa, the major town on the Estonian island of Saaremaa. "Kingissepp" was a communist agent's family-name, which replaced the Estonian name. The city reverted back to the Estonian name, Kuressaare, after Estonia regained independence. As another example, Leningrad has again become St. Petersburg. Semiotically, both of these instances tell of invasions that lack the constituent of physical force.

The conceptual invasion of a territory that stresses the importance of cities, and their potential as images of propaganda, has often paid great attention to proper names and their semiotic power. But there is another, quite popular technique of executing and expressing conceptual invasion. In fact, this can be closely related to the previous subfield: the case of the "First, Second, and Third" Rome can serve as an example here. I am referring to the very frequent practice in cartographic representations whereby a city is placed in the center of a map, thereby intimating a similar world-structure in the physical realm. This way of semioticizing not only a country, but the whole world as organized around a common center can be traced vividly, for example, in the Christian tradition of cartography. Conceptual invasions have frequently attained spatial form by means of artistic representations.

These kinds of maps are, in this respect, of special interest, since they "officially" share the genre of both document and artwork. This means that they belong both to the category of the utopian, because they reflect the values of cultural ideals, and to the sphere of the ideological, which uses them as a filter that insures "correct" products of "accurate" communication. Therefore, when studying maps like those above, one must pay attention to the part that exceeds the purely cartographic. The additional "artistic" images that appear in such maps are actually inherent and influential to the cartographic elements, inasmuch as they exhibit both the utopian and ideological factors that originate from a society's world-view and thereby influence the composition of such artifacts.

As we know, the Age of Discoveries brought with it great output in the field of utopian creativity (e.g., in literature). Therefore, any cartographic labor was also an attempt to match the physical (territorial) and cultural reality with what had been imagined to be discovered. Thus the act of invasion, the territorial aspect of which those maps represented, was finally resolved only by means of those representations.

Invasion of time

What has been said thus far applies primarily to territorial invasion and to the ideological conquest of space, as well as their representation in documentary works that can also be characterised as artistic. The arts can also acquaint us with invasion of another nature or, more correctly, with another subject of invasion. And that subject is Time.

The invading of time underlines the peculiar role of art as a mediator of invasion, because it is basically the arts alone to which this type of invasion can be related (though one might argue about the possibility of distinguishing between invasion of time and conceptual invasion). The core of territorial invasion is the subjection of a given area to the invaders' ideological system and conception of culture. But the nature of the invasion of time is different, for one reason, because of the gradation of steps in the act of invasion. More importantly, whereas the physical act of conquering a territory gains its *significance* via representation, the invading of time obtains *only* on the representative level.

What kinds of representations attempt to invade time? The answer is, utopian art, and in both of its meanings: (1) unconsciously (or unintentionally) utopian art, the explication of which was pointed out above; and (2) consciously (intentionally) utopian art. To the latter category belong works labeled nowadays as "science fiction". But keep in mind that utopian fiction, the forerunner of science fiction, actually began with the start of European discoveries. Of course, science fiction also explicates the third type of invasion (and the third type of relation between the arts and the act of invasion); namely, the invasion of topical subjects, the "official" beginning of which can be traced to Mary Shelly's *Frankenstein*. I say more about this below. Of present interest are utopias such as those envisioned by More, Swift, and others.

To proceed, we first consider the difference between spatial invasion and the invasion of time, as those two phenomena appear in the sphere of the "cultural", which is the key domain for invasion and its actualization through the arts. Although fictional representations of utopia came along with the conquests of lands considered "utopian", those representations also had an aspect uniquely their own. The utopias of More, Swift, and others all share the characteristic of invading the future: they conquer the future by fitting it into a conceptual schema of their own design. In addition to these "classic utopias", nowadays we all encounter claims and invitations to chronological invasion, beginning with children's cartoons and "screens between different time zones", and ending up with the implicit presupposition that the proper "cultural insider" should be able to differentiate between the "serious" time machines proposed by great thinkers of Western cultural history (e.g., H. G. Wells), and those nonsensical ones used daily by TV supermen. The situation is also largely the same retrospectively, as exemplified by historical novels or by any attempt to reconstruct history. So when we talk about the arts as a means (sphere, key, technique) by which utopian consciousness tries to capture the future, we are entering the temporal dimension of invasion.

Invasion intertwined

At this point an important observation must be made: no invasion of time can be executed without a parallel or correlative invasion of space. This assertion can be exemplified by the illustrations in Figure 4, which were taken from certain fictional works:

Figure 4. Invasion of topics of discourse by means of invading time, and by projecting a new conceptual realm into an alternative spatial order: (a) Utopia insulae figura (woodcut, first edition of Thomas More's Utopia, 1516); (b) part of a map representing the world of Winnie the Pooh (1988).

Figures 4a and b express the same kind of invasion. The one illustrating More's *Utopia* shows a place that reacts against the existing social order; it is a "positive utopia" depicting the ideal arrangement of society. Figure 4b depicts the world of Winnie the Pooh, which in its own way also represents the fictional reality of "a better world". It is important to notice that the fictional invasion of the utopian can never actually avoid tying itself with spatial expression; for the latter is in immanent connection with the invasion of time. One difference between the above illustrations is that, in order to reach the kind of utopia shown in Figure 4a, one has to use physical means (a ship) by which to transcend physical reality. The universe of Winnie the Pooh, however, can be entered by the conceptual "leaps" of mental labor. From this it follows that, while the representations of actual invasions tell us about the implicit core of the cultural, invasions of the utopian represent another conception of culture. Invasions taking their impetus from the representative status of the arts, are about to represent a new conception of (or about) the culture and the cultural.

This point is also vividly exemplified by the genre of science fiction, which features, e.g., little green men, unidentified flying objects from other planets, Biker Mice, and the like. Science fiction tends to represent visions of the future but can hardly ever do it without designing new and/or alternative spatial settings as well. To do so means creating an alternative conception of the cultural *oikumene*, and therefore shows again the tight interdependence of invasion and the "cultural", an interdependence made visible by means of artistic representations. This last fact points to the inadequacies of the definitions of "invasion" which began this paper. For in its semiotic mechanisms and its significance in the economy of a society's culturo-historical facts, an event of armed force becomes a meaningful act of invasion only *after* its explanatory representation.

References

Dictionary of English Language and Culture (1992). London: Longman Group.
Jansson, Jan (1658). Magellanica, in: *Novus Atlas*. Amsterdam.
Milne, A.A. (1988/1926). *Winnie the Pooh*. New York: E.P. Dutton.
More, Thomas (1516). *Utopia*. Trans. Ralph Robinson. Birmingham, UK: 1869.
Ricœur, Paul (1986). *Lectures on Ideology and Utopia*. G.H. Taylor (ed.). New York: Columbia University Press.
Webster's Encyclopedic Unabridged Dictionary of the English Language (1996). New York: Gramercy Books.

Niilo Kauppi

Cultural arbitrariness and linguistic bias

> *Because the sign is arbitrary, it follows no law other than that of tradition, and because it is based on tradition, it is arbitrary.*
> (Saussure 1959: 74)

Ferdinand de Saussure's linguistics is one of the main, albeit neglected, sources of inspiration for Pierre Bourdieu's social theory. Combining Saussure's notion of linguistic arbitrariness with Marx's idea of the social and class nature of culture, Bourdieu revises traditional sociology of culture and science, as well as Marxist cultural analysis. Though some linguistic inventions, such as arbitrariness and levels of structure, provide Bourdieu with fundamental instruments for the examination of society and for a critique of all forms of social domination, his interpretations are, while fruitful, also debatable. By contrasting Saussure's idea of a linguistic arbitrary with Bourdieu's idea of a cultural arbitrary and by examining the relationships between Lévi-Strauss's and Bourdieu's structuralisms, I discuss here the problems related to the linguistic-theoretical bias in Bourdieu's theory.

1. Saussure's arbitrary sign

According to Saussure, the linguistic sign is arbitrary and relational. Signs such as "-ing" form monemes, as in "walking," which in turn form syntagms like "The dog is walking." The reasons why the moneme "walking" is formed from a specific letter combination (which includes "-ing") are arbitrary. There is no logical or conceptual reason that would explain the use of "-ing" rather than some other combination of letters. In Saussure's view, arbitrariness is the fundamental fact of the linguistic sign (Mauro 1972: ix).

Saussure acknowledged the social nature of signs, although his conception of society was quite rudimentary. For him it consisted merely of a collection of individuals and conventions (Saussure 1959: 68), and the social mass is not consulted when signified and signifier join together in *langue*. The role of the social mass is an unconscious one, tied to the reproduction of language. Language is imposed and inherited. The individual user of language is always faced with a synchronous state of affairs – history does not exist for him/her. Changes in language depend not on the will of individuals but on immanent linguistic laws. Because linguistic signs are arbitrary and rely on social conventions rather than logic, they change constantly. Because they are independent of individual wills, they change, but they cannot be changed. They are intangible, but not unalterable (Mauro 1972: 108 n. 1).

For Saussure, *langue* does not exist without use, although use meant for him the execution of pre-existing rules. Echoing Durkheim's famous social fact (*fait social*), he stated:

> ... for the realization of language, a community of speakers (*masse parlante*) is necessary. Contrary to all appearances, languages never exist apart from the social fact, for it is a semiological phenomenon. Its social nature is one of its inner characteristics. (Saussure 1959: 77)[1]

Saussure strived to create an immanent rather than empirical science of signs. The radicalization of the difference between *langue* and other sign systems enabled him to protect the immanent character of linguistic research, which concerns *langue*, not the social uses of language.

> ... further reflexion suggests that the arbitrary nature of the sign is really what protects language [*langue*] from any attempt to modify it. Even if people were more conscious of language than they are, they would still not know how to discuss it. The reason is simply that any subject in order to be discussed must have a reasonable basis. It is possible, for instance, to discuss whether the monogamous form of marriage is more reasonable than the polygamous form and to advance arguments to support either side. One could also argue about a system of symbols, for the symbol has a rational relationship with the thing signified (see p. 68); but language [*langue*] is a system of arbitrary signs and lacks the necessary basis, the solid ground for discussion. There is no reason to preferring *sœur* to *sister*, *Ochs* to *bœuf*. (Saussure 1959: 73)

If the example of *sœur/sister*, *bœuf/Ochs* is indisputable, the example of symbols raises some questions. The choice between *Ochs* and *bœuf* seems logically unmotivated, whereas the same cannot be said of symbols such as the balance as a symbol of justice, as Saussure argues. Symbols are not totally arbitrary for him.

> One characteristic of the symbol is that it is never wholly arbitrary ... The symbol of justice, a pair of scales, could not be replaced by just any other symbol, such as a chariot. (Saussure 1959: 68)

According to the Genevan linguist, justice, which is represented by a set of scales, could not be represented by a chariot.[2]

Human traditions and laws are based on natural relationships between things (Saussure 1959: 75). From Saussure's viewpoint, there is some logical ground to argue that the symbol "balance" should represent justice, in distinction to other human institutions. The same could be said of other social constructs, such as fashion or, more generally, cultural taste.

> Unlike language, other human institutions – customs, laws, etc. – are all based in varying degrees on the natural relations of things; all have of necessity adopted the means employed to the ends pursued. Even fashion in dress is not entirely arbitrary; we can deviate only slightly from the conditions dictated by the human body. Language [*langue*] is limited by nothing in the choice of means, for apparently nothing would prevent the associating of any idea whatsoever with just any sequence of sounds. (Saussure 1959: 75–76)

According to another well-known Saussurian principle, the value of certain objects or actions as parts of a syntagm acquire their meaning in relation to the system of which they are part. For Saussure, inspired by the example of Walras's economic analysis and eager to protect the synchronic aspects of linguistic analysis, value and meaning were totally systemic: value is the result of the system in which the elements take part.

> ... language [*langue*] is a system of pure values which are determined by *nothing except the momentary arrangement of its terms*. A value – so long as it is somehow rooted in things and their natural relations, as happens with economics (the value of a plot of land, for instance, is related to its productivity) – can to some extent be traced in time if we remember that it depends at each moment upon a system of coexisting values. Its links with things give it, perforce, a natural basis, and the judgments that we base on such values are therefore never completely arbitrary; their variability is limited. But we have just seen that natural data have no place in linguistics. (Saussure 1959: 80; my italics)

Value is tied to the arbitrary and relational nature of the system. "Arbitrary" and "differential" are correlative qualities of sign systems. Identity derives from these characteristics. Synchrony is, for Saussure, totally dissociated from diachrony. It is the synchronic solidarity of one element with the other elements that dictates its value.

> ... in language [*langue*] there are only differences *without positive terms*. Whether we take the signified or the signifier, language [*langue*] has neither ideas nor sounds that existed before the linguistic system, but only conceptual and phonic differences that have issued from the system. (Saussure 1959: 120)

In contrast to Bourdieu, for Saussure this principle was the result, not the starting point of scientific research.

2. Bourdieu's sociological interpretation of Saussure

> *Every established order tends to produce ... the naturalization of its own arbitrariness.*
> (Bourdieu 1977: 164)

The parallel between linguistic and social systems is the foundation of Bourdieu's sociological interpretation of Saussure's *Course in General Linguistics*. Social and linguistic sign systems are thought to be identical in terms of their properties and functioning. For Bourdieu, both are arbitrary and relational entities.

> Indeed, if the highway code (like the linguistic code) imposes its authority without much discussion, it's because with rare exceptions, it decides between relatively arbitrary possibilities (even if such possibilities – like driving on the right or on the left – may cease to be arbitrary once they have been made objective and incorporated into the habitus). In this case, the collective profits of calculability and predictability linked to codification win out, without any need for discussion, over the interests – nil or, at most, minor -associated with choosing either option on its merits. (Bourdieu 1990b: 83)

The arbitrary means the conventional (cf. Bourdieu and Passeron 1990: xx). For instance, the calculus "1 + 1 = 2" is not arbitrary for Bourdieu and Saussure. On the other hand, shaking hands when meeting somebody is arbitrary. Thus the arbitrary, not the nonarbitrary, is conventional, contrary to what some commentators have argued (e.g., LiPuma 1993: 28). For Saussure as for Bourdieu (1990a: 7), arbitrariness and differentiality are two correlative properties of social sign systems.[4]

The sociological interpretation of Saussure's linguistic arbitrary is the foundation of Bourdieu's notion of the *habitus*. For culture to be social, it has to be arbitrary; the cultural arbitrary is social (Bourdieu 1990a: 69), or a "pure *de facto* power" (Bourdieu and Passeron 1990: ix). A basic idea of Bourdieu's social theory is that the objective truth of the dominant culture is that it is arbitrary (Bourdieu and Passeron 1990: 23). This objective truth cannot be "deduced from any principle" (Bourdieu and Passeron 1990: xx).[5] To this formal argument Bourdieu adds social and historical determinants, and to linguistic structures he joins sociological variables, as Nicholas Garnham points out (1986: 425):

> Bourdieu, in the Durkheimian tradition, sees symbolic systems, as such, as arbitrary, undetermined taxonomies, structuring structures in the sense that they do not reflect or represent a reality, but themselves structure that reality. As in the Saussurean model of language, such systems are based upon "difference" or "distinction." However, he criticizes the idealism of the Durkheimian/Saussurean tradition by stressing that these systems, although arbitrary in themselves, are not arbitrary in their social function which is to represent, but in a misrecognized form, the structure of class relations. Indeed it is their very arbitrariness that allows them to do this, since if they were not arbitrary they could not be the object of class struggle. They represent class relations

and in the same movement disguise that representation because their logic is that of "distinction."

Bourdieu's point of view wavers constantly between social arbitrariness (the background) and social necessity or determinism (the foreground). Everything is arbitrary, thus everything is socially motivated. Social signs are arbitrary, thus they are historically and socially necessary.

Bourdieu has also borrowed from Saussure the idea of a linguistic structure in which value is formed negatively through the relationships that elements have with each other. The following passage, from *Distinction*, exemplifies the assumption that meaning arises through difference and forms in a system of relations. This assumption is transformed in Bourdieu's theory into a general heuristic principle:

> It is no accident that each group tends to recognize its specific values in that which makes its value, in Saussure's sense, that is, in the latest difference, which is also, very often, the latest conquest, in the structural and genetic deviation which specifically defines it. Whereas the working class, reduced to "essential" goods and virtues, demand cleanness and practicality, the middle class, relatively freer from necessity, look for a warm, "cosy", comfortable or neat interior, or a fashionable and original garment. (Bourdieu 1984: 247)

In contrast to Lévi-Strauss's interpretation, Bourdieu offers an alternative social-scientific interpretation of Saussure. By rejecting the division between internal and external linguistics (Bourdieu 1977: 170), he combines elements of Saussure's *langue* and *parole* (cf. Bourdieu 1993a: 32). Still, the dominant social-scientific interpretation of Saussure's ideas has been that presented by Lévi-Strauss (1958). Bourdieu has often criticized the objectivist bent of Saussure's linguistics. He interprets the preeminence of *langue* as an example of objectivism, which considers actualization as an appendix to an ahistorical essence, *langue* (Bourdieu 1977: 23; 1990a: 33). Obviously, contingency means social contingency, not logical or linguistic contingency. For Bourdieu the rules of language require *parole*, the practical use of language, which he gives preeminence over *langue*. This is the main difference between Bourdieu's and Lévi-Strauss's interpretations of Saussure (for an elaboration of these, cf. Kauppi 1998).

Although Bourdieu has severely criticized the theoretical and objectivist tendency of Saussure's work (cf. especially Bourdieu 1977: 23–25) and some of Saussure's social-scientific followers (notably Bourdieu's teacher, Lévi-Strauss), Bourdieu, in a way, comes closer to Saussure than to Lévi-Strauss in his conception of the role of the language user. On the other hand, by emphasizing the arbitrary nature of signs, Bourdieu highlights the domination conveyed by all signs.

Bourdieu's interpretation of Saussure differs in at least four respects from that of Lévi-Strauss. For Bourdieu, the social is the semiological in the sense that all social systems (or fields) are differential entities in which the value of one element is formed through the relational network in which it is embedded. The concept of field enables the scholar to phenomenologically bracket part of reality and proceed to an immanent analysis of an area of social activity. In some sense, Husserl and Saussure require one another. Not surprisingly, Bourdieu's main work is entitled *Distinction*. Distinction is the quasi-transcendental principle that governs social life, the merciless and endless struggle for social value. Distinction comes close, in its theoretical function, to other terms in vogue in France in the 1960s: *différance*, distribution, and so on. The social fate of an object or activity that carries distinction is to lose both value and distinction. In a sense, value is a syntactic property. The value of an object or activity depends on its frequency. The second difference between Bourdieu's and Lévi-Strauss's interpretations of Saussure is that for Bourdieu all social systems are arbitrary. They do not follow any universal principle such as logical reason or biological necessity (Bourdieu and Passeron 1990: 10). The third difference has to do with conceptions of power and meaning. Bourdieu analyses power in society through the idea of the cultural arbitrary. Power creates meaning and distinction. The imposition of a cultural arbitrary, a kind of symbolic violence, is arbitrary both in terms of content (for instance, "red" signifies "stop" and "green" signifies "go") and in terms of imposition (people will consider "red" to signify "stop" as legitimate as any other alternative). Bourdieu's analysis is reminiscent of Durkheim's analysis of classifications: power struggles mostly involve battles over classifications and their contents. Bourdieu does not separate synchrony and diachrony from one another as Lévi-Strauss does. Fields develop historically. Unfortunately for Bourdieu's social theory, dynamic models do not accommodate well to Saussure's synchronic principles.

3. Problems with Bourdieu's interpretation

The basic problem with Bourdieu's use of linguistic ideas is his view that Saussure meant by "arbitrary" the nonexistence of "natural" or logical reasons in the articulation of acoustic images as semantic substances. This idea was further developed in phonological research by scholars like Trubetskoy (1964), and Lévi-Strauss (1958) inflated this principle to cover all signs and communication. But are other sign systems totally arbitrary, consisting only of negative differences?

A Saussurian reading of Bourdieu's cultural and social arbitrary raises the following question: is it legitimate to consider social systems as having qualities similar to *langue*? (cf. Fougeyrollas 1983: 54.) For Saussure, this kind of generalization would have been illegitimate, as only *langue* fulfilled the necessary requirements of an immanent and differential system. Social conventions, excluding *langue*, were not arbitrary for Saussure. A *langue* is not the same kind of social product as other symbols in a specific society. For if linguistic signs are part of a limited linguistic inventory (the alphabet, for instance), this does not mean that social signs belong to a limited inventory. A *langue* or a phonological system, for instance, is a closed and relatively stable system of signs. The same cannot be said of the social world and its signs. Social signs are unlimited in number – new ones are constantly invented and old ones pass away. As far as one knows, there is no social alphabet, in the sense of the building blocks of social life. Consequently, there are no pertinent features, because these require knowledge of a totality. The limits of social life are not as clear as those of an alphabet. Despite these objections, both Bourdieu and Lévi-Strauss assume the existence of a system consisting of a limited inventory of elements.

A further difficulty is related to the combination of signifier and signified. When signifier and signified are combined they form in Saussure's view a positive entity, a *fait positif* (Saussure 1959: 121). Distinction replaces difference. But in that case we are not talking about *langue*, but about *langage*, or language (cf. Saussure 1959: 121). The catch is, from a Saussurian point of view, that *langage* is not a closed, theoretical entity like *langue*. Ideas developed in the context of an analysis of *langue*, such as the notion of differences without positive terms, cannot be transferred as such into the context of *langage*. For instance, there is no immanent logic of the system of automobiles, because the determining factor of the system's elements is not the relations between signs as such but their social use by individuals. A Saussurian would say there might be negative differences on the two levels, that is, the signifiers and the signifieds, taken separately. The brand Toyota CX might obtain its "meaning" in relation to other Toyota models (SX, L, Camry, etc.) and other brand names (Mazda CX, for instance). Likewise, at the level of signifieds, a Mercedes Benz can be differentiated from a Volvo or a Lexus. But automobiles as signs – that is, as combining these two levels and as embedded in multiple social relationships – do not necessarily constitute a system in the Saussurian sense of the term, because the system is highly motivated, not unmotivated, and it is not immanent. In other words, a sign's value in this system is not determined solely by the system, but also, say, by technological factors (cf. Cole and Griffin 1980: 354–355). If the elements do not constitute a system in the Saussurian sense, they cannot form part of an arbitrary and differential structure. Nor would value be a purely relational property.

Given the characteristics of social systems, it might be that the degree of arbitrariness of the signs to be examined depends more on the cultural proximity of the subject (the researcher) to the object of research or, more generally, on the synchronic and/or diachronic distance between observer and observed, than on the internal characteristics of social systems as *langue*. For instance, a bodiless observer such as a computer might not be able to understand how the bodily basis of human activities could possibly influence the degree of motivation of human sign systems. But a human observer would understand this. Another example: for an observer living in the twentieth century the historical conditions of the appearance of certain social institutions, such as the highway code, might have faded away. But this does not mean that these historical conditions never existed or that they are arbitrary. It could be, that, as time goes by, a loss of understanding of historical conditions (that is, of motivation) takes place. Increasing opacity increases the likelihood of considering social signs as arbitrary, and, consequently, "the appearance of arbitrariness is therefore an effect of history" (Hodge and Kress 1993: 206). Signs are both necessary from the point of view of the individuals using them and relatively arbitrary from the point of view of an outside observer, because for the latter they could equally well be different. For an outside observer familiar with the culture s/he studies, sign systems are both arbitrary and motivated (Kauppi 1995: 387–395) instead of arbitrary but unmotivated.

4. *Conclusions*

For a critical sociology committed to unmasking all forms of social domination, the idea of arbitrary signs is extremely useful, because it anchors the theoretical system and its neologisms on a stable and indisputable basis. However, qualifying a norm as arbitrary does not clarify human motivation, emotional and ethical investment, and the reasons for certain actions. The strength and weakness of Bourdieu's idea of a cultural arbitrary lie in its populism: because of its arbitrary nature in the technical sense of the term, dominant culture does not have to be investigated and it can be *a priori* judged as arbitrary in the ordinary sense of the term. This interpretation helps to hide causal relationships behind a screen of abstract terminology and pseudo-explanations. What is needed is a discussion of the social and psychological factors that influence social action and behavior.

Notes

1. Unfortunately, the dominant interpretation of Saussure is that of Lévi-Strauss, which emphasizes the langue aspect of Saussure's work and thus leads to a static structuralism. Bourdieu subscribes to linguist Emile Benveniste's critique of Saussure's conception of the arbitrary. For Benveniste, the relationship between signifier and signified is necessary, not arbitrary. What is arbitrary is the relation of the sign to reality (Benveniste 1971: 43–48).
2. This example is, however, highly questionable. Obviously, the meaning of justice would be different if it were represented by a chariot (for instance, it would then symbolize the justice of a god or a king) rather than by scales. Perhaps both symbols (chariot and scales) are both logically arbitrary and socially necessary. The symbol of the scales might be embedded in an ideal of equality rather than one of the

benevolence of the ruler. But this embeddedness is a highly arbitrary factor, in the sense given the term by Saussure and Bourdieu.
3. For Saussure, signs varied in degrees of arbitrariness. Indexical signs (for example, smoke as the sign of fire) are less arbitrary than verbal languages. Symbols are less arbitrary than icons or indices, because in them there is "the rudiment of a natural bond between the signifier and the signified" (Saussure 1959: 68). 5. Except the principle presented by Bourdieu and Passeron, of course – which is, that the social is not logical. If the social is the area of arbitrariness and not of logic, then how can it possibly form the object of a scientific study? It would seem that, from the premises of Bourdieu's and Passeron's research strategy, it follows that the social world could not be scientifically studied at all.
4. Except the one presented by Bourdieu and Passeron of course – i.e., that the social is not logical. If the social is the area of arbitrariness and not of the logical, how can it possibly be the object of a scientific study? It would seem that from the premises of Bourdieu's and Passeron's research strategy it follows that the social world cannot be scientifically studied at all.

References

Benveniste, Emile (1971). *Problems in General Linguistics*. Trans. Mary Elisabeth Meek. Coral Gables, FL: University of Miami Press,
Bourdieu, Pierre (1977). *Outline of a Theory of Practice*. Trans. Richard Nice. Cambridge, UK: Cambridge University Press: Cambridge.
– (1984). *Distinction*. Trans. Richard Nice. *A Social Critique of the Judgment of Taste*. Cambridge, MA: Harvard University Press.
– (1990a). The Logic of Practice. Trans. Richard Nice. Stanford, CA: Stanford University Press.
– (1990b). *In Other Words: Essays toward a Reflexive Sociology*. Trans. Matthew Adamson. Cambridge, UK: Polity Press.
– (1993). The Field of Cultural Production. Randall Johnson (ed. and introduction). New York: Columbia University Press.
Bourdieu, Pierre and Passeron, Jean-Claude (1990). *Reproduction in Education, Society and Culture*. Trans. Richard Nice. Beverly Hills, CA.: Sage.
Calhoun, Craig et al. (eds.) (1993). *Bourdieu: Critical Perspectives*. Chicago, IL: University of Chicago Press.
Cole, Michael and Griffin, Peg (1980). Cultural amplifiers reconsidered. 343–364. In: Olson (ed.).
Fougeyrollas, Pierre (1983). *L'obscurantisme contemporain: Lacan, Lévi-Strauss, Althusser*. Paris: SPAG-Papyrus.
Garnham, Nicholas (1986). Extended review: Bourdieu's *Distinction*. *The Sociological Review* 34(2): 423–433.
Hodge, Robert and Kress, Gunther (1993). *Language as Ideology*. London and New York: Routledge.
Kauppi, Niilo (1995). From indexicality to multiple sign processes: Anthropological knowledge reconsidered. *Semiotica* 104(3/ 4): 387–395.
– (1998). Merkin arbitraarisuus ja motivoituneisuus yhteiskuntatieteissä [The arbitrariness and motivation of signs in the social sciences]. *Synteesi* 1: 80–85.
Lévi-Strauss, Claude (1958). *Anthropologie structurale*. Paris: Plon.

LiPuma, Edward (1993). Culture and the Concept of Culture in *A Theory of Practice*. 14–34. In: Calhoun et al.
Mauro, Tullio di (1972). Introduction. I-xviii. In: Saussure (1959).
Olson, David R. (ed.) (1980). *The Social Foundation of Language and Thought: Essays in Honor of Jerome S. Bruner*. New York and London: Norton.
Saussure, Ferdinand de (1959). *Course in General Linguistics*. Trans. Wade Baskin. New York: Philosophical Library.
– (1972/1916). *Cours de linguistique générale*. Paris: Payot.
Trubetskoy, N. S. (1964). Principes de phonologie. Trans. J. Cantineau. Paris: Klincksieck (1939).

Maarja Pärl Lõhmus

Approaches to media semiotics: Journalism in social context

Journalism in society – society in journalism

The need to communicate numbers among such other basic human needs as nutrition, shelter, and warmth. Journalism came into being when the fundamental need to communicate was not only satisfied but also adapted to different social purposes. (Today we buy a newspaper to take part in communication, although we get something more in the bargain.) The multifarious utilization of man's communicational needs and the creation of new ones constitutes the history of journalism. The principal means and purveyor of the need to communicate is the journalistic text.

The journalistic text is the vehicle by which various interest groups express themselves and influence the public. The media constitute a public field of struggle for journalistic texts in two senses: firstly, as the public sphere, where texts appear, circulate, and acquire meanings through semiosis and discourse. Secondly, as the space within a text, the struggle at the level of its inner structures. The concept of *text* has a central position. Based on language and reflecting the coexistence of many codes, the text, while expressing a semiosphere, simultaneously shapes it.

The struggle for influence over society through journalism continues to make itself felt. The most serious struggle in society concerns the definition and interpretation of social processes. Different interest groups try to insert their ideas into the text, either directly or indirectly. Thus, journalism is essentially the field of mediating ideas and the means of establishing and consolidating ideologies:

Dominator(s) ------ Dominating ------ The dominated
                              ideology(ies)

The situation is complicated by the large number of interest groups and intersections of their various competing directions. The empirical view of communication theory is that the "truth" of the first source and its interpretation have a decisive meaning. Later interpretations cannot do away with the original interpretation, but have only a kind of sharpening effect on it. Thus, the battle ensues for quick interpretations of events and phenomena. The basic issue is, whose story will be published first and in what way.

Journalism is one of the few practices whose ideas and myths affect different public fields. In terms of Bourdieu's conceptual system, journalism is the arena of all struggle for political and symbolic power, for the determination of exchange values. Symbolic power is a covert and transformed (i.e., misrecognized), transfigured and legitimated version of other forms of power. Contemporary myths that are spread by the press form a part of every established ideology.

Interest groups whose texts do not proceed from the dominant or established ideology must use more complicated structures to express their ideas. The more closed the situation in the social battlefield and the more difficult the access to publicity, the more complicated is the inner structure of the text and the more intensive are the text's inherent problems.

Suppose that we are seeking objectivity, then on the first level we meet semantic problems, on the second level shared rules concerning particular texts. On the third level, however, we observe general ethical rules (cf. Habermas). Journalistic texts do not generally aim for objectivity, since the application of rational principles in them is inconsistent.

Each text forms a "cloud of meanings" which in turn is a part of semiosis (cf. Biber 1988). The semiosis includes all possible meanings of the language, as well as shades of meanings in different discourses and different contexts of the linguistic environment.

The state of a society and the semiotic use of the language spoken in it are interconnected. The more closed the situation in social (public) battlefields, the richer the semiosis; it becomes more active, bringing inner potentialities into play. The density of semiosis generates more meanings. The struggle in a closed society goes on in terms of a hyper-dense semiosis. With the opening of society, the semiosis expands and becomes thinner.

The journalistic text, *as an active text*, is a social phenomenon located in the realm of conscious, intentional acts. At the same time, something in the text may remain unconscious or unintentional (and some, Lévi-Strauss and Jung among them, have argued that the unconscious forms a deeper structure that affects all people in the same way). Still, the journalistic text expresses primarily the *conscious* activities of interested groups, though journalists do not always recognize in what sphere of domination they are working. It is characteristic of the text that, apart from what is intentionally expressed in it (objectivity, unambiguity), something additional is always "left over" (subjectivity, ambiguity). The struggle in the text is obvious even if it is not expressed in it.

Consider the model shown in Figure 1. I use the notion of "model" in a very general sense, as an analogue of the cognized object which replaces the object in the cognition process. The questions are these: Who participates in the struggle for information and interpretation, and what are the relations between the participants? In what kind of battles (subjective, realistic, symbolic) do journalistic texts participate? I also want to explain with the help of the model these functions that cause structural differences in and between media, in both closed and open societies. The model does not conceive of media as independent phenomena but as part of the struggle for ideas and for domination. (Even the most independent publications present texts that express evaluative manners of thought.)

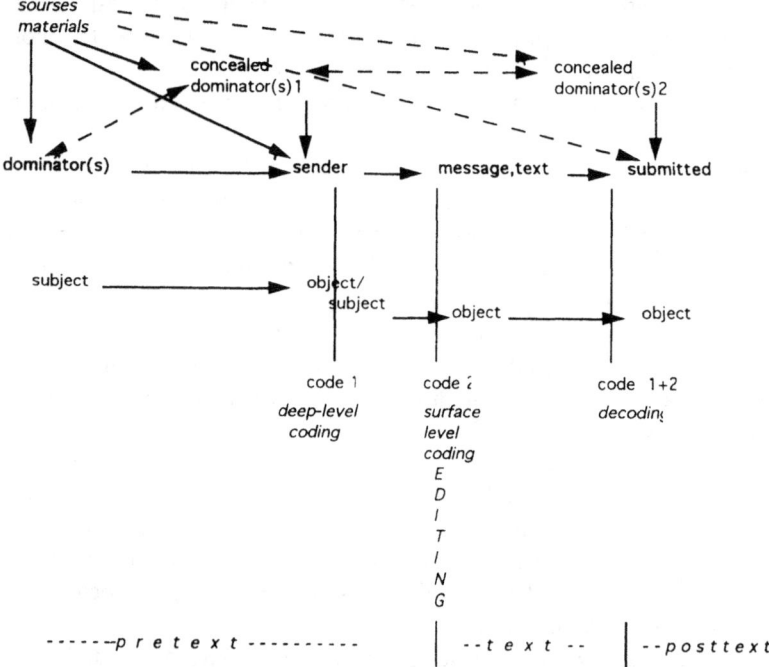

Figure 1. Model of the field of struggle in media.

The combatants in these symbolic battles are as follows:

(1) *Dominators* (overt and hidden) wish to make sure that their ideas will reach the public through the journalistic text.

(2) *Concealed dominator(s) 1*, represent (independent) attitudes towards other dominators.

(3) *Sources and materials* exist independently of the participants on the battlefield and the battlefields themselves, but the main struggle involves the issue

of how to code them. This coding takes place in the phase of the pre-text (to be discussed below).

(4) The *sender* codes the material and sources in some way (independently or under duress) using the journalistic message. In this complex semiotic situation, the central role is played by the author, who him/herself becomes a separate sign (and code) in the field of texts. (Senders can be dominators, concealed dominators, authors, interpreters-editors). Depending on the society, environment, publication, and sender-author, the coding may take place only once (code 1), being the deep-level coding. Basic coding in the media, however, can also be completed by additional codings (code 2), which in essence are surface-level codings.

(5) The *message*, or *text*, is a result of the struggle and also an instrument of that struggle (text as institution; text as instrument). It contains some manner of thought which has been coded in a specific way. The journalistic text can be very effective in advocating different social interests. It is both the means of influence and the object of the struggle for influence. Texts on the battlefield require symbolic meaning as the representatives of corresponding discourses. The appearance of one or another text assures that one or the other discourse has sprung forth in society. (In a closed society, such an appearance has been called "the front line" and journalists, the senders of the texts, the "soldiers of the ideological front".)

(6) The *submitted* are the recipients who turn to journalism in need of communication and who are submitted to the power of journalistic texts. In the process of decoding the texts, they often cannot discern the different structures hidden in the code.

(7) The *concealed dominator 2* represents other (independent) attitudes towards the dominators, material, and topic. It is a journalistic message that by its very existence influences those who are submitted.

A text on the symbolic battlefield moves through three phases: *pre-text*, *text* (itself), and *post-text*. The struggle about and for the journalistic text takes mainly place in the first phase, in the pretext (see Tarasti (forthcoming), on the "pre-sign").

Self-domination takes place in media. Media may also want to change themselves into an existential judge. The media as a group may wish to change the participating subjects in the battles into objects, trying itself to become irreplaceable and the only link between the dominator and the submitted. The media aspire towards ever greater power in order to make the dominators depend on them.

Maarja Pärl Lõhmus

Struggle in the text

Every text contains a tension that results from its essence and becomes apparent at different levels: (1) Grammatical tensions are chosen parts of the sentence and the connections between them. (2) Semantic tensions are components of the content of the text and the overall interconnectedness of those components. (3) Semiotic tensions are the relations between the text and the semiosis around it, between codes and discoursive whole.

Thus the text has its inherent parameters, the alteration of which changes the text itself. This kind of change can be used in the struggle over the text. Struggles within the text mainly concern its inherent meanings and signs – i.e., the codes.

The potential energy of the text to influence is essential. All the tensions in the text form this potentiality of the text if all semantic possibilities are present in the text. The potentiality of the text is what makes it useful in symbolic struggles.

There is no tension in an unambiguous text. With the occurrence of another idea tensions arise, which concern the different interpretations of the text. Thus the struggle for different semantic interpretations of the text and the utilization of the text as a whole breaks out. This struggle is two-sided: The *external problem* of the struggle concerns, for example, which one of two of the three possible meanings would be accepted. The *internal problem* of the struggle hinges on the fact that all the meanings of the text cannot be unambiguous and expressed in one way only. The difference in meanings creates the inner tension of the text, and the characteristic feature of the text is its meaningfulness.

The struggle in texts is connected to the problem of coding and decoding: what is the "real text"? what language-system (codes) are used in the text, and what is the thought-system behind it? The more complicated the *deep-level (text) code* of the sender (code 1), the greater the inner tension of the text. The more the text has *surface-level codes* (code 2), the greater its inner tensions, the more divergent are its inner directions. The potentialities of the text may even contradict one another (thus the influence of a strongly edited and censored text is small).

Editing and censoring of the text means forcing it to submit to new codes. In this way, the inner power of the text is weakened. In the tension between code 1 (deep-level coding) and code 2 (surface-level coding), the inner conflict in the structure of the text may come into being, appearing now as a weakening of the text's potentiality. The conflicts and inner tensions between different codings are the greater the more differences there are between codes 1 and 2. If the sender (code 1) and the editor (code 2) happen to be the same person, inner (role) conflicts may arise in him/her, since he/she, as one person, is required to code dualistically (on cognitive dissonance, see Festinger 1957)

The text that undergoes repeated codings cannot be complete. Additional coding changes the text. Surface-level codes prevent the decoding of the deep-level code, reduce the influence of the deep-level coding and make it impossible to receive the text in its completeness. The following tendency can be noticed the more we have contradictory surface-level codes, the greater is the destruction of the deep-level code structure (code 2). Each coding (code 1, code 2, etc.) separately may be carried out on the basis of orderly rules. Yet their combined influence may produce an absolutely disorderly code or a code of unrecognizable regularity.

Every code should have its own key for decoding (Eco 1977; Hall 1980). Many codes together, however, do not present the necessary code-structure for decoding.

The recipient decodes with codes 1+2, which is the sum of different codes, but this doesn't lead to the necessary code structure for decoding. The recipient finds it difficult to differentiate and decode the sum of the codes.

One of the most important assumptions of censorship is that it can program the text with different codes. But for decoding there is only one code in which the sum of components does not correspond to the complexity of the component codes.

The journalistic text as the centre of struggles in society

Today, a very interesting problem concerns the kind of texts that societies prefer and produce. How should one characterize a society in which texts circulate, what kind of structures (as codes) emerge between (types of) texts and society.

What is the content of the struggle taking place in media? The reasons for inner struggles between dominators and dominated often center on interpretations of existential problems – "world-view", "perception of time", "experiences", "events". Other contested issues concern what exists in this world, how phenomena are related to each other, and what are the hierarchies of value (cf. Gerbner 1969).

In a closed society, the text rarely becomes a public battlefield. Instead, the struggle takes place in the text's structure, between signs-codes, on more of a "hidden" level.

In sum, the text is an "external" struggle between dominators for interpretation of signs and codes that are "internal" to the text itself. The struggles may be real and/or symbolic. Editing in journalism denotes (directly or indirectly, consciously or unconsciously) a situation where the thoughts and sources used are previously censored and controlled, and from which "unsuitable" material has been removed. Manipulation and censorship (concealed or open) take place in all phases of editing: in choice of topics, in interpretation, in developing relations in a text and in shaping context, and in performing the text.

Useful for decoding is the ability to recognize the most important parts in the whole of the text – the real "message" and its content – and the skill to make generalizations regarding the whole text on the basis of a very small part of it. In practice this means the communication, coding, and decoding of "imaginations" in a text between "concealed dominator" and receiver (whom the text dominates). Because it is very complicated to determine these imaginations, the dominators establish control over texts that demand the ascertaining of imaginations and possible associations. Censorship of the established discourse take place as the structural analysis of texts and imaginations (concerning texts); the imagination of imaginations is controlled.

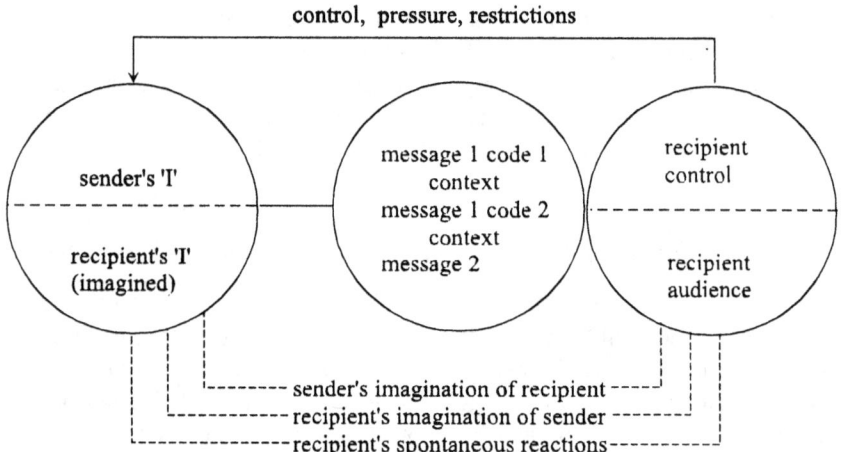

Figure 2. Background of media process.[2]

From the point of view of editing, the imaginary media process is contradictory, containing ambiguity in regard to the established ideological discourse and considering the recipient who have adopted a defensive position towards journalism.[1]

In a closed society the battlefield of texts may give an impression of "openness" to the observer-recipient. By studying simultaneously texts of different discourses, and by establishing their mutual relations, it is possible to create new, more complicated "codes" and, consequently, a certain "openness", which might not obtain in separate textual types as such, but which are opened by the recipient.

Notes

1. In a media process between sender and recipient, there is an imagined, reciprocal "guess-work" absorbed into the text, at the same time as its critical analysis. In "editing", the (imagined) recipient is an ambivalent phenomenon. As for the "editor", he is both an ordinary recipient (*alter ego*) and a controller placed higher up in the hierarchy, who guarantees journalistic discourse and is responsible for sustaining the established, dominant ideology.
2. My model of media process combines Jacobson's, Lotman's, and Maletzke's communication-models.

References

Biber, Douglas (1988). *Variation Across Speech and Writing.* Cambridge, UK: Cambridge Univ. Press.
Bourdieu, Pierre (1977). *A Theory of Practice.* Cambridge, UK: Cambridge University Press.
– (1991). *Language and Symbolic Power.* Cambridge, UK: Polity Press.
Eco, Umberto (1977). *A Theory of Semiotics.* Thetford, Norfolk: Love & Brydone.
Festinger, Leon (1957). *A theory of cognitive dissonance. Dissonance.* Evanston, IL: Row, Peterson.
Gerbner G. (1969). Towards "cultural indicators": The analysis of mass mediated public message systems. In: *The Analysis of Communication Content.* New York: Wiley.
Hall, S. (1980). Encoding/decoding. In: *Culture, Media, Language.* Hall, Hobson, Lowes, Willis (eds.). London: Hutchinson.
Jakobson, Roman and Halle, M. (1980/1956). *Fundamentals of Language.* The Hague: Mouton.
Lotman, Juri (1984). Tekst v tekste [Text in Text]. *Trudy po znakovym sistemam* 18: 3–18.Tartu.
– (1992). *Kultura i vzryv* [Culture and Explosion]. Moskva: Progress.
Tarasti, Eero (forthcoming in 1999). *The Enchanted Signs.* Bloomington, IN: Indiana University Press.
Vygotski, Lev (1979/1934). *Thought and Language.* Cambridge, UK: Cambridge University Press.

Viktor Shibanov

Ethnofuturism in Udmurtia

Udmurtia is an average dependency of Russia and a center of the armament industry. It lies just to the west of the Ural Mountains, and its capital city is Izhevsk. Though it has a population of over 1.6 million people, less than a third of them are Udmurts. During the Soviet period a lot of factories, especially those producing armaments and metals, were concentrated in Udmurtia, and crowds of skilled Russian personnel were transferred there to work. The biggest employer in the capitol city is the Kalasnikov machine gun factory, called Izhmash, which manufactures those rifles and submachine guns often favored by the world's guerrillas. Because most people who live in Udmurtia are Russians, the Udmurtian culture used to and still does represent itself mostly as a "shadow" of the Russian one.

In this article I describe one fast-growing cultural phenomenon in today's Udmurtian literature. Estonian scholars and Finnish professor Kari Sallamaa call it *ethnofuturism*. A group-essay which appeared in the journal *Synteesi* has this to say about the phenomenon: "The idea of ethnofuturism is to combine two different sides of culture. Some particular culture is partly its people's ancient, stratified, independent tradition; at the same time it reveals features of a newer, modern world-class culture. Within this connection between these two elements hides naturally the vitality of culture. Ethnofuturism asks the question, Does a smaller population group have any future in culture?" (Pärl-Löhmus et al. 1994). Thus, ethnofuturism is characterized by oppositions such as past / future, village / city, ancient culture / modernism (postmodernism), and the like.

Literary ethnofuturism of present-day Udmurtian appears in works such as Sergei Matveev's novel, *The Fool* (1995), and in Lidija Nankina's short story, "Au-au! or Curved Lines in Heaven" (1993). It is also present in the poetry of Erik Batujev, Rafit Minekuzin, Mihail Fedotov, and Pjotr Zaharov, and in the prose of Oleg Tsetkarjov, Nikolaj Samsonov, and Ar-Sergi. For these writers, the future of culture, or ethnofuturism, means most of all returning to their national past. Without doing so, it would be impossible for them to reform their lost identity.

In the 1920s, Udmurtian culture and literature gathered momentum and national tendencies arose. Then came Stalinism (1930–1950) and post-Stalinism (1950–1970), which rendered the situation of Udmurtian writers difficult and did away with all forms of national literature. By 1937 the national writers of Udmurtia had been captured and most of them executed. This meant victory for so-called socialist realism. At this point, any nationalist tendencies either had to be masked or channel themselves into the forms of socialist realism. At that time some prevalent symbols in literary texts were the Communist Party, its employers and ideological goals, sunrises and flourishing gardens (cf. Schibanov 1996). Only Flor Vasiljev (1934–1978) in his poetry and Gennadij Krasilnikov (1928–1975) in his prose elevated the style and use of symbols to a new level.

Ethnofuturism is the strategy and set of shared goals that guides Udmurtian writers of today to create their own unique works. Every new tendency or "movement", including ethnofuturism, lies dormant within its predecessor; it therefore breaks its ties to tradition from the inside. It separates itself from the one that gave birth to it and begins to live an independent life of its own. After *perestroika*, ethnofuturism in literature arose in Udmurtia. You will find affinities with postmodernist ideas in some of its distinguishing features: (1) Ethnofuturists see today's world as absurd and chaotic, and the former, socialist world as a kind of preposterousness. (2) Both the subject and his/her ways of thinking are considered fractious and "de-centred". (3) Traditional ancient myths are borrowed, fragmented, and mixed with other types of discourse. In what follows I consider each of these features.

Today's world as preposterousness and chaos

According to Lévi-Strauss, the world of myth consists of nature (or chaos) and culture (or universe). To say that socialist realism was analogous to ancient myths meant that, within its own world, socialist realism had its own senseless chaos and organised universe. After *perestroika*, the situation was reversed: the former chaos became universe, and the former universe became chaos (see Leiderman and Lipovetskij 1991). People who were once classified as positive – such as civil servants, militia, communists, doctors, etc. – are now considered negative. And vice versa: those who were earlier understood as undesirables – schizophrenics, prostitutes, vagrants, alcoholics, etc. – have now become positive figures.

In new Udmurtian literature the action takes place in a world that could be defined as chaotic. Preposterousness reigns in both the city and the countryside. The philosophy of preposterousness was well represented in Albert Camus's 1942 work, *Le mythe de Sisyphe: Essai sur l'absurde*. The hero, Sisyphus, pushes a gigantic piece of rock up a mountainside, then the rock rolls back down. Sisyphus pushes it up again, and once again it comes down. This process repeats itself endlessly, demonstrating Sisyphus's faith. According to Camus, this story has a particularly important meaning in today's absurd world, in which every human being has the same destiny as Sisyphus. One finds variants of this story constantly repeated in Udmurtian ethnofuturist literature. Among many other texts, this situation is described in Pjotr Zaharov's poem, "Metamorphoses", and in Nikolai Samsonov's short story, "Destiny".

In Zaharov's "Metamorphoses", the hero takes a nail and hammers it into the wall of his sauna. Then he hangs his ladle on it. He drives a second nail into the wall and hangs his sponge on it. He takes a third nail, a fourth, a fifth, sixth, and so on. All of a sudden his neighbour shows up. The curious neighbour observes the other man's actions, then goes home and starts to hammer nails in the wall of his own sauna, upon which he hangs his ladle, sponge, etc. Viewing our lives as both funny and ridiculous, Zaharov repeats in his poem Camus's idea of the absurd Sisyphus.

Nikolaj Samsonov's short story, "Destiny", tells about a fellow named Oberjan who in the 1930s, in order to save his own life, served as an informer for the NKVD (KGB) by giving that agency information on persons considered "dangerous". Working in a small village all his life, Oberjan has performed his duties well, including his job as a KGB informer. When the story begins Oberjan is already 80 years old, and he is ready to die. He tries to commit suicide but fails: death won't take him to the other side because Oberjan has committed so many sins. Oberjan even builds himself a coffin, but when he lies down in it he realizes that the coffin is too small for him. After couple of days he makes another coffin that is bigger and longer than the first one. But again, it does not fit him. He makes a third coffin and a fourth one, a fifth, a sixth, and so on (again the Sisyphus motif!). But all in vain: each new coffin is too short for his body. The problem is that, in order for Oberjan to die, he must first make up for his sins by seeking absolution from those victims on whom he has informed. A central figure in the story is one special birch tree, which hums and rustles even though no wind is blowing. In the course of the story, the Devil, the "evil one" from mythology, keeps showing himself, peering from behind the branches of the birch.

In Oleg Tsetkarjov's stories "The Blue Dove" and "The Noose", as in his new novel, the action takes place in a city of today, located at the center of the armament industry. Abiding chaos shows up in the miserable life of youths who live in the dormitories: the suicides, fears, and threats that armament factories spark among the common folk – these are the main themes in Tsetkarjov's stories. An interesting example of the ethnofuturist view of the fragmented subject (discussed below) is Tsetkarjov's comparison of men with knitting. One hero of the short stories says, "after work I walk down the road and see that all around there is knitted work, seams, knitted work, no humans!"

Fragmented subject and fragmented thought

The consciousness of today's human being is like a shattered mirror. One cannot reconnect those splinters and fragments, and each shard reflects images of different worlds. Similarly, a piece of art is structured by many parallel elements. These can come from every possible level of reality or textuality, from different literary styles and traditions, from different forms of discourse (cf. Smirnov 1994).

The loneliness of man is the starting point of Sergej Matveev's poetry. This theme most shockingly appears in the poem, "On a birthday". Around a table sit three persons who are looking back on their lives. Who are they? A modernist might identify the first person as the ego, the "I", and the other person as his "shadow" (a kind of *Doppelgänger*). The third might be "an empty seat", possibly another "I". In "On a birthday" the hero of the poem talks about himself in all of these forms.

The preposterousness of today's life also shows up in Matveev's prose works. It is seen, for example, in the disparate segments of his novel, *The Fool*. The book consists of three parts. The first part is highly erotic, featuring seven girls who manage the hero's life for him (Valentina, Galina, Vera, Tatjana, Oksana, Natalja, and Anna). Delirium and babble form the other two parts. Yet despite the powerful contrast between the parts of the book, it is dominated by the consistency of postmodern logic.

Alla Kuznetsova is another poet whose work exemplifies the "multiple" nature of today's subject. Here is one of her most well-known poems, called "I'm like a horse":

> I'm like a horse.
> There's a heavy load on my back -
> I'm a fly who gets stuck in a spider's web
> I don't know how to get clear of the strong web.
> Here I am, I suppose, a spider.
> I bite into myself and I am eating myself away.

Also of note is the work of Lidija Nankina, especially her story called "Au-au! or Curved Lines in Heaven". The main character is a 33 year-old prostitute named Elena, an unmarried writer who lives in her own apartment. The story takes place at the beginning of 1990s and mostly in Udmurtia in a city of today. But the *chronotope* of the story also includes Afghanistan, where a war is going on and where Elena's husband was killed; a beach by the southern sea, where the American singer Madonna performs; an imaginary erotic restaurant in which a three-eyed creature is serving customers as a waiter; etc. (on the "chronotope", or time-space segment, see Bahtin 1986: 121–123, 284–290). The main thread of the story begins when Elena meets a young female cabdriver who seems very familiar to her. The girl, whose name is Ljalja, knows everything about Elena's secret night life and about her writing. "Is this girl an assistant of the KGB?" Elena wonders. Her suspicion grows stronger when Ljalja breaks into Elena's apartment and takes a shower, acting as though it were her own home. Suddenly Elena senses that this strange girl is in fact her own daughter, who has come back from the dead. Elena had gotten an abortion after her husband had died in Afghanistan, so Ljalja did not have the chance to be born into the real world. But the ghost of Elena's unborn child goes on living. Interestingly, time, for Ljalja (the ghost), moves backwards, going from future to past (there are from 3 to 4 different cycles of time moving in parallel in the story). So instead of growing, Ljalja gets younger all the time. At first she transforms into a small child, and finally she disappears (!), closing one of the several time-cycles in the story.

From the above examples, it is clear that the works of today's young Udmurtian writers display "preposterousness" and "multi-stylistic discourse" (in Russian science: *polistilistika*). To close, let us consider briefly the ethnofuturists' construction of myth in their writings.

Mythological motives

The preposterous and absurd world has long been a subject of European literature. But in the ethnofuturism of Udmurtia, "indigenous" Udmurtian mythological subjects and themes are also beginning to grow and develop. Even though the consciousness and thought processes of today's subject might be fragmented, and even though today's world can be construed as chaos, we can draw positive strength from the ancient myths. (That is why we must not yet think about Udmurtian "postmodernism", but rather ethnofuturism). Mythological symbols abound in new Udmurtian literature. As examples, one can mention Ar Serg's black raven (in the story, "Kristja and the raven"); Oleg Tsetkarjov's tree of the world (in the short story, "The noose"); Lidija Nankina's child of the world, which instead of growing keeps on getting younger (as mentioned above, in the story "Au-au! or Curved Lines in Heaven"); Mihail Fedotov's devils and water trolls (in a collection entitled *Pain*), and so on.

Though space prevents me from analyzing those symbols in detail, scholars such as Jurij Lotman (1994), Aleksej Losev, and Igor Smirnov (1994) agree that many of today's ways of thinking are based on ancient myths. The philosophy of life based on Udmurtian tradition and mythology survived even in the form of socialist realism, existing in the subconscious and appearing only on the semiotic level (cf. Vasiljev and Shibanov 1997). In the 1990s, after *perestroika*, new Udmurtian writers consciously combined mythological ways of thought with (post)modern ways of thinking. Together they form a new and original literary whole – ethnofuturism.

(Translated by Seppo Koskinen)

References

Bahtin, Mihail (1986). *Literaturno-krititseskije statji*. Moskva: Hudozhestvennaja literatura.
Camus, Albert (1942). *Le mythe de Sisyphe: Essai sur l'absurde*. Paris: Gallimard.
Kuznetsova, Alla (1995). *Lushkem jaraton* [Intim]. Izhevsk: Udmurtia.
Leiderman, M. and Lipovetskij. N. (1991). Mezhdu haosom i kosmosom [Between chaos and universe]. *Novyj mir* 7: 240–257.
Losev, A. (1991). *Filosofija. Mifologija. Kultura* [Philosophy. Mythology. Culture]. Moskva: Polititseskaja literatura
Lotman, Jurij (1994). *Izbrannyje trudy* [Selected works]. 3 vols. Tallinn: Aleksandra.
Matveev, Sergej (1994). *Lul* [Soul]. Izhevsk: Udmurtia.
– (1995). *Shuzi* [Fool]. Izhevsk: Udmurtia.
Nankina, Lidija (1996). *Vajobyzh kar* [Swallow's nest]. Izhevsk: Udmurtia, pp. 126–176.
Pärl-Lõhmus, Maarja; Kauksi, Ulle; Heinapuu, Andreas; and Kivisildnik, Sven (1994). Etnofuturismi: Ajatustapa ja tulevaisuuden mahdollisuus [Ethnofuturism: A way of thinking and an opportunity for the future]. *Synteesi* 4: 5–8.
Samsonov, Nikolaj (1991). Shundyberganjos [Sunflowers]. Izhevsk: Udmurtia, pp. 152–191.
Shibanov, Viktor (1996). "Über die Poetik der udmurtischen literarischen Utopie des XX. Jahrhunderts". Part 7. 174–177. Jyväskylä: COIFU.
Smirnov, Igor P. (1994). *Psihodiahronologika: Psihoistorija russkoj literatury ot romantizma do nashih dnej*. Moskva: Novoje literaturnoje obozrenije
Toporov, Viktor (1995). Mif. Ritual. Simvol. Obraz: *Issledovanija v oblasti mifopoetitseskogo*. Moskva: Progress – Kultura.
Vasiljev, Sergej and Shibanov, Viktor (1997). *Pod tenju zerpala* [Under the shadow of *zerpal*]. Izhevsk: Udmurt University Press.

SIGNS IN HUMAN BEHAVIOR

Heikki Majava

Ethnic identity in the light of an ancient myth: Psychoanalytic and semiotic interpretations of the Finnish Kullervo-legend

1. Introduction

Psychoanalytic traditions of research in war phenomena can be divided into three developmental stages: first, the analysis of oedipal neuroses, as found in the writings of Sigmund Freud (1930) and Edward Glover (1946); second, Money-Kyrle's Kleinian interpretations (1937) of paranoid persecution anxiety and Wilfried Bion's group dynamics (1961); third, Franco Fornari's (1974) and Vamik Volkan's (1994) researches, which view war as a paranoid grief reaction.

Psychoanalysts have proposed different ways of preventing wars. Glover and Fornari suggest that a world government, such as the United Nations, should seek to enable normal grief-work instead of the anxiousness produced by pathological persecution anxiety. Yrjö Alanen (1980) has presented a family-therapeutic, transactional model for international conflict resolution. Mohammed Shaalan (1987) and Vamik Volkan (1994) have elaborated a new negotiation strategy for ethnic war situations, which Volkan calls "second track diplomacy" and which consists of group workshops that act out psychodynamically the actual negotiation stage. Shaalan has explored the religious denominations and Volkan the mythologies beyond ethnic wars and conflicts.

Coming closer to the position of the present paper, Tor-Björn Hägglund (1985) has presented an oedipal-analytic interpretation of the mythic Kullervo: when the hero, in his oedipal fantasy, killed his father, he lost the possibility of identifying himself with and internalizing the "father-king". And so Kullervo roamed, seeking vengeance the rest of his youth, full of narcissistic rage and merciless hate toward women's "inner space" and their capacity to give birth.

Ethnosemiotic perspectives are new for these aims. *Kalevala* mythology has not previously been interpreted psychoanalytically in relation to the dynamics of ethnic war. In what follows, the verses of Kullervo's legend are explained in psychoanalytic terms, then discussed according to aspects of semiotics, psychiatry, and social history.

2. Psychoanalysis of the Kullervo legend

2.1 The basic mistrust

The psycho-social setting is a fishing quarrel and envy between two brothers: Untamoinen, a popular leader from central Finland, and Kalervo, a Carelian man of note.

> Untamo let down his nets
> in Kalervo's fishing ground;
> Kalervo looked to the nets,
> gathered the fish in his bag. (31: 19–22)

Untamo subdues Kalervo and his army, sparing only one pregnant woman out of the whole clan. Shortly thereafter, the unhappy mother gives birth to a boy.

> Then the little boy they swaddled,
> And the orphan child they rested
> In the cradle made for rocking,
> That it might be rocked to lull him.
> The child rocked in the cradle,
> the child rocked, his locks wafted:
> he rocked one day, he rocked two,
> till soon by the third
> when that boy kicked out
> kicked out, tensed himself
> he burst through his swaddling bands
> got on top of his cover
> smashed the rocker of limewood
> ripped up all his rags. (31: 83–96)

According to Erik Erikson (1969), muscular maturation leads to two simultaneous sets of modalities: holding on and letting go. The basic conflicts of these modalities can lead to either hostile or benign outcomes. To hold can become a destructive and cruel form of retaining or restraining. To use Erikson's language, Kullervo's precocious locomotion-genital hyperactivity can be interpreted as a lack of adequate holding capacity. This, in turn, serves as a protective mechanism against the Oedipal phase, which becomes too much for Kullervo because of his early deprivation.

2.2 Sorcerers of mind

Already at three months old, as a boy no more than knee-high, Kullervo begins to think to himself:

> Would I were to get bigger
> to grow stronger in body
> I'd avenge my father's knocks
> I'd pay back my mother's tears! (31: 108–111)

When unconscious motives of war were examined according to the frames of individual psychology and group analysis, it was noticed that war represents a kind of normality, but also insanity in its regressiveness. War is the result of a psychotic process, concludes Glover (1946: 3). Swords and spears and other primitive weapons represent genital-sadistic fantasy, manual fire-arms anal sadism, warfare with chemical and nuclear arms moral sadism in its omnipotence and threat of annihilation.

Money-Kyrle has adapted Melanie Klein's theories of war and political life. When at the level of fantasy a child is persecuted by external sources, we speak about persecution anxiety, because the child feels the threat of an enemy which he himself has created. When these enemies are internalized, the child experiences them as foes from within. In a manic process, the child gains a feeling of power from being an evil-object himself. Money-Kyrle considers this process a prototype of the adult's psychology of war.

2.3 Spoiling, shaming, enslaving

When growing up, Kullervo failed at all his assigned tasks. Therefore Untamo, his foster-father, tried to destroy him in various ways, first hanging the boy on a tree (like Oedipus!) and then selling him as a slave to Ilmarinen.

> Nothing comes of this toiler!
> Whatever work I set him
> he stupidly spoils.
> Shall I take him into Russia,
> Shall I sell him in Karelia? (31: 359–363)

Outer control at the phallic stage should be firmly reassuring. The infant must attain the basic faith that existence – which is the lasting treasure saved from the rages of the oral stage – will not be jeopardized by sudden violent wishes, demands, or eliminations. Kullervo, lacking outer control over his inner threats of oral rage and greediness, risked being taken to the East, the archetypal threat of the Finns. There, the wife of the blacksmith Ilmarinen becomes Kullervo's external threat, when she maliciously bakes bread for him with a stone inside it, before sending him out to herd the cattle.

He slipped his pack off his back
took the loaf out of his pack
looks at it, turns it over;
then he puts this into words:
"Many rolls are fair on top
very smooth of crust
but have husks within
chaff beneath the crust." (33: 72–80)

2.4 Memories spring forth from the grief

The knife skidded on the stone
stubbed against the piece of rock
and the blade sheared off the knife
snapped off the dagger.
Kullervo, Kalervo's son
looks at his dear knife
and fell weeping;
he uttered a word, spoke thus:
"One knife was brethren
one iron was love -
goods my father got
my parent laid up
and I broke it on a stone... .
How shall I repay the wife's laughter
and wench's taunts... ?" (33: 85–99)

In this most dramatic episode, the stone inside the bread symbolizes both the deceitful mother-figure and the inner threat of oral greed. The knife is a representative of the lost object, what Winnicot calls the transitional experience (1953), which here distinctly represents the absent father. The knife gave Kullervo the capacity to deal with his feelings of loss and grief, control his masculinity, and soften his depressive anxiety.

The present psychoanalyst (Tähkä 1993) calls this representation – which is the third major form of internalization – "memory formation", which, among other functions, has the special purpose of helping one cope with the loss of an object, such that the child receives the illusion of the presence of the absent mother or father. Culture, too, has memory mechanisms, such as language and poetic tradition.

2.5 Individuation through escapism

Kullervo escapes from the homestead of Ilmarinen and wanders through the forest. Wandering sorrowfully toward Carelia, he first meets the Old Woman of the Forest and then a young maiden who has lost her way while gathering berries.

Psychodynamically, wandering is the counterpart of intimacy. It is a means of distancing oneself from the hatred of the superior object-image, the father, connected here with the relation between the step-father, Untamo, and the father, Kalervo. The danger of this stage is isolation, the avoidance of contacts that commit one to intimacy. In the etiology of psychopathology, as Erikson has written, this disturbance can lead to severely narcissistic problems of character. Prejudices thus developed are utilized and exploited in politics and in war (Erikson 1969).

Kullervo and the maiden have never met before and thus do not recognize each other. Kullervo drags the maiden into his sled, bribes her with silver, then makes love to her.

> There he sported with the maid
> touched up the tin-breast
> under the copper-bright cloak
> on top of the speckled fur. (35: 153–156)

Afterwards, when the couple identify themselves as brother and sister, the maiden throws herself into a torrent of water to drown. Kullervo then hurries to his native home, relates his sister's terrible fate to his mother, and proposes ending his own life also.

> Woe my luckless me, for my days
> and woe, wretch, for my horrors
> that I have used my sister
> and spoilt her my mother bore!
> Woe my father, my mother
> woe, woe my honoured parents!
> What did you create me for
> and why carry this mean one?
> I would have been better off
> had I not been born, not grown
> not been brought into the world
> not had come to this earth; (35: 173–184)

Kullervo, bitterly regretting his incestuous act, became like the "Guilty Man" described by Heinz Kohut (1977). He was driven to this state of mind by massive Oedipal-neurotic ambivalence:

> As for me, I don't know now
> cannot guess nor grasp at all
> where to bring about my doom
> and where, wretch, to cause my death -
> in the mouth of howling wolf
> in growling bear's jaws
> or the belly of a whale
> or a sea-pike's teeth? (35: 337–344)

The cape of Finland could safely hide Kullervo, as his mother says:

> Do not go my boy
> to the mouth of howling wolf
> to growling bear's jaws
> nor the belly of whale
> nor a terrible pike's teeth!
> There's lots of room in Finland
> and within murky Savo
> for man to hide from his crimes
> to feel shame for evil deeds
> to hide for five years, for six
> for nine years in all
> till time brings mercy
> and the years ease care. (35: 345–358)

2.6 The internal armies

Step by step the hero is becoming a tragic loser. He resolves, above all else, to avenge himself on his step-father Untamo. Here we witness the moment when the "Guilty Man" psychically regresses to the status of "Tragic Man". Kullervo builds up narcissistic glory in the destructive elements of his bitter soul, filling his self with war and death.

> I'll not go into hiding
> this evil one will not flee!
> I will go before doom's face
> to the doors of grave's farm
> to the great places of war
> to the killing-grounds of men ... (35: 364–369)

According to Franco Fornari, war represents a social institution whose function is to deal with those paranoid and depressive anxieties that lurk in every man. Nightmare and real object fuse in enmity with each other, to the point that war serves our sense of reality. In the case of depressive psychopaths, killing may represent verification of one's own separateness, notes Matti Tuovinen (1973).

Finding the real enemy is part of our search for realities and a sense of safety. According to the Kleinian school, the schizo-paranoid phase is institutionalized by war, such that internal, psychotic anxiety turns into an external danger. In paranoid grief-work, the dead love-object is not mourned for; instead, the goal is to kill the enemy that is considered the destroyer of the love-object. War is an existential event, where both love-object and enemies are needed (Volkan 1994) and where fantasy and reality walk hand in hand.

2.7 "War is a pleasant disease"

Kullervo prepares for a long war and leaves home joyfully, for no one but his mother remains to miss him. In a highly dramatic dialogue with her, Kullervo sings his song of praise for the war:

> I'll not then sink in a swamp
> nor fall on the heath
> in the ravens' homes
> on the crows' acres, when I
> sink down in places of war
> drop on battlefields.
> It is sweet to die in war
> fair to die in sword-clash!
> War is a pleasant disease:
> a boy comes off suddenly
> goes off without suffering
> falls down without growing thin. (36: 25–36)

Kullervo takes his sword and sets to making ethnic war. He slaughters Untamo's whole tribe and burns all the houses to ashes, leaving nothing but the hearthstones.

When on his return home Kullervo finds the cabin empty and his entire family killed, he bursts into tears. He takes his dog, steps into to the forest at the place where he once met his sister, and ends his remorse by throwing himself on his sword, following this intimate dialogue with it:

> Kullervo, Kalervo's son
> snatched up the sharp sword
> looks at it, turns it over
> asks it, questions it;
> he asked his sword what it liked:
> did it have a mind
> to eat guilty flesh
> to drink blood that was to blame?
> The sword... answered with this word:
> "Why should I not eat what I like
> not eat guilty flesh
> not drink blood that is to blame?
> I'll eat even guiltless flesh
> I'll drink even blameless blood."
>
> Kullervo, Kalervo's son
> the blue-stockinged gaffer's child
> pushed the hilt into the field
> pressed the butt into the heath
> turned the point towards his breast
> rammed himself upon the point
> and on it he brought about
> his doom, met his death. (36: 319–346)

Ethnic identity in the light of an ancient myth

Figure 1. "Kullervo's Death," painting by Mjud Metshev (printed by permission)..

3. The interpretation of the holy myths

After Kullervo's death, Väinämöinen, an archaic father figure in the Finnish national mythology, gives posthumous advice to the readers of this legend:

> Do not, folk of the future,
> bring up a child crookedly
> with someone stupid lulling [him]
> a stranger sending [him] to sleep!
> A child brought up crookedly
> or a son lulled stupidly
> won't come to grasp things,
> have a man's understanding,
> though he should live to be old
> or should grow strong in body. (36: 351–360)

Väinämöinen's advice is medically sound, and one can imagine its origin in the mind of the collector of *Kalevala*, doctor Elias Lönnrot, since it fits well the mentality of a country physician amidst poetic pathos. For though the origin of *Kalevala* lies in folk poetry, its overall shape and structure are the work of Lönnrot (Kuusi 1977).

Folklore researchers also ask why only particular ethnopoetic materials are selected and transformed for the purpose of national identity, while other sources go unused (Siikala 1994). French cultural sociologists would call this transformation an "interruption", a "disturbance" of the myth, the "engraving" of the "unfinished" oral voice in the literary text, accomplished by lifting the narration out of its original, "holy" surroundings (Arppe 1995). In myth-analytic interpretations one must distinguish between mythologic-symbolic and historical realities without mixing them. We must be prepared to elaborate new political or clinical ideologies and mythologies, if we give the myths such totalising explanations.

3.1 A myth-analytic interpretation of Kullervo

In this study, war has been analysed on the basis of a Finnish national legend, Kullervo. Its mythology offers rich substance for interpreting the disastrous character and warlike attitudes of human beings. In psychoanalytic language, these interpretations are as follows: the defects of early-childhood holding, oral frustration and rage, phallic hyperkinetic defensiveness against the Oedipal phase, the birth of mental "sorcery" and images of the enemy, the lack of the ability to grieve, antagonisms between autonomy and shame, relations of intimacy, isolation, and destructiveness, as well as familiarity and estrangement.

Kullervo's knife, as a metonymy of the absent father, represents an ultimate object-loss. When the father's knife was broken the prerequisites for productive grief-work and its connection to memory formation were lost.

3.4 Violence versus war

Kullervo psychically regresses into the Tragic Man and starts to fill his self with war and death, no longer grieving over his real or symbolic lost objects. His aim is to kill the enemy, which he considers to be the destroyer of his love-objects. Socially Kullervo was ungrounded, and he had failed at all his duties, which group-analytically means that the task structure in his life was replaced by the more regressive organizations of dependency, pairing, and fight-flight defenses. His dominating motives became revenge and destruction, culminating in homicidal and suicidal acts.

This moment has been captured in the outstanding Kalevala-paintings by Axel Gallen-Kallela (1901). The painter "interrupts" the oral myths by interpreting them. In the painting *Kullervo Leaving for War*, he is presented as a brave national hero, who is departing to do battle against hostile troops (Figure 2). He is not depicted as just any tragic man or as a loser. The symbolic reality is "interrupted" and made to serve the historical reality, which was to aid the purposes of the national independence movement.

In clinical terms, Kullervo fell prey to a malignant narcissistic psychic disorder. He felt the grandiose need to be a hero and he demanded respect, but he met only with icy scorn. Kullervo's suicide seems to be an ecstatic one, preceded by the mental states of trance, shame, and penitence. After his deep, life-long melancholia, arising from repeated real and symbolic object-losses and bitter disappointments, the pathos of revenge matured in his heart, and he sought to purge that sentiment by waging war and destruction with the edge of the sword. In the Kullervo-legend the object of the war, the enemy's image, is shrouded in mystery. Psychologically, this points to the collapse of external realities in the mind of a human being who is preoccupied with homicidal and suicidal acts. This is the "blind" pathos that exceeds both ethos and logos.

In Finnish national-romantic paintings and musical compositions, Kullervo's homicidal activities have received decorative, national-hero interpretations, while his suicidal activities have been resolutely repressed. These repressions have correspondences in our everyday frames of reference and in our attitudes toward life.

4. Summation

Ethnic conflicts constitute the main type of war phenomenon of our time. This is reflected also in psychodynamic studies of war phenomena, where the spectre of

Figure 2. "Kullervo Leaving for War", painting by Axel Gallen-Kallela.. (Printed by permission from Suomen taiteen museo Ateneum, Helsinki, and Kuvataiteen keskusarkisto, Helsinki.)

global nuclear war has been replaced by questions of ethnic conflicts having regional, religious, transcultural or transgenerational consequences.

Psychoanalytic research traditions concerning war start from Sigmund Freud's oedipal analysis, where the father represents the enemy and war is the competition for ownership of the mother. Later psychoanalysis considers war to be simultaneously normal and insane in its regressiveness; war is the result of a psychotic process that can be described as the manic projections of persecution anxiety.

The lack of the ability to grieve and the complications of the mourning processes are the basic concepts in psychodynamic therapies. These help us also to understand group dynamics, even international conflicts, explaining why entire nations are, historically, unable to grieve (Volkan 1994). The consequences of the ability to grieve, or lack thereof, remain from one generation to the next in the cultural memory mechanisms, which today form the objects of anthropological, folklorist, and ethnosemiotic research.

Missing or paranoid grief-work, in the metapsychology of the bitterness of the Tragic Man, are basic concepts of current psychodynamic therapies. These concepts of individual psychoanalysis, along with knowledge of emotionally regressive group reactions, help us to understand ethnic conflicts.

In Kullervo's legend, the loss of an object, the lack of grief-work, and the paranoia which substitutes for that lack, are the universal narrative themes. And Väinämöinen's sage advice shows sharp insight into, and empathy with, early holding experiences and their influence on the psycho-social development of the child. The metaphors in this legend might provide mental maps for the physician, psychotherapist, or educator.

Sciences and arts can transform and "interrupt" oral myths for the purpose of interpretation. Yet by doing so they risk false generalizations or the dual danger of totalism and reductionism – the Scylla of too much fantasy and the Charybdis of too much reality.

References

Achte, Kalle ym (1989). *Suomalainen itsemurha* [Finnish suicide]. Yliopistopaino. Helsinki: Yliopistopaino.
Alanen, Yrjö (1980). On the psychology of the nuclear war. *Psychiatria Fennica*: 107–112.
Arppe, Tiina (1992). Pyhän jäännökset. Ranskalaisia rajanylityksiä [The Remains of the Holy. French border crossings]. In: Mauss, Bataille, Baudrillard (eds.). 120–124. Helsinki: Tutkijaliitto.
Bion, Wilfried (1961). *Experiences in Groups and Other Papers*. London: Tavistock Publications.
Broms, Henri (1984). *Alkukuvien jäljillä. Kulttuurin semiotiikka*. Juva: WSOY.
Erikson, Erik (1969). *Childhood and Society*. Middlesex: Penguin Books.

Freud, Sigmund (1991/1930). *Civilization and Its Discontents.* In: Sigmund Freud, Standard Edition, vol. 21. 59–145. London: The Hogarth Press.
Fried, Risto (1978). Environmental rootedness and low self-esteem as factors in Finnish suicides. Paper presented at the Ninth International Congress Suicide Prevention and Crisis Intervention. Finnish Association of Mental Health.
Fornari, Franco (1974). *The Psychoanalysis of War.* London.
Gallen-Kallela, Axel (1901). *Kullervo Goes to War.* Fresco in the Old Student House, Helsinki.
Glover, Edward (1946). *War, Sadism and Pacifism.* London: George Allen & Unwin.
Hägglund, Tor-Björn (1990): *Oidipus iänikuinen* [The Eternal Oedipus]. Jyväskylä: Gummerus.
Kalevala: An Epic Poem after Oral Tradition by Elias Lönnrot (1989). Trans. Keith Bosley. Oxford, UK: Oxford University Press.
Kohut, Heinz (1977). *The Restoration of the Self*. New York : International Universities Press.
Kuusi, Matti; Bosley, Keith; and Branch, Michael (eds.) (1977). *Finnish Folk Poetry: Epic*. (=Suomalaisen kirjallisuuden seuran toimituksia/Publications of the Finnish Literature Society.) Helsinki: Finnish Literature Society.
Metshev, Mjud (1975): Kullervon kuolema, grafiikka teoksessa Kalevala [Kullervo's Death, graphic in: *Kalevala*]. Petroskoi: Karjala-kustannus.
Money-Kyrle, R.E (1937): Development of war: A psychological approach. *British Journal of Medical Psychology* 16: 219–236.
Shaalan, Mohammed (1987). Political psychiatry: A developing need for the profession. *American Journal of Social Psychology* 7(3): 173–176.
Sibelius, Jean (1996). *Kullervo*, Opus 7. Turku Philharmonic Orchestra, Jorma Panula (cond.). Naxos 8553756 [compact disc].
Siikala, Anna-Leena and Vakimo, Sinikka (eds.) (1994). *Song Beyond the Kalevala: Transformations of Oral Poetry*. (= Studia Fennica Folkoristica 2.) Helsinki: SKS.
Tarasti, Eero (1979). *Myth and Music: A Semiotic Approach to the Aesthetics of Myth in Music, Especially That of Wagner, Sibelius and Stravinsky.* The Hague, Paris, New York: Mouton.
Tuovinen, Matti (1973). *Crime as an Attempt at Intrapsychic Adaptation.* Oulu: Acta Universita Ouluensis.
Tähkä, Veikko (1993). *Mind and Its Treatment.* Madison: International Universities Press Inc.
Volkan, Vamik (1994). *The Need to Have Enemies and Allies: From Clinical Practice to International Relationships.* New Jersey: Northvale.
Winnicott, Donald (1953). Transitional objects and transitional phenomena. In: *Collected Papers*, 229–242. New York.

Tuomo Jämsä

Signs and meanings in education

1. Introduction: a contradiction between the whole and the part

There are two main schools of thought concerning curriculum design: differentiation and integration. The objectives of differentiation are bound up with scientific specialisation, and they emphasize the strict division of material into autonomous subjects. Today, a tenacious holding to the (wrongful) notion that school subjects are different and separate partly reflects the 'information shock' and overspecialization that make us know more and more about less and less, and become more and more alienated – like some kind of civilised idiots – from the great indefinable nucleus of life. In point of fact, the grounds for a strict division of subjects are illusions.

As a social institution, the school is conservative – as are all social institutions. The subjects taught and learned at school are roughly the same as they were decades ago. Yet today the producers of knowledge (researchers) are more numerous than ever before. Syllabi and textbooks generally lag badly behind the times and convey an irrelevant image of information in different fields.

The conveyance of information should not be called *education* but *schooling* (cf. Cunningham & Shank 1997). As for schooling, we should remain ever aware of the fact that we stand on the threshold of a revolution. We should evaluate again what is important in the information of our own era. Is the old division into subjects of instruction still relevant today, or should we plan a curriculum based on themes or projects that would make our children and ourselves better adaptable to the present cognitive frames? The same problem concerns the contents of the rest of our objectives of schooling and the make-up of those objectives as a whole.

The demands for integration are relatively new. A large school reform – the *peruskoulu* (basic school, grades 1–9) – took place in Finland in the 1970s, starting in Lapland in 1970 and reaching Southern Finland a few years later. At the lower level of the new school, in grades 1–6 (and especially the first two grades), there already existed a tradition favouring integration. In the 1920s

Aukusti Salo, a Finnish educationalist, had planned the first phases of instruction on the principle of what he called 'wholeness'. The organisation of the basic school is more for integrative learning in grades 1–6 than in grades 7–9. The *class teachers* work in grades 1–6, instructing in all or nearly all subjects in one or two classes. In turn, the *subject teachers* work in grades 7–9. As their title suggests, they regularly instruct in only one or two subjects in which they specialize.

The history of the basic school has been marked by different kinds of experiments. The teachers have internalised change in itself as characteristic of the new school and the readiness to change as characteristic of a good teacher. From a semiotic point of view, the supremacy of signifiers typifies the recent history of the Finnish school system. Its development has resembled that of modernistic movements in general, with the dominance of signifiers and the subjection of signifieds.

Early in the 1980s, the Finnish basic school discovered the value of integrative education. The theoretical basis of integration was expressed in a 'thematic syllabus' or – to use a more practical term – 'thematic instruction'. That phase peaked in a few years, just as former and later 'new' ideas had come out and then disappeared. The principle of integration is, however, too valuable to be forgotten, and cannot be compared to the pedagogical fashions with which it was competing. In the 70s we had a purely centralized model in school administration. Since then, we have made an about-face in our school policy. In the 1990s' spirit of decentralisation, every municipality, and even every school, enjoys the right to realise a curriculum of its own. Since the 70s, thematic teaching has been mainly practised in the first two grades of elementary instruction.

As yet Finland has no preparatory classes, or pre-schooling. Children start school at the age of 7 years. The assumption that thematic teaching is most suitable at the beginning of basic school, less suitable in grades 3–6, and least suitable at the upper level in grades 7–9 with subject teachers responsible for instruction, is largely due to the old structure of the school administration and the old division of teachers into class teachers and subject teachers. That, in turn, reflects the old, essentially quantitative view of the child's typical cognitive development.

The value of information is largely measured by the amount of it. Hence textbooks, especially those for grades 3–4 on the humanities and the natural sciences, already take on the appearance of encyclopedia articles. They are full of details and short incoherent sentences that prove quite difficult to read even for an adult. Instruction becomes, in a quantitative-cognitive sense, more demanding grade by grade. The ranking of teachers reflects this view. The teaching staff constitutes a pyramid with a university professor at the top and a teacher of the two first grades at the bottom. Nursery school teachers were considered to be almost outside of the educational system. But today the appreciation of early education is slowly rising, with the education of nursery-school teachers having gained acceptance as part of university curricula some years ago.

The historic emphasis on the quantitative side of knowledge makes pupils and teachers forget that it can be estimated from a qualitative point of view, too. Qualitatively, the amount of information is not decisive; significant instead is the value of the knowledge, its utility in helping one understand the physical and psychic worlds. The development of versatile pupils requires as vast a general survey of life, the environment, and the self as possible. Instruction based mainly on quantity of information easily leads to fragmentation.

Traditional school work, with its lessons and specified texts, stresses details instead of wholes. I vividly recall my preparation for the public final examination of Finnish 'high school' (*lukio*) 35 years ago. Then, for the first time in my 12 years of schooling, I had the feeling that I had gained a deeper understanding of many things taught to me during all those years. For the texts of the lessons had seemed to have very little in common. After a few years at school, the atomization of schoolwork probably contributes to the well-known extinguishing of learning willingness in many pupils. The qualitative view of knowledge that is highlighted here stresses that the value of matters to be learnt would depend on their significance, on how they provide pupils a basis for understanding themselves and the world around them. Instead of atomism and a plethora of fragmented pieces of information, a qualitative approach would engage fewer but more integrated items. The main focus would go to the synthesis that information could provide and to understanding. Versatility and integration in the pupils' development, depth of understanding – these would be the main objectives. The cognitive side of teaching should not be separated from other areas of human development. It should instead them.

2. A path into the whole

2.1. Semiotics used pedagogically

As a means of instilling a holistic view of the world, semiotics is highly applicable to educational integration, yet efforts in applying semiotics to schooling are relatively few. It was recommended for school for the first time, as far as I know, in 1947 by Charles Morris (Morris 1971: 274–324). Morris proposed – without giving a detailed description – an implicit use of semiotics in primary education and an explicit use of it in secondary education.

At the university level, semiotics has been taught since the 1970s, pioneered by Thomas A. Sebeok at Indiana University. In Finland, at the University of Helsinki, lecture series on semiotics have been delivered by Eero Tarasti since the early 1990s. These last have proven very popular, and today students there can choose semiotics as a separate element of their studies. In Finland, semiotics has also been taught in lecture courses at the universities of Joensuu and Vaasa. In 1992, a segment on semiotics, which included lectures and practicums, was included in the basic Finnish studies in the Savonlinna Department of Teacher Education at the University of Joensuu. Since then, the course has been realised every year. Thanks partly to the course, several masters' theses and a few doctoral dissertations with a semiotic frame of qualitative analysis have been completed or are under preparation.

Semiotics has constituted the most important background idea in the program of aesthetic and communicative education in the Training School of Savonlinna. That school is like the other schools that belong to the Finnish system of the basic school, but it boasts a more qualified staff than is generally the case. Moreover, the school serves as a training institute for student teachers. The class lecturers of the Training School and the lecturers in didactics of different subjects of the Teacher Education Department attend student teachers' training lessons, guiding the students before and after them.

Savonlinna Training School was in the early 90s one of the Finnish 'aquarium schools' – a term used of the schools that were to design new syllabi. At that time the schools in the basic system were considered to be too similar, and a move toward individualization, or profilization, took place. The Training School of Savonlinna and the Savonlinna Department of Teacher Education chose art, communication, and technology as their common profile areas. The curriculum booklet for aesthetic and communicative education in the Savonlinna Training School, entitled *Merkkejä ja merkityksiä* (*Signs and Meanings*), appeared in 1993. Music, drama, visual arts, and the Finnish language were represented. The introductory part of the curriculum comprises the author's view of the possibilities of applying semiotics to education in arts and communication (Jämsä 1993a). In addition, the booklet includes my efforts to apply semiotics to instruction in pupils' first language (Jämsä 1993b). In the summer of 1994, I delivered a paper on the same topic at the Imatra Meeting of the Semiotic Society of Finland.

Though I have made no thorough overview, it seems to me that the value of semiotics in the practice of schooling and in educational research is growing little by little. In Germany, I noticed an educational semiotic endeavour in the instruction of geography. The pupils had to interpret signs on the map by translating them into their corresponding referents in nature, and to predict weather changes on the basis of cloud formations (Schmauks 1994: 93–114). The most important sign of the growing significance of semiotics in educational is undoubtedly the activities of an association of American educational researchers (AERA), with Donald J. Cunningham and Roger Shank at the head, and with special interest groups (SIG) within the association, such as Semiotics and Education, and Arts and Learning. Above all, I have been following the energetic interest in semiotics in art education, especially work by Deborah Shank-Smith and her group (e.g., Smith & Shank et al. 1995).

2.2. 'Sign', the key concept of education

Education is a fundamental process in human life. The word education derives from the Latin original *exducere* (> *educere*), which means 'to bring out', as in bringing forth actualising what lies inside of an individual as a possibility. Education implies that what is possible may become actual and what is actual may again become potential. As such, life is education, a dialectics between becoming and non-becoming. (The existential semiotics of Tarasti [1996: 11–49] can aptly describe this process.)

We normally see the process of education 'von oben herab' and conduct ourselves more or less actively as educators. We should feel our responsibility. For me, education means giving the growing individual as optimal circumstances for learning as possible, and intervening only when absolutely necessary. I said, 'the growing individual'. We have grown too used to attaching the notion of 'education' only to children and youngsters. Traditional thinking sees education as an institution, consisting of actions by those who have the power of education, performed on those who do not have it. We do not often think of education in the context of adults and old people. In my view, education is a central, self-steering process, which continues throughout life. Thus, education is not only growth, except in a metaphorical sense. In principle, it can be a state of non-growth, too, if a certain optimum is reached and a new stage of development – or better said, life – lies ahead. But above all, education is creative. It deals with rules of fuzzy logic if it has rules at all. It is an adventure. The process of education as a nuclear process of humankind is basically indefinable.

By education I mean 'the active side of changing and non-changing, the side that can be influenced, as opposed to the passive side, which is steered by genetic and other innate programs'. Existentialism, with Kierkegaard perhaps as the first and Sartre as the best-known representative of the doctrine after him, emphasised that existence precedes essence; that is to say, feelings, thoughts, and actions constitute the individual who feels, thinks, and acts. Indisputably, nature plays a role in all this. Nevertheless, the process of education in a broad sense makes individuals what they finally are. The process is more general than is regularly supposed.

As pointed out by Cunningham (1992: 179), semiosis guides life, and both he and Roger Shank (1997) stress the presence of signs everywhere. They are not confined to the things considered signs in language, but are all things and all possible worlds. We have no direct relationship with the 'real', which is always mediated by signs. This makes our worlds unsure and relative. Cunningham (1992) denies, however, the ultimate solipsism proposed by Sebeok. He seems to join the philosophers of today who explain our intentionality on the basis of beliefs. All processes of life are sign processes; they are semiosic. Shank and Cunningham (1997) cite John Deely, who defines semiosis as the process of building up structures of experience via the use of signs. In their view, there are two primary modeling systems: language and logical inference. As is well-known, Peirce divides logical inference into three types: deduction, induction, and abduction. Cunningham and Shank (1997) consider deduction to be inference from sign to sign, induction to be the application of signs so as to understand some phenomenon, and abduction, correspondingly, the invention of signs to make sense of some new experience. Shank and Cunningham (1996) emphasise abduction as an essential tool for semiosis. According to them, there are six models of abduction. The most important feature of abduction seems to be, in a way, that open structures become more closed. They attain meaning, yet meanings are always more or less open.

The primary code or sign system to be learnt is, roughly speaking, that of things. It begins before birth. The feelings are possibly derived from the reflections of the fetus in the womb. A new-born child learns to know the 'index language' of things, that is, to connect a certain perceptive structure with a certain experiential structure. Both structures are primarily open but become more closed in the course of time. A certain level of closedness is necessary before the central feature of the 'Umwelt' – the feature of recognition – is possible. Recognition means that a baby connects a certain figure with a certain experience. In fact, primary codes are many, but the code of things is the most important one.

In my view, language is only a secondary code. Language acquisition presupposes the primary code. Both codes develop partly in parallel. Naming, as an essential operation of language, is not possible, though, if the one who names does not have things to be named (on the primary code, see Jämsä 1996).

The child applies abduction to his experiences. Elements of consciousness develop little by little, and can be called constructs. This corresponds to the constructivist theory in educational research. As Shank and Cunningham (1997) point out, educational constructivism can be made more explicit by placing it into semiotic frames. Constructivist theories of learning should emphasise semiosis. Our educational agencies in nursery schools and the early grades of basic school should take into account how children acquire as signs those things that they learn. Abduction can even be the most important tool in teaching. A normal course of development in pupils is that first they are eager to learn and then their motivation wanes. The reasons for this are many, one of the most important of them being that the methods of instruction rely too much on deduction and induction, and too little on abduction. Pedagogical alternatives – such as the German 'Waldorf-schule' – have generally had better success, because they use methods of instruction that are based on an educational view of the pupil as a whole.

3. An outline of semiotic didactics

3.1. The model of language

Although the Peircean form of semiotics is more versatile, I will concentrate on the Saussurean one. But I want to emphasize that, between the two theoretical perspectives, no borderline exists that could not be crossed. Actually, they are variants of each other. The term semiotics is attached to Peirce because he used it, and the term semiology to Saussure because he, in turn, preferred it. I recently found in the Library of the State of Niedersachsen and of the University of Göttingen a book by Kurt Sprengel printed in Halle in 1801 and entitled *Handbuch der Semiotik*. At the very beginning, Sprengel writes, 'Semiotik ist die Lehre von den Zeichen des widernatürlichen Zustandes. Man kann sie auch Semiologie nennen, aber man muss in diesem Falle mehr die Theorie der Zeichen als die gesamte Lehre davon verstehen' ('Semiotics is a doctrine of signs reflecting a state against nature. It can be called also semiology but in that case you have to understand it more as a theory of signs than the whole doctrine of them'). In the preface to his book, Sprengel (1801: 1–5) mentions a German forerunner – Gruner – whose classical work appeared in 1774. Semiotics developed from the interpretation of medical symptoms. But as we can see, a theory of sign interpretation existed, too. Thus, we continue a long tradition.

Peirce's semeiotic, as he called it, is triadic whereas that of Saussure's is dyadic. That Peirce had one category more is due to the fact that one coordinate of Peirce's diagram was called the 'object'. This does not imply, however, that Saussure could not have spoken about objects, or referents, as well.

Thus, I consider semiotic didactics to be based on the dualism of signs. Dualism is, for various reasons, more illustrative. In the spirit of the dualism of signs, we can say, in a nutshell, that signs have two sides: the signifier and the signified. In linguistics, as a Saussurean tradition that was developed by the Prague Circle in the 1920s and later by the Dane Louis Hjelmslev (cf. Koerner & Asher 1995: 207–268), the dualism of signs used to be called the principle of double articulation. In that context the word 'articulation' means not 'a way to speak' but 'the hierarchy of the central elements'. Because the terms signifier and signified are not very illustrative, I suggest, for pedagogical reasons, that the term signifier be replaced by the term sign (in Finnish: *merkki*) and the term signified by the term meaning (in Finnish: *merkitys*). Peirce performed a similar trick by using the term sign instead of the more usual 'representamen' – never mind that a sign in Peirce is actually a triadic and in Saussure a dyadic whole. In the frames of our dichotomy 'sign – meaning', we can first characterise 'signs' as constituted by sounds and letters. In linguistics, signs are called morphemes. Signs are signs because they mean something. For example, the sign 'flower' can have the meaning of 'bloom, blossom'.

A speaker or writer expresses the sign by joining together, in his utterance or writing, the sounds or letters that make up the sign. Sounds and letters belong to the physical world; they can be heard or seen. The counterparts (models) of sounds and letters in the psychic world are called in linguistics phonemes and graphemes. The phonemes /f/ + /l/ + /a/ + /u/ + /reductive e/ and the graphemes /f/ + /l/ + /o/ + /w/ + /e/ + /r/ in these successive orders enable us to distinguish that sign from others.

The meaning of a sign consists of the thought and feeling that each person combines with the sign. As a nucleus of thought, as a denotation, the meaning of the sign 'flower' is the concept of it. As a feeling, however, and as having a number of connotations, the meaning in question depends on many things: on the context in which the sign occurs, in which the addresser and the addressee are personally present at the moment of communication, on their earlier experiences involving the sign, and so on.

Concepts belong to the psychic world; they cannot be heard or seen, but only understood. Because psychic entities are largely unconscious, we do not know precisely the basic nature of concepts. We may assume, however, that concepts are made up of components – logical atoms, as Bertrand Russell termed them – that are similar to phonemes enabling us, in a certain composition and order, to distinguish a particular concept from other concepts. Successions of concepts express thoughts, and thoughts are actually propositions. As Ludwig Wittgenstein (1963) says in his *Tractatus logico-philosophicus* (originally, *Logisch-philosophische Abhandlung* (2.0272), 'Die Konfiguration der Gegenstände bildet den Sachverhalt' ('The configuration of things forms the proposition'). In my view, propositions are relations, and relations are composed of one or more arguments and a relator: xR(y)... I would distinguish two kinds of propositional meanings: context-free and contextual. The sentence 'It is hot here!' always has the same meaning nucleus, but the contextual meaning varies. For example, the contextual meaning can include the speaker's attitude that a window should be opened, the air conditioning started, and the like. The contextual meaning coincides with that of speech acts.[1]

Signs are not only single morphemes. In a discourse, what is the signifier and what the signified depends semiotically on the identification of the relation between them. The colloquial use of the word sign largely corresponds to the semiotic use of it that is suggested here, and supports the use of the terms sign and meaning in the syllabus. For instance, when someone says in English, 'This is a sign of his industry', he regards the meaning of the word 'this' to be a sign, the meaning of which is indicated through the expression 'his industry'. This process is similar in Finnish and apparently in many other languages. Thus, there seems to be a good reason for adopting the word sign in place of the Saussurean term signifier and the of-word ('sign of something') with the interpretation of it as a meaning, in place of the Saussurean term signified.

Signs have no fixed boundaries. Words, sentences, paragraphs, or texts – all these may be identified as signs. The sentence 'The flower is blue' can be interpreted as four consecutive signs: the, flower, is, blue, or one and only sign referring to a certain thought and to a certain feeling. Similarly, textual wholes such as novels, short stories, and poems can be identified as signs with certain meanings. When speaking about the theme of a text or analysing the title of it – as we traditionally do at school – we interpret a textual whole as a sign with a certain meaning.

So-called post-structuralism, with Jacques Derrida as perhaps its main representative, has criticised Saussurean structuralism because of its supposed rigidity in regard to oppositions between signs and meanings. Derrida's 'deconstruction', based largely on his interpretation of Peirce, highlights the infinity of both signs and meanings in every text. I do not see any deep contradiction between structuralism and poststructuralism, if a decisive difference does indeed exist. Besides, Peirce surely stresses the continuity of the signs we identify as meanings and he calls interpretants. Meanings (or interpretants) are so numerous that they can lead to nihilism – or, better said, to nothingness. But as Madison (1988: 113) points out, Derrida misreads Peirce, ignoring the fact that Peirce often speaks about a 'final interpretant'.

3.2. The codes

All expressions – verbal, pictorial, musical, dramatic, balletic – can be dealt with primarily as representative and secondarily as communicative. Being representative means in this connection that the expressions in question have counterparts or objects that precede or presuppose them. I am for philosophical realism because it is hard for me to understand that in the end nothing stands behind this immense sea of signs. And I am for Kantian transcendentalism when supposing that we do not know what the basic structures of the world are like. Cunningham (1992: 169) emphasises that we have no direct contact with things.

But expressions are communicative as well. Being communicative does not mean only that signs are conveyed from one human source to another. Communication derives from the Latin word *communis*, common. In communication, objects become common with subjects. It means that the act of cognition – when 'I am becoming aware of a certain thing' – is an act of communication. Lotman's model of autocommunication (cf. Broms & Kaufmann 1988) describes human cognition in general, and from a pedagogical point of view, it is a valuable tool in semiotic didactics. The term reflectiveness, stressed recently by educational researchers and in semiotics, for one, by Norbert Wiley (1994), seems to coincide with the content of the term autocommunication.

In the usual sense, to communicate is to transmit signs. The addresser – speaker or writer, artist, musician, playwright, actor, or dancer – transmits signs that are to be observed by an addressee, someone who listens to, reads, or watches the message. The sender of the message cloaks his thoughts and feelings in signs; the receiver of the message uncovers the same signs and rediscovers the thoughts and feelings in them.

Verbal, pictorial, musical, dramatic, and balletic expressions are realised in sign systems, or codes. Every code has a 'dictionary' and a 'grammar' of its own. Dictionaries are inventories of signs peculiar to each code. Grammars comprise rules according to which signs are used. Although language has a decisive status in the semiotisation of the world, we must not exaggerate its significance. Codes are, in my view, autonomous. That there seems to be a higher semiotic structure common to all codes does not imply that verbal language should be the model for all of them. The structuralist thesis of difference implies, from another point of view, a thesis of indifference. Apparently, a general logical-conceptual order of the world is repeated in the orders of the different codes.

It is beyond my competence to present all the different codes. Yet I can try to sketch some semiotic traits of aesthetic codes from a linguistic point of view. The 'phonemes' of the pictorial code are surface or mass elements. The counterpart to the phoneme in the pictorial code seems to be a unit composed of points and colours. Points and colours make up lines and surfaces. Points, lines, colours, and surfaces are easy to understand as signs when they refer to particular things or persons. Traditional pictorial signs are figures representing physical entities: a mouth, an eye, a tree, a lake, and so on. It is more difficult to recognise that the elements and wholes of nonfigurative art are signs as well. Their meanings are open, whereas those of representational art are more closed. Besides, artists like to create new things and cling to them by imagining them as 'monadic signs', on a typically post-structuralist view. Those kinds of paintings resemble music more than they do visual art.

I would argue, however, that figures – whether they describe things or not – are inseparably linked with colours. The relation between figures and colours resembles the one between thoughts and feelings, that is, between rational and emotional meanings.

Music illustrates the core of all codes, the importance of relations, the relative differences between dynamics, intervals, pitches, etc., of sounds. Musical signs give an impression of their monadic character. But this is perhaps illusory. When we watch a thing, say a radio receiver, we implicitly see the form and quality of it in opposition with the corresponding features of other representatives of the same thing and, then, with those of different things. Thus, what we see is one kind of 'symphony'. Things give us the impression – an illusion – that they speak directly to us. Sign and meaning in music are, in a context-free sense, inseparably intertwined. Contextually, the meanings of musical signs – especially those attached to feelings – can go very deep. Musical signs may iconically refer to outside of the work. For example, iconic sections occur in Einojuhani Rautavaara's *Cantus arcticus* and in Beethoven's 'Pastoral' Symphony. The music of the romantic era particularly stressed the importance of a connection between the level of sign and that of meaning.

The dramatic code represents a total expression. It is composed of speech, facial expressions and gestures, body language, motivated expressions, and actions. The total dramatic message includes the architectonic and pictorial expression of the stage as well. Peculiar to dramatic communication is the code of actions. Actions are dramatic signs. A sign of the code of actions might be, for example, to knock at the door or to move from one part of the stage to another. The sign of knocking has, of course, the meaning of 'trying to come in', and the sign of on-stage motion might have the expressly contextual meaning of 'the reason for which the motion is done'.

Balletic communication (together with music) may appear as an independent art of dramatic expression – the dance. The signs of dance are motions and may be unconventionally or conventionally figurative. The moves of classical ballet are based on artistic conventions; those of modern dance are largely not. Music and motions together constitute in both kinds of ballet a discourse of signs, a discourse in which meanings are realised above all through plastic impressions.

3.3. Semiotic didactics

The semiotic outline for a communicative and aesthetic syllabus can be compressed into a few principles:

1. Languages and arts belong together. They are – except as representations of a transcendental world – means of communication. Verbal and aesthetic social messages presuppose someone who says something and someone who receives the message. From a didactic point of view, it is also important to take account of autocommunication, that is to say, the transmission of the sign of an object into the experiential world of a subject.

2. Each language and art represents a code of its own. Every code has a 'dictionary' and a 'grammar'.

3. 'Dictionaries' are inventories of signs and are composed of signs peculiar to the code. Signs are morphemes in verbal communication, figures in pictorial communication, sequences of tones in musical communication, and so on.

4. 'Grammars' are composed of rules concerning how signs can be used.

5. Signs are signs because they mean something. Sign and meaning are inseparably joined together.

The principles listed above might be applied to education more or less implicitly starting with elementary instruction. The semiotic outline, presented above, could be used explicitly as a pilot program of semiotics, linked, say, to instruction in one's native language, at the upper level of comprehensive school in forms 7–9 or in secondary school thereafter (comp. Morris 1971).

The syllabus suggested here is based on the model of language. It need not imply, however, ignorance of the aesthetic codes proper. On the contrary: instruction should pay attention to the semiotic metatheory of codes regarding the similarities and differences between them. The goal is the pupils' deeper understanding of language and arts and, along with it, other content-fields of education. Semiotic didactics helps to instill the sense that everything is basically part of one and the same unity. This makes it easier for a pupil to understand connections between different things.

Aesthetic education as such has deeper significance for a child than education in the usual cognitive subjects. As Rudolf Steiner, founder of the Waldorfschule, writes in one of his notebooks (Tautz 1995: 116), 'Die Eindrücke der Schönheit verbinden allein den Menschen mit seiner Kindheit und über diese mit der Ewigkeit... Sie sind das, was gebraucht wird, um den Mut zu bekommen, über die Erkenntnisgrenzen hinauszuschreiten... Die Schönheit verbindet das "Ich" mit dem Leben.' ('Only impressions of beauty connect the human with his childhood and through these with eternity... They are what is needed for getting the courage to cross the boundaries of cognition... Beauty connects the "I" with life.') We need not accept Steiner's religious 'Weltanschauung' in order to understand and, in principle, to accept the theoretical prerequisites for art education in the Waldorf schools. Arts and handicrafts form the basis of the Waldorf pedagogy. Art education divides into two main areas: musical-poetic and plastic-designing. As Steiner expresses the ultimate functions of the two areas, the musical-poetic one links children with the ideal essence of the world, and the plastic-designing one, by stressing the pupil's physical involvement with materials, highlights the child's feeling for his basically inexpressible connection with the world (Jünemann 1985: 232–240). Aesthetic education and, to a large part, even instruction in the native language, which is not cognitive but aesthetic, accepts the unique value of imagination. As André Gide once said, 'I have lived many lives, of which the real one is the tiniest of all.' Imaginative processes are typically abductive. We might speak of abductive dialectics – in Chomskian terms – between competence and performance, and – in Saussurean terms – between langue and parole. In fact, imaginative abduction is realised in a much wider sense. It is dialectics between the given and the ungiven, the latter being typically a 'terra incognita', a set of signs giving shape to the unknown.

In passing, I just mentioned Steiner's 'Weltanschauung'. There is a cycle, and if you do not accept the 'Weltanschauung', then you do not accept art education as a part of it. In connection with religions, we traditionally feel obliged to make a commitment. This is because social institutions have adopted religions as essential parts of their use of power and requisite commitment. We commit ourselves in different degrees to different things. Religions represent an ancient, artistic-mythical way of interpreting the world. Their roots go back to the dawn of human development, and in the long course of time, everything unessential falls away. Russian philosopher, Aleksej F. Losev, emphasises in his posthumous book, *Die Dialektik des Mythos* (1994), that all explanations of the world, scientific ones included, are nothing other than myths. In freedom, without social commitment, the positive values of religions are stressed. Religious interpretations of the world are actually similar to poetic ones.

The basic principle concerning the essence of a language is that of the double articulation, which takes shape here as a doctrine of sign and meaning. In principle, it is present in all codes. Because of the autonomy of each code, it is good to inquire if the division into signs and meanings really exists; for example, in connection with music, nonfigurative art, architecture, and design (I give examples of codes not dealt with here before). In such cases, the instructor should perhaps stress that meanings are not always the same, but in fact seem to be connected with the signs of the code in question. This implies that there are visual, musical, dramatic, etc., meanings.

Pupils regularly have a dualistic epistemological view of everything learned at school. All is right or wrong. The analysis of two levels of discourses should lead the pupils to understand that the 'digital' (or 'closed') model in the definition of meanings obtains only rarely, whereas the 'analogical' (or 'open') model suits most cases. This kind of epistemology at school can liberate a pupil from the well-known disastrous lack of self-reliance, and help him regain the joy of learning and participation shown by children in the early stages of schooling. There is no higher goal of education than the construction of consciousness, and that consciousness can be closed or open. Our objective is to promote openness by all means.

Attempts to discover meanings – for example, by listening to classical music – are important for children in many respects. I have spoken before of the division of meanings into those that are context-free and those that are contextual. In education, especially in the early stages, the contextual meanings are more important. Finding them is always a result of problem-solving or abduction. When listening to a piece of music, children may be asked: What do you hear? Does it resemble a certain shape (round or angular, a line or a circle, etc.) or a particular colour? Can you say why it resembles it? Do you feel the music is glad or sad, strong or weak, sure or unsure? And so on. Questions provoking children's awareness of a piece of art are innumerable. The instructor should agree with the children at the very beginning that they need not look for right answers but for different ones, which are interesting because they are personal. The goals of musical, visual, verbal, etc., education is to make the codes in question a familiar part of the child's life, and to arouse love for the arts, the verbal art of expression, and the immense diversity that they represent.

In early education, at nursery school and in preparatory classes for school proper, metacognitive skills especially should be considered cautiously and with a gradually increasing stress. Metacognition is valuable in many respects. Its unique value is based on the fact that it encourages the child to become familiar with the area of culture he should learn and – more importantly – to understand roughly the general conditions of the context in question and above all his own status in relation to it. Educational research has pointed this out in the context of learning to read and write, but it should be accentuated in every context of learning. In the context of learning to read and write, however, its significance is perhaps more obvious than in most others.

According to the prevailing view of educational research, the child should be aware of the language he uses before he becomes able to learn to read and write. The principle in question is called linguistic awareness. To promote the meta-comprehension of a language, it is possible – from the point of view of our semiotic didactics – to use the term sign (as well as 'sound') in the instruction of reading and writing, and to stress the existence of the term meaning as its partner. As stated above, sounds constitute a sign if they together mean something. Thus, the most important questions the teacher can ask a pupil that is in the process of identifying successive sounds are these: Do those sounds form a sign? Do they mean something? In the Finnish phonological system, opposition prevails between a long and short sounds of both vowels and consonants. The writing system of Finnish is very consistent with this opposition: a short sound is always shown by one letter, a long one by two letters. Thus, the instructor can ask, for example, 'Is *pu* a sign? Does it mean something?' The answer is, 'No.' Then, the instructor asks, 'But what about *puu*? Does *it* have a meaning?' This time the answer is affirmative. The word *puu* means a 'tree' (as a living plant) or 'wood' (as a material). By the way, it is perhaps interesting for English-speaking people to note that, in a country of vast forests and where wood traditionally enjoys high status as a material, the language uses only one word where English needs two. Similarly, we can pay attention, say, to the pairs *kuka/kukka* (*kuka*? = 'who?', *kukka* = 'flower') and *tuka/tukka* (**tuka* is an empty place in the lexical system of Finnish and means nothing; *tukka* means 'hair' as a collective term).

In learning the contexts of reading and writing, it might be profitable for the instructor and the children to make trips downtown, where the pupils could get familiar with the ways in which letters are represented in the names of shops, buildings, and so on. At the same time, they could observe the pictures and other icons by which shops and businesses inform one of their presence. A broad understanding of the contexts in which reading and writing are needed is necessary for the awakening of linguistic awareness. Cunningham (1992) tells about Freire's pioneering work in the 60s, in the instruction of Brasilian peasants to read and write. Freire wished them to understand why reading and writing were important even for them. He took the peasant culture as a whole into account and taught his pupils self-esteem, to understand that they – despite all the denigration they met with in their daily life – were something to be valued in themselves. Freire's pupils made trips to their people. They designed posters in which the features of their culture gradually appeared. The pictures of the posters together with the texts helped them to understand the similar functions of pictures and texts in general.

Freire (1970) had the insight that the appreciation of human culture in general depends on whether a people appreciates themselves and their own culture. When Heitor Villa-Lobos designed a Brasilian program of musical education in the 1920s, he saw its main object to be 'the awakening of the feeling of Brasilian nationality' (Carvalho 1993: 70). Education starts with self-esteem. In the nineteenth century, it was shown that the Finns had a history and a culture with an extraordinarily rich folk poetry behind it. When national self-esteem had been awakened, it was only natural that an institution of instructing the people – called *kansakoulu* ('the people's school') – would be founded in the 1860s.

Contextual learning, i.e., pragmatics, is the key word in applying semiotic didactics. The varying use of signs in different contexts might also be illustrated (except in verbal and aesthetic codes), for example, in traffic instruction. Traffic lights function according to a simple code that might be observed and rehearsed during the downtown trips mentioned above. Traffic and general behavior in the city area are regulated by many kinds of pictograms, too. Otto Neurath, an Austrian philosopher of the Vienna school, designed a large inventory of pictograms, many of which were taken into civic use (cf. Bernard & Withalm 1996).

The observation of traffic can moreover teach children to understand that the interpretation of signs depends in many cases on the context. For instance, what different meanings can the sign of a car's blinking direction light have? It usually means, 'I am going to turn to the right/left'. In the context of highway driving, if the car ahead is blinking the right-sided direction light to the driver behind, it could be interpreted as, 'The highway is now clear for you to pass me.' If the car from behind has passed and is blinking the right turn-signal, then it means, 'Thanks'. The interpretation of the use of the different car lights in different contexts may help children to understand – besides traffic – the functional principles of different codes.

Finally, I would like to accentuate the practical implications of the double articulation in the instruction of the native language and the arts. In performative skills such as writing and speaking or drawing and modeling, pupils easily become anxious because they are traditionally required to produce a complete piece of work at once. My advice, on the basis of double articulation, is simple. In the first stage of the work, we should feel free and glad because we find ourselves alone before the richness of the content, an implication necessarily following the principal openness of meanings. In the first stage, pupils should concentrate on content – how to convey it – and take no care of the form. The first stage of conveying content may include many smaller phases, and it is the most important stage. In the second stage, when a pupil has as a clear a view of the content as possible, that content will be given a cloak of signs. This kind of procedure can make the artistic work easier and, hopefully, add joy to the process. And I would emphasize – more than anything else – the pedagogy of joy.

Note

1. Speech act theory, an essential part of pragmatics today, was introduced by John L. Austin in his posthumous book, *How to Do Things with Words*.

References

Austin, John L. (1962). *How to Do Things with Words*. Cambridge, Mass.: Harvard University Press.
Bernard, Jeff and Withalm, Gloria (hg.) (1996). *Neurath-Zeichen*. Wien: Institut für Sozio-Semiotische Studien.
Broms, Henri and Kaufmann, Rebecca (1988). *Semiotics of Culture*. Helsinki: Arator.
Carvalho, Angela Maria de (1993). *Konzeption und Rezeption von Heitor Villa-Lobos Projekt einer musikalischen Volksbildung*. Dissertation. Freiburg: Erziehungswissenschaflicher Fachbereich.
Cunningham, Donald J. (1992). Beyond educational psychology: Steps toward an educational semiotic. *Educational Psychology Review* 4: 165–194.
Cunningham, Donald J. and Shank, Gary D. (1997). *Semiotics: An Introduction*. In press.

Freire, Paulo (1970). *The Pedagogy of the Oppressed*. New York: Herder and Herder.
Jünemann, Margrit (1985). *Der künstlerisch-handwerkliche Unterricht*. Stefan Leber, Die Pädagogik der Waldorfschule und ihre Grundlagen, vol. 1, 232–240. Darmstadt: Wissenschaftliche Buchgesellschaft.
Jämsä, Tuomo (1993a). Semioottista teoriataustaa [A semiotic background theory]. Erkki Savolainen (ed.): *Merkkejä ja merkityksiä* [*Signs and Meanings*], 9–12. Joensuu: Joensuun yliopiston kasvatustieteiden tiedekunnan opetusmonisteita, 27 [Handouts in the Faculty of Education at the University of Joensuu].
– (1993b). Äidinkieli [The first language]. Erkki Savolainen (ed.): *Merkkejä ja merkityksiä*, 13–22. Joensuu: Joensuun yliopiston kasvatustieteiden tiedekunnan opetusmonisteita, 27.
– (1996). Semioottinen näkökulma oppimiseen, erityisesti lukemaan ja kirjoittamaan oppimiseen [A semiotic perspective on learning, especially on learning to read and to write]. *Aikakauskirja Äidinkielen Opetustiede* [*Annual Review of Didactics of the Primary Language*] 19–20: 12–23.
Koerner, E.F.K. and Asher, R.E. (eds.) (1995). *Concise History of the Language Sciences: From the Sumerians to the Cognitivists*. Cambridge, UK: Pergamon.
Losev, Aleksej F. (1994). *Die Dialektik des Mythos*. Hamburg: Meiner.
Madison, G.B. (1988). *The Hermeneutics of Postmodernity*. Bloomington: Indiana University Press.
Morris, Charles (1971). *Writings on the General Theory of Signs*. The Hague: Mouton.
Russell, Bertrand (1992). *Collected Papers*, VI. London: n.p.
Schmauks, Dagmar (1994). *Semiotische Prozesse bei der Planung und Durchführung von Wanderungen*. Klaus Robering (hrsg.). Zur Semiotik von Wort, Ton und Karte, 93–114. Arbeitspapiere zur Linguistik 31. Berlin: Institut für Linguistik.
Shank, Gary and Cunningham, Donald J. (1996). Modeling the six modes of Peircean abduction for educational purposes. Paper presented at the annual meeting of the Midwest Artificial Intelligence and Cognitive Science Conference, Bloomington, IN. Internet 21 October 97: php.indiana.edu/6modes.html.
– (1997). Why semiotics is good for education. Article on the Internet 21 October 1997: php.indiana.edu/shtcrs.html.
Smith-Shank, Deborah et al. (1995). Semiotics and art education. Unpub. ms.
Sprengel, Kurt (1801). *Handbuch der Semiotik*. Halle: Johann Jacob Gebauer.
Tarasti, Eero (1996). *Esimerkkejä: Semiotiikan uusia teorioita ja sovelluksia* [*Examples: New theories and applications of semiotics*]. Helsinki: Gaudeamus.
Tautz, Johannes (1995). *Lehrerbewusstsein im 20. Jahrhundert: Erlebtes und Erkanntes*. Dornach: Verlag am Goetheanum.
Wiley, Norbert (1994). *The Semiotic Self*. Cambridge, UK: Polity Press.
Wittgenstein, Ludwig (1963). *Tractatus logico-philosophicus: Logisch-philosophische Abhandlung*. Frankfurt am Main: Suhrkamp.

Hannu Lauerma

Inside out – from verbal imagery and inner voice to verbal hallucinations

A model of schizophrenic hallucinations and related cognitive deficits based on sensori-motor disintegration

Introduction

> *The concept of imaging is rather like one of doing rather than receiving.*
> (Wittgenstein 1980)

Both subjectively and according to the results of neurophysiological research, a qualitative difference exists between intensive verbal thoughts, or "inner speech", and true verbal hallucinations. Although transient hallucinations may occur, say, as a result of prolonged sleep deprivation among healthy subjects, persistent verbal hallucinations still are prominent hallmarks of mental illness.

From a phylogenetic point of view, processes like language and other intrapsychic or interpersonal communication are complex series of muscle activity. These include speech, signing, gesturing, touching, and mimicry. Emotional interaction, mediated by facial expressions and music-like qualities or prosodies of spoken language, is of utmost importance because it carries messages that are not to be mediated by verbalization and may reveal material that is inconsistent with verbalizations.

Weimer (1977) has argued that the mental or cognitive realm is intrinsically motoric, like all the nervous system, and that there is no sharp separation between the sensory and the motor components of the central nervous system. According to this motor metatheory, the mind is intrinsically a motor system. The sensory order by which we are acquainted with external objects as well as ourselves, and the higher mental processes which construct everything mental, is a product of what are, correctly interpreted, constructive motor skills. Without concrete or imagined movements there is no speech, words, gestures, or communication of any kind. All the engrams of the brain and ideas of the mind can be understood as feed-forward mechanisms that serve to prepare the organism for some selective subset of possible experiences or movements.

Movement research in psychiatry
– a conflict of paradigms

> *Outspread fingers often show fine tremors ... The expression of the face, vacant, immobile, like a mask, astonished, is sometimes reminiscent of the rigid smile of the Aeginetans... Simple movements are stiff, slow, forced.*
> (Kraepelin 1919)

> *Namentlich der Gang ist oft auffallend. Schon das Zusammenspiel der Arm- und Beinbewegungen ist oft gestört, manche Kranke halten auch die Arme beim Gehen steif. Besonders wichtig aber ist, dass oft die Füse zeitlich vie räumlich ganz unregelmässig gesetzt werden.*
> (Bleuler 1911)

Since the beginning of our century, clinicians have known that an early sign of incipient schizophrenia can be a loss of the natural gracefulness of body movements. It has been estimated that 10 to 25 percent of schizophrenic patients have visible abnormal body movements that are not related to antipsychotic drug treatment, which may cause similar phenomena. Abnormally rapid eye movements, saccades, during attempts to follow a moving object smoothly are observed in approximately 50 to 80 percent of patients, 40 percent of their first-degree relatives, and 8 percent of normal subjects (Grebb and Cancro 1989). By viewing home movies of adult-onset schizophrenic patients and their healthy siblings filmed during their childhood, judges who were blind to the psychiatric outcome of the subjects could reliably identify the pre-schizophrenic subjects (Walker and Lewine 1990).

The question arises of whether movement disorders seen in a significant subgroup of schizophrenic patients have anything to do with the pathogenesis of other schizophrenic symptoms, or whether they should be considered an epiphenomenon without significance for those patients who do not exhibit clinically significant motor disturbances. In other words, could a movement disorder, visible in only some patients but subclinically present in others, be an expression of a more fundamental cognitive disorder with implications for thought disorder? Certain symptoms, such as the delusion of being made to say or do something by an external force, could share the same neurocognitive mechanism with involuntary movements. Verbal hallucinations, obsessions, and certain involuntary movements share unintendedness as a property and thus might have similar pathophysiological mechanisms.

Since the division of neuropsychiatry into two medical specialties, neurology and psychiatry, the view that extra-pyramidal and catatonic symptoms in schizophrenia are essentially different from one another has been considered uncontroversial. This view is based on two lines of reasoning. Pathologically, extra-pyramidal symptoms are thought to be side-effects of neuroleptic drugs and reflect interferences with the function of the basal ganglia. Catatonic symptoms, on the other hand, are by definition an expression of an unknown disease process of schizophrenia. Phenomenologically, extra-pyramidal and catatonic symptoms show broadly different characteristics. The former tend to be less complex and purposeful than the latter; the areas of clinical overlap between them are not great; and their mutual similarities have been considered to be limited to external appearances. However, the large number of individual abnormalities subsumed under the term "catatonic" varies from what could be called simple disorders of movement to more complex disorders of volition; very complex disorders of overall behavior, and disorders of speech. The justification of clear demarcations seems to be questionable. The assessment of catatonic symptoms has not acquired accuracy and phenomenological rigour, and to distinguish them from extra-pyramidal side-effects is not always easy (Lund et al 1991). In certain cases, it may be both clinically and theoretically impossible and unjustified to distinguish between drug-induced disorders and primary neuropathological or psychogenic phenomena (Heikkilä et al 1992). Medication may also normalize some aspects of motor abnormalities. These abnormalities are usually considered mannerisms, controlled by the patient's will, thus having an explanation on what is called a "higher" emotional-cognitive, psychological level. However, it is difficult to define and standardize complex series of movements, and we cannot yet reliably distinguish between mannerisms not due to primary movement disorder but to personal will, and primary abnormalities of the motor system.

Rogers (1993) concludes that the importance of studying psychiatric movement disorders and the psychiatric aspects of neurological movement disorders, so as to understand idiopathic psychiatric disorders, is increasingly recognized. Motor disorders of drug-naive schizophrenic patients as well as neuroleptic-induced movement disorders are of special interest for the following reasons: 1) movement programming is a fundamental part of our cognitive system, and the two body halves differ from each other as clearly as the two cerebral hemispheres do; 2) movement analyses enable description of dissectable neurocognitive behavioral components, and they can be reliably replicated; 3) the most important forms of human communication are entirely based on motor activity. Motor disorders in schizophrenia may represent cognitive disorders of largely distributed neural networks. Mental dysequilibrium and positive psychotic symptoms, which usually fluctuate, would emerge when these networks are critically overloaded.

The division of movements into totally voluntary and totally involuntary may be justified in clear or extreme forms of movement, yet dichotomizing is inadequate. Volition is essentially a subjective experience and it is difficult or impossible to assess directly. Usually we have a clear view that our movements are voluntary, yet there are numerous, complicated combinations of movement of which we are not aware. Besides this, a number of movements, such as spontaneous facial expressions, are elicited by emotions and are not voluntary or explicitly controlled by our will. Table 1 is a simplified classification of movements, aimed at helping us to understand the theory concerning movement abnormalities in schizophrenia.

Table 1. Normal movements in man (modified from Marsden 1982).

Type of movement	Movement control
"Most automatic" or reflex	Automatic, no intention
"Least automatic" or voluntary	Plan
Fast or ballistic	Timing by will, preprogrammed, open-loop
Feedback from periphery	Continuous programming, closed-loop

The ability to recognize and correct errors during motor tasks cannot be explained solely by a closed-loop model involving sensory feedback. Error-correcting behavior also depends on the monitoring of internal, self-generated cues. Several investigators have suggested that some aspects of schizophrenic symptoms could be explained by an impairment of the ability to monitor one's own cognitive processes. According to a movement analysis study, schizophrenic patients are deficient in the ability to monitor their motor behavior internally (Malenka et al 1982). It has been concluded that a derangement of feedback can account for many of the classic pathological features of schizophrenia. For example, a motor act that was performed without corollary discharge or inner monitoring could well be perceived as having been generated by an outside agency. The same holds true for a thought.

In advancing his "conflict of paradigms" hypothesis, Rogers (1985) implied that emphasis on the distinction between intrinsic and drug-induced movement disorders may be misplaced because of overlap not only in the observable characteristics of these disorders, but also in the underlying neuropathology. According to this view, there is no fundamental distinction between "neurological" movement disorders and catatonic "psychiatric" disorders: their demarcation is illusory, and reflects the historical divergence of neurological and psychiatric traditions.

According to McKenna et al (1991), the contradiction of views concerning the relationship between primary neuropathology and drug-induced movement disorders was very pronounced in the 1960's, but the case for clinical unrelatedness gained ground and, most unfortunately, ultimately acquired the status of orthodoxy, despite evidence to the contrary. Reiter (1926) described a series of dementia praecox patients whose symptoms match the modern definition of schizophrenia, with a large variety of extra-pyramidal disturbances but normal cerebrospinal fluid findings and no macroscopic abnormalities of post-mortem brains. Owens and Johnstone (1982) assessed 411 patients with chronic schizophrenia, and found that approximately half of 47 neuroleptic-naive patients showed evidence of involuntary movements such as those of tardive dyskinesia. These movements were indistinguishable from those seen in neuroleptic-treated patients. Also, a retrospective examination of schizophrenic patients' case notes, which antedated any possible use of neuroleptics, clearly demonstrated frequent extra-pyramidal disorders.

Rating 75 schizophrenic patients, McKenna et al (1991) divided catatonic phenomena into negative phenomena, which reflect a deficit of activity, and positive phenomena, which entail abnormal activity. They found a highly significant correlation between tardive dyskinesia and "positive" catatonic phenomena and a weaker but significant correlation between Parkinsonism and "negative" catatonic symptoms. According to Liddle (1991), the authors could have much more convincingly confirmed the latter association if they had not been so careful as to include the most prevalent negative catatonic item, marked underactivity, which is similar in character to the hypokinesia in Parkinsonism. When schizophrenic patients who had never been medicated were examined by the use of instrumental measures, rigidity and tremor were observed in 29% and 37% of the patients, compared to 4% and none in healthy controls (Caligiuri et al 1993). Duration of illness was significantly correlated with tremor amplitude. Early treatment of acute psychoses and the profound effects of neuroleptics on the motor system may thus overshadow subclinical, extra-pyramidal dysfunction of a primary nature.

From verbal imagery to hallucinations: sensorimotor disintegration

Hoffman (1986) has attempted to develop a cognitive-processing model of schizophrenia by conceptually linking verbal hallucinations and speech disorganization. The latter is often referred to as "loose associations". According to his model, schizophrenic speech disorder is a disturbance in generating multipropositional discourse plans that specify communicative intentions. The major components of the claim that such language-planning disruptions induce verbal hallucinations are as follows: 1) verbal hallucinations are verbal images that are accompanied by a feeling of unintendedness; 2) research findings support the hypothesis that disruptions in language-planning processes associated with schizophrenia can cause verbal images to be experienced as unintended; 3) if such images are discordant with concurrent cognitive goals then the experience of unintendedness provides the basis for the sustained conviction of a non-self origin. Hoffman argues that there is a significant negative correlation between verbal hallucinations and some negative symptoms of schizophrenia such as akinesia, which implies that inactivity causes a decrease in hallucinations.

As Flor-Henry (1986) concludes, numerous empirical investigations demonstrate, by amplifying the activity of laryngeal musculature, that during hallucinations there is activation of the vocal apparatus: in essence, subliminal vocalization that is perceived by the subject as externally projected and alien. Also silent thinking and silent reading in normal subjects are associated with subvocalization and laryngeal electromyographic activation, but this activity is not perceived as non-self-derived. A model of poor monitoring of one's motor or cognitive activity in schizophrenia is in keeping with the findings of Malenka et al (1987). Hallucinations, obsessions, and certain involuntary movement disorders share unintendedness as a property and thus might have similar pathophysiological mechanisms. Most hallucinating schizophrenic patients report that the voices disappear during mouth-opening maneuvers, which precludes subvocalization (Bick and Kinsbourne 1987). Because the hypnotically induced hallucinations in normal subjects do not seem to be affected by the mouth-opening maneuver (Levitt and Waldo 1991), a comparison of these two types of hallucinations and their laterality should prove to be of interest.

Several authors' criticism against Hoffman's theory is justified, however. Experimental research does not uniformly support his model, and furthermore, hallucinated non-verbal sounds – such as the sound of steps, musical hallucinations, etc. – would have to be of different origin, since it is hard to believe that they could be caused by subvocalization of any kind. They could instead be "audible memories", the neural origin of which would be distinct from "voices". Musical hallucinations may be more often a symptom of ear disease than one of psychiatric disorder.

During sleep, hallucinations and sensori-motor disintegration take place simultaneously. At the beginning of REM-phases, with the increasing activity of hallucinatory information processing, motor inhibition is further increased by the spinal mechanism. These processes may either share common mechanisms and possibly also be causally linked, or be purely coincidental. The latter case seems improbable.

An obvious need exists to reintegrate movement research with psychiatric research. One area of interest is movement lateralization. The role of left-hand movements in left hemi-neglect based on right-sided cerebral lesions is well documented, as is the relatively greater dysfunction of the left, verbal hemisphere in schizophrenia. Manual tasks requiring "dexterity" – i.e., well organized occupational therapy – might enhance normalization of perceptual asymmetry in a way that is also typical for antipsychotic medication. The validity of some psychiatric and neurological concepts has to be re-evaluated to enhance dialogue between the two different scientific traditions that seem to use different language to describe the same phenomena. Especially, the classical concept of catatonia seems to be of very limited scientific value.

References

Bick, P.A. and Kinsbourne, M. (1987). Auditory hallucinations and subvocal speech in schizophrenic patients. *American Journal of Psychiatry* 144: 222–225.

Bleuler, Eugen (1911). *Schizophrenie*. Leipzig und Köln: Deuticke.

Caligiuri, M.P.; Lohr, J.B.; Jeste D.V. (1993). Parkinsonism in neuroleptic-naive schizophrenic patients. *American Journal of Psychiatry* 150: 1343–1348.

Flor-Henry, P. (1986). Auditory hallucinations, inner speech, and the dominant hemisphere. *Behavioral Brain Science* 9: 523–524.

Grebb, J.A. and Cancro, R. (1989). Schizophrenia: Clinical features. In *Comprehensive Textbook of Psychiatry*, Kaplan and Sadock (eds.). 757–777. Baltimore, MD: Williams and Wilkins.

Heikkilä, J.; Raitasuo, S.; Lauerma, H.; Mölsä, P. (1992). Katatonia ja pahanlaatuinen neuroleptioireyhtymä kehitysvammaisella potilaalla [Catatonia and malignant neuroleptic syndrome in a mentally handicapped patient]. *Duodecim* 108: 1120–1124.

Hoffman, R.E. (1986). Verbal hallucinations and language production processes in schizophrenia. *Behavioral Brain Science* 9: 503–517.

Kraepelin, Emil (1919). *Dementia Praecox and Paraphrenia*. Edinburgh.

Levitt, E.E. and Waldo, T.G. (1991). Hypnotically induced auditory hallucinations and the mouth-opening maneuver: A failure to duplicate findings. *American Journal of Psychiatry* 148: 658–660.
Liddle, P.F. (1991). Commentary on the modified Rogers scale and the 'conflict of paradigms' hypothesis. *British Journal of Psychiatry* 158: 337–339.
Lund, G.E.; Mortimer, A.M.; Rogers, D.; McKenna, P.J. (1991). Motor, volitional and behavioral disorders in schizophrenia 1. *British Journal of Psychiatry* 158: 323–327.
Malenka, R.C.; Angel, R.W.; Hampton, B.; Berger, P.A. (1982). Impaired central error-correcting behavior in schizophrenia. *Archives of General Psychiatry* 39: 101–107.
Marsden, CD (1982). The mysterious motor function of the basal ganglia. *Neurology* 32: 514–539.
McKenna, P.J.; Lund, C.E.; Mortimer, A.M.; Biggins, C.A. (1991). Motor, volitional and behavioral disorders in schizophrenia 2. *British Journal of Psychiatry* 18: 328–336.
Owens, D.G.C. and Johnstone, E.C. (1982). Spontaneous involuntary disorders of movement: Their prevalence, severity, and distribution in chronic schizophrenics with and without treatment with neuroleptics. *Archives of General Psychiatry* 39: 452–461.
Reiter, P.J. (1926). Extrapyramidal motor-disturbances in dementia praecox. *Acta Psychiatrica et Neurologica Scandinavica* 1: 287–304.
Rogers, D. (1985). The motor disorders of severe psychiatric illness: A conflict of paradigms. *British Journal of Psychiatry* 147: 221–232.
– (1993). Movement disorders. *Current Opinion in Psychiatry* 6: 113–116.
Walker, E.F. and Lewine, R.J. (1990). The prediction of adult-onset schizophrenia from childhood home movies of the patients. *American Journal of Psychiatry* 147: 1052–1056.
Weimer, W.B. (1977). A conceptual framework for cognitive psychology: Motor theories of mind. In: *Perceiving, Acting and Knowing*, Shaw and Bransford (eds.). 267–311. Hillsdale, NJ: Erlbaum.
Wittgenstein, Ludwig (1980). *Remarks on the philosophy of psychology*. Chicago: The University of Chicago Press.

ARTS I: MUSIC

Erkki Pekkilä

Ethnomusicology and media reality

Ethnomusicology, which was once the study of traditional music then, later, of popular music, is today undergoing many changes. Among recent research paradigms in the discipline, Jeff Todd Titon has listed such things as new-found interest in representations, authorship, gender, ethics, epistemology, Marxism, feminism, self-inspection, applied ethnomusicology, and the world seen as a text (Titon 1995: iv). These new interests arise not only from within the discipline, but also reflect changes in our daily life and culture, which in turn affect our research objectives. The pressure for change can also be seen in exchanges that took place in 1997 between Henry Kingsbury, Anthony Seeger, and Jeff Todd Titon in the journal *Ethnomusicology*, under the title "Should ethnomusicology be abolished?". The answer was – if a bit tentatively – "No". Still, those exchanges and some recent trends in research encourage us to re-evaluate views of what ethnomusicology is, and to reconsider the anthropological approach that has been so popular since the 1970s, in the Americas and many other countries, Finland included.

This is not to accuse music anthropology, the dominant approach to ethnomusicology for the last three decades, of being old-fashioned. Even today the principles laid out in Merriam's (1964) classical book on music anthropology remain sound for ethnomusicological study. That book and ethnographies in general have their place in the study of modern culture. But ethnography alone is not enough. We need something else.

In my view, the study of modern culture must emphasize three domains of research: communication theory, semiotics, and ethnography. Communication theory lays the groundwork for study of electronic media and related phenomena. Semiotics is the science with which we study meanings. Ethnographical descriptions are a way of discovering the perceptions of sender and receiver.

I will now discuss in some detail what has led me to my present views. The meaning of many basic ethnomusicological concepts, such as field-work, informant, society, music culture, and so on, is changing. And this change relates more widely to the concept of empiricism in general. When Alan Merriam (1982) was doing field-work in Zaire in the village of Lupupa Ngye, he was surrounded by something like "an ethnographic reality". People there lived face to face with each other, making music, and generally participating in social behaviors and transactions. But when we study modern culture, the empirical reality does not present itself so clearly. For instance, in Robert Walser's (1993) study of heavy-metal music in an urban context, the empirical reality seems to be a mixture of the reality created by media – phonograph records, fan magazines, television, mass concerts – and so-called "empirical" reality, which in this case means social behaviours such as taking lessons in heavy-metal guitar playing or simply meeting other people.

Also problematic in the study of urban culture is the concept of the key-informant. In traditional ethnography one way to collect information is to conduct interviews. This is also, of course, a relevant method in the study of urban culture: interviews with performers, audiences, fans and so on, mirror a certain kind of reality. But to this reality we must add another one – the reality created by the media.

Media reality comes about partly though stories in newspapers and magazines, which can take the place of interviews as sources of information. In many cases, one has access to ready-made newspaper articles, such as published interviews. An interesting question here is whether this kind of information is as pertinent or as valuable as that gathered by the traditional interview. When the researcher interviews a performer face-to-face, a discussion takes place between two persons such that the informant can really be regarded as passing along information. But the interview done by a journalist who is only collecting material for his "story" presents quite another kind of situation. This interview will be distributed widely, to thousands or even hundreds of thousands of readers. It is not a mutual exchange of thought, because such an interview is tailored from the beginning for the public and their needs. In a magazine story people can read what they want to hear about the performer or the star. It is not a report of a discussion but a metatext that helps to subsidize the myth of stardom. It is not a description of a reality, but a reality unto itself.

The traditional conception of society has also been problematized. We used to think that a musical culture was more or less a group of people practising a certain kind of music. Originally, this was a folk-music society or tribal culture society. At some point, especially in the field of urban anthropology, the concept of society changed so as to become understood as an ethnic minority living in an urban area (e.g., see Nettl 1978). We can trace a similar line of thought in the sociological concept of sub-culture and in Bourdieu's class theory. Nowadays the very concept of society has become obscure. Listeners to a certain type of music do not form a clearly delineated society of people who live near or even know each other. A society of, say, heavy-metal music fans is not a society in the traditional sense, but rather a network of people drawn together by traditional electronic media or even the Internet. Today a music society is a global network of people in contact with each other through products of mass culture such as compact discs, music videos, and meta-texts created by the media.

Music is not what it used to be. Folk music no longer needs to be transmitted aurally and orally, but may be passed along through phonograph records and compact discs. Popular music is no longer necessarily something transmitted through sound recordings alone, now that music videos perform this task. Ethnic music is no longer necessarily the music of tribal cultures, since it has become a kind of cross-cultural, "fusion" music transmitted through the media. Even Western classical music is no longer what it used to be, for behind it operate mechanisms similar to those in popular musics: marketing, performers, stardom, and various extra-musical, commercial, and media matters have become more and more important to the once-rarefied domain of classical music.

Ethnomusicology must face the fact that our surroundings have dramatically changed. We do not live in a folk culture or in an ethnographic reality, just as we no longer inhabit an industrial society, but rather a post-industrial one. Media reality, which has replaced ethnographic reality, is fragmented into such fields as music, the press, national and local radio stations, television, records, satellite TV, compact discs, background music in shops and restaurants, and more. Postmodern media reality does not concern only popular music; rather, it is all-invasive, touching more or less all music. Clearly, the ethnomusicologist studying modern culture faces a landscape that is quite different from the one we traditionally encountered.

We cannot study media culture and media reality in the same way as we did ethnographic reality. The traditional ethnographic reality was studied by field-work, that is, by interviews with key-informants, taking photographs, making on-site recordings and videocassettes, describing, reporting. Media reality, however, differs radically from the old ethnographic one. Media reality itself produces the texts that we used to create by field-work: television and newspaper stories, photographs, music videos, television and radio programs, reports, stories, oral reports, commentaries. The media record, mould, and produce their own sound documents, which they distribute to the world. For these and other reasons just given, media reality must be studied differently than ethnographic reality.

A central reason for the change in music is the phonograph record. In traditional tribal communities the consumption of music was collective. All the people had a similar social background, culture, tradition, beliefs, and norms, and they all listened to the same kinds of music. When music was transferred to the phonograph record, something changed. As Cubitt has noted (1991: 44), the music was liberated from its historical and cultural connection and it became, in a certain sense, "pure".

The "purity" of music has all kinds of effects. For one, the phonograph record has, to some extent, broken the contact between performer and listener. In small venues featuring folk or other kinds of music, for example, the public could applaud, whistle, tap their feet, and sing along to encourage the performer. But you cannot communicate with a phonograph record, because the communication goes in only one direction, from performer to audience. The feedback that once obtained at live performances now takes place mainly in the form of buying records and thereby affecting sales. This is not direct communication. The performer does not know his audience, and the audience knows the performer only through the media. What was once dialogue has become a monologue.

The fact that music is no longer tied to its cultural background also makes possible "crossovers" (e.g., Beethoven played by rock bands; country artists singing rock music, and so on) and all kinds of stylistic fusions, examples of which can be found in much so-called world music (e.g., the Gipsy Kings, purported to play Andalusian music, in fact play a mix of disco, flamenco, and rock-and-roll). Purity in music does away with historical authenticity and at the same time encourages eclecticism and stylistic borrowings.

The "purity" of music liberates the public, too. Music mediated by phonograph records is not tied to social class and sub-culture in the same way it was in traditional cultures. In media culture, a person may live physically in the same "society" as those around him, but still belong to a completely different culture of taste than that of one's neighbour. (For instance, a student of mine tells the story about his two younger brothers, one of which listens to "hip-hop" and the other "grunge". Both brothers have different musical preferences, and both wear different kinds of clothing as emblematic of their respective taste-cultures.)

Small-town Finnish hip-hop culture probably can be seen as a certain kind of sub-culture. This kind of culture, however, does not spring from the society or social class, as Bourdieu describes (1984). A paradoxical strain in these new taste-cultures is their non-existent connection to tradition (Finnish hip-hoppers cannot count black reggae, soul, and rap as part of their historical musical heritage). A young person feels free to change his or her taste in one night, from grunge or hip-hop to something else – quite unlike the case in traditional cultures, where one remains tied to certain habits and norms. This is the way fragmented and postmodern taste-cultures are formed, and traditional theories of culture cannot explain it.

The separation of music from performance turns conventional conceptions of music anthropology upside down. Music is no longer a result of behaviour and something that lives "in" or "as" culture. It is now a mere "musical sound", which lives in its own hermetic state. Music can be seen not as a performance but as a compact disc or cassette tape lying on a retailer's shelf. Music circulates freely from one place to another without being tied to its historical background and the culture where it was born and developed. For instance, hip-hop in the United States may exist as a sub-cultural phenomenon linked with black urban communities; but in Finland it is no more than a kind of "pure" music with no clear connection to its own background.

The phonograph record has also caused music-making to become an industry. Jacques Attali has argued that the phonograph record turned music into a commodity that could be bought, sold, and traded (1985: 88). Music, originally a non-material thing, was materialized, or "reified", and transformed into an object for commerce and profit. Attali also notes that, as music became an industry, there came into being a new society of mass reproduction and repetition (ibid.).

Mass media and the phonograph record turned music into a commodity that is fabricated and consumed on the terms of the market economy, thus making the listener or receiver a consumer. This situation divides music more and more into two sides: production and market. The former consists of the performer, producer, record companies and so on; the latter is the listener, the audience, and consumption in general. Listeners can of course be seen as something more than consumers; they are individuals having music as a hobby, representatives of certain tastes or sub-cultures, social classes or musical micro-worlds. But this does not negate the fact that in a modern or postmodern market economy listeners are, in the last analysis, consumers. Marketing has become increasingly important in the mediation of music, and the consumer has become more and more the focus of marketing activities.

Modern technological advances have brought a new dimension of "estrangement" to the making of music. A vocalist may never even meet the instrumentalists, but instead sing on top of pre-recorded background tapes. Musicians may not know each other, but go to a studio and record their parts separately. In many cases, musicians are no longer necessary, since one person may compose and record all the music on a computer in his home studio. In this sense, the making of music has already become a semi-industrial activity, giving substance to Adorno's (1994) vision of a "culture industry".

The reality has in fact exceeded his vision. Adorno (1984; 1991) rejected the term "mass culture" because he took "culture" to mean something that people actively make, which he thought was not the case in the passive consumption of popular music. He thus replaced the term "mass culture" with that of "culture industry", as better describing the passive consumption of popular music. For Adorno, the culture industry was based on mechanical replication and commercial exploitation, which made the culture a commodity and the consumer a passive object. The culture industry, in Adorno's view, combined the arts of the elite and the common people – to the undoing of both – and it created a false star-cult based on self-deception and pleasure-seeking. The culture industry inculcated passivity and regression, and created aesthetic emptiness, all this finally leading to totalitarianism.

Adorno did not, however, regard the role of songwriters as being an industrial activity, because he thought composition took place according to more or less traditional methods. Industry did not mean the rationalisation of the production process but only that of distribution (Adorno 1991: 22). But although Adorno was extremely pessimistic, even he could not envision that the production of music would also become a highly industrialized activity.

The most conspicuous feature in this process is the division of labor. Such division can be seen most clearly in industrial music-making on a large scale, where production consists of an incredible amount of people performing different tasks. As Rein et al. note (1987: 40–44), the production of music in the industrial state includes such job categories as talent agent, personal manager, publicist, professional coaches, business and financial manager, market researchers, product planner, advertising specialists, publicity agents, venue consultants, and so on. The division of labour is highly diversified, which justifies the view that culture is not only industrialized but fabricated and manipulated as well.

Nowadays the culture industry does not concern just popular music but extends into classical music, too. Decca Records marketing manager, Didier de Cottignes, goes so far as to say that the politics of marketing can affect the public's musical taste (quoted in Nieminen 1996: 57). For example, record companies used to limit themselves to producing music by Bach, the Viennese School, and other traditionally famous composers. When the companies began also to record less-known compositions by famous composers, as well as the music of lesser known composers of earlier eras, the demand for this kind of music skyrocketed. Sociologically, this indicates a change in musical taste. The fact that marketing can affect taste indicates how tightly linked are the processes that sustain modern media-society and market-society.

The nature of modern consumer society has been well described by Baudrillard (1988: 29): we abound in things and surround ourselves with objects. Instead of interacting with other people, we constantly deal with things. This view also applies to music, in the sense that we no longer communicate with other people by performing, playing, and listening to music. Rather, we communicate with different kinds of objects: CDs, cassette tapes, and records, as well as musical meta-texts such as newspapers, magazines, tabloids, and books containing stories about music and interviews with performers.

Baudrillard (ibid.) also speaks about our living in a postmodern society that is filled with objects and their rhythms. Postmodern society watches objects come and go, whereas in traditional cultures it was the objects that remained from one generation to another. This observation extends to culture and music as well. Musical style used to remain more or less stable from one generation to the next. In comparison, the life of musical works and even musical genres is very short nowadays. We can watch the birth, short life, and death of a hit tune on the sales charts

In modern consumer- and media-society the making of music is a chain of communication with consumers on one end, producers on the other, and music in the middle. The music cannot be understood without the other two links in the chain. Music does not live in a "culture" but in this communication chain.

It is worth remembering that the term "communication" has at least two different meanings. First, communication denotes the emitting of messages (like telephone calls) from sender to receiver. Secondly, communication refers to those images and associations that are born in the receivers' minds, as Klopf and Cambra have observed (1989: 14). John Fiske points out that these two ways of understanding communication are in a certain way value-based (1990: 29). In the first meaning, communication is seen as a more or less mechanical process wherein the sender emits a certain message to the receiver; in the latter, communication is viewed as an activity that creates meanings, i.e., as a semiotic phenomenon. In music studies many people think that, in musical communication, the creation and relaying of meanings and artistic ideas are more important than the structures of the production chain. This may be the case in classical music, but not necessarily in popular music. At least in the most commercial forms of popular music, marketing and all kinds of background work seems at times to have even more importance than the product itself.

This explains why in popular-music research the study of the product itself or the meanings given to it by the audience may not be enough. Studies of both production and reception are also necessary, and this involves communication theory and semiotics.

Communication theory views popular music from the production side. In media culture, this side is equivalent to the composer or the performer in classical music. In a market economy, the unique author has been replaced by a team or a collective. It seems also that the structures of production vary with locale, musical genre, and so on. This variability highlights the need to search out the different production structures, which can be done quite objectively by case studies and by researching the links and their functions in the communication chain. In this context, it is interesting to study, in addition to the big record companies, also various small record companies, since many of these continue folk-music and communal ways of production.

The next link in the chain, after the product, is the music itself. But the music cannot be understood without knowledge of the receiver, since music does not begin to exist until it reaches the listener. The study of receivers proves difficult because they represent psychological or subjective experiences. Popular music features so-called "hooks", which are key words and key melodies encoded by the senders. Hooks do not contain any meanings in themselves but they catch the receiver's attention, evoking different kinds of associations, affects, and interpretations in the mind. The experience of the individual is here more important than the product. The study of the receiver or the consumer is the study of the subject, the person experiencing music. And when we explore the receiver, semiotics enters the picture, in the form of the study of musical meanings.

In this way, classical communication theory (which studies structures of the production chain) and semiotics (which studies meanings) do not exist apart from each other but in a complementary relationship. While communication theory studies the facts, semiotics accounts for the meanings that the individual or the culture attaches to music.

Traditional ethnography does have its place in the study of modern culture. The study of structures of musical communication is necessary, but it is only the first phase. When the links in the production structures have been explicated, we can concentrate on what is inside the different "boxes" of the communication model. In this work of explanation, ethnographic description is a useful tool.

In sum, we live inside the market and the media, which together create a reality that is more complex than the old ethnographic one. There is no music culture or ethnographic reality in a traditional sense. Instead of music, there are only electronic recordings accompanied by metatexts concerning music. Instead of culture, there are only interviews, newspaper and magazine articles, concert reviews, radio programs, and concert advertisements.

The reality that is built upon these is fragmentary. It does not arise "naturally" as the output of members of a culture, but is pressed upon us by corporate senders. Self-made or domestic culture does not exist in a media-society riven with the conflicts of commercialized clockwork versus consumer, institutions versus citizens, media versus people, sender versus receiver. The importance of communication theory and semiotics in explaining this fractious scene cannot be overemphasized.

References

Adorno, Theodor W. (1984). Yhteenveto kulttuuriteollisuudesta [Conclusive summary of the cultural industry], *Tiedotustutkimus* 3: 21–28.
– (1991). *The Culture Industry: Selected Essays on Mass Culture*. London: Routledge.

Attali, Jacques (1985). *Noise: The Political Economy of Music*. Manchester: Manchester University Press.
Baudrillard, Jean (1988). Consumer society. In: *Jean Baudrillard: Selected Writings*. Mark Posner (ed.). 29–55. Cambridge: Polity.
Bourdieu, Pierre (1984). *Distinction: A Critique of the Judgement of Taste*. Trans. Richard Nice. Cambridge, MA: Harvard University Press.
Cubitt, Sean (1991). *Timeshift: On Video Culture*. London: Routledge.
Fiske, John (1990). *Introduction to Communication Studies*. New York: Routledge.
Kingsbury, Henry (1997). Should ethnomusicology be abolished? *Ethnomusicology* 41(2): 243–249.
Klopf, Donald W. and Cambra, Ronald E. (1989). *Personal and Public Speaking*. 3rd ed. Englewood Cliffs, NJ: Norton.
Merriam, Alan P. (1964). *The Anthropology of Music*. Evanston, IL: Northwestern University Press.
– (1982). *African Music in Perspective*. New York: Garland.
Nettl, Bruno (1978). *Eight Urban Musical Cultures: Tradition and Change*. Urbana: University of Illinois Press.
Nieminen, Janne (1996). Taidemusiikki äänitteellä: Ääniteteollisuuden tuotantoketju ja -prosessi taidemusiikin nä kökulmasta [Classical music on sound recordings: the production chain and process from the point of view of Art music]. MA thesis. Department of Musicology. University of Helsinki.
Rein, Irving J. (1990). *High Visibility: The Professional Guide to Celebrity Marketing*. Oxford: Heinemann.
Seeger, Anthony (1997). A reply to Henry Kingsbury. *Ethnomusicology* 41(2): 250–252.
Shannon, Claude E. (1964). *The Theory of Communication*. Urbana, IL: University of Illinois Press.
Titon, Jeff Todd (1997). Editor's farewell. *Ethnomusicology* 39(3): v-vi.
– (1997). Ethnomusicology and values: A reply to Henry Kingsbury. *Ethnomusicology* 41(2): 253–257.
Walser, Robert (1993). *Running with the Devil: Power, Gender, and Madness in Heavy Metal Music*. Hanover, MD and London: Wesleyan University Press.

Anne Sivuoja-Gunaratnam

Music as narrative discourse[1]

Narrativity as a tool of human comprehension

I share the view of many scholars, that narrativizing is essentially a human way of (re)constructing reality for oneself (see Bruner 1991: 5, 8–9; White 1981). Narrativity is our attitude towards the world around us: we conceive and explain it through innumerable narratives.

Jerome Bruner assigns a very special place to narrative: it is one of two modes of thought, the other one being that of argumentation. These modes of thought are complementary and irreducible to each other. Their structural properties are different, and even though their aim (human cognitive functioning) is the same, they reach that end in different ways. The argumentative mode of thought deals with formal logico-scientific truths, as abstract and general as possible. The narrative mode of thought is concerned with human conditions and intentions, which can be very complex and contain inner contradictions. (Bruner 1986: 11–43.) In a later study, Bruner goes so far as to claim that

> narrative comprehension is among the earliest powers of mind to appear in the young child and among the most widely used forms of organizing human experience (1991: 9).

The value of narrative comprehension becomes crucial when one confronts discourses that seem not to employ any conventional structures of communication. In studies of (post)modern music, narrative is often pressed into service as an analytical tool (see Nattiez 1990: 257; Pasler 1989 and 1991; Heiniö 1988: 15–17 and 1989: 133–134). This appeal to narrative is not so much because of the overwhelming 'story-like' quality of (post)modern musical compositions, as compared, say, with some classical or romantic pieces. Rather, it points up the lack of other options available for the description of these pieces. Nevertheless, some musicologists have strong reservations about musical narrativity, and for different reasons (Kramer 1991: 143; Nattiez 1990). These objections are voiced most elegantly by Carolyn Abbate,[2] who, despite her skepticism, is ready to admit that

> [p]erhaps the idea of a dramatic plot is so central to human cognition, to our rationalization of experience, that we cannot resist pursuing the analogy of plot and music, even when it results in generalities, in mechanistic explanations (Abbate 1991: 46).

Even though narrative apprehension reflects, if not universal, then at least common, transcultural, and natural attitudes of people towards the world, self-identification, the processing of emotions and experiences, and so on (Barthes 1982: 251–254; White 1981: 1), such a basically human approach can be further developed and refined for analytical purposes, in order to avoid trite interpretations and hollow conclusions. In the case of (integral) serial compositions, where even an experienced listener is unlikely to follow the *serial* unfolding, it is crucial to discover a level of analysis that supports his or her efforts to construct a cohesive narration.

Referential meaning and musical narrativity

But how could music narrate a story? How would we know the content by just listening to a piece? And if we perceive the music as telling a story, who guarantees that it is the right story we have in mind, the one intended by the composer?[3] History has shown that composers' explanatory programs can remain concealed, as in the case of Alban Berg's *Lyric Suite*, whose secret story of unfulfilled love between the composer and Hanna Fuchs-Robettin was not made public until the late 70s (see Floros 1992: 235–291). Thus audiences were deprived of the 'right' story for over 50 years, but not of the narrative experience of this music, because musical narrativity has practically nothing to do with the 'storyness' or programs of musical discourse (cf. also Heiniö 1989: 133).

Narrativity in music does not necessarily require a prefabricated, extramusical story or program – such as the creation of the universe, *The Sorcerer's Apprentice*, or a young musician's fantasies – the understanding of which would be indispensable in order for the listener to make the correct connections between certain sonorous events and passages in the tale. Nor does musical narrative need to depict psychological states such as joy, sorrow, desperation, or melancholy (see Kramer 1990: 190–203; Kivy 1984: 169–181; Salmenhaara 1989: 55–58). Musical narrative *can* do this, but it is not obliged to do so. Musical discourse is not something for which a narratologist would desperately be looking to find a referential content,[4] be it psychological, emotional, historical, or whatever.[5] Hence musical narrative is not a subclass of musical representation, although it may well exploit extramusical connotations (see, however, Kivy 1984: 159[6]).

The narrative mode becomes activated by the listener as an interplay or dialogue between his or her narrative competence[7] and the piece, without recourse to descriptive titles, whether of entire works – e.g., *The Bard, Transfigured Night, Tasso* – or of particular movements – such as the boasting of Goliath or the Israelites' joyful victory, in the *Biblical Sonatas* of Johann Kuhnau (see also the 'March to the Scaffold' or 'Dream of the Witches' Sabbath' in Berlioz's *Symphonie fantastique*; and the chapter on 'Music as Narration', in Kivy 1984:

159–196). A descriptive title, a motto, or an annexed program may surely add a semantic (referential) dimension to the piece, but without either decreasing or increasing its narrativity.

'Narrative' is not a conclusion

As stated above, narrativity is viewed here as an innate human response to being in the world and a way of processing mental content, experiences, and the like. This situation applies to music, too, for musical narrativity permeates the Western musical tradition, and its absence is rare (see also Pasler 1989: 233–235). But if almost all music is narrative, then how can narrativity be other than a trivial concept?

Indeed, Carolyn Abbate reproaches the term narrative for its 'interpretive promiscuity':

> Broad definitions of narrative ... are so broad as to enable almost all music, all parts of any given work, to be defined as narrative (Abbate 1991: xi; see also 28, 45–46).

She believes that such all-inclusiveness impoverishes the analytical power of the term, the ultimate danger being the mechanical application of a narrative model.

In this context, let us recall Roland Barthes's rhetorical question in his 'Structural Analysis of Narratives': 'Must we conclude from this universality that narrative is insignificant?' (1982: 252). Is there a danger in having a very extensive paradigm of musical narratives and a very small number of pieces that can be categorized as non-narrative? I don't sense the danger Abbate warns about. In fact, there is nothing negative in the supposed 'interpretational promiscuity' of the term, because 'narrative' is not the end or the conclusion of any analysis or interpretation. On the contrary – it is just the beginning.

To ask, as does Abbate (1991: 28–29), whether or not a composition is 'narrative', as though that were the endpoint of analysis, is a rather unfruitful and somewhat strange line of inquiry. The parallel in literary criticism would be to declare a certain literary/fictional text or passage thereof as narrative, and to shut off the inquiry at that point. It is simply not very interesting whether something – a piece of music, a literary work, a dance performance, a painting – is conceived as narrative. The really interesting questions concerning narrative of any kind are qualitative: how the narrative has been constructed, how its boundaries are defined, how it is mediated, how the subjective identities become transformed, how time has been manipulated. What counts is the elaboration of the narrative model and its skillful application.

As just mentioned, there exists a scantly populated category of non-narrative pieces. In those works, recognizable and recurrent patterns, figures, motives, and themes are annihilated, while at the same time musical memory is negated: 'Works without narrativity shun any organizing principle and try to erase the role of memory' (Pasler 1989: 233, 247–248; see also, Stoianova 1978: 236–252). Such musical discourses are often generated by a method that inhibits the will of the composer, for example, by total serial matrices or by chance operations. In my view, such pieces constitute highly interesting attempts to break out of the prison-house of narration and narrativity.[8]

The problem of the narrator

Adopting a narratological approach to music does not entail the utilization of each and every narratological concept in the analysis of a single piece. To do so would be practically, if not virtually, impossible; for there are many narratologists – Genette, Greimas, Brémond, Barthes, to name but a few – and each one has developed complex and elaborate narratological models. The competent narratologist must choose from a plethora of terms and concepts, and decide which ones would be most apt for describing a particular situation. The assessment of the narratologist's choices falls ultimately to the reader.

There are many narratological concepts, among which are point of view and narrator, that are crucial to lots of novels, but which are quite rarely applicable to music in a fruitful way (see, however, Hatten 1991 and Abbate 1991: 3–60). A narrator is presupposed for literary discourse by many scholars (e.g., Genette 1983: 64–69; Ricœur 1985: 95–99). But must we similarly assume that musical discourse requires a narrator, one responsible for enunciating the piece? Perhaps the claim for a narrator would be more justifiable if we did not try to anthropomorphize him or her. In fact, it might be easier to accept the concept of a narrator in musical discourse if we could treat *it* – not him or her – as a logical but invisible and, paradoxically, *mute* agent presupposed by the utterance, which is the piece of music itself (cf. also Kramer 1990: 187–188). Certain literary authors, for instance, Ernest Hemingway in *The Killers,* Elias Canetti in *Die Blendung* (in English, *Auto-da-fé*), and Gustave Flaubert in *Madame Bovary*, tried to erase the narrator by positioning the narrative agent outside the diegesis of the narrative proper and by offering no information about this agent. In such instances the narrator is however automatically presupposed by the fact of the text being given. There seems to be little use for such *extra-diegetic* narratorship in music (on narrative levels, see Genette 1986: 227–262), for in many cases such a mute agent would not give any new insights into the narrative mechanisms of a musical piece. This is why in this study the category of narrator remains unexplored.

Instead, musical discourse will be understood here as analogous to Benveniste's 'historical narration' or 'history', which is characterized by the absence of a narrator:

> No one speaks here; the events seem to narrate themselves ... the narrator does not intervene, the third person is not opposed to any other and it is truly an absence of person. (Benveniste 1971: 208–209)[9]

I would find the concept of narrator meaningful only in such cases where actual narrative utterances take place *within* a piece, where the narrator, and possibly the audience as well, is built-in or evoked. Such would be the case with Gurnemanz's long monologue in the first act of *Parsifal*, in which he relates the story of Amfortas's fall. His narrative has a built-in audience on stage (four squires, the knights, and Kundry).[10] But he is not responsible for producing *all* the musical discourse in the opera. In Genette's terminology, Gurnemanz would only be a second-degree (or intra-diegetic) narrator, the first-degree (or extra-diegetic) narrator remaining as an unarticulated, logical agent. The first-degree narratorship cannot be attributed to Richard Wagner, who is the author (both librettist and composer), but not the narrator[11]. As another example of diegetic narratorship, one could mention Einojuhani Rautavaara's opera *Thomas* (1982–1985), in which the chain of events presented on stage are in fact projections of the protagonist's (Bishop Thomas's) mental activity (Sivuoja-Gunaratnam 1992: 91–98).

For Abbate, the virtual absence of a narrator is enough to prove that musical discourse is non-narrative. She claims that musical narration is 'a rare and peculiar *act*, a unique moment of performing narration within a surrounding music' (Abbate 1991: 19; her emphasis). Her insistence on the performative act of narration requires a subject of enunciation (i.e., narrator), who is positioned within the utterance and who performs the narrative act. Admittedly, such moments are scarce in music. Those rare acts of the diegetic subject are always indicated by specific, context-bound gestures in the musical discourse, signaling a transposition into the narrative mode (Abbate 1991: xii).[12] Tarasti is of the same opinion when he writes that, "'narrativity is a secondary modeling system' that does not manifest in all musical discourse. The narrative nature of the discourse must be foregrounded somehow, for instance, by breaking the rules of syntactical structures." (Tarasti 1994: 30–31.) Only such a narrative 'transposition' would license the researcher to promote a narratological approach to that piece. Yet what if these ruptures and disjunctions in the musical discourse were already part of a larger musical narration, which would conceal within itself a second-degree or embedded narrative, marked in the discourse by one of the aforementioned, musico-semiotic devices?[13]

Abbate argues that Dukas's *The Sorcerer's Apprentice* only 'allows a single instance of narrating' (1991: 30; cf. also 56–60). But this single instance, which for Abbate is a certain sonority ('that sound'), seems to lack the most crucial component – the narrative proper – for it has hardly any duration, and narrative is 'irreducibly durative' (Bruner 1991: 6). In her elaborate analysis what Abbate is really deciphering is the evocation of a communicative act, that is, an enunciation, which may *cue* a narration and hence be 'narrative' in its thrust, but which, in fact, is not a narration itself.

Musical narrativity as a time-bound chain of musical events

Music is a temporal art, to such an extent that perhaps its most basic parameter is not pitch, harmony, or timbre, but time or temporality (Rowell 1987: 183[14]; Kramer 1988: 1–9). According to Igor Stravinsky

> ... music is a *chronological* art, as painting is a *spatial* art. Music presupposes before all else a certain organization in time, a chrononomy... (Stravinsky 1970: 28; emphasis his).

Music unfolds in time and is conceived as a process of sonorous events. As Nattiez writes:

> Musical 'discourse' is placed in time. It comprises repetitions, returns, preparations, expectations, resolutions, and on the level of melodic syntax ... techniques of continuity. One is tempted to speak of musical narrative on account of the existence of this syntactical and temporal dimension of music (1990: 244).

But Nattiez is only *tempted* to do so, and in his article 'Can we speak of narrativity in music?' he reaches a negative conclusion:

> I have tried, in fact, to show that *in itself*, and as opposed to a great many linguistic utterances, music is not a narrative and ... any descriptions of its formal structures in terms of narrativity is nothing but superfluous metaphor (Nattiez 1990: 257; emphasis his).

Contrary to Nattiez, I wish to prove that musical narrativity – be it a metaphor or not – is far from superfluous.

The core of any kind of narrativity lies in the dynamic identity of musical entities projected into a temporal dimension (cf. Nattiez 1990: 257; Ricœur 1994: 113–168; Heiniö 1988: 15–17). These two aspects – entities and time – are often referred to in definitions of narratives. For example, Robert Scholes defines narrative as

> the symbolic presentation of a sequence of events connected by subject matter and related by time (Scholes 1980: 209).

For Claude Brémond the minimal condition for narrativity is that a subject[15] has undergone some kind of transformation between times T and T+n (1973: 99–100).

These definitions are mainly intended for literary discourse, but they can also be applied with ease to music, because it is the transformation of musical identities in a temporal continuum that most tightly unites music with other narrative arts.[16]

For Stoianova (1978: 219–221), determined and directional linearization is a crucial feature of musical narrativity, which runs from the initial impulse until it reaches its end, the terminal point (*fin-objectif*). Like Stoianova, Newcomb also stresses the importance of functional events appearing in a prescribed order, and he further elaborates plot types that particularly characterize the music of Schumann and his contemporaries (Newcomb 1984 and 1987). In his most inclusive definition of narrativity, Tarasti asserts that it is

> ... a competency that involves putting temporal events into a certain order, a syntagmatic continuum ... [which] has a beginning, development, and end, ... a sort of arch progression (Tarasti 1994: 24).

Tarasti is referring, with his 'arch progression', to what Barney Childs calls a narrative curve, which

> [t]he Western Europe intellectual and cultural tradition has seemingly found most fundamental [as] a basic structural organization of a work of time art, what might be called a *narrative curve* (1977: 195; emphasis his).

What is more important in the narratological analysis of a particular piece is to decipher how the musical *sign system* functions: the way the musical narrative is organized, how its energies are regulated and channeled, how time is manipulated, whether or not figures (themes or motives, for instance) are foregrounded in the discourse and, if so, what happens to their identity in the course of musical events, how are they developed or possibly destroyed. The asking of such questions constitutes a semiotic inquiry, because they try to decipher the sign systems that articulate a musical piece as a narrative. They do not deal with referential or representational matters, in the sense of establishing and investigating links between sonorous events and possible semantic contents.

Notes

1. The article is based on chapter 5.2. in auhtor's book *Narrating with twelve tones. Einojuhani Rautavaara's first serial period* (1997)
2. Even though many of Abbate's ideas will be submitted to criticism in what follows, they have been crucial to the development of my own model. Without her well-articulated discussion of narrativity and her elaborate analyses I would not have been able to find my own voice.
3. This question is spelled out in Abbate's title '*What* the Sorcerer Said' (1991: 30; emphasis mine), the interrogative pronoun referring to the content of a narrative utterance.
4. Pasler introduces here the analogy of signifier (the musical discourse) and signified (the semantic content), in 1989: 235–237.
5. In no way do I wish to negate the possibility of semantic structures in music (see especially Grabócz 1986; Monelle 1991 and 1995; Hatten 1994). The main point is

that narrativity doesn't depend on musical semantics. For experimental semantic analyses see, for instance, Nattiez 1973: 251–256 and 1990: 246–248.
6. Kivy (1984: 159) claims that 'Narrative music, to be sure, is only a subclass of a representational kind' but after a couple of sentences notes that his view is 'over restrictive ... and guilty of overemphasis in our insistence on the dependence of the narrative on the propositional.' I totally agree with the latter statement.
7. I presume that all human beings, including composers and their audiences, are entitled to live in the prison-house of narration and narrativity.
8. See Sivuoja-Gunaratnam 1997: 152–161 and 200–227 for further discussion.
9. Furthermore, Benveniste's 'history' employs certain typical verb tenses which are absent from 'discourse', which he defines as '... every utterance assuming a speaker and hearer, and in the speaker, the intention of influencing the other in some way. ... [A]ll the genres in which someone addresses himself to someone, proclaims himself as the speaker, and organizes what he says in the category of person' (Benveniste 1971: 207–211).
10. Narrative acts furnished with intra-diegetic narrators and intra-diegetic narratees are typical of the narrative mechanism of *Parsifal*.
11. Narrator – in musical or whatever discourse – must also not be confused with implied author, nor with what Cone calls the implicit musical persona of the composition, who 'is a projection of his [the composer's] musical intelligence, constituting the mind, so to speak, of the composition in question' (Cone 1974: 57). Contrary to Anglo-American narratological tradition, Genette has strong reservations about the notion of an implied author (1983: 93–107).
12. One very typical evocation of an intra-diegetic narrative act would be the use of recitative-like texture within an instrumental piece.
13. About embedded or metadiegetic narratives, see esp. Genette 1986: 228–234 and 1983: 55–64.
14. Rowell (ibid.) considers tonality as the strongest expression of temporal force in Western music; temporality being thus more primary than tonality.
15. For music, a motive, theme, or other musical gesture or figure that possesses a degree of individuality as compared with its context.
16. See Ricœur 1985: 29–30, who however does not mention music in his list of narrative media; cf. also Pasler 1989: 241–244 and Nattiez 1990: 257.

Bibliography

Abbate, Carolyn (1991). *Unsung Voices: Opera and Musical Narrative in the Nineteenth Century*. Princeton, NJ: Princeton University Press.
Barthes, Roland (1982). Structural Analysis of Narratives [1966]. Trans. S. Heath. In *A Barthes Reader*, ed. Susan Sontag. 251–295. New York: Noonday Press.
Benveniste, Emile (1971). *Problems in General Linguistics* [1966]. Trans. M.E. Meek. Miami Linguistics Series 8. Coral Gables, FL: University of Miami Press.
Brémond, Claude (1973). *Logique du récit*. Paris: Seuil.
Bruner, Jerome (1986). *Actual Minds, Possible Worlds*. Cambridge, MA and London: Harvard University Press.
– (1991). The Narrative Construction of Reality. *Critical Inquiry* 18/1: 1–21.
Childs, Barney (1977). Time and Music: A Composer's View. *Perspectives of new music* (spring-summer) 15/2: 194–219.

Cone, Edward T. (1974). *The Composer's Voice*. Berkeley and Los Angeles: University of California Press.
Floros, Constantin (1992). *Alban Berg. Musik als Autobiographie*. Wiesbaden: Breitkopf & Härtel.
Genette, Gérard (1983). *Nouveau discours du récit*. Paris: Seuil.
– (1986). *Narrative Discourse* [1972]. Trans. J. Lewin. Oxford: Basil Blackwell.
Grabócz, Márta (1986), *Morphologie des œuvres pour piano de Liszt: Influence du programme sur l'évolution des formes instrumentales*. Budapest: MTA Zenetudományi Intézet.
Hatten, Robert S. (1991). On Narrativity in Music: Expressive Genres and Levels of Discourse in Beethoven. *Indiana Theory Review* 12: 75–98.
– (1994). *Musical Meaning in Beethoven: Markedness, Correlation, and Interpretation*. Bloomington: Indiana University Press.
Heiniö, Mikko (1988). Lastenkamarikonserteista pluralismiin. Postmoderneja piirteitä uudessa suomalaisessa musiikissa. *Musiikki* 1–2: 3–139.
– (1989). Post-modernism: An Approach to Contemporary Finnish Music. Proceedings from the Nordic Musicological Congress, Turku, Finland. 15–20 August 1988. *Musiikki* 1–4: 130–139; printed in abbreviated form in *FMQ* 4 (1988): 16–24.
Kivy, Peter (1984). *Sound and Semblance: Reflections on Musical Representation*. Princeton, NJ: Princeton University Press.
Kramer, Jonathan D. (1988). *The Time of Music: New Meanings, New Temporalities, New Listening Strategies*. New York: Schirmer.
Kramer, Lawrence (1990). *Music as Cultural Practice, 1800–1900*. Berkeley, Los Angeles, Oxford: University of California Press.
– (1991). Musical Narratology: A Theoretical Outline. *Indiana Theory Review* 12: 141–162.
Monelle, Raymond (1991). Structural Semantics and Instrumental Music. *Music Analysis* 10/1–2: 73–88.
– (1992). *Linguistics and Semiotics in Music*. Contemporary Music Studies 5. Reading and New York: Harwood Academic Publishers.
– (1995). Music and Semantics. In *Musical Signification. Essays in the Semiotic Theory and Analysis of Music*, ed. E. Tarasti. 91–107. Berlin and New York: Mouton de Gruyter.
Nattiez, Jean-Jacques (1973). Y-a-t-il un diégèse musicale?. In *Musik und Verstehen*, hrsg. P. Faltin and H-P. Reinecke. 247–257. Köln: Arno Verlag & Hans Gerig.
– (1976). *Fondements d'une sémiologie de la musique*. Paris: Union générale d'éditions.
– (1990). Can one speak of narrativity in music? *Journal of the Royal Music Association* 115/2: 240–257.
Newcomb, Anthony (1984). Once More 'Between Absolute and Program Music': Schumann's Second Symphony. *Nineteenth-Century Music* 7/3: 233–250.
– (1987). Schumann and Late Eighteenth-Century Narrative Strategies. *Nineteenth-Century Music* 11/2: 164–174.
Pasler, Jann (1989). Narrative and Narrativity in Music. In *Time and Mind: Interdisciplinary Issues*, ed. J.T. Fraser. 233–259. Madison, WI: International University Press.
– (1991). Postmodernism, narrativity, and the art of memory. *Contemporary Music Review* 7: 3–32.
Ricœur, Paul (1985). *Time and Narrative*. Vol. 2 [1984]. Trans. K. McLaughlin and D. Pellauer. Chicago and London: University of Chicago Press.

– (1994). *Oneself as Another* [1990]. Trans. K. Blamey. Chicago: University of Chicago Press.
Rowell, Lewis (1987). Stasis in music. *Semiotica* 66–1/3: 181–195.
Salmenhaara, Erkki (1989). Musiikin suhteesta todellisuuteen. *Musiikkitiede* 2: 47–65.
Scholes, Robert (1980). Afterthoughts on Narrative II: Langugage, Narrative, and Anti-Narrative. *Critical Inquiry* 7: 204–212.
Sivuoja-Gunaratnam, Anne (1992). Nature versus Culture in Einojuhani Rautavaara's opera *Thomas*. *ITR* 13/2: 89–106.
– (1997). *Narrating with Twelve Tones: Einojuhani Rautavaara's First Serial Period (ca. 1957–1965)*. (=Humaniora, vol. 287.) Helsinki: The Finnish Academy of Science and Letters.
Stoianova, Ivanka (1978). *Geste – texte– musique*. Paris: Inédit.
Stravinsky, Igor (1970). *Poetics of Music in the Form of Six Lessons* [1942]. Cambridge, MA: Harvard University Press.
Tarasti, Eero (1994). *A Theory of Musical Semiotics*. Bloomington and Indianapolis: Indiana University Press.
White, Hayden (1981). The value of narrativity in the representation of reality. In *On Narrative*, ed. W.J.T. Mitchell. 1–23. Chicago: University of Chicago Press.

Eero Tarasti

Jean Sibelius as an icon of the Finns and others: An essay in post-colonial analysis

Introduction to the topics

In this century all Finns – not just musicologists – have grown up amidst a Sibelius cult. In the 1970s and 1980s attention focused on yet another Finnish "icon", the Sibelius biographer Erik Tawaststjerna, the very incarnation of the Sibelius cult. When he spoke one got the impression that the spirit of the great master still dwelt on earth, for Tawastsjerna was like a direct link to the world in which Sibelius had lived. When Tawaststjerna's biography of the composer was finally completed, Seppo Heikinheimo, the main music critic for the *Helsingin Sanomat*, wrote that Sibelius was now a "picked bone". But he was wrong. For after Tawaststjerna came a new flurry of Sibelius studies, including many academic dissertations. First versions of many of the composer's works were recorded, which till then the family had banned from performance. And congresses took place, at first only in Finland, but soon spreading to other important music centers such as Paris, London, Berlin, and New York.

On their own, however, musicologists, record companies, and even illustrious conductors can neither create a national cult nor revive one. While Finland has always had a Sibelius cult, it has recently gained fresh momentum triggered by the national turning-inward of the 1990s. Patriotism again has become fashionable, along with its accompanying national spectacles and ceremonies. A timely example of the renewed Sibelius cult was the concert series entitled *Sibelius in Memoriam* held in the fall of 1997 at the Kallio Church in Helsinki to commemorate the fortieth anniversary of the composer's death. For that event, Osmo Vänskä conducted the Lahti Symphony Orchestra in performances of the composer's seven symphonies.

For a semiotician the occasion had two sides. On one hand, the musical signifiers afforded the ear a new and fresh experience (as one can verify by listening to the recording of the symphonies as played on the memorial concerts). On the other hand, at the level of signifieds one experienced a national spectacle of sorrow, as if Sibelius had just then reached the peace of the grave. Newspapers publicized the concert on black-gilt pages, and those who attended found themselves before an altar above which hung a huge, candle-lit picture of the composer. The phenomenon thus had a purely musical aspect that brought about completely new qualities in the interpretations by Vänskä and the Lahti Symphony Orchestra. At the same time, one could so strongly experience the social-semiotical aspect that it bracketed, so to speak, the musical qualities in the signifiers and put greatest emphasis on the musical content, or signified. That content was Sibelius as an iconic figure with whom the listeners identified at the same time as they experienced a strengthening of their selfhood and community. Here I endeavour to show that these two seemingly unrelated phenomena are in fact intimately connected.

Although we should like to take an iconoclastic attitude toward all cults, we need not at the same time reject the positive aspect of iconisations that have the power to catalyze new and liberating sign processes. (For instance, the completely new Sibelius interpretations at the aforementioned concerts broke the hold of well-worn clichés about his music.) Even giving up the ideology of national togetherness and taking a critical position towards certain regressive phenomena of Finnish contemporary culture, one would find that these phenomena are not as simple as they first appear.

The fact is that we find ourselves again at the center of a Sibelius cult. How can this be explained? The present cult differs, of course, from the one that began in Solemnity Hall of Helsinki University in 1892 at the premiere of the *Kullervo Symphony* and that continued almost uninterrupted in Finland and the Anglo-Saxon world until the death of the composer and even beyond. Naturally these various cults arose partly from different grounds, and my objective is to analyze such differences. (How, for instance, does the American Sibelius cult differ from the Finnish one?) On the other hand, the contemporary Sibelius cult, spinning out its pseudo-myths, no longer produces "primal" mythicism but only a kind of second-order "mythologism". Of course today we are immersed in the postmodern age when everything has been experienced and nothing is taken seriously any longer. And yet the present Sibelius cult – like Finnish neopatriotism – is a deadly earnest matter.

Many phenomena of Finnish contemporary culture can be understood only if one takes into account a remarkably broader context than the one which we normally consider as our purview. The Finnish connection to that broader world is simply this: *colonialism* – and *post-colonialism* as its continuation. The latter form of critique belongs to the conceptual arsenal of the 1990s, along with deconstruction, postmodernism, gender studies, and others. But while theories of post-colonialism have seen great use in various fields, particularly in English literary studies, they have not (yet) been much applied to music.

I encountered ideas about colonialism years ago when studying the Brazilian "Sibelius", Heitor Villa-Lobos. In one treatise on Latin American literature there appeared the term "the colonialized imagination" (Franco 1973). Third-World people do not know how to appreciate their own achievements, leaders and "icons", but put stock only in the values and models imported from outside their native lands (for example, from Europe). Even back then it struck me that the term "colonialized" suitably described certain phenomena in Finland, particularly the Finnish sense of national inferiority and worship of everything foreign. But only now have I come to realize that the colonial heritage expressly concerns Finland. The theme is now more topical than ever, and since Europe can be divided into colonizers and colonized, there is no doubt to which category a country like Finland belongs. Post-colonial theories thus do not apply only to the so-called "Third World" but also to highly developed countries that have been spiritually "colonialized" or trapped within a "colonialized imagination". It is my intention to prove that, to a great extent, Finnish culture finds itself in that situation.

Nationalism, too, can be interpreted in connection with colonialism or in relation to an imperial, subordinating center of power from which a smaller nation attempts to liberate itself. In doing so, nationalism underlines its own Otherness and distinctiveness by enlisting the aid of all possible discursive practices. Yet nationalism can also be the discourse of the colonizer when the latter is in an expansionist phase of occupation.

Colonialist models are essentially based on the opposition between dominant and dominated. Taking discursive practices captive, the dominants occupy the *langue* of communication while the dominated are permitted to produce new *parole*s only within specified limits. Thus the dominant/dominated categories are two subject positions as regards the *langue* and *parole* of a culture. Since *parole* consists of signifiers and signifieds, the only way to erase the aforementioned dominance relationship is to create radically new signifiers and signifieds that would "explode", so to speak, the colonialist scheme of communication.[1]

To take some concrete examples, colonialism is surely the right term for describing the cases of both Estonia and Finland. In Estonia the years 1944–1990 saw not so much the sovietisation of that society but rather its colonialisation. The Finns, however, believe that colonialism does not concern us, at least after 1917, the year Finland gained its independence. In fact, it has concerned and still concerns us. Patriotism is a reaction to colonialist ideology, which is distinctive, racist and essentialist. All representations of Finland in Russian art, for example, situate us in the colonialist and exotic category of Otherness, from the sorcerer in Glinka's *Russlan and Ludmilla* to Glazunov's *Finnish Rhapsody* and Solov'iev's

Saimaa poems. Finland is – and must be – viewed as *en dehors*, outside the Slavic cultural sphere proper. Yet patriotism always stems from colonialism, originating first as a justifiable striving for independence, as occurred in the Baltic countries at the beginning of the 1990s. Yet even when the real physical threat of colonialist suppression has withdrawn there remains an imagined post-colonial threat. An Anti-Subject is concocted because patriotism must always have one. Nationalism in all its forms is an ideology of distinction which determines itself as a subject (i.e., the people) in relation to something not-subject or anti-subject. Nothing threatens Finland physically, so where does this zeal for national distinction originate? The answer is, from inner uncertainty. A patriotism that serves to replace the lack of inner certainty is as dangerous as the colonialist-expansionist patriotism that seeks to impose its own culture on others. In Finnish neopatriotism, however, nationalism does not expand, but is rather a form of discourse that performs the function of pure autocommunication. Europe's present phase of "community" calls for an ethics of loyalty and solidarity (in the manner of Solov'iev and Josiah Royce). Instead, the turn has been toward an ethics of distinction. This is characteristic not only of Finland but of many other European countries as well.

The foregoing reflections have a place in a new theory under construction which I call *existential semiotics*. Iconic behaviour and the experiences of colonialism link my theory to social practices. For instance, the word "icon" in recent social usage refers to "cultural icons" who are persons or phenomena that have attained the status of "concepts" inasmuch as they have assumed a permanent place and signification in people's everyday thinking. The semiotic denotation of the term – as in Peirce's "icon" – has nothing to do with this meaning, except that one is perhaps easily inclined to identify oneself with icons. Nor does this new usage relate to icons as paintings, although the extremely sophisticated conventionality of visual icons, fixed as it is on certain rules, might also be a permanent feature of iconic behaviour. In what follows, however, I present my own theory on the formation of icons in the recent, popularized sense of the term, believing that the Sibelius cult might yield itself to study from this new perspective.

Keys to iconic behaviour

One way a dominated community can heighten its self-reliance, consciousness, and freedom from the dominant, is by means of semiotic formations called idols and icons. As noted above, the term icon must be understood here in its purely socio- or psychosemiotic context.

An icon is a sign-complex that provides the sound, body, smell, the identifying essence of something, an essence which one can neither name nor analyze. Therefore icons can be dangerous: in them one gives his/her "double", simulacrum, or *Doppelgänger* the right to speak for oneself. An icon acts as an emancipated, concretized "double":

Subject 1 (Ego) – Double/Icon – Subject 2 (Other)

The idea of "double" originates with Marcel Proust in the volume *The Prisoner* from the series *A la recherche du temps perdu* (*In Search of Times Past*). There the author presents his theory of "doubles" with whom we in fact communicate much more than with physically real persons.

Icons maintain their command over people precisely through the "doubles" that they pretend to be. That is why communication with icons is always reflexive, introverted, non-transcendental. The subject believes that in the icon his or her double is speaking, whereas the icon in reality is always the Other. It is the negative Other insofar as the subject does not realize that it is the Other but still wants to retain it as his/her own "double". The concept of a "double" is crucial to every social interaction. In some sense the double is a sign sent by the Other, but at the same time it is an image produced by the subject as a part of his/her psychic reality. To some extent the double is always "first" as the Other, but "second" when it is transmuted into a part of the Sameness of the subject.

The subject believes itself really to be dealing with the Other, although during the semiosis the double, the sign which was originally sent by the Other, becomes more and more a part of himself. Yet the original double always lurks in the background, threatening at any moment step to the fore and break the double created and nurtured in the subject's mind. The more the imagination of the subject becomes invested in the double, the stronger the double is iconised. In the end, the subject can no longer react to the Firstness of the Other. Although Elvis is dead, his fans believe he lives. When news of the death of Stalin, such an undeniable Anti-Subject, reached the prison camps, inmates broke into tears. Another example is the movie *Diva*, by the French film producer Beneix, which describes a young boy, a music lover, who worships an opera singer on the basis of her recordings and operatic roles. In some cases where the subject has itself become an icon, he starts to behave according to his own "double" – as did Sibelius.

Icons and idols are semiotic formations. They are doubles in which the dominated has knowingly and often with much respect and adoration abandoned him- or herself to the power of the dominant. This typically takes place as the imitation of the most ephemeral parts of the icon, such that these minutiae become more significant to the imitator than does the weightier conduct of the idolized figure. Very often an icon is somewhat "mythical" or unreachable, someone whose capabilities exceed those of the average person. One can nonetheless identify with the icon by imitating such relative trifles as his or her everyday mannerisms and routines. In Finland one hears numerous such anecdotes about Marechal Mannerheim and his mannerisms, which were considered signs of something exquisite – as is also true of many other national heroes, including Sibelius. It is characteristic of present-day media communication to magnify even the most trivial things into matters of great importance. Everyone wants to be a specialist in everything. Thus a dominant media must fashion the messages to suit those which it dominates. Control over the dominated can be sustained only if the dominant adapts itself to the world-view of the dominated.

Narratives about icons and idols may be classified as belonging to the folklore category of *legends*, which as a rule include some "miraculous" event. Legends can tell about the world of both benefactors and malefactors, and in them we also find anti-icons and anti-idols toward which we assume ambivalent attitudes. Even such negative types qualify as icons, and to follow their stories transports the reader, detaching him or her from everyday life with that horror mixed with admiration which we display in the face of the bizarre and the unusual.

Are icons in any way positive forces? Or is iconoclasm à la Roland Barthes always the right attitude to take? In the icon the subject escapes from existential responsibility and relinquishes his or her power of decision and rationality to someone else. Naturally there is pedagogical or educational iconism and idolatry. One learns by imitating a goal or an ideal with which one tries to identify iconically. Yet this process also necessarily involves a detachment from the icon, which occurs when the educational process is completed and the properties of the icon are shifted to the subject. In pedagogical iconism genuine communication takes place in the form of the student striving to reach the other (for example, a teacher) with which he or she wants to "meld". False iconism, however, such as that which occurs in the media, does not involve growth or aspirations toward true iconicity or the essential qualities thereof. Rather, it has to do with immediate identification that takes place without intellectual effort and without the existential input of a subject which is at the same time always emancipatory.[2] The genuine iconic process includes a kind of self-negation by making itself unnecessary. Teachers encounter this frequently when once-unquestioning pupils in time become aggressive opponents. And students often stop smiling and aiming to please when they realize that the teacher has power over them, especially if they receive unwanted pedagogical criticism.

The iconic relationship is thus one of power, and one might use the concept of an *iconeme* by which to describe such subordination and domination. But the matter has two sides: There is the iconised (*iconisé*), the one who believes in and strives for identification with the icon. And there is the iconising agent (*iconisant*), who acts so as to bring others into an iconising activity. It is essential to realize that the iconising agent might very well exercise power without even knowing it or wanting to do so. In semiotic terms, the iconisation process exercised by the *iconisant* does not necessarily include the modalities of "will" and "know". That process may instead function solely according to the modality of "can", or ability, which an icon might even enact unknowingly. The person or group that believes in the one iconised is always a willing subject; that is to say, they want the icon. It is also a believing subject, one who trusts in the icon. And most often it is a subject who "can"; that is to say, one who has the ability to reach the icon or the level of "can" and "know" which the icon represents. (But not always: there is also frustrated iconic behaviour and the iconoclasm that follows from it.) Sometimes the wanting subject, for example, a group, can pressure one into believing in its leader even though the individual subjects do not want to do so (as happens in totalitarian and authoritative communities). And there is the case of the not-knowing subject, that is, a person who does not even know that he or she has accepted the iconising relationship although behaving in accordance with it. It is the task of the semio-analyst to become conscious of iconising behaviour, to recognize and reveal it, whatever the consequences may be.

Iconising behaviour, whose apparent goal is to strengthen the subject, can in fact enfeeble it unless the subject becomes conscious of the fundamental unreachability of the icon's Otherness. As mentioned above, in the social field of *Dasein* icons often stem from nationalism. Congeneric, autocommunicative patriotism apparently strives to bolster national identity by means of flags and songs. But such patriotism only makes that identity weaker, finally destroying it from within. If nothing threatens the community, then where does such a reaction come from? In iconic behaviour one does not create meanings; one does not enter into signifying processes nor make semiotic acts. For this has already been done long ago, by the icon and the subject. Pavarotti performs in a stadium, for those who cannot sing. Congenial music has been created by the great composers of previous centuries, on whose iconisation most of contemporary music culture rests. Thus from the viewpoint of our subject, the iconising behaviour belongs to the category of event and not that of act.

Analysis of the Sibelius cult

The Finnish Sibelius cult started precisely at the first performance of the *Kullervo* Symphony in Solemnity Hall of the University of Helsinki in 1892. Despite the fact that this cult became an essential part of Finnish national history, it has received little systematic study, though some tentative efforts have been made in this direction. Among them was the project by Philip Donner and Juhani Similä on the analysis of Sibelius as an idol, in which the authors used a method developed by the Finnish folklorist Matti Kuusi (see Donner and Similä 1982:

33–49). According to Kuusi, "idols are wish figures, real or fictive, which personify what we dream, admire, appreciate, aspire, desire (or fear)" (quoted in Donner and Similä 1982: 18). The objective of Donner and Similä was not to break the Sibelius myth as such, but only to investigate the composer as an ethnomusicological and musico-cultural phenomenon, since "his personality accumulates the crucial values of Finnish art music". Yet their essay did not constitute a probative analysis but rather a general mapping of the phenomenon, as such sufficient to irritate, among others, Erik Tawaststjerna, who viewed the authors' work as an attack on his Sibelius biography. Donner and Similä's study suffered also from the scantiness and disparity of their material (which might have been compensated for by the presence of some integrating theoretical view).

Among later studies one finds Anni Heino's analysis of the public image of Sibelius as presented by Finnish newspapers, and Matti Huttunen's articles on Sibelius as a national figure in several articles. Naturally the monumental history of music in Finland by Dahlström, Heiniö, and Salmenhaara deals with this side of Sibelius. The centrality of Sibelius is undeniable, and therefore Volume 3 of the history, written by Erkki Salmenhaara, represents a story in which the central plot consists of the composer's various phases. Deviations into side plots occur, concerning things that took place between Sibelius's "heroic acts". The plot almost follows the narrative scheme by Claude Brémond, with the As in the diagram representing Sibelius's story:

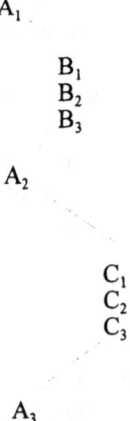

In the fourth volume, however, written by Mikko Heiniö, the principal narrative no longer focuses on Sibelius. The main protagonists are now other Finnish composers over which this central figure casts his "shadow". Heiniö uses this last term instead of the word "cult", tracing that shadow along three lines: first, Sibelius as the object of national reverence; second, the "shadow" of Sibelius; and third, the new Sibelius reception. The personality cult namely took another, more "figurative" form in the later Finnish Sibelius reception. At first people spoke about the immortal idea of the symphony, in which regard the dominated Finns directly adopted the canonized view of the dominant: the symphony was the summit of art music; it was absolute and hence of higher order than programmatic music; and it was based upon immortal suprahistoric thinking (Heinio 1997, vol. 4: 64). The "myth of the symphony" later turned into the myth of "organicism", which to date no one has analysed in detail. Particularly in the remarks of the Finnish "Pro-Sibelius", Joonas Kokkonen, the notion of organicism plays a central role and has even shifted to academic discussions about the musical texts themselves.Having sketched a brief history of the Sibelius cult in Finland, I next deal with the reception of the composer in verbal texts, both Finnish and foreign, that portray him as an icon and idol. These sources often do not include visual "texts", whose existence is laudably mentioned, however, by Donner and Similä. (Well-known is their analysis of a photograph that shows the baby Sibelius and his mother in a Madonna and child pose, made possible by the fact that the photo was retouched so as to remove Sibelius's sister from it!) We do find exciting visual iconisations, such as the painting by Eemu Myntti that represents Sibelius as Väinämöinen, in which the composer's features are blended with those of the ancient Finnish god.

In what follows, however, I draw on certain verbal "toposes" as found in texts dealing with Sibelius as an icon, examine them in the light of post-colonial musicology and semiotics, and end by offering some ideas as to how new signifiers can be revealed behind these icons, signifiers that hopefully can liberate us from dominant/dominated relationships.

Sibelius icons in Finland

Typical expressions of Sibelius iconisation can be found in texts by Sulho Ranta, Martti Similä, Ilmari Krohn, and other contemporaries. It is crucial to see the icons in the dialectics of the categories Sameness/Otherness. Who are the "we" of music and arts, and who are the "others"? Sulho Ranta, the Finnish composer, a fervent, European-minded modernist in the 1920s, writes on Sibelius's birthday in 1945 in a style that is understandable in the context of that memorial event:"We Finns are always aware of the greatness of Sibelius as the national composer... we understand as well his breadth as a composer, his universal view that recognizes no limits. Yet only the Finnish Sibelius is our Sibelius" (Ranta 1946: 11). In terms of what we understood above by the *langue* and *parole* of music, Ranta elsewhere recognizes that *parole* can only with great difficulty become a new *langue*. The dominated does not alter its subordinate position by creative acts solely within the framework of the dominant *langue*. Ranta writes about the difficulty of penetrating to the area of *langue*; as is typical of him, he underlines the nationality of the dominated:"Every nation, every country sees the great men of its art mostly as national artists and fighters... Nevertheless, the domains of the great arts are limitless... Shakespeare, Goethe and Beethoven are great world citizens of art... Purely national art... does not easily become such a common property. Such an art has its own atmosphere, in which it grows in the easiest way and breathes most naturally. Yet even it has... possibilities of being accepted in very broad areas." (Ranta 1946: 13) So Ranta wrote in his essay, "Jean Sibelius as a European and Global Phenomenon". The life of the composer-hero follows a certain narrative scheme in which the initial phase is constituted by the assumption of the dominant *langue*; the second phase is the production of one's own *parole* within its limits; and the last phase the creation of one's own *langue*. These phases can be found in the following words of Ranta: First, "those seeds which were rooted in Sibelius's mind during his student time... bore fruit only later". Second, "Fifty years ago Finland needed a Finnish composer, and Sibelius knew his place... the result was Finnish, national art". Third, "Only when we had been able to show Europe that the distant Finland is a country that has its own culture, only then could even Sibelius get relief [from bearing the national standard], sink his thoughts inward, and let the goals of his art carry him still further away".

In Ranta's text the most crucial act of the hero-idol is seen as the legitimizing of his home country ("only when we had been able to show") to the Other, which is of course Europe. Throughout the entire text Europe appears as the Other of the Finns – the Other which determines what is valuable and what is not. On the other hand, the acceptance of the German view of culture as innate Spirit (*Geist*), as a matter of inwardness (*Innigkeit*), is revealed by the statement that the new *langue* emerges only from a sinking into oneself (on *Innigkeit*, see especially Taruskin 1997: 251). The new *langue* is not created by means of external activities such as manifestoes, schools, or outwardly dramatic acts, but by a turning or looking inward. In semiotic terms, the modality of "appearing" of the art is subordinated to that of its "being".

Ranta later returns to the idea of the "symphony" in the twentieth century (his references to gender are of course intended neutrally): "Those men, who really wrote symphonies did them as symphonists, certainly as perspicacious, struggling composers. They did not listen to the fashionable sounds of the new music; by 'they' I mean of course Jean Sibelius and Carl Nielsen, who were independent." (Ranta 1946: 248)

We could in this context complete the classification of idols by Matti Kuusi, adding to it the category of the "fighter" and "inner seer", which perhaps merges with Kuusi's type 1, the creator and pioneer; type 3, messiah but not martyr; and type 6, the skillful artist. This idol hero distinguishes himself by the symphony, which "did not die, but it was the property of only a few". Only certain iconic figures can ably compose symphonies. For if the "symphony is of all the forms of composition the highest, the most expressive, durable and extensive, it is also the most demanding and frightening" (Ranta 1946: 248–250).

Another kind of topos is formed by personal meetings with the iconised figure, when even the slightest signifiers convey the gigantic signified of the icon. Such was the case with Ranta, but more particularly with Martti Similä in his *Sibeliana*, published in 1945. In that book, every statement by the composer takes on enormous proportions, along with his every gesture and expression. Similä was a pianist and conductor who was very devoted to Sibelius's music. When he played his piano sonata (perhaps somewhat overdramatically) at Sibelius's home in Ainola, the master looked keenly at him and said: "I wonder whether you understand me when I say that my style is ascetic". The story continues:"We sipped mocha and smoked our Havanas in all quietness. Then suddenly, almost as if mid-thought, [Sibelius] stood up and walked vehemently, sometimes from one corner of the room to the other. This was truly not the jovial pondering of an old priest. No, like a lion did he step." (Similä 1945: 36)Similä spins out the mythologisation of Sibelius's music with a type of discourse that was very common at that time: "As the background of his seven symphonies there is the deserted nature of the North, and at the same time an austere and mild, autumnal grey, or the reflections of the calm beauty of a summer day. In the first and second, and even in the third symphony, from this soil arises the heroic figure of the young master-composer, in the first two [symphonies] as strong, in the third already much acquiesced, and in its final hymn, one might say, in the serenity of antiquity." (Similä op. cit.: 19)Similä had no doubt that the hero of the symphony was the composer himself. Such a view was not only the main content of popular texts such as his, but also that of scientific discourse. This is well illustrated by the analyses of Ilmari Krohn.

Krohn was a composer and musicologist, the first to hold the chair of musicology at the University of Helsinki. His study on *Der Stimmungsgehalt der Symphonien von Jean Sibelius* (1945) can be interpreted in the light of both colonialism and iconisation. Krohn experiences the Second Symphony in particular as depicting Finland's struggle for independence and proposes that it be called the *Finlandia* or the *Suomi* symphony. When dealing with motifs and tone colours – i.e., the musical signifiers – he determines as their main content or signified the political fight in which "the Russian dominant power tried to deprive Finland of its autonomy and free cultural development". In Krohn's view, the symphony predicts the liberation of the fatherland with the help of German brothers-in-arms. For Krohn, music thus has the ability to forecast social events, a view nowadays held by many (for one example, see Jacques Attali's 1985 book, *Noise*). Krohn says that "the main key of D major corresponds to this view. As the dominant of the dominant it represents higher activity, and its symbolic colour fits well with the expression, which depicts the fervent patriotism." He thus views the musical signifiers as if they existed in a ready-made framework. Krohn elsewhere compares the Second symphony to the First, noting that when Sibelius adopts the necessary compositional technique – the *langue*, as we could say – then the difference in his subsequent symphonies must appear on the level of the contents – or in the *parole*. Every master achieves more certainty in the technical sense by mastering the *langue*. The better he can handle it, the less effort the work of composition requires. In the end, the composer acquires a coherent unity of idea and form.

In Krohn's writings there is no doubt about what constitutes the *langue* of music, which he describes in his monumental treatise on musical form (1911–1937). Musical *langue*, in his view, is a neutral way to express ideological and aesthetic ideas. On the level of these ideas he takes an anticolonialist stance. But when he reduces the Sibelian text to a Wagnerian leitmotif table and a straightjacket of strictly metrical analysis, he is taking a very "Germanic" attitude. In other words, what he wins in content, the level of the signified, he loses elsewhere, on the level his own discourse. Thus Krohn's logic follows that of the musical dominant or hegemony despite his efforts to be an anticolonialist. This impression is intensified by his dry, Germanic style of writing that allows no intuitive flights of fantasy. The very unfolding of the analysis in his writing (or as the French put it, his *écriture*) – that alone and in itself constitutes the taking of a certain position or standpoint. The deconstructionists have taught us to read musicological analyses, as well as verbal texts, in this way. Krohn's analysis of the Second Symphony culminates in a diagram in which every theme and section of the symphony is provided with its "signified":"Introduction: *treues Tagewerk der tiefen Volksschichten (Strebemotiv);* the main phrase: *Fremde Kultur der Oberschicht (Ziermotiv und Blütemotiv)*; transition: *vereinigende Liebe zum Vaterland (Mahnmotiv und Vaterlandsmotiv);* subordinate theme: national awakening (*Weckrufmotiv und Funkenmotiv)*... Development: awakening of the national consciousness (*Aufbruchsotiv)* into the diligent striving in all disciplines of the cultural life", etc. (Krohn 1945: 207)

In contrast, some texts seem in retrospect to be completely free from the iconisation of their object although they were interpreted as such in their time. One of them is Bengt von Törne's *Sibelius: A Close Up,* published in English in 1937. Törne's work sparked one of the most (in)famous anti-iconisations of Sibelius, Theodor Adorno's *Glosse über Sibelius* (1938). What in von Törne's tiny book could have prompted Adorno's enormous rage? For indeed, Törne's account was written in an amazingly objective style as compared to the overtly mythologizing texts on the subject by other Finns. The book reports on encounters between von Törne and Sibelius, and these meetings do not contain more idolizing than one generally finds in those between a young composer and older maestro. Von Törne writes:"I had the unique opportunity to be in touch with a man from which at every moment radiated the influence of a great genius. But in Sibelius there is not a trace of the constraint of the great figures in the tragedies by Corneille or Racine. He is rather related to the heroes of Shakespeare: at the same time human, great and humorous." (von Törne 1965: 93)

One of Adorno's main arguments was directed against the notion that Sibelius's closeness to nature could directly dictate his style of composing. Here Adorno echoed politically backward ideas in the Germany of the 1930s. According to the musical progressivists, music could by no means be based on any return to "nature", since in music even nature is negated by culture as a *zweite Vermittlung*, or form of mediation. When von Törne coming from the Baltic sea depicted landscapes upon his arrival in Finland, Sibelius answered him: "And when we see those granite rocks, we know why we can deal with the orchestra as we do" (op. cit.: 90). This statement seemed to be transmuted into an iconising form in the obituary by Yrjö Kilpinen: "So is Jean Sibelius's life-work like a mighty lighthouse standing on the solid granite rock of Finland, a lighthouse whose bright radiance is seen everywhere in the world" (*Uusi Suomi*, 1 October 1957). (It is sad, in a way, that Adorno's reasoning in this instance comes close to the position of semiotics, in the sense that cultural texts are always arbitrary and conventional "social constructions" that cannot be based upon or justified by appeals to a "nature" that motivates compositions in a directly indexical way. The fault lies in the fact that Adorno uses his Hegelian-semiotic logic in a tendentious way, in the manner of the dominant, as did his ideal composer, Schoenberg. Adorno did not accept that for any composer, even Stravinsky, nature could form the source of aesthetics. In his shortsighted conjectures about aesthetics Adorno proves himself to be an adherent of colonialist discourse though his persuasive rhetorical style often conceals this fact.)

What probably irritated Adorno even more was Sibelius's judgements about those other "gods", Richard Wagner and Gustav Mahler, which had been canonized by the German musical hegemony. Von Törne says this about Mahler: "He clearly aspired to broad epic vision, and his intentions are supported by an irreproachable technical skill and experience. Yet all these great properties do not benefit him at all since in these gigantic works there is no life, since they have been written without inspiration" (von Törne 1965: 68). Von Törne quotes Sibelius's criticisms of Wagner's heavy-handed rhetorical style, himself adding that there is in music nothing further removed from the character of Sibelius than Wagner's overloaded baroque. "Sibelius's personal aversion against him was multiplied by the conviction that the influence of this master and his school on music history had been completely devastating" (von Törne 1965: 53). Sibelius even said, according to von Törne, that "Wagner reminds one of his earlier friend, then enemy, Nietzsche, who always gives the impression of being a servant elevated to a baron." (From these anti-Wagner statements of Sibelius one might have anticipated a good deal of the later negative Wagner reception in Finland. Many composers saw it as their duty to take the same position as Sibelius (see, e.g., Kokkonen's writings). Even the third volume of *Music History in Finland* provides the picture of Wagner with the following text: "Wagner fever was a disease from which only a few musicians of the turn of century were spared. Likewise Sibelius had his own Wagner crisis." (Salmenhaara 1997: 98)

The real value of von Törne's book lies in the small observations he makes concerning the signifiers of Sibelius's music, especially the composer's orchestrations and tone colours. The author claims that Sibelius's great merit was to create so-called "Nordic" instrumentation. To von Törne, this had nothing in common with a "search for dark Wagnerian colours". Rather, the pale darkness that unites one day with the next had through Sibelius gained its expression in Nordic music. The accompanying score examples lend a ring of authority to von Törne's discourse.[3] They exhibit those new sound colours and timbres which Sibelius had invented, though in some ways they may be seen to echo Wagnerisms; for instance, the intriguing dark tone colour in the First Symphony that sounds in the low register of the oboes and clarinets (von Törne: 114). On the other hand, this passage also evokes the *Romeo and Juliet* of Tchaikovsky, a connection further underlined in the performance by the Lahti Symphony Orchestra under the direction of Osmo Vänskä, who requires that an unprecedented exactness be given these musical signifiers.

Sibelius as seen by others

In Finland it was believed that, after René Leibowitz's article, "Jean Sibelius, le plus mauvais compositeur du monde", all French reception of the composer would have followed along the lines of Adornian, pro-serialist (anti-tonalist) critique. Yet this was not the case, as proven by articles published in France even before Leibowitz's in France.[4]

As early as 1954 Jacques Lonchampt wrote in the *Journal Musical Français* a positive report on "Jean Sibelius et la solitude". To his mind Sibelius's music had remained too long in obscurity in France, unlike in England or Scandinavia where the composer's music was well-known. (In turn, another French historian, Paul Collaer, interpreted this predilection of the English as a sign of their bad taste.) Lonchampt considered Sibelius's symphonies mystical and impressive, thoroughly Finnish, but not in any descriptive sense. He remarks that if to French ears Sibelius's music sounds almost contemporary, it in fact dates from the turn of the century. Lonchampt particularly emphasizes the importance of the Fourth Symphony, which for him fulfills the universal values of the musical "dominant": "*Ce qui frappe dès que l'on est parvenu à se familiariser avec l'extraordinaire langage de la 4ème symphonie, c'est la prodigieuse concentration de la pensée.*" [What is striking, as soon as one has grown comfortable with the quite extraordinary language of the Fourth Symphony, is the prodigious concentration of thought.]

Precisely the same opinion surfaces five years later, when Pierre Vidal writes in the same journal about the Sibelius festival in Helsinki (Vidal 1959). Vidal first quotes the iconising statement of a Sibelius biographer who called the composer a magician who received his inspiration from his connection to the forces of nature. At the same time Vidal remarks that this statement only emphasizes the fact that one should not always imagine Finland's forests and lakes when listening to Sibelius's music, because geographical location does not matter when the musician's expression reaches the sublime. Vidal thus clearly takes an anticolonial view, even admitting that Sibelius was able to create a new musical *langue*: "He has forged his own language, and every work is a new problem to him. His overwhelming national popularity has never led him to make any concessions to public taste as far as his own aesthetic development was concerned. This development was a long journey on the way towards the ideal of beauty and classical completeness, which he fully obtained in those works whose admiring inheriters we are."Here the voice of one central dominant, France, is speaking, and it wholeheartedly accepts Sibelius expressly on the level of *langue* as a composer who must be evaluated by the same universal criteria of rationality as any other European composer.

In September of 1955 Jacques Lonchampt published another long article in the aforementioned journal about the Sibelius festival in Helsinki, and again we find no trace of a colonializing attitude in the text. However, the graphic artist of the journal, André Lebon, provided the article with a cartoon that depicted Sibelius as a young and old hero among other heroes from *Kalevala*, as if the composer were a mythical figure of the same dimension. In the humorous pictures Väinämöinen is shown carrying Finland's flag behind the young Sibelius, then he is chasing Aino, Lemminkäinen is shooting an elk, and finally Kullervo is pictured shepherding lambs in the courtyard of Ainola where the aged maestro is sitting with a top hat on his head and a stick in his hand. The cartoon portrays Finland as an exotic Otherness for which the verbal text gives no basis.

Eero Tarasti

Figure 1. (*Journal Musical Français* 29.9.1955.)

Leaving Europe behind, we find one of the most interesting chapters in the history of the Sibelius cult to be his reception in the United States, about which Otto Andersson published a book, *Jean Sibelius i Amerika* (Andersson 1960). It is known that Sibelius visited the Norfolk festival in 1914 and during the same journey received an honorary doctorate from Yale University. The critiques and reviews collected by Andersson show to what extent the rise of the Sibelius cult in the United States was dependent on the work of certain conductors.

Even so, the reception of Sibelius in America was not unanimously positive at the beginning. When in 1904 Wilhelm Gericke conducted the Second Symphony in Chicago, one critic had this to say: "In any case the symphony is thoroughly boring and austere, there is not that passionate melancholy typical of Tchaikovsky's music, but it is rather gloomy and repressive."[5] Philip Hale, who wrote abundantly about Sibelius in the *Boston Herald* newspaper, wondered whether the boring austerity of the symphony was due to the "local colour" of Finland or to the emotional life of the composer (Andersson 1960: 14). In the *Boston Journal* one read that "the symphony belongs to a lonely, distant, original country and that it manifests the impact of austere lakes, deep forests and deserted hills". Even for America the nature topos drew the central arguments, either for acceptance or rejection. Philip Hale wrote the following in the *Herald Tribune*:"Sibelius's music if of his own country. It evokes lonely meadows, storm-driven firs, wild sounds, which lonely wanderers hear far away from habitation, bitter defiance and agitated struggle. Even if there sometimes occur joyful moments, they are but coarse jests and suddenly the knives are revealed. Yet in this savage music there is also something feminine and lovely. The softer passages express moderate complaint or silent whispering: one hears the sounds as forecasting a war."

The Americans had the ability to step outside the European dominant/dominated dichotomies, as shows the critique of Louis C. Elson after the performance of the First Symphony in 1907 under the direction of conductor Karl Muck who had moved from Berlin to Boston. Elson namely argued that leadership in orchestral music had shifted clearly to the North. The Russians, Norwegians, and Finns seemed to have something to say, whereas the Germans and the French had abandoned themselves to the search for rare modulations and dissonances.

Not all American texts about Sibelius contain competent musical judgements, however. Some reveal a dilettantish competency in the cultural semiotic sense by their foregrounding of hidden stereotypes. When the *Scènes historiques* were conducted by Adolf Tandler in Los Angeles, the program notes gave the following information about Finland:"Sibelius's music is incomprehensible for the one who does not know Finnish history and its strange mythology. The Finns are a mixture of Mongols and Western racial elements. From the West they have received power and self-reliance, from the East slowness and mysticism. Finnish music, like the Finnish character, is the result of a painful struggle against harsh natural conditions, a life or death fight, which ends with the jubilant triumphs of life. They move and think slowly, and they do not have much sense of humour. It is harder for them to understand a pun than it is for the Englishmen or the Scottish; in spite of this they sing; there is singing everywhere, and also dancing. But the song is plaintive and the dance lacks joy. They both express the sorrow that rests upon Finland. This is true of Sibelius's music as well..." (quoted in Andersson 1960: 45.) In this racist and essentialist form of colonializing discourse, Sibelius is depicted as something that expresses the national character and race, not as an independent composer or man in his own right. Naturally the Americans were influenced by the scant English literature on Sibelius, such as the work of Rosa Newmarch, who viewed the composer as the product of two cultures, one of which lay in the distant past – obviously in Finnish mythology – and the other being modern European culture (ibid.: 47). Sibelius was thus not conceived as European in the same way as its "proper" musical masters, but as something strange and thus also fascinating.

The nature of Sibelius criticism in the United States later changed as the image of the *Kalevala* receded into the background. As Otto Andersson says, attention turned toward the "universal features" of Sibelius. The aforementioned Philip Hale, who had started his criticism along those same lines, wrote after the performance of the Seventh Symphony: "Sibelius would probably have written in the Sibelian style whether he had lived in Rome, Paris or Chicago" (ibid.: 110). Another critic thought that Sibelius's originality did not lie in the fact that he was born and lived in Finland, but in "the mystic human quality, which can be called phantasy [or] congeniality".

These qualities, musical signifiers in all their immediacy, spurred a re-evaluation of Sibelius's music. As noted at the start of this essay, my theory of post-colonial discourse proposes that this is an avenue whereby the dominated can overcome its subordinate position and find a new *parole* or even a new *langue*. The critics with the best ears could correctly "read" these signifiers. Among them was Olin Downes (1886–1995), music critic for the *New York Times*, who has been studied exhaustively by Glenda Dawn Goss in her treatise, *Jean Sibelius and Olin Downes: Music, Friendship, Criticism* (1995).

Downes gloriously represents the first post-colonial music critics (which attitude was also reflected in his judgements about Villa-Lobos, though the analytic depth of those latter writings did not extend so deeply as his writings about Sibelius). Downes's evaluations are colourful because he applies to Sibelius an array of categories and criteria, some of which are even opposed to each other, as one may expect according to the works in question and the various places and times the critic heard them. Among his categories we find the following, taken from the 1945 Finnish version of his book on Sibelius:

1) *Truth*. Downes says: "I dare to believe… that I was permitted – as early as when I had much less experience than today – to see a part of that unwavering truth and to feel the force of eternity, which is in Sibelius's music" (Downes 1945: 18). Thus Downes experiences the composer's music as "true speech", an expression used at the same time by the Russian musicologist, Boris Asafiev. However, the essential nuance of Downes's statement is the relation of Sibelius's music to the category of timelessness. Whereas music in general is only an insignificant piping amidst the noise of the age, some of it can touch truth via the sensibility of our instinct, thinks Downes. Truth is an instinctive, intuitive category, not a rational one. Thus Downes' statement would in fact be an iconisation of Sibelius insofar as it makes reference to the irrational category of truth, yet it does so completely outside the national, colonial position.

2) *The Tragic*. Downes writes the following about the First Symphony: "I felt the pulse of the primal forces full of life; I heard the voice which had faded away from all contemporary music; I felt the grasp of the tragic, which is felt in every

artistic creation, that tragedy which is an essential ingredient of life and of its ending, [the end] of all human destinies" (1945: 21). The tragic quality of Sibelius is therefore not that of an individual people and its representative, but tragedy in the Aristotelian form handed down by Western aesthetics. Accordingly, Sibelius's music can be assessed according to the aesthetic categories of Western culture, thus taking part in the sphere of Sameness.

3) *Instinctiveness*. Downes compares Sibelius to a beast: "To my mind you are reminiscent of an animal". He then says, "I conceived that he listens with the still unspoiled ears and genuine instinct of an animal ... he is able to find combinations with which he conveys to us these sounds in all their purity" (ibid.: 32). This statement could be considered an essentialist exploitation of the myth of the Noble Savage, for in it Sibelius is placed outside Western rationality, into the category of the natural or the instinctive. One variant of this category is the appearance of race in Sibelius's music, which in Downes's view is a positive feature: "He has been able to interpret the obvious ... racial marks in a way that has made specialists rank him as the next great symphonist after Brahms and Beethoven." Interestingly, Downes did not see the appearance of race and the continuation of the *langue* as mutually exclusive, as they were usually seen in European colonial discourse. Here emerges what is perhaps a typically American viewpoint: freed from the heavy load of tradition it can combine things in the most surprising ways and by doing so also find something really new.

4) *Stimmung*. A crucial notion in Heidegger's existential analysis, this is Downes's new category. Like the ambiguous German term itself (variously defined as "mood", "tuning", "voice"), *Stimmung* cannot be reduced to a particular feature in the work, but is present everywhere in the music: "The most successful traits of the First Symphony are its freshness, energy and irresistible force, and above all *Stimmung*... This *Stimmung* is felt in the symphony to such an extent that, although the work might not contain one original bar, it would nonetheless declare the arrival of a new gigantic figure to the arena of music" (ibid.: 57).

5) *Masculinity*. As early as the First Symphony this category appears: "A man has spoken there, who has said everything he had to say, and who knows that further persuasion would be useless and vain". And Downes says this about the Second Symphony: "This is the true symphony, written by a true man, a man who has the entire North behind him". The category of masculine virility, which appears, among other places, in Wagner (though to a lesser extent than one might suppose), also forms part of Sibelian aesthetics. It shows up quite clearly, for example, in the *Jägermarch* and at the beginning of the third movement of *Kullervo*, in the austere sound of the male choir. Also the end of the Finale of the Violin Concerto, when the violin scurries up and down on a chromatic scale,

evokes for Downes the "call of an ancient raging war hero". And the Third Symphony should have a "manly and direct interpretation" (ibid.: 72). On the other hand, Downes resorts to an anti-gender critique when he describes *Tapiola* as heroic yet at the same time devoid of eroticism.

6) *The Rhapsodic*. Concerning the Violin Concerto, Downes states: "Although Sibelius follows a strict form, he is yet rhapsodic, like an ancient bard... The extensive cadences emphasize and enrich the rhapsodic nature of the music" (ibid.: 70). In an astounding way Sibelius could thus be joined to that category of rhapsody which Vladimir Jankélévitch, while opposing the myth of organism and symphonic ideals of the German romanticism, held as one important form in Liszt, Albeniz, Debussy and other estimable composers.

7) *Communality*. "It is music for people and nation and not only for specialists and critics." It is noteworthy that here communality does not mean, say, the Finns as a nation, but rather Everyman, the average music listener, who by his solidarity with the community understands music's ability to appeal to anyone. This is of course also the shortest way to iconicity and idolisation.

8) *Loneliness*. As the near opposite of the previous category, a metamorphosis takes place in Sibelius's later symphonies such that the composer seems detached from the communality in the sense that he is no longer writing music of "the memory of the ancestors". "He looks deeply into his innermost self. He thinks and speaks aloud in all his solitude" (ibid.: 80). Discussing the Fourth Symphony, Downes speaks about the "absolute loneliness of the soul". To his mind, in that symphony Sibelius is not having a dialogue with an implied listener but is simply thinking aloud: "If the listener does not like it, then so be it". Sibelius has withdrawn into what is called in semiotic terms the "idiolect", that individualizing element of the artist who strives to be innovative within given style constraints, and which must often be interpreted as breaking away from the *langue* represented by the dominant. This view of Sibelius's "loneliness" in music history is one of the leading themes in Downes. In his criticism of Cecil Gray's book on Sibelius, Downes states that Sibelius does not conform to any traditional mould of a composer: "He has absolutely nothing in common with any of his contemporaries ... he is in reality not in any relationship with any other composer, living or dead" (ibid.: 153). Therefore the ordinary comparative devices do not fit in his case.

9) *Anticolonialism*. Downes admits that one hears in Sibelius's music the spirit of perpetual rebellion, but states that many consider it only the result of national conditions. This he considers a mistake, since Sibelius extends far beyond local patriotism: "In Sibelius the whole North rages against this dwarfish Lilliputian race and age. He is not the prophet of one country, but of the entire world, and he fights for all those who cannot forget where they have come from" (ibid.: 149). In

this way Sibelius represents precisely that voice of the subaltern, which has been repressed by colonial discourse.

It is true that Downes relates Sibelius to the power centers of European music, but only as their negation: "Without saying anything about Schoenberg or Stravinsky ... Sibelius continues the shaping of his own, deeply fresh and inimitable style... It achieves what Paris and Vienna have been chattering and reasoning about: purely musical discourse, in which there is no romantic dross nor oversaturation of colour" (ibid.: 103). Downes states ironically that Sibelius "was educated with German harmony and orchestration – a good education as such, if it does not kill" (ibid.: 52).

10) *Phenomenal Qualities*. Downes could represent verbally that aspect of Sibelius's music upon which its rebellious content is based; namely, the new qualities of the signifiers that as yet had no pre-established signified. Roland Barthes emphasized in his descriptions of music that "Only the metaphor is exact". Here one might add: not just any metaphor, as Downes seemed to understand.

For instance, the metaphor of colour forms a central category in his analyses. He writes about *En Saga*: "Listen to the strange orchestral colours! Timpani ... are absent. The distant rumble of the big drum and the vibrating figures of the violins, dividing and further dividing among themselves, make the dimness sink down over everything, a dimness through which the flute or the flashing horn penetrates for a while. An immensely heavy motif rises out of the darkness. The instruments ruminate gloomily. They start to grumble and rumble." The variety of metaphors in Downes's descriptions is both apt and multi-faceted. Here, for example, he describes the Second Symphony: "In the first movement bright colour changes take place, particularly when the recapitulation starts. The orchestra becomes transparent, some instruments are trilling, it seems as if the sun might appear between the clouds" (ibid.: 63). Sometimes he also names the colours, as when portraying the end of the Fourth Symphony: "The strings play A-minor chords more and more quietly, ever more grey, until the music has faded away like a seagull in the dusky sky."

It is crucial to note that Downes' descriptions, though couched in extremely figurative language, are not impressionistic criticism in the ordinary sense of the word. Behind them stand quite clear musical concepts, and aesthetic categories and positions.

The Musical Signifiers

In many respects, Downes was as a precursor of semiotic music analysis. He does not describe musical signifiers in traditional syntactic terms, since that would reduce the music's essential qualities to some dominant *langue* on the discoursive level. Instead he describes with amazing exactitude the phenomenal qualities of music. In what follows we extend Downes's analysis with further categories, some of which appear in his own texts, but amplified here with further argument.

To examine Sibelius as an object of post-colonial musicology, one must first examine what immediate qualities of Firstness his music contains and what kind of metaphors it spontaneously evokes. On this Firstness level such signifiers would be the gestures in themselves. As such they have not yet been sublimated to serve "spiritual" – read: colonialised – discourse in the Adornian sense (for colonial discourse has given itself the right to define what is spiritual, profound, beautiful or generally "universal" in art). Gestures in music are always to some extent corporeal. What kind of body, then, speaks in Sibelius's music? Is it a virile, Wagnerian body? Or is it an androgynous one, inclined to Nordic melancholy and Arctic hysteria? Certainly it is often a relatively heavily-moving, often cumbrous body, with rare flashes of quick motion. Joseph Gingold, the famous violin professor, has spoken about the "brooding quality" in Sibelius, but adding that it was a noble, sublime brooding. Excessive repetition that approaches the persuasive powers of incantation forms one of the most constant features of Sibelius's music. Leo Normet uses the term "driving force" to describe this trait, which could of course be determined also as but one variant of desire. Normet also finds an "arabesque" quality in Sibelius's music, which links it to another artistic phenomenon of the time, *art nouveau*. Moreover, Sibelius's music transforms itself over time, particularly in his symphonies, becoming more and more of a linear art, a "linear counterpoint" (and precisely during those years when musicologist Ernst Kurth coined the term).

Although the term comes from the visual arts, *chiaroscuro*, or the play of light and darkness, is another phenomenal quality of Sibelius's music. For instance, the sound of the violins in the upper register in the *Andante festivo* allows them to be recognized immediately as a kind of "Lohengrin sound". This is a cultural unit in Western art music and at the same time an immediately experienced quality, a Firstness, which penetrates our senses with unquestionable certainty. Likewise, darkness has its place in Sibelius's music, as one hears, among other places, in the brooding timbre of the opening of *Kullervo* and the overall dark sonority of the Fourth Symphony.

To the light/dark opposition we can add the category of lightness/heaviness. Sibelius's music is seldom light in the sense of playing with ambivalencies, parody, irony and the grotesque. The signifiers of his music represent what they stand for in an amazingly univocal way. Sibelius did not listen to the advice of Hugo von Hoffmansthal's countess in in *Der Rosenkavalier*: "*Leicht muss man sein / Mit leichten Händen nehmen und halten, halten und lassen / und wer nicht so sind, den straft das Leben*". [One has to be light / With light hands take and keep, keep and leave / and who are not such, they are punished by life]. The composer's skill was of course put to the test of lighter salon music, but even there his specialty was the Valse *triste* and other toposes of death (Lemminkäinen in *Tuonela*, *The Swan* of Tuonela, The Death of Melisande, and other programs). Yet Sibelius's texture is not always heavy, despite the eternally sounding tremolando. Enacting Ruskinian ideas of power, Sibelius's themes rise up and surge forward, always meeting heavy resistance, their final elevation and dispersal always earned by a previous struggle now sanctified by a reward. To speak in such terms leads us "naturally" to another category of Sibelius's music, that of desire.

So well conceptualised by recent gender analysis, desire is a directly experienced quality of music. In Sibelius's works one clearly feels this quality in the actorial "desires" of his themes. In some cases Sibelius tags his discourse with masculine virility, sometimes again with feminine "softness". In all studied opinions his first symphonies contain "Tchaikovskian" topics, which in recent research have been linked expressly to the description of the history of desire.[6] But in Sibelius desire is also neutralised by a sublimation that transmutes it into something else altogether. If one takes as the signifier of musical desire the inner indexicality of the discourse – that is, the marked impression of continuity, forward motion, striving, tension and release – then one should add to it the presence of a certain iconic gesturality.[7]

Sibelius produces a musical discourse in which desire appears as a marked quality. But he also includes its neutralisation – not the straightforward repression of desire, but areas that stymy, freeze, depersonalize and deactorialize it. In the *Swan of Tuonela*, for instance, the English horn appears "neutrally", without the original feminine-erotic connotations it has in Berlioz's music (this is almost analogous to the linguistic fact that the Finnish language has only one word, *hän*, to indicate both he and she, *il* and *elle*, or *er* and *sie*).

The neutralisation of the subject of desire in Sibelius's music appears together with the phenomenal category of presence/absence. His music often gives the impression of a bare landscape without a living soul on it, as at the beginning of the Violin Concerto. A certain gender neutrality also becomes more pronounced in the Sibelian discourse the further we go in his output. The category of desire manifests itself according to euphoric/dysphoric aspectual semes that are especially noticeable in the shift from dysphoria to euphoria, as occurs in the simple but effective narrative program of *Finlandia*. Naturally euphoria is indicated by a softness of sound, rhythmic regularity in the corporeal sense, the avoidance in all musical parameters of abrupt or sudden contrasts. Dysphoria is represented by all the dissonant elements and by everything that aspectually overloads the musical signifiers. While this category often glides by unnoticed on a more sophisticated or "rational" level, it is also a phenomenon to be experienced as Firstness.

Conclusion

In sum, Sibelius's musical signifiers – and indeed, all signifiers – constitute a store from which the dominant discourse chooses those that support its arguments. All the signifiers may serve as material for the dominant in its inexorable striving for mastery. Often this mechanism is so subtle that it demands a particularly careful and revealing reading. The dominant selects those features that are contrary to its own criteria of Sameness, which, given the privileged position of the dominant, are taken to be universal criteria.[8] What is really the "same" in the dominated, according to the criteria of the dominant, is foregrounded as a sign of the expansion of the categories of the "same" of the dominant. The attitude obtained is something like, "My, my, (s)he attained that level, even though (s)he represents an external, non-cultural Otherness." On the other hand, the admission of a certain degree of Sameness, such as the acceptance of Sibelius by music historians as having the same status as other great symphonists, is also a proof of the applicability of one's own criteria even outside the boundaries of Sameness, a proof of the continuation of one's own "tonosphere" outside its proper limits. The dominant can always say, "The best of 'them' have almost reached the level of what we take as the norm in our own music." Unfortunately the history of music, art, and culture in a history of exclusion.

Yet when the dominant wishes to deny access to its sanctuary to any of the dominated who aspire to enter, then it looks to find those signifiers of *parole* that do not fit with the *langue* but rather which break from it. These signifiers may be greatly admired by the dominant, which focuses on their great originality and uniqueness. But at the same time this kind of admiration guarantees their exclusion from the "Pantheon" as exotic peculiarities. Such errant musical signifiers can satisfy the consumer's need for variety and novelty, but for this very same reason they cannot represent the discourse of Power and Sameness.

Notes

1. I deal at length with problems of disrupting colonialist schemes of communication in my forthcoming book, *The Enchanted Signs* (Indiana University Press).
2. The notion of "intellectual effort" comes from Henri Bergson. I am indebted to Kristian Bankov for calling my attention to this connection.
3. In a discussion with Erik T. Tawaststjerna, Tawaststjerna's son, he, however, denied von Törne's biographical statements about Sibelius by characterizing them as the ramblings of an old and talkative story-teller. Yet von Törne, at least in his earlier writings, was a serious music aesthetician and composer.
4. I am indebted to the Parisian musicologist Pierre Vidal for bringing to my attention certain articles on Sibelius written in France during the early part of this century.

5. I have not been able to find the original articles. Therefore all the translations into English from the books by Andersson and Downes published in Finnish are my own.
6. On the origins of certain themes in Tchaikovsky's symphonies, see Timothy Jackson (forthcoming).
7. See Richard Taruskin's (1997) analysis of orientalism as a semiotic category in Russian music.
8. The "universal" criteria that the dominant seeks to impose should not be identified with the transcendental criteria of existential semiotics, however, which are the same for both the dominant and the dominated. (See my forthcoming book on existential semiotics.)

References

Adorno, Theodor (1938). *Glosse über Sibelius*. (Review of Bengt von Törne's *Sibelius: A Close Up.*) *Zeitschrift für Sozialforschung* 7: 460–463. (Published also in *Impromptus*. Franfurt am Main 1968.)

Andersson, Otto (1960). *Jean Sibelius Amerikassa*. Keuruu: Otava. (Originally published in Swedish: *Jean Sibelius i Amerika* [*Jean Sibelius in America*]. Åbo: Bro, 1955.)

Attali, Jacques (1985). *Noise: The Political Economy of Music*. Trans. Brian Massumi. Minneapolis, MN: University of Minnesota Press.

Dahlström, Fabian; Heiniö, Mikko; and Salmenhaara, Erkki (1995). *Suomen musiikin historia* (4 volumes) [Music History in Finland]. Porvoo: WSOY.

Donner, Philip and Similä, Juhani (1982). "Jean Sibelius – teollistumisajan musiikkimurroksen idolihahmo" [Jean Sibelius – an idol figure in the transition of music in the period of industrialism], in: Vesa Kurkela & Riitta Valkeila (eds.), *Musiikkikulttuurin murros teollistumisajan Suomessa* [The transition of music culture in Finland in the period of industrialism]. (=Jyväskylän yliopiston musiikkitieteen laitoksen julkaisusarja A: tutkielmia ja raportteja No. 1.) Jyväskylä, pp. 33–49.

Downes, Olin (1945). *Sibelius*. Edited and translated into Finnish by Paul Sjöblom together with Jussi Jalas. Helsinki: Otava.

Goss, Glenda Dawn (1995). *Jean Sibelius and Olin Downes. Music, Friendship, Criticism*. Boston, MA: Northeastern University Press.

Heiniö, Mikko (1995). *Suomen musiikin historia, osa 4: Aikamme musiikki* [Music History in Finland, Vol. 4: Contemporary Music]. Porvoo: WSOY.

Heino, Anni (forthcoming). MA thesis, Department of Musicology, University of Helsinki.

Jackson, Timothy (forthcoming). *The Cambridge Handbook on Tchaikovsky's Sixth Symphony*. Cambridge: Cambridge University Press.

Jankélévitch, Vladimir (1955). *La rhapsodie. Verve et improvisation musicale*. Paris: Flammarion.

Kilpinen, Yrjö (1957). Sibelius's obituary, *Uusi Suomi*, 1 October 1957.

Kokkonen, Joonas (1992). *Ihminen ja musiikki* [Man and music]. Helsinki: Gaudeamus. (See particularly the article "Ooppera taidemuotona" [Opera as an art form], pp. 196–201.)

Krohn, Ilmari (1911–1937). *Musiikinteorian oppijakso* [A Course in Music Theory]. Porvoo: WSOY.

– (1945–46). *Der Stimmungsgehalt der Symphonien von Jean Sibelius* (2 vols) (=Suomalaisen tiedeakatemian toimituksia. Sarja B ; 57, 58.) Helsinki.
Leibowitz, René (1955). *Sibelius, le plus mauvais compositeur du monde.* Liège: Dynamo.
Lonchampt, Jacques (1954). "Jean Sibelius et la solitude", *Journal Musical Français* (21 octobre).
– (1955). "Helsinki et le festival de Jean Sibelius", *Journal Musical Français* (29 septembre).
Ranta, Sulho (1946). Jean Sibelius eurooppalaisena ja yleismaailmallisena ilmiönä [Jean Sibelius as a European and global phenomenon]. In: *Sävelten valoja ja varjoja: toinen kirja musiikista ja muusikoista*, 13–18. Porvoo: WSOY.
Similä, Martti (1945). *Sibeliana*. Helsinki: Otava.
Taruskin, Richard (1997). *Defining Russia Musically: Historical and Hermeneutical Essays*. Princeton University Press.
Törne, Bengt von (1965/1945). *Sibelius: A Close Up.* Helsinki: Faber & Faber. (In Finnish: *Sibelius. Lähikuvia ja keskusteluja*. Helsinki: Otava.)
Vidal, Pierre (1959). "Un IMF à Helsinki, de Festival Sibelius 1959", *Journal Musical Français* (9 octobre).

ARTS II: THEATER AND CINEMA

Ilkka Niiniluoto

Film and reality

Cinema has become an inseparable part of the modern world. Perhaps more effectively than any other form of art, it is able to record and capture reality. But it also creates an illusory and fictive reality. The narrative language of film, based on pictures and sounds, enables one to make representations that are sometimes characterized as "dream-like", sometimes even "more real" than the world itself.

The diverse relation between film and reality is the challenging and controversial basic question of film studies. It is argued in this paper that Charles S. Peirce's semiotics helps to show how films can function as signs or representations referring to reality.

Film theory: Ontology and semiotics

The task of film theory, or "the philosophy of film", is to present an analyzed and argued conception of what kinds of entities films are (cf. Andrew 1976; 1984). Thus, it attempts to answer the question, What is cinema? (cf. Bazin 1967) Since films as works of art are more like processes than objects, we can also present the question in the following form: How is a film? (cf. Goodman 1976) These problems concerning the "essence" or "way of being" of films belong to the ontology of film (see Jarvie 1987).

The representative and communicative function is related to films as cultural objects. As works of art in general, films function as signs which refer to something "external" to themselves.[1] Thus, the semiotics of film is a part of film theory (see Wollen 1970; Lotman 1976; Peters 1981). Semiotically, films are conceived as significant "texts" constructed in the "language" of cinema (see Mast and Cohen 1979).

The problems of the ontology and semiotics of film are already apparent in the usual distinction between animated, documentary, and fictional films. As a cartoon, animation differs from the forms of film based on photography, since the method of producing the film material itself is different. Documentary and fiction, in turn, are distinguished from each other on the basis of their relations to reality, but this "issue of realism" is problematic in many ways (see Armes 1974; Mast and Cohen 1979; Williams 1980).[2]

The ontological and semiotic questions in film theory are not just topics of academic discussion. They also have an important influence on the creation and assessment of films. This is demonstrated by the various programmatic statements concerning the realism debate, made by great film directors (among others, Dziga Vertov, Sergei Eisenstein, Robert Flaherty, Roberto Rossellini, Eric Rohmer, Pier Paolo Pasolini, Andrei Tarkovski, and Jean-Luc Godard) and critics (André Bazin).

The issue of realism

The discussion on the relations between film and reality is regularly reduced to principal philosophical problems. This is especially clear in Andrew's surveys (1976; 1984), whose central theoreticians base their views on some philosophical doctrine or a philosophically interpreted research programme of cultural study: Hugo Munsterberg and neo-Kantianism, Rudolf Arnheim and Gestalt psychology, Sergei Eisenstein and dialectical materialism, Béla Balász and formalism, André Bazin and Catholic existentialism, Siegfrid Kracauer and naturalism, Christian Metz and semiology, Henri Agel and phenomenology. Since France has been the center of film theory, the discussion of the past few decades has mainly relied on the traditions and new trends of Continental philosophy – such as Marxism, psychoanalysis, hermeneutics, phenomenology, existentialism, structuralism, semiotics, post-structuralism, and deconstruction.

In contrast, my own field, so-called analytic philosophy, has achieved almost nothing of interest with regard to film. If the subject has been touched at all, instead of the usual silence, the tone has been negative: Gilbert Harman condemns the semiotics of cinema as fruitless (see Mast and Cohen 1979); Roger Scruton (1983) considers photography and film as "pornographic" media which cannot create representative art – except for the plot of a film.[3]

The disinclination and incapability of traditional analytic philosophy to approach the problems of cinema are perhaps understandable. Before Charles W. Morris (1930s) in the United States revived the approach to semiotics by Charles S. Peirce at the end of the nineteenth century, and before Nelson Goodman published his influential work The Languages of Art (1968), analytic philosophers concerned with the philosophy of language did not have any notion of language available that could be useful in dealing with film.

Film as a language differs in significant ways from natural language, as has been emphasized since the 1960s by Christian Metz (see Mast and Cohen 1979). For example, it does not have smallest significant elements corresponding to the phonemes and morphemes of natural language. On the other hand, film does not structurally correspond to the formal languages of logic, in which the analytic tradition – that of Frege, Russell, Wittgenstein, Tarski, and Carnap – has sought its models of language. These languages have been assumed to possess a well-defined syntax (grammar) and a semantics following "Frege's principle": the meaning of a sentence is a function of the meanings of the words functioning as its parts. This kind of simple principle of compositionality is not applicable to the language of film, which utilizes context-sensitive techniques of montage in editing.

Influential philosophical schools have also claimed that the entire realism debate must be rejected as "metaphysics". Thus, the Vienna Circle in the 1920s urged that the question of the existence of a reality "external" to human cognition is a pseudo-problem caused by misuse of language. Similar criticism of "metaphysical realism" or "objectivism" has also been presented on the basis of Husserl's phenomenology, which "brackets" the external world and focuses on studying human intentional acts and the "life-world" constituted through them and determined by human interests and ways of experiencing. These ways of thinking are still defended by many analytic philosophers, among them "internal realists" (like Hilary Putnam), and "neopragmatists" and "constructivists" (like Nelson Goodman).

Inside analytic philosophy, there is, however, another trend which has, in its way, aimed at rehabilitating the status of ontology. This view is manifested in critical scientific realism, which urges that interaction with objective reality enables human subjects and communities to achieve more and more accurate and "truthlike" knowledge that "converges to the truth" about the world (see Niiniluoto 1987). The realist agenda has, in part, gained support from Alfred Tarski's logical semantics, and from possible-worlds semantics as developed by Jaakko Hintikka and others since the 1950s (see Hintikka 1967). Since the 1970s, it has been applied to the semantics of fictive expressions (cf. Niiniluoto 1986).

Analytic philosophy has excelled in aiming at conceptual clarity, but in taking up philosophical questions it has not been as bold as Continental philosophy. It is curious that, precisely now that interesting tools and results concerning the realism debate – which includes the problem of film realism – can be found in analytic philosophy, the Continental structuralist, post-structuralist, and "postmodern" semiotics has arrived at a contrary situation.

Andrew describes the situation as follows. Contrary to the American trend relying on Peirce, the French semiotics of film "brackets reality". Signs or signifiers (signifiants) refer to other signs or signifieds (signifiés) in human mind or culture, but discussion of the relation between language and reality has been eliminated. "Not only are film images and sounds no longer to be thought of as fragments of reality, they now do not even refer to the real" (Andrew 1984: 58).

At the background of this situation lies the manner, typical of European semiology, of operating with a two-place semantic relation, signifier-signified, instead of Peirce's triadic relation, sign-object-interpretant.

Formalism and realism

In 1958 André Bazin presented his famous distinction between those film directors "believing in picture" and those "believing in reality". The former are usually called formalists, the latter realists. A corresponding distinction can also be made among film theoreticians (Andrew 1976).

The formalist tradition of film was initiated at the beginning of our century, when the directors of the first dramatized films (George Méliès, Edwin S. Porter, and D.W. Griffith) started to develop a specific expressive language for film narration. The schools of silent film, according to Bazin (1967), developed these tools to perfection. The German Expressionists turned film into a decorative photographic art of stage settings, lights, oblique angles of view, close-ups, and plastic composition (Josef von Sternberg). The Soviet school (Sergei Eisenstein, Vsevolod Pudovkin) enriched the expressive power of the language of film, its ability to create new meanings, through the montage technique and the utilization of metaphors (cf. Eisenstein 1965; Lotman 1976).

In 1932 Rudolf Arnheim, a classic proponent of formalist film theory, saw the heart of film to lie in how images distort the perceived object: precisely the limitations of the picture (such as framing of images, two-dimensionality, absence of colour and sound) make possible active selection and the "creative organizing of the raw sensual material", through which cinematic art is realizable (see Arnheim 1958; Mast and Cohen 1979). Arnheim's view is an extension of the formalist theory of photography, according to which photographs – through the choice of frame, angle, hole, lighting, and paper – are works of art comparable to paintings, in which the conscious changing of reality, not its mechanical copying or representation, is the measure of the artistic process.[4]

Bazin opposes formalism with the realistic view that "the meaning of a picture lies in what it reveals from reality, not in what it adds to it". During the period of the silent film, the realistic trend was represented, for Bazin, by Robert Flaherny's documentaries and by Erich von Stroheim, who was the most ardent opponent of "picture expressionism and artificial montage" and who, in his film The Greed (1924), "views the world so closely and intensively that its ugliness and cruelty are, in the end, revealed". The silent film was, however, a "cripple" compared to the more realistic sound film, whose triumphs of artistic maturity for Bazin are, among others, Jean Renoir's "poetic realism", John Ford's westerns, the deep and accurate description of Orson Welles's Citizen Kane (1941), and Italian neorealism (Roberto Rossellini). Film realism in Bazin's sense can be seen as a continuation of the realistic theory of photography, where the camera is the medium through which reality itself is reproduced or copied onto the film.

In 1840 Edgar Allan Poe admired the daguerreotype technique, which had been invented the preceding year, since by means of it we reach "reality better than by any other means" – the picture is "INFINITELY more accurate in its reproducing ability than any painting by a human hand". The same magical sense of reaching reality, of capturing time and movement, was present in the Lumière brothers' film of a train arriving at a station in 1895. This sense of respecting and admiring reality is visible in Flaherty's documentary on Eskimos, in the newsreels of Vertov's "Kino-Eye", in the poetic pictures of raindrops on apple blossoms in Alexander Dovchenko's film The Earth (1930), in the Rossellini film-crew's rides on the streets of occupied Rome, or in cinéma-vérité films describing life in the cafés of Paris.

With respect to photography, a similar attitude toward reality has vividly been described by Roland Barthes in his book Camera Lucida (1990). He begins by telling about how he was astonished when seeing the photograph taken in 1852 of Napoleon's brother Jerome: "I am watching eyes which have seen the Emperor." For Barthes, "each photograph is a piece of evidence of presence" – contrary to a painting or a language. The "noema" of photography may, according to him, be called "This-has-been".

Peter Wollen (1977) has criticized this kind of esthetics of realism of a "monstrous fallacy" that "truth lives in a real world and can be picked up by a camera". This realism is, according to his insightful remark, an "outgrowth of romanticism" – lacking interest and respect toward scientific knowledge.

In accordance with the Christian-existentialist tradition, the world is, for Bazin, religiously interpreted: reality is the presence of God, and God is the real creator or subject of the film. A similar element of holiness as woven into reality is visible in Robert Bresson's films.

A skillful maker of films may describe the world as interpreted through myths even in cases where he or she does not believe in them. Pasolini's The Gospel according to St. Matthew (1964) is a description of the story of the Gospel by a non-believing Marxist, together with a 2000-year tradition of myth, which produces a far more effective and genuine, religiously charged picture of Jesus than does any Hollywood Bible spectacle. Pasolini's films Oedipus and Medea, which picture the reality of myths, have the same effect.

Hence, realism in film is relative to the creator's conception of reality. Some forms of realism may set the task of art parallel to the one of science as seen by scientific realism: to seek knowledge about reality and to control reality by means of knowledge. Examples of this could be provided by Kracauer's film theory of "rescuing reality", socialist realism (cf. Basin 1979), and the so-called informative conception of art. On the other hand, scientific realism typically sees science as aiming at the correction, through theoretical concepts irreducible to observations, of the conception of the world which we obtain in everyday experience and perceptions. Thus, science transcends photography and film in so far as they are concerned with recording different experiences of reality related to sense perception.

Relativity in the concept of reality makes it possible to interpret many different trends of art as "realistic". For example, Impressionism in painting, whose influences are seen, e.g., in Renoir's film Un partie de campagne (1936), is related to a positivistic or phenomenalistic view of the world as a totality of perceptual experiences. Cubism is connected with the phenomenological doctrine of the constitution of the life-world by "meanings" of intentional acts, that is, "noemas"; in the field of film, German Expressionism can be regarded as a corresponding view. Surrealism can also be understood as a form of radical realism inspired by psychoanalysis, which – in the manner of Bunuel's Un chien Andalou (1929) – attempts to picture dream-like hallucinations springing from human unconscious mental life.

Drawing a boundary between formalism and realism in film theory is, thus, an extremely problematic matter that depends on our philosophical conception of reality – of ontological and epistemological presuppositions. Bazin's distinction between directors believing in picture or reality is a useful simplification which needs additions and more sophistication.

For example, Roy Armes (1974) divides film into three main lines: (1) realism, i.e., "revealing of reality"; (2) illusion, i.e., "imitation of reality"; (3) modernism, i.e., "questioning of reality". Realism, in his sense, includes the documentary tradition from Louis Lumière, Robert Flaherty, and John Grierson to contemporary TV realism, Vertov's Kino-Pravda, von Stroheim, Renoir, Rossellini's neorealism, and the cinéma vérité of the 1960s. Griffith, westerns, Charles Chaplin, the heritage of Hollywood, Alfred Hitchcock, and Walt Disney's animations belong to the tradition of illusion. Representatives of modernism (or, according to other thinkers, "postmodernism") include those who experiment with the expressive possibilities of film, such as Eisenstein, Expressionism, Luis Bunuel's Surrealism, Alain Resnais's films that fragmented time, Jean-Luc Godard, and underground films.

According to radical formalism, a film is a "text" produced by means of a camera (or cartoons); it is analyzed purely syntactically, independently of representational relations of reference. For a realist, the relation of this text to what it expresses externally to itself is important. In this case, we need not be concerned with a documentary "recording" or revealing of the actual world, but with a "visualization" of an imagined world (cf. Peters 1981: 9).

In the following sections, I try to approach the problem of film realism by utilizing the basic concepts of Charles S. Peirce's semiotics.

Film as index of reality

In Peirce's semiotics, signs have a "triadic" structure: a sign is "something which stands to somebody for something in some respect or capacity" (CP 2.227). The reference of an interpreted sign to its object may be based on three different things: in the case of indices, there is a natural causal relation (smoke is a sign of fire, the odour of a cat is a sign of a cat); icons are in some sense similar to their objects (e.g., pictures, diagrams, metaphors); symbols rely on a convention accepted by the linguistic community (e.g., words of natural language; the word "cat" is a conventional sign of a cat).

Some attempts have been made to analyze the special nature of cinema by means of Peirce's theory of signs (see Peters 1981; Wollen 1977), and Peirce himself made some brief remarks about photographs as indices and icons.[5] In my view, Peirce's theory does provide a good instrument for considering the referential relations of films (cf. Mast and Cohen 1979). Armes (1974), following Wollen, even bases his whole tripartition between realism, illusion, and modernism of film on what type of sign (index, icon, or symbol) is dominant in each case.

Film realism in the sense of Bazin and Barthes – when animation and other artificial ways of producing pictures are excluded – is essentially based on the indexical nature of the images of a film. The existence of a photograph presupposes a real causal relation between the object and the film. A photograph is evidence for the existence of the object in front of the camera at the moment of the shooting of the picture – for what has been here and now. Hence, a film can be considered a "text" that is in an indexical relation to what has happened in front of the camera.

On the other hand, a photograph as a trace of its object, as a projection of reality for us, also expresses the non-existence of the object, as Stanley Cavell especially emphasizes (1979). In this respect, John Wayne on the screen is in a similar status as the products of imagination: if I imagine what my friend David is doing in Berlin just now, David as imagined is, according to Sartre, a part of "nothing" (cf. Niiniluoto 1986). Film, however, distinguishes itself from imagination – from "fantasy" in Scruton's (1983) disparaging sense – by its indexicality: my perceptions of John Wayne as Ethan Edwards in the film The Searchers reduce through the camera to the causal influence of Wayne himself.

Film as icon

An index need not in any way be similar to its object – smoke does not resemble fire. However, photographs and films have, in addition to their indexicality, the nature of Peirce's icon: they represent their objects in the form of picture. Through the "eye" of the camera, reality is reproduced on the film, which, when projected onto the screen, produces an observable picture in motion which is similar to its object. Iconicity is, therefore, an essential feature of the possibility of film realism.

In semiotics, the concept of icon has been considered problematic because of the difficulties related to, among other things, the notion of similarity. In his famous critique of picture, Umberto Eco proposes that icons are also culture-bound representations whose codes must be learned (see Mast and Cohen 1979).

For analytic philosophy of language, Eco's thesis is not surprising: the doctrine of Wittgenstein's Tractatus (1921) of language as a picture of reality has been made more precise by the concept of isomorphic correspondence, which is always relative to a given "key" (see Stenius 1964). The notion of similarity (or resemblance), too, can – despite Goodman's nominalistic criticism – be usefully defined (see Niiniluoto 1987: Chapter 1). Moreover, we can sensibly talk about degrees of similarity – iconicity is not a matter of either-or. Hence, the distinction between icons and symbols can still be maintained: an interpreted picture (contrary to a conventional sign) refers to its object on the basis of similarity. (In this case, the object is an object or state of affairs in reality, not a perception of reality.)

Eco may be right in claiming that a two-dimensional photograph literally has no properties of its three-dimensional object. Correspondingly, a film-strip as a physical object is not, in itself, similar to its object. Still, a film or a screen appropriately interpreted may function as an iconic representation similar to reality.

Yet the watching experience also belongs to the pictorial nature of film: a film becomes a film only when being watched. Is, perhaps, the perceived film in the mind of the spectator an icon of reality? Answers to this question depend essentially on what kind of a philosophical theory of perception we advocate. According to representational theories, in perceiving a tree I perceive a sense datum which, in one way or another, represents the tree. However, direct realism (which I consider better argued) regards the tree as a physical object, as the real object of my perception. Depending on its truthfulness, my perception gives more or less adequate information about it.

A realistic theory of perception supports a thesis of the ontology of film, which could be described as ultrarealism. Semioticians have sometimes characterized film as a "language without a code" consisting of "natural signs". Pasolini (interviewed by Oswald Stack, 1969) expresses this idea by claiming that cinema expresses reality by means of the reality itself, not by means of symbols, so that the "semiology of film" corresponds to the "semiology of the signs of reality".

I can perceive a tree directly through my eyes, through a window, as reflected in a mirror, as a photograph through my own camera, or through a film shot by Pasolini's camera – just as I can hear the voice of my friend directly, over the telephone or on the radio. For an ultrarealist, film provides a mediated but, still, direct connection with reality. In the film The Searchers, I see John Wayne, not a picture of Wayne, as I see my wife at home over dinner – the only difference lies in the longer and more complex causal chain from the object of the perception to my perception here and now. The screen is not a painting representing the world or a picture together with its frame, but a "hole into reality" (Jean Mitry).

Ultrarealism's worship of reality is manifested in the documentary tradition of film and in Bazinian esthetics. Even though it reaches something essential about the nature of film, as a theory of film it has notable limitations. A one-sided emphasis on the indexicality of film may lead to a denial of the possibility of the entire film art: for Scruton (1983), photography and film are based on a causal relation, not on intentionality; hence, as representative art they are as impossible as an art of mirror images.

Pasolini's ultrarealism does not take into account the fact that dramatized films are "pictures of pictures of pictures" (Peters 1981: 20): the camera records a picture of actors visualizing a story that describes a (real or fictive) history. In the film October, Eisenstein may denote the square of the Winter Palace by the square of the Winter Palace; however, in his film Reds (1981), Warren Beatty denotes St. Petersburg by Helsinki; in his film The Gospel according to St. Matthew, Pasolini does not denote Jesus by Jesus, but by a Spanish amateur actor, Enrique Irazoqui.

The verisimilitude of cinema

It is well known that a film may "cheat" the spectator by creating an illusion of reality. When I think I see the bleeding villain falling with a thump on the street of a tumble-down western city, penetrated by a bullet fired by the hero, there "really" was, in fact, only a bang without a bullet, red tomato ketchup, a stuntman, and a paperboard stage setting in a Hollywood studio. In another sense of illusion, happy-ending stories give a distorted and romanticized picture of the world and of "real life".

In film realism, what is essential is not what happens in front of the camera but what is recorded by the camera. For example, shots of different times and places may be combined into the same scene on the filmstrip. Verisimilitude (in French, vraisemblance) is not dependent on what is real but on what the spectator feels to be real. In order to achieve a sense of verisimilitude in front of a camera, one often has to manipulate the dramatized reality: a fight must be exaggerated, so as to make it seem genuine.

In Godard's film Little Soldier (1960), it is stated that "film is the truth 24 times per second". It must be kept in mind, however, that a picture does not in itself state or assert anything about the world. The verisimilitude of a fictive film is, thus, an illusion of reality, an iconic representation of a fictive world. Von Sternberg, a master of stage setting and lights, magically creates by means of film – for example, in his Blue Angel (1930) – an artificial "dream-world", whereby "the iconic feature of a sign independently of indexicality" is emphasized in film (Wollen 1977: 86; Armes 1974).

The vraisemblance of film is, thus, different from the truth-likeness of scientific realists (cf. Niiniluoto 1987): the former is verisimilitude relative to a fictive world, or relative to the spectator's beliefs and expectations, the latter relative to the actual world.

Fiction, symbols, and reality

The basic nature of fictive art was authoritatively expressed by Andrei Tarkovski in 1967. A film begins, according to Tarkovski, from the moment at which the director "sees through his mind's eye the figure of the future film". He then shares with the spectators this personal pictorial composition and way of experiencing the existing world, as if he were revealing his most secret dreams (see Tarkovski 1986). The main idea of film art is "time captured in its concrete forms and phenomena", which is loyal to the "truth of life".

Let us consider Francis Ford Coppola's film The Godfather (1972), based on Mario Puzo's novel of the same title, as an example of fiction. What kind of referential relations does it have to the world? In Figure 1, the situation is illuminated with regard to the scene in which Vito Corleone dances with his daughter at her wedding in New York in 1947.

Firstly, it may be noticed that the pictures on the filmstrip and on the screen, as well as the picture experienced by the spectator, are in an indexical and iconical relation to the stage set by Coppola in 1971, on which the smiling, made-up Marlon Brando dances with Talia Shire. Thus, the spectator "really" sees Marlon Brando dancing amidst stage setting and other actors. In accordance with the illusion of the film, however, the spectator's experience is wholly different: he or she sees the Mafia boss Vito Corleone dancing in New York in 1947. The content of this experience thus partially describes a fictive possible world, in which a person named Vito Corleone is dancing in 1947. The spectator's perceptions are not in an indexical relation to this imagined world, which Coppola, the director, has seen "through his mind's eye". However, the picture Coppola has, by means of his film, conjured up into the spectator's mind is, in a trivial sense, an icon of the fictive New York – though Puzo, the author, may himself have originally imagined everything differently.

How is it possible that, in watching the film The Godfather, I see Vito Corleone instead of Marlon Brando? It is not necessarily a matter of self-deception: I see Corleone although I know that Brando acts in this role and thereby represents him. Jarvie (1987) emphasizes, following Munsterberg, that cinema does not deceive the spectator: it is not a matter of a false belief, but of "voluntary illusion".

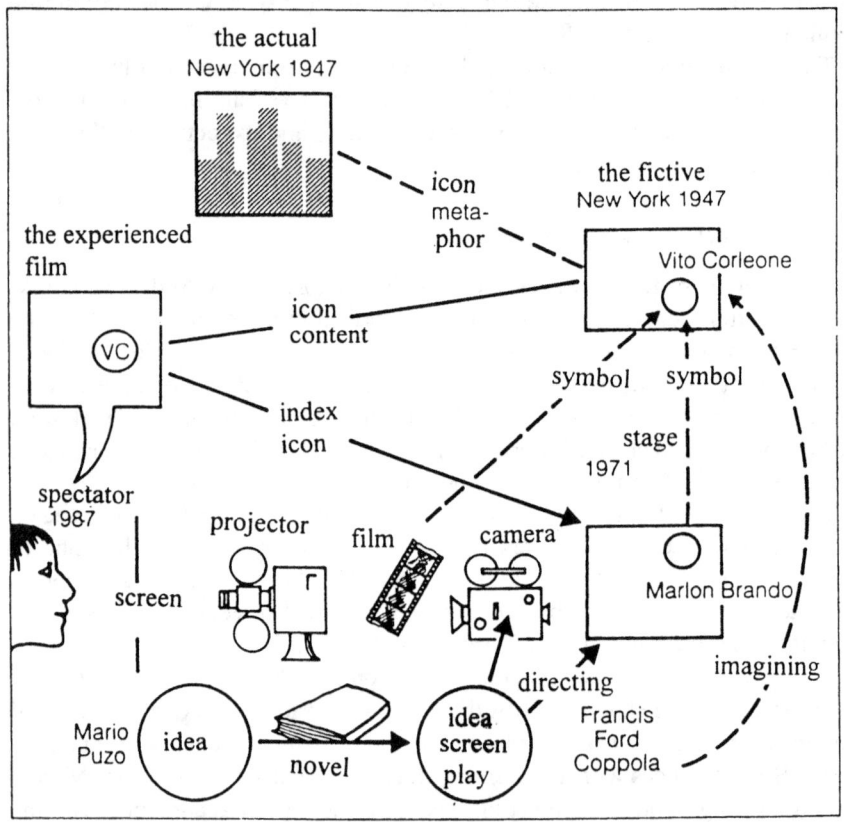

Figure 1. The Godfather and reality.

Hence, we may say that, on the basis of a silent convention between the director and the spectator, Marlon Brando is a sign referring to the fictive Mafia boss. I can understand the film only if I accept this convention from the beginning. Thus, we can say that Marlon Brando – as well as Brando's image on the filmstrip

– works as a conventional sign, as a symbol in Peirce's sense, which refers to the fictive entity Vito Corleone.

The language of dramatized narrative films thus includes, in addition to indices and icons, the level of "codes" or symbols. Hence, all types of signs of Peirce's tripartition are relevant in film semiotics.

In the language of film, narrative codes that the director may use as his or her personal means of expression have a special significance. Business negotiations in a darkened room and the daughter's wedding in the brightly lit yard create a contrast, which expresses the dark background and the well-lighted facade of the godfather's double role. The analysis of a film is often precisely an interpretation of these kinds of expressive means. Even though they are usually based on different metaphors and indirect references – or "connotation" of signs – they may, if established, rise to the status of a generally adopted, conventional sign in Peirce's sense, i.e., a symbol. In this spirit, Peters (1981) emphasizes that each film creates a unique symbol system or code of its own through its multi-layered language of expression.

The above-mentioned symbols are included in the story: they refer to the fictive world of The Godfather instead of the actual world. What about the "realistic" nature of the film The Godfather in the sense of the relation between the imagined New York and the actual New York? It is clear that this kind of a relation exists, since the Mafia is a real phenomenon. Although Vito Corleone is a fictive character, he resembles in many respects the real godfathers of New York – and thus functions as their icon. More generally, we may say that Vito Corleone "symbolizes", in a metaphorical form, organized crime as a whole. Furthermore, it is possible to consider the moral message of The Godfather, by interpreting the Mafia boss as leading and taking care of his "family", as a metaphor of the President of the United States.

Through fictive films, an artist has enormous liberty in creating reality, in illuminating his or her own imagination by means of narration. The most absorbing questions in interpreting individual films are related to what the director meant (if he or she even knows) by the metaphors he or she invented. Those metaphors that connect the story with some actual or potential features of our world are often the most exciting ones. These kinds of metaphors relate fiction to reality and thus produce the core of film art, in Tarkovski's sense: "To make a man face his limitless environment, meet an innumerable number of other people, relate him to the world."

Ilkka Niiniluoto

Notes

This paper is based on my article "Elokuva ja todellisuus" [Film and reality] published (in Finnish) in Synteesi 1–2 (7) (1988): 90–107. I am grateful to Mr. Sami Pihlström for assistance in preparing the English version.
1. According to Goodman (1976), works of art function as "symbols". I prefer to speak about "signs", and to reserve the concept of "symbol" for the specific use in Peirce's sense.
2. In this paper, I concentrate on semiotic questions, without entering into systematic discussion of the ontological status of films.
3. For positive exceptions, see Cavell (1979) and Jarvie (1987).
4. Arnheim makes a distinction between watching the real world and watching the screen. On the watching of pictures as a complex perceptual process, see Gombrich, Hochberg, and Black (1972).
5. See CP 2.281, 4.447, 5.554. I am not trying to interpret Peirce's original texts here, but rather I am freely using his ideas and distinctions for my purposes.

References

Andrew, D. (1984). *The Major Film Theories: An Introduction.* Oxford: University Press.
– (1984). *Concepts in Film Theory.* Oxford: Oxford University Press.
Armes, R. (1974). *Film and Reality: An Historical Survey.* Harmandsworth: Penguin.
Arnheim, R. (1958). *Film as Art.* London: Fuller and Fuller.
Barthes, R. (1990). *Camera Lucida: Reflections on Photography.* New York: Noonday.
Basin, Y. (1979). *The Semantic Philosophy of Art.* Moscow: Progress.
Bazin, A. (1967). *What Is Cinema?* Berkeley: University of California Press.
Cavell, S. (1979). *The World Viewed: Reflections on the Ontology of Film.* Enlarged Edition. Cambridge, MA: Harvard University Press.
Eisenstein, S. (1965). *Film Form: Essays in Film Theory.* Cleveland, OH: Meridian Books.
Gombrich, E.H.; Hochberg, J.; and Black, M. (1972). *Art, Perception, and Reality.* Baltimore and London: Johns Hopkins University Press.
Goodman, N. (1976). *The Languages of Art.* Indianapolis, IN: Hackett.
Hintikka, J. (1967). *Models for Modalities.* Dordrecht: D. Reidel.
Jarvie, I. (1987). *Philosophy of the Film: Epistemology, Ontology, Aesthetics.* New York and London: Routledge & Kegan Paul.
Lotman, J. (1976). *Semiotics of Cinema.* Ann Arbor, MI: University of Michigan Press.
Mast, G. and Cohen, M. (eds.) (1979). *Film Theory and Criticism: Introductory Readings.* 2nd ed. Oxford: Oxford University Press.
Niiniluoto, I. (1986). Imagination and fiction. *Journal of Semantics* 4: 209–222.
– (1987). *Truthlikeness.* Dordrecht: D. Reidel.
Peirce, C.S. (1931–35). *Collected Papers.* Vols 1–6. Cambridge, MA: Harvard University Press.
Peters, J.M. (1981). *Pictorial Signs and the Language of Film.* Amsterdam: Rodopi.
Scruton, R. (1983). *The Aesthetic Understanding.* London: Methuen.
Searle, J. (1979). *Expression and Meaning.* Cambridge: Cambridge University Press.
Stack, O. (1969). *Pasolini on Pasolini.* London: Thames and Hudson.
Stenius, E. (1964). *Wittgenstein's "Tractatus".* Oxford: Blackwell.

Tarkovski, A. (1986). *Sculpting in Time: Reflections on the Cinema*. London: Bodley Head.
Williams, C. (ed.) (1980). *Realism and the Cinema: A Reader*. London: Routledge and Kegan Paul.
Wollen, P. (1970). *Signs and Meaning in the Cinema*. London: Thames & Hudson.

Henry Bacon

Actors as characters, characters as actors, in audiovisual fiction

The three levels of personage

In his study of French poetic realism of the 1930s, *Mists of Regret*, Dudley Andrew, elaborating on Roland Barthes's ideas in *S/Z*, proposes three primary categories as regards "the way any character is constructed in relation to his/her surroundings":

1) theatrical: an actor on a set or stage;
2) fictional: a character in a locale;
3) poetic: a figure in a milieu.

Style, genre conventions, star-system, and the like as well as the idiosyncratic qualities of a given film might cue one of these *levels of personage* to be more pertinent than others, but all three are present in all fictional films. In a Hollywood film the fictional (diegetic) level predominates, but the first level is present in the use of the star-system. There is also the figure of an "entity made up of actor and role, but going beyond both to function as a magnet for a host of values, qualities, and concepts that the ... viewer engenders in the course of interchange with the text" (Andrew 1995: 237).[1]

In writing about theatre Brecht advocated breaking what in film theory is called the diegetic illusion and foregrounding the fact of representation in order to make the spectator focus intellectually on the ideological implications of the fiction. Perhaps he rather overstated his point in pitting intellectual attitude against emotional involvement. The richness of film experience stems to a great extent from being able to appreciate a film on all three levels of personage simultaneously. Spectators of a mainstream film will be swept away by the action and emotions displayed in a film even as they recognise and appreciate the performances of actors familiar to them from various other films and film culture in general. Also, it belongs to the basic competence of film spectatorship to be able to understand certain actor-bound characteristics as not belonging to the fictional character. The most obvious example is the use of the language of the primary audience instead of the native tongue of the character – a talent called for much more in the theatre which is by nature a far more presentational form of art than cinema. Furthermore, depending on his/her sophistication the spectator will also be able to see symbolic dimensions in the film, that is, to see the actor/character as a figure in a landscape.

In other types of film, say, European art films, these patterns vary considerably. Sometimes their relationships can be foregrounded, as when the same actor assumes the roles of several characters. This happens, for example, in Bertolucci's *The Conformist* in which Dominique Sanda has a triple role and even more excitingly in the same director's *The Spider's Stratagem* as Giulio Brogi is throughout the film identically dressed both in the roles of father and son. The interaction between the two first levels becomes even more prominent in the extremely rare case when two or more actors play the part of a single character, as do Carole Bouquet and Angela Molina in Bunuel's *That Obscure Object of Desire*. Such devices are bound to have implications also on the third level.[2]

The third level might well develop within the confines of the enfolding of the plot, but it might also become so prominent that it temporarily and sometimes even completely eclipses plot logic. This may take place due to the foregrounding of features starting from mise-en-scène and ending in more specifically cinematic elements such as camera movements and montage. In Andrew's words, "figural personages, as opposed to characters, are by definition 'achronological' and appeal to the passions rather than the 'actions' or quests of the audience" (1995: 237). This can take place partly in conjunction with the first level thus partly short-circuiting the second level, the level of the plot. Andrew's example is Jean Gabin whose character to a considerable extent set the tone of the films of poetic realism.

In order to gain a fuller understanding of how the three levels of personage interact it is useful first to focus on the crucial second level, the way fictional characters are conceived in audio-visual fiction. To penetrate deeper into this question a comparison with literary fiction and the addition of yet another set of conceptual tools will be enlightening.

The motivations of characters

It is often fruitful to compare the devices available for different narrative arts, in this case literary and audiovisual fiction. In his article "What novels can do that films can't (and vice versa)", Seymour Chatman points out that while in novelistic description "the possible number of details is absolutely determined", "in filmic representation the number of details is indeterminate since what this version gives us is a simulacrum". Turning this into an advantage, literature enjoys the privilege of indeterminacy, non-commitment to specific appearances, while it can also qualify its descriptions in a way that cinema can't; for example, "a twenty-five-year-old ... stately villa". As opposed to this, the fate of cinema is to present particular outer characteristics. On the other hand, as our perception is usually guided by narrative interest, we do not concentrate on the entire wealth of visual details a film offers (see Chatman 1980: 123 and 125).

In contrast to literary fiction where the starting point of character formation is usually his/her name, in audiovisual fiction it is the character's outer appearance, determined primarily by the physiognomy of the actor. To this are added various traits such as clothing, mannerisms, other patterns of behaviour, items belonging to the character, and the like. Furthermore, the character, through his/her behaviour and interaction with other characters, is given a number of traits. The more traits, the rounder the character, and since traits are repeatedly displayed, the character gains in consistency and substance. If traits are added or changed during the course of the plot, the character develops. And while in the popular genres traits can fairly easily be listed, in more complex films they become less easy to define and number. Characters in such films are thought to be realistic.

In seeking to understand how traits serve to build characters in various contexts the concept of *motivation* turns out to be extremely useful. Thinking out motivations is defined by David Bordwell as the procedure by which "the spectator justifies a given textual element". Motivation can be *compositional, realistic, intertextual*, and/or *artistic*. If a given cinematic element is necessary for the basic unity of the work, development of the plot, or thematic coherence, then its motivation is said to be compositional. If the element accords with the spectator's perception and/or understanding of the real world, the motivation is realistic. The motivation is transtextual if it derives from established ways or practices of representation such as genre conventions. Finally, the motivation of an element may be artistic in that it serves specifically expressive purposes. Particularly the first three categories of motivation usually function together as a mixture, although it could be argued that all films serve also some expressive purposes, however rudimentary they might be. Mainly, however, this motivation is evoked only when the three others cannot furnish a satisfactory explanation for a given feature (Bordwell 1988: 36).

From the point of view of character formation the film audiences of our time are accustomed to what is taken with more or less justification as (in the normal sense of the word) psychological motivation.[3] This is what keeps the story rolling. In the scheme of textual motivations this belongs to the realm of realistic motivation. We think that the way the character acts is plausible, if we feel it is the way a person in such and such a situation conceivably would act. The problem here, of course, is that conceptions of what is plausible human behaviour do change from one cultural environment to another and as time passes. Films become dated, and we might find it difficult to watch without an ironic smile on our lips a film which the original audiences may well have thought heralded a whole new dimension of realism. Thus in our experience other categories of motivation gain ground at the expense of the realistic in respect of this film.

In any case, a basically competent spectator, even one not trained in critical appreciation of films and unable to formulate his/her intuition, is aware that also compositional motivation (pardon the pun) influences the behaviour of the characters even in contemporary mainstream films. Furthermore, genre expectations in conjunction with the way the film opens cue the audience as to what extent and in what sense the diegetic world with its characters is supposed to be considered a realistic representation of real-world people and how much scope there is for flights of fancy. The most obvious case is the farce, where characters tend to be fairly flat so as not to slow down the plot mechanism with unduly complicated psychological problems. Another typical example is the situation when a character does something implausibly stupid only to end up in danger. A paramount example can be found in Mark Robson's horror film *The Isle of the Dead* where the hero actually says to the heroine: "There's a homicidal maniac around. You'd better stay alone."

On the whole, in genre films characters might have a fair dose of colour, usually thanks to good performances by charismatic actors, but they nevertheless conform to stereotypes. Transtextual motivation is in operation making things easier for everyone. Character formation is unproblematic because so much is already there before the film begins and no one apart from misguided critics expects anything more. Everything is predictable, goodies are goodies and baddies are baddies. Or to be more precise, the goodies are usually Americans and the baddies gangsters, hooligans, or members of nations with which the United Sates happens not to have been on good terms with at the time of the film's making. All in all, transtextual motivation is ethically doubtful because it involves a trivialization of moral issues and a stereotyping of cultural, ethnic, sexual, and various other differences.

Artistic motivation is perhaps the least pertinent of the four as regards character formation. This is because understanding characters relates back to questions of mimesis, understanding the story as a way of modelling the real world. The question we face here is that of a shift in the balance between realistic and expressive tendencies. Are the characters representative rather than individual? The characters might be reduced to caricatures in order to make more emphatic the point that they stand for some feature of human existence, a social group, or some other such abstraction. Examples abound in the Soviet films of the 1920s in which characters are often representative of social classes rather than individuals. Thus when artistic motivation predominates we are reducing the second level in Andrew's scheme into a mere plot mechanism, moving from following fictional characters in action into observing figures in a landscape.

But we are moving too fast now. There is still a lot to be learned about the second level and the way it functions in the artistic whole of a film. It is high time to ask why we should take interest in fictional characters in the first place?

Understanding real and fictional people

The legitimate pursuit conducted by structuralists and semiotician of various description to reveal the codes which guide cinematic perception was perhaps necessary to guard film studies against naive conceptions of realism. But as it would, the pendulum swept outrageously far to the other end. A generation of semiotically orientated films scholars (and even more so, cinematically orientated semioticians) were blinded to the analogies filmic perception has with natural perception. Recently, however, many scholars have made the point that not everything we perceive on the screen is coded. As Toben Kragh Grodal writes in his masterly doctoral thesis *Cognition, Emotion and Visual Fiction*:

> Images in film and television do not reflect the natural world: they come to us through cultural systems of representations. But some of the basic skills needed to understand film and television are identical with the abilities necessary for natural visual perception. A face or a tree is immediately recognizable by means of innate perceptual mechanisms plus fundamental human experience, even for persons without any previous experience of film and television. (1988: 73–74)[4]

This is not to deny that, say, the image of a face or an entire human body has a sign function in the filmic discourse. On the first level of personage, it is indexically linked to the actor, who plays the role of the fictional character. On the second level it has an iconic function as we recognize it as a representation of a human being in a given situation. And finally it has symbolic functions as we become aware of metaphorical aspects of his/her behaviour or fate on the third level.[5]

From the present point of view the iconic aspect, the second level, is of special interest. It would appear that in audiovisual fiction, understanding characters is tied not only to our natural perception of human beings but also to the way in which we make or try to make sense out of the behaviour of our fellow men – much more so than in literary fiction. Or as Murray Smith argues in his excellent book *Engaging Characters*, both understanding real people and cinematic characters is based on the same *person schema*. Paraphrasing Clifford Geertz, Smith argues as follows:

> ... the narrow, fundamental category of the human agent (on which culturally specific developments are based) may be taken to include:
> 1. a discrete human body, individuated and continuous through time and space;

2. perceptual activity, including self-awareness;
3. intentional states, such as beliefs and desires;
4. emotions;
5. the ability to use and understand a natural language;
6. the capacity for self-impelled actions and self-interpretation;
7. the potential for traits, or persisting attributes. (Smith 1995: 21)

This does not mean that these features would have to be thought of as "natural" or "biologically determined". But it does appear that "there are certain regularities in human physiology and in the physical environment which all human societies face, which have given rise to common conventions and practices" (ibid.: 22).

Smith's thesis is that we bring these assumptions also into our understanding of fictional characters. While in literary fiction we might be given detailed knowledge of the thoughts and psychological states of the characters, understanding characters in audiovisual fiction is by far more analogous to the real-life situation of trying to make sense out of the behaviour of our fellow men. This understanding is conditioned by many other schemata covered by the concepts of compositional, transtextual, and artistic motivation; nevertheless, our ability to relate fiction to our real-life experience is an essential aspect of narrative competence. We do not take fiction for reality; there is no "suspension of belief" because fiction by definition is not a matter of belief. So why do we so often feel emotional about what happens to fictional characters in their fictitious lives? Because through what we experience as realistic motivation the same mental faculties which govern our engagement and relationship with real people is activated. We take fictive situations seriously because we recognize them as representations of genuine human situations in which people for whatever reasons will have to act in one way or the other and bear the responsibility for the consequences.

As I encounter other human beings, I expect them to have their own consciousness and perceptions, emotions, values, and understanding of the world. In short, I think of them as subjects with their own point of view. Their subjectivity is in a sense absolutely beyond me, but on the other hand the fact that I usually do understand why they behave in the way they do suggests that we are alike in some fundamental ways, and that within limits I can simulate their mind and point of view in my own mind. Also, my knowledge of the factors that determine human behaviour in general, gained through experience and factual as well as fictional accounts of what being a human being is all about, will assist me in gaining an understanding of my fellow men.

Similarly, when following audiovisual fiction I perform an act of simulation in my mind. As in doing this I take into account the above-mentioned conditions which bracket the fictional experience from our real life situations, this mental operation could be, as Gregory Currie has suggested, called *off-line simulation*. Currie explains:

> Running off-line is, exactly, a matter of severing the connections between our mental states and their perceptual causes and behavioural effects. A belief run "off-line" isn't really a belief, just as a monarch who has been deposed is no longer a monarch... with off-line simulation, states of imagining function as internal surrogates of beliefs because they retain belief-like connections to other mental states and to the body. Imagining, like beliefs, can lead to decisions and can cause certain kinds of bodily sensations. (1995: 149–150)

"Empathetic reenactment of the character's situations" furthermore allows us to think of the story from the point of view of the character, his/her involvement in a given situation. In a mechanical way this takes place even if the characters appear stereotypical and the story trivial. But if the film succeeds in engaging us, if it stimulates our mind into performing the activity of simulation with any degree of intensity, the fictional characters take on life – in our minds. As a rule, however, we do not lose ourselves in the protagonists, but "we might be said to imagine *ourselves in the situation* (as distinct from imagining *being the character in the situation*)" (Smith 1995: 80).

To penetrate into the thorny question of spectatorial identification Smith inaugurates the concept of a *structure of sympathy*, with which he designates the *levels of engagement* that we have with fictional characters (ibid.: 5). First of all, *recognition* is the process by which the spectator constructs the characters. Secondly, inasmuch as the "spectators are provided with visual and aural information more or less congruent with that available to characters, [they] are placed in a certain structure of *alignment* with characters." Finally, *allegiance* is the level of engagement at which "spectators respond sympathetically or antipathetically towards a character or group of characters". (Ibid.: 62 and 75.) The intensity of allegiance varies as the story proceeds and it includes an evaluation of the moral status of the character within the fiction.

Spectatorial identification is an extremely interesting and complicated issue, but here it will be discussed only to the extent that it affects the understanding of characters. It is obvious that what Smith calls *structures of sympathy* within fiction influences the way we simulate characters in our mind. Smith writes:

> The typical functioning of empathy – of simulation and mimicry – is thus twofold: first, to act as a searchlight or probe in our construction of the narrative situation; and secondly, to generate in the viewer, in somewhat attenuated form, the predominant emotions of the characters in the story world. They function to "attune" the spectator to the emotional tenor of the narrative. (Ibid.: 103)

Thus our construction of the character is by no means a purely intellectual issue. On the contrary. The historian W. B. Gallie has compared following a story to following a game, to make the point that it is not a question simply of understanding the rules but also of the ability to empathize, to understand the motivations of the characters. (1964: 37-39)

Characters and plots

In mainstream films, as a rule, the first impression we get of the main characters is fictionally true. Their goals are usually set forth early on and they keep the story going until the very end. If there are any discrepancies they are interpreted as moments of weakness. As opposed to this, in certain kinds of fiction we have the cliché of the false friend, who at the critical moment turns out to be a traitor. But such developments seldom surprise us these days. On the whole we are given right from the start of the film a firm basis by which to assess plot development. Many features relate to the character's profession and his/her relation to it. Often traits or skills or experiences referred to early on during the film turn out to be important at crucial moments. The paradigmatic example is the opening of Alfred Hitchcock's *Rear Window*, where a single, smoothly sweeping shot tells us the protagonist's profession (photographer), his present situation (he has broken his leg, probably in the course of his work), and some of on going concerns (problems with his girlfriend). His photographic equipment will help in developing the plot (telephoto lens used as a telescope) and eventually save his life (blinding the attacker with flash bulbs).

In an art-film understanding the characters often becomes a problem. Part of the film's strategy might be to leave to the audience the effort of figuring out why the characters behave as they do. This is often achieved by means of elliptical narration, as in many films by Robert Bresson and Krzystof Kieslowski. There is an interesting example of this also in David Hare's *Paris by Night*, as the heroine (Charlotte Rampling) in one scene is reduced to tears and immediately after that is seen opening the door to her potential lover, now perfectly composed. It is left for the spectators to figure out, party on the basis of what has been seen before but above all in terms of their understanding of human behaviour, as to what kind of psychological process she has gone through. Another device that calls for such a conscious act of interpretation is the kind of taciturn acting, almost non-acting, which is Bresson's trademark as well as that of Aki Kaurismäki. This kind of yielding to the first level of personage usually serves expressive purposes on the third level.

Characters evolve not only as monadic units but also through their interrelationships. The status of the characters in the fictional world they inhabit is determined primarily according to the way other characters relate to them. What they say about each other often tells more about themselves than about the character under discussion, but in certain plot situations the spontaneous reactions of other characters may give weight to an entrance or a sudden, striking gesture. This is a standard device in depicting persons of exceptional authority such as Napoleon as seen by Abel Gance or Ivan the Terrible in Eisenstein's film of that name. But it is an indispensable device also on a more mundane level. Just before the dinner scene at Donnafugata in Visconti's *The Leopard* the entrance of the Sedaras is almost over determined. As the father Don Calogero arrives, the mocking exchanges between the prince and his sons cue the spectator not to take him seriously even before he is first seen. But when his daughter Angelica arrives a little later, she takes everyone by surprise with her beauty.

This scene in *The Leopard* is also a good example of how various cinematic devices can be used to give the desired impression of a character. The idea we gain of Don Calogero on the basis of what the other characters, starting from the hero of the film, say of him is amply confirmed by the slightly clownish acting of Paolo Stoppa as well as by various other cinematic devices. We see him arrive from the visual point of view of the prince and his sons, literally looking down at him from their position at the top of the staircase. Even the music seems to mock him. He is made to appear out of place in the brilliant palaces of the aristocracy to which his fortune opens all the doors. But when Angelica arrives at the door of the big splendid living room, all action stops and a beautiful, romantically longing melody emerges from the soundtrack. Conversation halts and the effect on everyone is underlined by showing it in a rapid series of close-ups of all the main characters. As Angelica walks forward the camera follows her as she passes exquisite flower arrangements with which she is thus metonymically associated. She has come to stay and adorn the place with her presence. Claudia Cardinale may or may not strike us with her beauty, but in the world of *The Leopard* her extraordinary loveliness is a fictional truth. But what is crucial here is that we have been guided very affectively into appreciating the concerns and values at issue.

The way the characters are introduced and developed by different cinematic means can almost surreptitiously lead us to seeing them in a particular way that serves purposes beyond immediate narrative needs. Edward Branigan gives an interesting example in his *Narrative Comprehension and Film*. Applying a highly elaborate scheme of narrative levels to Hitchcock's *The Wrong Man* he points out how the protagonist Manny (Henry Fonda) has been shot "as if" taken by the police. By showing us Manny in this way, future events are anticipated because similar patterns will recur (Manny surrounded by two men) throughout the film and he will eventually be taken in by the police. It also suggests that "misperception could arise in quite an arbitrary and unprecedented way", particularly as a little later a siren calls to mind the police (Branigan 1992: 90–91). This is perhaps not exactly what Andrew meant with his third level, but it serves as an example of how cinematic representation may be used to make a point beyond the needs of depicting the diegetic world. This leads to the final phase of the present study.

Characters as functions and figures

Aristotle suggests in his *Poetics* that not the characters but the plot has to be universal. The characters may appear highly individual while the story might still be thought to have more general relevance.

In neorealist films this point is often made by first showing us groups of people gathered for one reason or another (working, looking for work, demonstrating) and only gradually the protagonist emerges as the centre of the film. Thus his story is made to appear to be representative, as if the camera might have started following some other individual just as well. In any case the universality of the plot is given substance and affective value by the infusion of individual flavour.

It might as well be argued, however, that characters are in the last instance mere plot functions and should be treated as such, in critical discourse at least. The formalist account above of how characters are formed and apprehended in audiovisual fiction has for the main followed these lines in presenting characters as bundles of traits and thus forming a part of the overall organization of the narrative discourse. Certain films actually cue us to adopt this attitude, as in Godard's *Deux ou trois choses qui je sais d'elle* where Marina Vlady is first introduced as herself and then as the fictional character whose role she is to assume. The diegetic illusion is then broken in multiple ways in order to demonstrate how factors such as the building of modern Paris and consumer culture force people to live in a certain way, lead them to various forms of prostitution (literal or otherwise), and the like. In films like this the characters are overtly subsumed under thematic or stylistic concerns; that is, the second level of personage is well nigh obliterated in order to foreground the third level.

Yet there is much more involved in this reductive view of fictional characters. The death of the character is only one among a number of casualties ranging from God through the author to the individual him/herself. Behind this tragedy without characters lies the idea of the self as a social construction, a mere process without substance. This may well be so, but it does not accord with the lived experience most of us appear to have of ourselves and our fellow men. It has to be conceded that this is a real, valid experience which should be accounted for when one tries to understand the psychological as well as the social and cultural functions of fiction (as well as when one pursues any branch of studies in the humanities). Discussing fictional characters and their doings as if they were real people serves a heuristic purpose which ties with the whole point about the function of fiction in our lives.

Henry Bacon

Paul Ricœur suggests in his *The Rule of Metaphor* that *mimesis* should not be understood as imitation of reality but rather as a way of modelling reality or some aspect thereof. The fictional world with all its elements can thus be thought of as a network of metaphors. So what really happens in fiction is that reality is being modelled through a systematic whole, the plot. Configuring a story, like inventing a metaphor, is simultaneously a way of redescribing and discovering the human world. We can think of fictional characters as metaphors of real characters, and correspondingly of our emotional reactions as being in a metaphorical relationship to our real life reactions. This view could be seen as a poetic view of the process of identification described by Smith in his book. This scheme, however, can be further elaborated by taking into account what we, with an inextricable mixture of cognition and emotion, understand the characters to stand for in a scheme wider than the confines of the narrative.

Third level implications abound in many genre films, perhaps most obviously in Westerns, in which the milieu is often one of the defining elements carrying a considerable part of the burden of connotations. Similarly *film noir* excels in creating an atmosphere of existential anxiety by placing characters into its shadowy settings. This feature is even more prominent in German Expressionist films in which the distortions of the settings and the characters serve emphatically expressive purposes to the point of subsuming the entire second level.

Among art films almost all of Michelangelo Antonioni's films could be subsumed under the heading of "figures in a landscape". Particularly in his films of the early 1960s the phenomenal world often appears like an abstract surface, which almost crushes the fragile humanity of the characters. At the other end we have someone like Peter Greenaway, a painter by training, who deliberately sets a system of one kind or other – thematic, graphic, numerical, statistical, playful, or whatever – against the narrative, leading us to focus on the audiovisual texture and seeing the personages as figures in a richly metaphorical landscape beyond any coherent spatio-temporal or causal schemes. In this case the second level of personage has lost its autonomy; it has been subjugated to the concerns which find their expression on the third level.

On the third level of personage there opens the sphere of interpretation. From hereon it is a question of meaning and sensations beyond the immediate thrill of being engaged with the characters as we are led through their story. This is a level of both sensuous impact and thematic interest, it is about how we abstract from the diegetic level themes which relate to our human interests, and it is why in the last instance we find the film effective, touching, provoking, compelling. We might be raised to this level by an exotic or a dreary locale, or we might be guided to it through the bleakest naturalism or the most extravagant fantasy. Various cinematic means might be used ranging from classical realism to the extremes of stylization.

It might appeal to our innermost desires or most deeply grounded fears. We might experience it poetically, sensuously, intellectually, or, ideally, with a mixture of all our faculties. But always we come to it through seeing characters embodied by actors as figures in a landscape.

Notes

1. "Levels of personage" is my own term. I use Andrew's concepts just as a starting point for treating issues only partly related to the ones he discusses.
2. The practice of more than one actor playing a single role is so unusual in the cinema, that it is automatically foregrounded as an artistic device. In turn, in the theatre it has always been standard practice and thus remains usually a first level phenomenon. It has to be specially cued to be mark it as significant. Alban Berg in the libretto of his opera *Lulu* specifies which roles are to be assumed by the same actors, as does Carol Churchill for some actors in her play *Cloud Nine*.
3. The word "motivation" does not refer to my categorizations. Unfortunately, because of standard usage the semantic overlap can not be avoided.
4. Barrels of ink have been spilt in arguments about how a two-dimensional representation could be understood simply on the strength of familiarity with its three-dimensional referent. I find it by far more mind-boggling that we are able to recognize the same face through a range of facial expressions, in a variety of lightings, and after it has changed over the years. We possess a tremendous capacity for interpreting visual data as encountered in natural perception, so it is hardly surprising that we are able to carry it over to pictorial representation – photographic representation in particular. It should also be remembered that stereoscopic vision is operative only at fairly close range. Our perception of three-dimensionality is actually to a high degree cognitive in nature and is based on certain visual cues reproduced indexically in the photographic image.
5. For making certain distinctions among filmic images and their functions, I am partly indebted to Kimmo Pentikäinen, who is working on this topic in his licentiate thesis.

References

Andrew, Dudley (1995). *Mists of Regret: Culture and Sensibility in Classical French Film*. Princeton, NJ: Princeton University Press.
Bordwell, David (1988). *Narration in the Fiction Film*. London: Routledge.
Branigan, Edward (1992). *Narrative Comprehension and Film*. London and New York: Routledge.
Chatman, Seymour (1980).What novels can do that films can't (and vice versa). *Critical Inquiry* 7(1): 121–140.
Currie, Gregory (1995). *Image and Mind: Film, Philosophy, and Cognitive Science*. Cambridge: Cambridge University Press.
Grodal, Toben Kragh (1994). *Cognition, Emotion and Visual Fiction: Theory and Typology of Affective Patterns and Genres in Film and Television*. Dissertation, University of Copenhagen.
Smith, Murray (1995). *Engaging Characters: Fiction, Emotion, and the Cinema*. Oxford: Clarendon Press.

Kari Salosaari

The signs of the player: A solution

Searching for a theatre language

About ten years ago[1] Keir Elam stated in his *The Semiotics of Theatre and Drama* that the question of theatrical polyphonic discourse has turned into a "semiotic philosopher's stone" which continuously keeps eluding the possibilities of contemporary theory. (Elam 1980, 48–49) There is reason to agree with him, adding the conclusion, however, that insufficient application of theory is, in fact, the primary reason for many of the dead ends that the semiotics of the theatre have come to.

The question of theatrical signs forms part of the problem concerning the expression system, and the study of these signs was initiated by certain members of the linguistic School of Prague (among them Petr Bogatyrev, Jiři Veltruský and Jindřich Honzl). Especially significant in the history of research is Honzl's thesis according to which almost all means of expression in the theatre can substitute each other, and therefore the characteristic that defines the theatrical sign must be "transformability". (Honzl 1971, 16–17)

After the Prague School, it was only in the wake of the Structuralist movement of the 1960's in France that the semiotics of the theatre started to make headway. Roland Barthes shared with the above-mentioned school the notion of the theatre as a complex system consisting of several 'sub-languages' (langues subsidiaires) which should be analyzed before attempting to form a picture of the system as a hole. (Barthes 1964b, 249; Barthes 1964a, 101) Umberto Eco, among many others, has delved into the question of how the player functions as a sign. A veritable turning point in the discussion was marked, however, by Tadeusz Kowzan's *Litérature et spectacle* (1970), in which the Polish scholar named 13 different expression systems. Some of these are articulated in space, others in time, and others still in both dimensions. Kowzan suggested that these subsidiary languages should be studied through their respective semiotics. The theatrical sign can be described as a kind of a common denominator, once the basic units of expression in each subsidiary system have been identified. (Kowzan 1975, 212–215)

Since then, the debate concerning the semiotics of the theatre has centred on whether or not these hypotheses and objectives are correctly formed. Juri Lotman figures among those who believe in the theatrical sign, but he bases his ideas on ad hoc examples instead of whole texts. He is more interested in the use of signs than in their definition and classification. Mihail Nadin has provided the most consistent and far-reaching application of Charles S. Peirce's sign theory to performance analyses; Jørgen Dines Johansen is also working along very similar lines. Erika Fischer-Lichte bases her three-part *Semiotik des Theaters* (1983) on Charles Morris' sign theory which, in turn, is a simplification of Peirce's system. In terms of performance analysis, however, it is not particularly productive. It seems that such scholars as Anne Ubersfeld, Patrice Pavis and André Helbo, who had already published pertinent material in the 1970's, have since then completely abandoned the segmentational method of research in theatrical performance and directed their attention rather towards the semiotics of the spectator. In his *Theory of Performing Arts* (1987), Helbo will not examine the theatre as a text and suggests, instead, that it be looked as an entity, comprising both the performance and the audience's experience of the same. Willmar Sauter, too, seems to consider such an extension promising.

Sets of signs or production of meaning?

The prevailing official definition of semiotics is "a science about signs, systems of signs, and their production and use". (Tarasti 1990, 5) A *doksa* such as this, one which is embedded in the tradition of philosophical semiotics and likewise dominant in the Moscow-Tartu school, will inevitably govern, to a large extent, the empirical application of semiotics. As I see it, the fact that the goals set by Barthes and Kowzan have not been reached in performance analysis is very much connected to this far too restricted view of semiotics.

According to the second major trend in the field, namely linguistic semiotics (Saussure- Hjelmslev-Greimas and the Paris School), the definition of semiotics as a sign theory is comparable to seeing linguistics as pure morphology, without any regard for semantics, syntax or phonology. The difference in the structure of the sign is known well enough: the triad sign of Peirce (representamen- object-interpretant) presupposes the existence of an extratextual referent and, thereby, an objective 'reality'. Saussure's binary sign (signified-signifier) speaks only of contents and expressions, and its employment in research leads to compliance with the principle of the immanence of the text, excluding both the enunciator (meaning understood as the interpretation of the author's intentions) and the receiver.

What then is left? Only the text which is divided into the levels of content and expression. According to the methods of Louis Hjelmslev, both of these would be distributed into the smallest possible parts in order to reveal the text's underlying system. (Hjelmslev 1969, 5) There are two major arguments against such a procedure. According to the phenomenological school of thought, the segmentation of perceptions into structural units loses sight of the gestalt of a signifying object. But is this really the case? If the intention behind this argument is that the textual level or discourse as a continuous process is overlooked by segmentational semiotics, it is certainly not true to say that it denies the role of either one in the production of meaning. However, structural linguistics would never have emerged if language had not been seen both as a process and a system. Explanation of the former presupposes knowledge of the latter or at least hypotheses of it. On the other hand, one must look for the system beneath the process. Thus, it is also possible to describe syntagmatic gestalts as structures, indeed even to identify poetic structures in the structural poetics as extensions of significant structures.

Those in support of the second counterargument find it difficult to acknowledge the existence of an objective intratextual meaning, because in their view the conscious subject actively adds to or subtracts from the meaning while reading. They refer to concepts such as 'framing' (Goffman) or other circumstances which allegedly change the content of signs constantly. This leads to the conclusion that everything is unique, thus disqualifying the existence of a theatrical language system (*langue*) that should be valid for all its users and receivers.

This argument is another effective pretext of avoiding the effort needed to uncover the system of the theatre. It is, first of all, in sharp conflict with the axiom of linguistic semantics which claims that meaning can be studied and revealed through the immanence of the text, without regard for conditions of its production or reception. Secondly, reference can be made to the concepts originated by A. J. Greimas of 'isotopy' (*isotopie*) and meaning effect (*effet de sens*). The concept of isotopy can be used to explain the different ways of reading prompted by a certain part of discourse: isotopy refers to the continuity of context-defining features, which actualizes certain features from the unit of content of a lower level. Thus, if one part of a text is read according to another isotopy, different features will become actualized in the unit. However, there are only a finite number of ways of reading a text. (Greimas-Courtés 1979, 118) The variation found in the reading of signs is partly explained by the concept of meaning effect which refers to the impression of 'reality' produced by the senses when brought into contact with meaning, i.e. the underlying semiotics. (*Ibid.*, 116) One structure can produce several different meaning effects in the minds of its receivers. This is why semiotics must concentrate on the description of structures and not on that of the effects.

The signs of the player: A solution

Analysis of a performed segment

Transposition of playing into an object of study

On 22 luly 1971, the first and second acts of Carlo Goldoni's comedy "Quarrels at Chioggia" (Le Baruffe chiozzotte, 1760), were videotaped in the Drama Studio of the University of Tampere. The play was performed by professional Finnish players as part of their supplementary training, and directed by Professor Rudi Penka (from the GDR). One of the best scenes recorded was the 12th scene of the second act, in which Isidoro, the court secretary, questions Checca, the fisherman's daughter, and attempts to marry her off.

It is not yet possible to include a videotape as part of a scientific article, and even if it were, it would sooner or later become imperative for the writer to define verbally how he sees each part of the tape. Even then, one could not speak of scientific description, but rather transposition of an audiovisual text into a verbal-graphic one. In my doctoral thesis entitled *Perusteita näyttelijäntyön semiotiikkaan* [Fundamentals in the Semiotics of the Player's Craft] (1989), my solution was to describe as coherently as possible the meaning effects provided by the tape, proceeding from the largest and most deeply embedded parts of the performance to the ones that were smallest in size and lay closest to the surface. In the following brief excerpt, from the semiotic point of view, only the content-substance and expression-substance are described. without separating one level from the other or the form from the substance, as is done later in this paper.

•

Isidoro has summoned Checca to act as a witness to a street brawl, but the girl's family has forbidden her to say anything. The questioning takes place in the office of the court, with Checca standing irresolute by the door at the back wall. Isidoro looks closely at her a long time from where he is sitting at his desk. Checca turns from her questioner towards the door which separates her from her family, who are waiting outside for her. Isidoro stands up, gives the witness a footstool and, requests her to take a seat. He then returns to his seat at the desk and leans back in his chair. Checca moves slightly closer to the stool, regarding it suspiciously, and turns slightly towards the door.

CHECCA: *I'm here, Your Honour.* (Striving to be pompous.)

The seated Isidoro raises himself and leans heavily forward, his weight on his foremost leg, extends his left hand abruptly, points his index finger towards the footstool and, bearing a look of exasperation, shouts:

ISIDORO: *Sit down.* (Venting the full measure of his impatience .)

Kari Salosaari

Checca quickly seats herself on the footstool, and only then does Isidoro lower his arm and, after a pause, continue his speech.

•

This sequence of action forms part of a scene lasting 6 minutes and 10 seconds, which is examined in my dissertation. From the point of view of dramatic tension, the moment contains the strongest element of conflict between the protagonists, which is one reason why it is ideal for studying the signs of the player. I will proceed to do this by presenting a cross-section of Isodoro's acting as he utters the words *Sit down*, an action lasting approximately 2 seconds.

Figure 1. *The positions of the players described graphically above.*

Surface level contents

According to the so-called 'standard theory' of the Paris School of semiotics, all production of meaning can be described by means of a *generative trajectory* scheme. The purpose of this scheme is to explain meaning contents, regardless of whether they are expressed in a verbal text or in *the natural world*, i.e. in the part of the perceptual universe conceived as a text. (A theatrical performance combines the two sources of meaning.) The procedure in generative trajectory is from the deep to the surface level, from the general to the specific, from the abstract to the concrete. The former continues to predominate over the latter as an isotope, while supplementary meaning is generated as more and more distribution occurs.

In this connection, I shall only state the extremities of my content description of "Quarrels at Chioggia", as it is just these elements which are relevant in the formation of signs, i.e.. in *semiosis*. The syntactic component of the scheme in this particular part of the play ends in the subject of persuasive doing present in the character of Isidoro who within the framework of *modalized communication* and through one of its acts that can be called 'opening the eyes' (*dessiller*), tries to make Checca see things his way. The utterance *Sit down*, as dramatic action, and as part of Isidoro's manipulation, belongs to this act.

In addition to deeper structures, the semantic component of the scheme produces *practice* as represented here by the 'questioning of the witness', in which Isidoro has the *figurative role* of questioner. This practice can also be described as eight consecutive figures of doing, e.g. (the questioner) 'indicates the place' – (the witness) 'occupies the place',[2] the figure which is focalized by the semantic content of *Sit down*.

On a deeper level, *modalizations of being* are structured by the thymic component of the schema: for instance, the value of NON-CULTURE represented by Checca is 'detrimental' to Isidoro and then transformed into a *passionate figure* "aggression" on the surface level. This state is both produced and occupied by the *passionate subject* inside Isidoro.

The character played, which is semiotically the *actor*, is therefore analyzed as a set of subjects and roles which define his doing and being. The actor in the discourse is an "empty space" which consists of various syntactic and semantic elements as well as their transformations. (Greimas-Courtés 1979, 7–8) This conception can also be applied to actors in a performance, although they are represented by the players and thus inhabit the natural world instead of the verbal text.

I would like to point out that formal description is made possible by the models originated by Claude Zilberberg for the purpose of identifying modalized communication. (Zilberberg 1980, 13–14) Therefore 'to open the eyes' can be represented by a structure in which doing, seeming and being determine each other: $f(p)(e)$ (faire-paraître-être). The persuasive subject makes (f) apparent (p) what is for him (e), while he tries to convince the interpreting subject.

On the basis of certain ideas suggested by Greimas, I have strived to achieve a similar exactitude in description of passions. Thus, "aggression" corresponds to the modal structure $S1 \underline{v} [S1 \rightarrow (S2 \wedge 0-)]$, if $S1$ = the subject of doing (Isidoro), $S2$ = the subject of being (Checca), $\underline{v}$ [e] = wanting to be, i.e. the modaluation 'desirable', $\wedge$ = conjunction, i.e. uniting and = 0–a dysphoric object. The object that Isidoro, in his passion, wants Checca to be joined to, thus takes on the semantic investment 'obedience' in this context, modally *not being able to not do* (*ne pas pouvoir ne pas faire*), i.e. $\overline{pf}$.

Thus both contents, 'open the eyes' (the actor's doing) and "aggression" (the actor's being) are divided into *semes*, i.e. the smallest possible semantic features, such as modalities and syntactic operations are. In the following I use the two contents for clarifying the player's signs.

Kari Salosaari

Structures of expression

The language theory of L. Hjelmslev emphasizes the principle of the description of a text always proceeding from the whole to the parts. As the largest parts are the level of content and the level of expression (because of the definition of semiotics), analysis of the content-form and expression-form must be carried through separately, and independently of the other. (Hjelmslev 1969, 98) Only then is it possible to answer the question of what is expressed in semiosis and how.

In examining the theatre as a complex system, T. Kowzan defines its different sub-languages largely on the basis of practical theatrical terminology. My classification is based on Hjelmslev's concepts of expression-purport, substance, and form. One purport can give substance to several forms, i.e. the semiotics which abstracts from purport a specific substance for its own use. (*Ibid.*, 52, 55–57) With the aid of these concepts, all theatrical expression can be reduced to seven purports, namely the human voice, body, psyche, width (*étendue*), planes, objects, and sounds. The first three of these function as material for the semiotics constituting the player's craft, which are: 1. verbal language (voice), 2. prosody (voice), 3. kinesics (body), 4. proxemics (body), and 5. psychosemiotics (psyche). It should be added, however, that in the signifying set the position of the last-mentioned diverges from that of the others. It is therefore possible to identify 16 different systems of theatrical expression or sub-languages which combine according to the principle of *syncretic semiotics* to signify the same content-universe.

In the above-mentioned example, verbal language (system 1) is, on the one hand, employed in the utterance *Sit down* (in Finnish, *Istu*), thus realizing the semantic figure 'to indicate the place' in the practice. On the other hand, *Sit down* is part of the act of modalized communication 'to open the eyes'. The substance of the expression is segmental articulation (in the Finnish language the phonetic sequence *i, s, t, u*), and only the linear organisation is valid.

I shall now proceed to examine the systems 2–4, which are to be set under the concept 'somatic'. Prosodically, the utterance is marked by loudness (<), transfer of stress (ᴗ) onto the second syllable (in Finnish, stress is normally on the first syllable), a pause (|) immediately following, as well as a quickening of tempo (→). If the last-mentioned is converted into the feature 'increase the density' (of the spaces between the phonemes), all the analysed parameters are spatial by nature, albeit auditively perceived. The influence of prosodics on the verbally produced phonetic sequence is shown in the following symbolic representation:

<→

Istu |

The signs of the player: A solution

On the kinesic plane, there are visible changes in the shape of Isidoro's body. The forward movement of the seated Isidoro, which involves his entire body, is followed by the thrusting gesture of the arm, an action rendered also deictic by the fact that it simultaneously points at the footstool. (I indicate both features with the symbol ⊣) Then this yields the expressive figures 'enlarge' (<) and 'release' (tension) (◁). The movements of both the body and the hand occur remarkably fast, thus increasing density. Facial expression can be divided into two figures, 'release' (◁) and 'harden' (∧) – with which, together with their oppositional terms, I have classified facial expressions preliminarily into four types. The pause in the prosody corresponds furthermore to the break in the 'releasing' tendency effected by the suspension of the movement of Isidoro's arm until Checca obeys him.

Proxemics is distinct from kinesics in that it is employed in examining the changes of body position in space. This system is not employed in the analyzed sequence, although spatial behaviour could be used in place of gestures: Isidoro could stand up, take a step closer to Checca or, on the contrary, move further away from her, etc.

If non-verbal expression is analysed with the help of the above features, which all involve the organization of elements in space, equivalences can definitely be found between the three somatic systems. This is made possible by the construction on the deep expression level of a double category *centrifugal (cf)-centripetal (cp), non-centrifugal $\overline{(cf)}$-non-centripetal $\overline{(cf)}$*. These four terms and their relations are generated by the *semiotic square*, which is used in the derivation of concepts in the generative trajectory schema. (Negated terms are here presented on the upper axis).

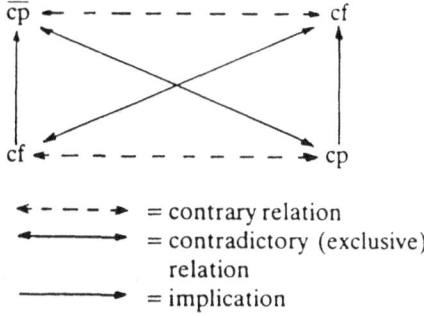

Figure 2.

The four values within the category can be presented in the intonation and melody patterns as follows:

Kari Salosaari

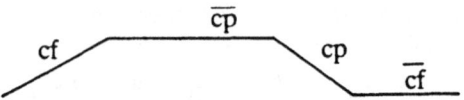

Figure 3.

A melody that keeps at a high-pitch ($\overline{cp}$) is by tendency more centrifugal than a melody that keeps a low pitch ($\overline{cf}$). Either a cf-tendency (e.g. up) or a cp-tendency (e.g. down) is discernible in all figures of the somatic system. My conclusion is that the former is the deep level which is variedly manifested by the latter. I shall return to the category in connection with sign analysis.

Constructing signs

The sign theory of the Paris School

The principle of the immanence of the text separates the sign theory presented by linguistic semiotics from Peirce's triad model in which the sign refers to an exterior object. The emergence of different signs depends on the kind of planes on which a semiotic system is formed. Verbal language is a *bi-planar semiotic system*: the content of the morpheme is constructed in another way than its phonemic sequence. According to L. Hjelmslev, both planes in *mono-planar semiotic* systems or in *symbolic systems* are conformal (as in chess). The *content-purport* produced by the expression plane can then be interpreted, but it does not have content-form. Hjelmslev sees the semiotics of music as an example of such a system. (*Ibid.*, 112–113)

A. J. Greimas adds to this, however, a third, *semi-symbolic system*, in which it is the categories of content and expression that are conformal and not the separate elements. In gestural semiotics, for example, the content category /yes/ vs. /no/ corresponds to the expression category /verticality/ vs. /horizontality/ (as a movement of the head). (Greimas-Courtés 1979, 343)

The semisymbolic sign can be presented formally as a correlation (≈) between two term-pairs, the one on the left representing contents and the one on the right expressions (see Figure 4).

The schema reads as follows: S1 is to $\overline{S1}$ as S2 is to $\overline{S2}$. S1 and $\overline{S1}$ contradict each other, as do S2 and $\overline{S2}$, whereas S1 and S2 are contrary to one another. This leads to the mutually exclusive alternative: if Sl, then S2; if $\overline{S1}$, then $\overline{S2}$.

The signs of the player: A solution

$$\frac{S1}{S1} \simeq \frac{S2}{S2} \quad \text{or, e.g.} \quad \frac{\text{"yes"}}{\text{"no"}} \simeq \frac{\text{'verticality'}}{\text{'horisontality'}}$$

Figure 4.

Hjelmslev also developed a tentative theory of *pluri-planar semiotic systems*. Of these, the *connotative* system has an independent content plane, but its expression plane is composed of *denotative semiotics* which in turn subdivides into its own planes of content and expression. This complex signifier is referred to as a *connotator*. According to Greimas, the connotator might just as well be a sign in an analyzed text as something in the substance of content or expression. (Dialectal areas are connoted by phonetic and not phonological features.) (*Ibid.*, 342)

Somatic sign

How can one establish a link between the surface level presented as communication acts and passions, and non-verbal systems of expression? The point of departure must be to assume that modal structures do not translate directly into expressions, but instead use tension structures as intermediaries. In my doctoral thesis, I have adopted certain ideas suggested by Greimas in developing the following categories for the description of *tension space* on the content plane. External or internal pressure, which acts as a stimulus to a tensile situation, is analysed in terms of SUFFICIENCY (SUF+)/INSUFFICIENCY. The latter can be further subdivided into 'too little' (SUF-) and 'too much' (SUF-!). The subject reacts to this kind of pressure by bringing about something which is of excess, the opposite of this being non-excess. The former can be divided into excess through increasing tension (EXC+) vs. excess through decreasing tension (EXC-).

The reaction to INSUFFICIENCY with both forms of EXCESS can best be understood by means of a simple action situation (e.g. the object of pursuit increases his speed or suddenly hides himself). The production of a modal communication act or passion can also be seen as a change in the field of tension. This has enabled me to show that each act and passion corresponds to a certain SUF- and EXC-value. Therefore both Isidoro's act of 'opening the eyes' and feeling of "aggression" has as its condition tension SUF-! (created by Checca's intolerable disobedience), and Isidoro reacts to this by means of both of these states, which, in the tension space, are represented by the value EXC+.

I shall now proceed to examine these categories of tension together with the deep level category of expression centrifugal/centripetal described earlier in this paper. My primary hypothesis is that the latter represents aspects of EXCESS in non-verbal expression according to the following code: EXC+: cf, $\overline{cp}$, cf + cp. EXC-: cp, $\overline{cf}$, $\overline{cf}$ + $\overline{cp}$.

Using the model of the semisymbolic sign explained earlier, it is first of all possible to examine the relationship between the modalized communication act 'to open the eyes' (EXC+) and the passion "aggression" (EXC+). Both share consequently a centrifugal tendency, but if the value of the passion is purely cf, both the anticipatory nature of the act and certain expression figures are more appropriately matched by $\overline{cp}$, which corresponds, for example, to a melody that keeps at a high pitch and blends with a feature of the centripetal tendency. This reasoning leads me to the observation that the act is expressed in prosody by the figures 'to increase the density', the transfer of syllabic stress, and the supporting pause; and in kinesics by the suspension of the thrusting arm together with its deictic function, as well as 'increasing the density' of the arm's movement. This leaves 'enlarge' as the expression of passion in prosody, and 'enlarge' and 'release' (the latter also visible with 'to harden' in the facial expression) to fill the same function in kinesics. Using the symbols presented in paragraph III.3, the somatic sign can be described as follows:

TO OPEN THE EYES ~ 2 $\overline{cp}$→ , ↙| 3 $\overline{cp}$↵,→
AGGRESSION   2 cf < 3 cf <, ◁ +∧

Figure 5.

As I have already noted above, the third expression system in the sign could be 4 proxemics. The same act or passion can manifest itself in all three systems simultaneously, in just two of them, or in one only. The fact that they can substitute each other, according to the choices made by the player, lends some support to Honzl's thesis on the transformability of theatrical signs. The somatic sign is only valid in the context into which it has been built. The permanent elements, however, are the tension aspects connected with acts and passions, as well as the rules according to which they become spatialised as values of the cf/cp category.

Psychosemiotics as a connotative system

Communication acts and passions can be analysed according to the same procedures on the basis of either a verbal or performed text. The latter differs from the former in that a human being is instrumental in its production of meaning. As a hierarchical, evolutionary structure, a human being contains both elementary and more highly developed levels. If the psychical level is postulated as extension of the somatic level, at least phenomenologically, it has to be examined in psychosemiotics especially from the viewpoint of the production of meaning. In this connection the hypotheses of depth psychology concerning psychic structures can provide psychosemiotic thinking with a more fruitful foundation than other schools of thought in this discipline. Neurophysiological functions remain outside the psychical subject's, as well as the spectator's field of perception.

Defining the position and function of the psychical level in the production of meaning is problematic. Psychical phenomena seem to be part of the content in relation to somatic expression (a trembling hand can express hysteria), yet experience has shown that it is possible, by psychical means, to express more profound dramatic contents: a player is probably capable of acting out any theme by hysterically exaggerating it.

As a solution I propose that psychosemiotics be seen as a connotative system according to Hjelmslev's conception (compare sign theory of the Paris School). This system invades, as a part of the player's constitution, as if from the outside in each performed text, part of which begins to manifest psychical forces simultaneously with other contents. The psychical level can thus be revealed in the signs of denotative semiotics, as well as in the substance of content and expression. A connoted content can in this case also be a structural description of the psychical state and expression of the player.

This definition of psychosemiotics means that connotated contents can be invested with elements provided by a psychological theory. Noteworthy in this connection is Leopold Szondi's (1893–1986) *Fate Analysis*. During more than ten years of research and experiments, much evidence has convinced me that Szondi's system is operative in studying the player's craft. It postulates the hypothesis of eight *drive factors* (hermaphrodite, sadist, epileptic, hysteric, catatonic, paranoic, depressive, manic) which represent the level of needs and which possess their own respective substances. The identification of two basic forms for each factor according to their situation in the *drive profile* yields another 16 drive tendencies. (Szondi 1960, 36–44)

I have stated in my research that these drive tendencies can be classified according to an EXC+/EXC- category (in expression furthermore according to a cf/cp category). The affirmation of the hysteric need (hy+: exhibitionism) increases tension, whereas the negation of this need (hy-: concealment of oneself) decreases it.

Psychosemiotic sign

On the basis of drive factors, on the one hand, and the meaning content of communication acts and passions, as well as by observing the binary tension values, on the other, it is possible to give a hypothetical description of the drive tendencies that affect playing. The connotator is, in this case, the somatic sign of an analysed act or passion. (If the expression-substance connotes psychical forces, it is possible to read this in the localization of tension in a specific part of the body or in the rhythm of expression.)

In the example under study, the act of 'opening the eyes' correlates on the psychical level to the cognitive action of the Ego. The paranoid enlarges and the catatonic reduces the Ego. Persuasion demands an exact objective in the imagination (p+ as paranoic tendency), as well as introjection of this wish as reality (k+ as catatonic tendency) during the communication. The tension values of both is EXC+.

The passion "aggression" belongs to the paroxysmal function of the psyche, and it refers to the use of crude (epileptic) and refined (hysteric) affects as defense mechanisms in situations of danger. Passion in this context corresponds to Szondi's structure of "hysterical rage", in which the epileptic has completely withdrawn from the foreground of the drive profile to the background (e0), and the affirmed hysteric need (hy+) can vent itself without the control of the former. The meaning effect produced here is of light, 'comical' rage.

The results from this study are shown in the following diagrams. In addition to abbreviations introduced in the foregoing, Sé = signified, Sa = signifier, Sé1↔Sa1 = denotative sign (whose parts are connected by a mutual presupposition or solidarity), Sé2↔Sa2 = connotative sign.

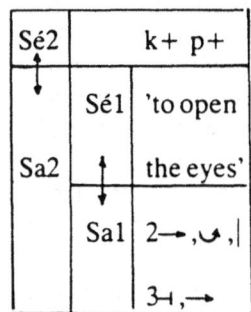 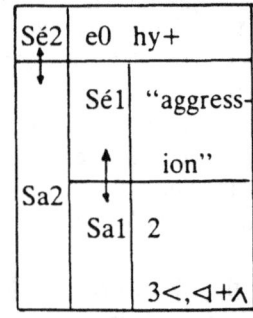

Figure 6.

Conclusion: integration of the player's signs

The verbal sign *Sit down* is still missing from the act diagram presented above. This utterance, which has an operative function in a modalizing way, has been generated as a result and extension of the enunciated enunciation (*énonciation énoncée*), which is the act of communication in the discourse. Just like the dialogue generally, a dramatic line simultaneously manifests other things in the discourse, in this case the semantic figure 'to occupy the place'. I do not consider such a relation a sign of the player, however, as it is not produced by him alone but also involves the semiotics of space and objects (the footstool and its location).

The utterance *Istu* (*Sit down*) is manifested in the phonemic sequence i,s,t,u which, as such, is merely linear and, according to tension, neutral value (this value can be marked $\overline{EXC}$). However, it becomes part of the tension space and thus a factor in modalizing action when the player spatializes the phonemic sequence in his prosody in the manner described earlier in this paper. Then the line is transformed into the value EXC+.

The player thus produces three kinds of signs, namely verbal, somatic, and psychosemiotic. They do not only exist side by side but also in layers and within each other. A hierarchical syntagm is thus produced, whose overall structure can be described using the model on the next page (SF= semantic figure, Re = line).

The figure below describes an action, which took a mere two seconds.

(Translated by Sari Hänninen)

5	EXC+ k+ p+		SF: 'to indicate the place'	5	EXC+ e0 hy+	
	EXC+ 'to open the eyes'				EXC+ "aggression"	
	Re: Sé					
	1 I,s,t,u					
2	$\overline{cp}\rightarrow,\smile,\mid$				cf <	
3	$\overline{cp}\dashv,\rightarrow$				cf <, ◁ +∧	
4						

Figure 7.

Notes

1. Structures of that kind are found and examined by Courtés in his article.
2. This article was originally published in *Nordic Theatre Studies. Yearbook for Theatre Research in Scandinavia.* No. 5/1992. Munksgaard.

Kari Salosaari

Literature

Barthes, Roland (1964a). Eléments de sémiologie. *Communications* 4.
– (1964b). *Essais critiques.* Paris: Editions du Seuil.
Courtés, Joseph (1980). La "lettre" dans le conte populaire merveilleux (1re partie). *Documents de recherche du Groupe de Recherches semio-linguistiques (EHESS) de l'Ecole de Hautes Etudes en sciences sociales.* Numéro 9.
Elam, Keir (1980). *The Semiotics of Theatre and Drama.* London: Methuen.
Fischer-Lichte, Erika (1983). *Semiotik des Theaters* 1–3. Tübingen: Günter Narr Verlag.
Greimas, Algirdas J. & Courtes, Joseph (1979). *Sémiotique.Dictionnaire raisonné de la théorie du langage.* Paris: Hachette. (In English: Semiotics and Language. An Analytical Dictionary.1980.Trans. Larry Crist et alii. Bloomington: Indiana University Press.)
Helbo, André (1987). *Theory of Performing Arts.* Amsterdam: Benjamins.
Hjelmslev, Louis (1969). *Prologomena to a Theory of Lanquage.* Trans. Francis J. Whitefield. Madison: University of Wisconsin Press.
Honzl, Jindřich (1971). La mobilité de signe théâtral. *Travail Théâtral* 4, 5–20.
Kowzan, Tadeusz (1975). *Littérature et spectacle.* La Haye: Mouton.
Salosaari, Kari (1989). Perusteita näyttelijäntyön semiotiikkaan. I osa: Teatterin kieli ja näyttelijä merkityksen tuottajana. [Fundamentals in the Semiotics of the Player's Craft. Part One: The Language of the Theatre and the Player as the Agent of Signification]. Tampere: Acta Universitatis Tamperensis. (Diss.)
Szondi, Leopold (1960). *Lehrbuch der experimentellen Triebdiagnostik.* Textband. Zweite Auflage. Bern: Verlag Hans Huber.
Tarasti, Eero (1990). *Johdatus semiotiikkaan. Esseitä taiteen ja kulttuurin merkkijärjestelmistä* [Introduction to Semiotics. Essays on the signs systems of art and culture]. Helsinki: Gaudeamus.
Zilberberg, Claude (1980). Notes relatives au faire persuatif. *Le Bulletin du Groupe de Recherches sémio-linguistiques (EHESS) de l'Ecole de Hautes Etudes en sciences sociales.* Numéro 15.

ARTS III: LITERATURE AND VERBAL SIGNS

Harri Veivo

Problems of reference in description

In this paper I address some problems concerning the relation between reference and spatial description in literature and try to sketch some elementary solutions to them. By "spatial description" I mean the description of locations as physical, social, and cultural spaces.

Questions concerning reference and the related theme of mimesis have been a central issue in recent literary research. In description studies, at least in the French context, the prevailing attitude has been to consider reference to extralinguistic reality as irrelevant or even erroneous. This attitude is based on the conception of literature as a self-referential linguistic activity with no direct relation to the extralinguistic realm. The roots of this conception may be traced back to Ferdinand de Saussure's theory of language and especially his conception of the linguistic sign. For Saussure, the linguistic sign is composed of two mental entities, the signified and the signifier, which are linked together by the language-system (*la langue*). Since the language-system is seen as an autonomous and self-sufficient system of internal relations, the extralinguistic domain does not play any role in the formation of the linguistic sign.

The impact of Saussure's thinking on structuralist and post-structuralist studies of literature since the 1950s is well-known. In description studies this impact is clearly manifested in several major works. Roland Barthes's "L'effet de réel" (1968; in 1993) and *S/Z* (1970) have been considered cornerstones of an antireferential approach to description. Barthes does not explicitly deny the text the ability to refer to the extra-textual domain, but he argues that literary descriptions signify above all social or cultural conceptions of reality. In the 1968 essay, Barthes claims that the concrete details that seem to establish a direct relation between the signifier and the referent are in fact literary devices that only signify the cultural conception of what reality is like: "c'est la catégorie du 'réel' (et non ses contenus contingents) qui est alors signifiée" (Barthes 1984: 186). Barthes baptizes this phenomenon the "illusion référentielle" and the effect produced by it the "effet de réel". A similar line of argumentation is followed in *S/Z* where Barthes claims that (traditional realistic) literary descriptions are subordinated to models used in visual arts. As such, they do not refer to an extratextual referent, but to a copy of a referent, to a reality already modeled by culture (Barthes 1970: esp. 61–62 and 172–174).

Denis Bertrand, in his study of spatial description in Zola's *Germinal*, uses the term "effet référentiel" instead of Barthes's "illusion référentielle" and "effet de réel". By this term he denotes textual segments that refer, by indexical means, to the extra-textual. Bertrand nevertheless follows Barthes in claiming that this extra-textual is not the reality as such, but always an already modeled conception thereof: "la référence n'est pas une référence au référent – tout simplement parce qu'un tel 'monde' est déjà une représentation" (Bertrand 1985: 29–30).

The antireferential stance is continued by Philippe Hamon in his book *Du descriptif* (1993), which is probably the most systematic study of literary description written in French. Hamon accepts Barthes's notion of referential illusion and takes as his starting point the idea that literary description must be seen as an intralinguistic activity, either as an amplification of a name or as an unfolding of signs belonging to the same paradigm.[1] For Hamon, the role of reference must be minimized also for methodological reasons: to accept the referent as a constituent part of description would dissolve the object of study, the descriptive text in general, to a plurality of domains, each having its own type of referent and thus its own logic.

Needless to say, all the writers mentioned above have made significant contributions to the understanding of literary description. Still, their approach also presents some difficulties.

Firstly, it may be argued that the excessive problematization of reference results in a limited understanding of the function of descriptions in a text. Characters, actions, and locations may all be described with linguistically similar devices. Still, extralinguistic knowledge, as Jørgen Dines Johansen reminds us, is always needed to understand the difference in meaning between linguistically similar phrases. "Charles loves Emma" refers to a fictional world, but "Charles loves Camilla" to the real world (Johansen 1993). Moreover, characters, actions, and locations have different narrative functions in the text – a character commits actions in locations, not vice versa.[2] This fact is reflected in the ways these are described.

Secondly, although it seems reasonable to claim, like Christian Jacob, that "l'espace ne préexiste pas aux pratiques, à la carte ni à la description: ils sont des constructions, des modélisations irrémédiablement distinctes de la réalité-référent" (1995: 13), we must recognize that there are degrees of generality and individuality. The reduction of a fictional referent to a cultural model, or an already existing representation, is contrary to a commonsensical understanding of fictional entities. Even if the anti-utopia of W, a totalitarian state devoted to sport in Georges

Perec's novel *W ou le souvenir d'enfance* (1975), has close intertextual relations to the tradition of both utopian and anti-utopian writing and is described with traditional rhetorical devices, this does not result in its being a cultural model, if by model we refer to general, repeated representations. W in Perec's novel is not reducible to coded representations; it is an individual fictional entity existing by virtue of Perec's text.

A dividing line must be drawn between the referent and the way the referent is described. The textual devices used to create reference – i.e., naming and description – may be more or less coded. The referent, on the other hand, may be individuated to varying degrees: in some cases we are dealing with cultural models, in others with individual entities. Separating the referent from the reference is a crucial move in understanding the nature of literary description. Meir Sternberg has said that "what distinguishes verbal or nonpictorial description is … the asymmetry between the spatiality of its object and the temporality of its presentation" (Sternberg 1981: 61). Text is linear and reading is temporal, but all the dimensions of a spatial object or location exist simultaneously. Spatial description may be an effort to overcome this discrepancy or it may use it to create rhetorical effects, such as the imitation of subjective perception. In all cases the difference between reference and referent is exactly what makes descriptions worth studying.

Description is thus referential activity. But how does the referent exist? And how does its mode of existence relate to description? Using examples from various authors, in what follows I try to see what insights recent theories of fictional existence might offer the study of description.

The possibility of fictional worlds

The theory of possible worlds, originally developed by Leibniz, has been one of the major issues in philosophy since the 1960s. In philosophy it has been applied mainly in analyzing counterfactual statements. Stipulating possible worlds as reference worlds permits the determination of truth-values for counterfactual statements that would be impossible to analyze if they referred to the actual world.

The theory of possible worlds has influenced several domains of research, such as linguistics, philosophy of science, and aesthetics. In literary research it has enriched reflections on fiction, which clearly is similar to counterfactuals in one respect: both are assertions about something that does not have physical existence. Despite this parallelism, in order to develop methods for fiction studies literary researchers have modified the philosophical theory of possible worlds in some major respects.

Philosophers have several opinions on the mode of being of possible worlds.[3] Some hold that possible worlds exist just like the actual world we live in.

Actuality is seen as an indexical notion: it refers to the world in which the individual using the word "actual" lives. Other individuals may live in other worlds, which are actual for them. Possible worlds thus exist in separate logical spaces where they all have physical existence. This modal realism is in some respects close to anti-realist views on the existence of possible worlds. Anti-realists claim that the notion of a possible world is irrelevant, since it presupposes a real world in relation to which the other worlds might be characterized as possible. For anti-realists, this presupposition is erroneous; they claim that we have no access to metaphysical reality, but only to relative world-versions.

The third attitude, known as moderate realism, covers several views that have in common the idea that possible worlds are constructions that exist in relation to the actual world. Possible worlds are seen as ramifications of the actual world; they are components of reality even though they do not have physical existence.

Moderate realism would seem to fit well the purposes of literary research. It could be claimed that the referents – that is, fictional entities – to which a text refers exist as mental constructions in a possible world related to the actual world. This basic insight is relevant, but it must be supplemented with several ideas stemming from the fact that fiction is a specific type of cultural practice.

In philosophy, possible worlds are seen as logically accessible from our world; that is, they may differ from the actual world but their mode of organization still follows logical principles. An illogical possible world is inconceivable in philosophy. In literary research, however, this point is problematic. Many texts defy our basic logical principles. Knight Agilulf literally does not exists but he nevertheless performs actions in Italo Calvino's *Il cavaliere inesistente*.

To understand the status of fictional worlds it is necessary to extend the field of inquiry and to consider fiction as a cultural practice. Many scholars have used notions and insights derived from speech-act theory to understand what kind of a linguistic activity fiction is. Gregory Currie (1985) and, with more sophistication, Marie-Laure Ryan (1991) have both proposed that fiction should be seen as a specific type of speech-act. When reading fiction, the reader engages in a sort of make-believe activity: the assertions in the text are assumed to refer to a fictional world instead of the actual world. Ryan has proposed that fictional communication should be understood as having a layered structure. When reading fiction, the actual reader is invited by the author to step to another level of communication in which a substitute speaker, the narrator, is making assertions to a substitute listener with whom the reader may or may not identify herself. The assertions the narrator makes refer to the fictional world; they are thus not assertions devoid of reference, but genuine speech acts having referents that exist as mental constructions. The reader of fiction is invited by this specific type of communication to mentally reconstruct the referents: "The rules of fictional transaction specify ... the invitation extended to the reader to reconstruct a universe on the basis of the pretended speech act" (Ryan 1991: 75).

Thomas Pavel has argued that the degree of commitment the reader has to the existence of these universes may vary. Physical existence or logical coherence are not successful criteria if we wish to understand how readers relate to fiction. For imaginary characters or events may have such an impact on our mode of thinking and life in general that it would be difficult to deny their existence on physical or logical grounds. In this sense, fiction is similar to other symbolic activities: "To be existent without existing is a sophisticated property equally shared by mathematical entities, unfinanced architectural monuments, spiritual emanation in gnostic systems, and fictional characters" (Pavel 1986: 31).

Pavel's proposal seems reasonable. Logical coherence, considered as an obligatory requirement of possible worlds in philosophy, does not enjoy the same status in literature. It is crucial for realistic texts, but in other cases it may be openly disregarded. Most scholars seem to accept the idea that there may be several ontological levels in the text.[4] The text may present some entities and situations as more real than others. Sophocles's *King Oedipus* is a classic example: Oedipus's conception of reality does not match with what the text presents as the real state of affairs. On the other hand, many contemporary works try undermine all conceptions of the real state of affairs the reader could get from the text. The idea that texts may refer to referents having different degrees of being, and that readers correspondingly assume varying degrees of ontological commitment, makes it possible to analyze fictional world construction without *a priori* judgments. Moreover, if we accept that fiction is a specific type of speech-act in which the reader is engaged in a game of make-believe, there seems to be no reason to deny that the reader can construct a fictional world in which fictional entities known only through the text exist in relation to actual entities known through experience and other sources. When we read Flaubert's *Madame Bovary* we presume that Normandy in the text is like the real Normandy except for the fictional locations Flaubert has invented. Logically speaking, Normandy in *Madame Bovary* is not the real Normandy, since it counts Yonville-L'Abbaye among its villages. But the reader knows he is reading fiction. For him the similarities between Flaubert's description of Normandy and the real region are more important than their dissimilarities. The similarities allow the reader recourse to extratextual knowledge about the entities described. Attention may thus be shifted from philosophical considerations to textual features and pragmatic aspects of literary communication.

Umberto Eco (1976, 1984) has proposed that the content of a linguistic sign should be enlarged to cover, in addition to the so-called essential properties, also such features as stereotypical knowledge, frames, and scripts. According to Eco, these are items of encyclopedic knowledge that are related to the sign by weak or strong codes. In this sense, an actual proper name conveys to the reader encyclopedic knowledge he can use to interpret the text. Mentioning "Paris", for example, is enough to active many conventional items of knowledge in the reading process, even though they are not explicitly mentioned. Reading can thus be considered as a dialogue between the text, the reader, and the encyclopedic knowledge embodied in language. Both Eco and Ronen (1994: 136) further hold that the properties related to a name cannot be hierarchized in terms of the essential and the inessential; any item of encyclopedic knowledge may be relevant or irrelevant. The way the reader uses encyclopedic knowledge to interpret the text depends on both the co-text and the context.

In Julien Gracq's novel *Le rivage des Syrtes* (1951), a fictional work if ever there was one, the narrator, a young officer, comments on his commandant's behavior in the following way:

> Le faste de la réception atteignit son comble quand il leur proposa une visite de la fortresse: le Roi-Soleil à court d'argent menant promener les traitants dans le parc de Versailles ne m'eût plus scandalisé; j'envoyai seller mon cheval et je m'excusai en me prétendant malade. (Gracq 1989: 610)

The passage mixes references to fictional and factual entities in a very interesting way. The story is located in a purely fictional world in the sense that it is never explicitly related to real geography. Logically speaking, the narrator with his pejorative remarks seems thus to be quite exceptional: he lives in a fictional world, but in some unexplained way he has knowledge of historical persons who existed in the actual world the reader lives in.

On the other hand, in *Le rivage des Syrtes* Gracq baptizes his fictional locations with names that sound very Italian. Moreover, the characters have Italian names and the city-state of Orsenna they live in has many similarities to eighteenth-century Venice. The reader easily locates Gracq's imaginary universe in some indefinite spot in actual geography and history, although strictly speaking it does not exist there. In this context, it is reasonable not to concentrate on logical inconsistencies, but to read the narrator's comment as an invitation to select from the encyclopedic knowledge related to Louis XIV, Versailles, and Italy those items that seem to be relevant for the understanding of the text. In this case, one of those items would be some notion of dignity proper to aristocratic societies and shared by the narrator, since it is the common element that establishes the unfavorable comparison between the commandant's real action in the fictional world and Louis XIV's imagined action in the actual world.

This example shows, I hope, that reference to the actual world functions as part of the text's strategy. I would like to emphasize that no far-reaching metaphysical assumptions are needed to maintain this argument. Reference to the actual world does not mean referring to factual reality, but, as Roland Barthes rightly claimed, to cultural models thereof. There is, however, a difference between the actual world and the fictional world: the former is a continuum that exists by virtue of a multitude of documents and experiences and is submitted to modifications; the latter is an individual entity existing solely by virtue of Gracq's text, even though readers gain access to it only through a creative reading process. In the reading process the reader, guided by the text, uses encyclopedic knowledge, that is, cultural models of reality, to construct a fictional world, which cannot be reduced to coded representations.

Incompleteness and reception

Fictional worlds thus exist as cultural artifacts embodied in linguistic texts. Readers have access to them through the semiotic channel constituted by the text. This focuses attention on the problematics of language.

Scholars who deal with the theory of fictional worlds usually assume without further elaboration that linguistic texts are interpreted in sufficiently similar ways by different readers.[5] I endorse their position and do not discuss the question any further here. Let it just be noted that the semiotic theory based on Charles Peirce's philosophy and developed in the literary context by Umberto Eco offers arguments to defend this basic assumption.

I will instead discuss another aspect closely related to the one mentioned above, namely, the incompleteness of fictional worlds. Fictional worlds may be considered necessarily and inevitably incomplete. Philosophers use the notion of completeness for entities of which it is possible to say whether they have any property x or not. Physically existing entities – for example, persons – are in principle complete; we can find out whether or not they are red-haired, if they have blue eyes, and so on. Fictional entities, on the other hand, are incomplete. Famous examples such as the number of Lady Macbeth's children or the colour of Emma Bovary's eyes show that it is often impossible to decide whether a fictional entity has certain properties or not. Texts remain silent on numerous points.

Readers thus always lack information because fictional worlds are incomplete. On the other hand, it is clear that readers supplement the information provided by the text. Many scholars have elaborated theories to account for this phenomenon. Umberto Eco (1979) has convincingly demonstrated that reading is cooperation between text and reader. According to Eco, the reader, guided by textual indications, fills the informational gaps in the text by using encyclopedic knowledge embodied in language. Eco has stressed that this interaction is guided by the text (1990, 1992). Recourse to encyclopedic knowledge in interpretation must always be justified with reference to the text.

Similar ideas are proposed by Marie-Laure Ryan (1991). She has introduced a pragmatic rule for reading called "the principle of minimal departure". According to Ryan, this principle refers to the fact that the world embodied in the text is considered to be similar to our world unless otherwise indicated by the text. For example, the reader supposes that laws of nature and habits of social interaction specific for the time described are valid in the fictional world even though they are not explicitly stated.

Eco's and Ryan's proposals indicate two important points. Firstly, the incompleteness of fictional worlds is relative: some informational gaps left by the text may legitimately be filled by the reader. Secondly, this necessary supplementation is largely guided by the text. Incompleteness may thus be seen as a problem of rhetoric, as Ronen has proposed (1994: 130).

It may be instructive to compare two very different texts in this respect. Philippe Sollers's *Drame* (1965) is an avant-gardist text presenting the aesthetics of the Tel Quel group. Its structure is based on an alternation of passages in which an extradiegetic narrator comments on the protagonist's actions and passages presented as written by the (male) protagonist to a female character. These passages written by the protagonist are very interesting. They contain many comments on and descriptions of how he feels and conceives of the surroundings in which he lives. Strong emphasis is put on bodily contact. On the other hand, the protagonist problematizes the relation between language and the extralinguistic realm. In this sense, the protagonist's text may be read as a metatextual commentary advancing Tel Quel's anti-representative aesthetics.

The third passage presented as written by the protagonist has the following description and commentary:

> Les immeubles ont l'air d'être entourés d'un air flottant (y a-t-il en ce moment quelqu'un pour le voir?). L'inachevé. L'inachevable. Un compte rendu noterait ici une métropole évidente, mais non, tu le sais: vent de plaine, rues désertes, amnésie généralisée (quelqu'un, en ce moment, oublie un infime détail). Voici la cathédrale. Des voitures tout autour, comme abandonnées, l'intérieur en désordre: vieilles cartes, vieux gants.... . Métamorphoses incessants: il suffit de passer des collines surplombant la mer aux ruelles du port. Du panorama géometrique à l'aveuglement mobile. Du centre au ralentissement des faubourgs. – Et ce langage: faux, borné par rapport à notre présence que je regarde au-delà des vitres se jouer en bas maintenant dans les reflets lumineux de l'eau sur la pierre, incessamment débordante, la même, renouvelée.... (Sollers 1990: 26–27)

The text thematizes the difference between the incompleteness of verbal description and the plenitude of visual perception. Language is seen as severely limited in comparison with the extralinguistic realm presented as visually perceived. Yet it is important to remember that this opposition is constructed by the text, inasmuch as the referents in relation to which verbal descriptions are incomplete exist only as evoked by the text. The text thus entertains two contradictory discourses. The first one constructs the referents by naming and description. The second one presents these referents as complex, visually perceived, extralinguistic entities and creates a discrepancy between the claimed incompleteness of verbal description and the assumed plenitude of referents.

For this to be possible, the text uses verbal descriptions in a very specific way. Signs such as "the cathedral" and "the small streets in the harbour" are related to numerous items of encyclopedic knowledge, since the average reader may be expected to know what a cathedral looks like. In Sollers's case, however, the text uses these items "negatively". The reader is not invited to directly supplement the verbal descriptions with encyclopedic knowledge, but to use encyclopedic knowledge to construct the pretended extralinguistic referents so as to make them complete. In this way, the text can oppose the incomplete description with that which is presented as the complete referent. The referent is, however, still constructed by description and encyclopedic knowledge. Sollers's anti-referential aesthetics presupposes reference.

In Georges Perec's *Tentative d'épuisement d'un lieu parisien* (1975) descriptive incompleteness functions differently. The text was originally written for a 1975 issue of the journal *Cause Commune* entitled "Pourrissement des Sociétés". It is not a fictional text: it describes a real location, La Place Saint-Sulpice in Paris. The text is represented as having been written in three days, 18–20 October 1974, in cafés around the square and on a bench in the square's center. Moreover, Perec gives to his text an openly factual status. His aim is to describe "le reste", that is, those things around the square that seem to lack importance to the extent that they usually remain unnoticed. In this sense, the purpose in *Tentative* is very similar to "Approches de quoi?", another article written by the same author for *Cause Commune* two years earlier. There Perec defined his project as follows:

> Ce qui se passe vraiment, ce que nous vivons, le reste, tout le reste, où est-il? Ce qui se passe chaque jour, le banal, le quotidien, l'évident, le commun, l'ordinaire, l'infra-ordinaire, le bruit du fond, l'habituel, comment en rendre compte, comment l'interroger, comment le décrire? Interroger l'habituel. Mais justement, nous y sommes habitués. Nous ne l'interrogeons pas, il semble ne pas faire problème, nous le vivons sans y penser, comme s'il ne véhiculait ni question ni réponse, comme s'il n'était porteur d'aucune information. Ce n'est même plus du conditionnement, c'est de l'anesthésie. Nous dormons notre vie d'un sommeil sans rêves. Mais où est-elle, notre vie? Où est notre corps? Où est notre espace? (Perec 1989: 11)

Perec thus intended in *Cause Commune* to write texts that would change the ways in which space is normally perceived and conceptualized. Truthfulness of representation is thus one key for the reading of *Tentative*.

Perec gives an interesting solution in *Tentative* to the problem of "How to describe the ordinary?". The text constructs a complex, three-layered referential system. Firstly, the text refers indexically to the extratextual realm, La Place Saint-Sulpice, presented both as an example of a typical Parisian square (the article in the title is indefinite) and as a specific real location (named in the text). Secondly, at the very beginning, the text gives a short pastiche of a conventional description of the square; that is, it refers intertextually to a body of cultural models of the square. This description is related to the rest of the text with the following comment: "Un grand nombre ... de ces choses on été décrites, inventoriées ... Mon propos dans les pages qui suivent a plutôt été de décrire le reste: ce que l'on ne note généralement pas, ..." (Perec 1988: 12). Thirdly, the main part of the text invites the reader to construct a referent consisting exactly of "the rest", that is to say, the details and events that are normally ignored.

The text juxtaposes two of these three referents – the pastiched conventional model and the one consisting of "the rest" – one against the other. Descriptive incompleteness is a crucial element in this antithesis.

The descriptive procedures used to describe "the rest" in the main part of the text are anti-conventional in the sense that they do not offer the reader any clear and complete conception of the place described. The descriptions consist of lists enumerating the things the writer sees from the place (mentioned in the text) where he is seated. They are often presented without explanatory comments. An example: "Le 70 va à la Place du Dr Hayem, Maison de l'O.R.T.F. / méhari verte / Le 86 va à Saint-Germain-des-Prés / Danone: Yoghourts et desserts" (Perec 1988: 16). The descriptions in passages like this remain very incomplete. We may infer from other parts of the text that "Danone" is probably an advertisement on a bus, but it could just as easily be some other text. Moreover, the buses, the car ("méhari", a special model based on the Citroen 2 CV), and the advertisement are not related spatially to each other nor to other entities described by the text.

This incompleteness makes recourse to encyclopedic knowledge indispensable. The reader has to supplement the information given by the text in order to be able to construct to a certain degree a coherent referent for the text. What happens is that the anti-conventional, incomplete description is conceived as closer to the extratextual realm than is the conventional representation.

On the other hand, the details and events Perec mentions complement the reader's encyclopedic knowledge. The text and encyclopedic knowledge thus structure each other. In this sense, descriptive incompleteness does not function to increase the discrepancy between the extratextual and the verbal, as in Sollers's text. On the contrary, it seeks to expose the deficiency in conventional representations. The description proposed by the main part of the text is conceived as "true", that is, as a truthful representation of an unconditioned perception of visual environment in comparison with the pastiched conventional representations.

Truthfulness here does not mean that the text would in its turn try to impose a true model of the square. On the contrary, Perec is acutely aware of the limits of his utopian project and of the inescapable subjectivity of perception. What the text does manage to do, however, is to expose the inadequacy of cultural representations in relation to individual experience. Descriptive incompleteness is the central means by which this goal is attained.

Concluding remarks

I have concentrated in both Sollers's and Perec's texts on the ways in which they use reference in spatial descriptions. In addition to this, they present other interesting subjects for analysis and discussion. For example, both texts contain intriguing cases of subjective spatial relationships: in *Drame* the protagonist identifies himself with the city; in *Tentative* the descriptive lists follow idiosyncratic hierarchies and intermingle with metatextual commentaries on the way the location is perceived by the writer. I suppose, however, that we can close (or start) the discussion here with the following remarks.

The theory of fictional worlds provides the study of description with several valuable insights. First of all, it is possible to analyze descriptions on a referential basis. Fictional entities' incomplete and often elusive nature due to their embodiment in linguistic texts does not make literature anti-referential. If we consider literature a cultural activity, that is, if we approach texts on both a formal and pragmatic level, it is possible to say that texts do refer to spatial locations in ways that are stable enough to form an object of study.

On the other hand, the relation between narration and description may be formulated in a new way. Narratological studies have usually either totally neglected description or granted it only secondary status as an interruption in the narration.[6] This attitude could be traced back to Aristotle's *Poetics* in which he argues that literature imitates action above all else. Aristotle, however, was writing about theatre, not poetry or prose. The difference lies in the fact that, although verbal descriptions do exist in theatre, they are not necessary for giving the addressee access to the world represented, whereas in prose or poetry fictional entities must be either named or described before they can commit acts or serve as locations. In this sense naming and description may be seen as necessary and essential constituents of narration.

If we furthermore consider narration in literary works to be based on a system of values,[7] it may be argued that naming is in many cases accompanied by a discourse expressing the values related to the named entities. Description is one of the means used for this purpose. Philippe Hamon has proposed that the fundamental level in description is constituted by axiologically organized logical schemes that structure the description with binary oppositions (Hamon 1993: 97–98). In this sense, it may be argued that descriptions construct worlds filled with values. Could it also be maintained that these values – that is, descriptions – make narratives possible?

Notes

1. For example, a description of a house is considered as a listing of signs belonging to the paradigm of house: roof, ceiling, walls, etc.
2. For a discussion of landscape descriptions from this point of view, see Chenet-Faugeras (1995).
3. For a good exposition of these philosophical positions see Ronen (1994: 21–26).
4. Ryan (1991), Dolezel (1988), and Eco (1990) have proposed theories and notions for split ontologies in the story.
5. See for example Ryan (1991: 15) and Dolezel (1988).
6. The article on description in Prince's *Dictionary of Narratology* (1987) clearly shows this tendency: it simply lists different types of description without considering its function in relation to other textual factors.
7. This idea is basic for Claude Brémond, who divides narrative sequences into two types, improvements and deteriorations (Brémond 1973), and to A. J. Greimas, who takes the relation of desire as the constituent element for the identity of the basic actants subject and object (Greimas 1966). Improvement, deterioration, and desire can be defined only with reference to a system of values.

References

Barthes, Roland (1976/1970). *S/Z*. Paris: Seuil.
– (1993/1984). *Le bruissement de la langue*. Paris: Seuil.
Bertrand, Denis (1985). *L'espace et le sens*. Paris and Amsterdam: Hadès-Benjamins.
Brémond, Claude (1973). *Logique du récit*. Paris: Seuil.
Chenet-Faugeras, Françoise (1995). Paysage et poétique. In: *Descriptions et créations d'espaces dans la littérature*. E. Leonardy and Hubert Roland (eds.). 31–52. Louvain-la-Neuve: Collège Erasme and Éditions Nauwelaerts.
Currie, Gregory (1985). What is fiction? *Journal of Aesthetics and Art Criticism* 43(4): 385–392.
Dolezel, Lubomir (1988). Mimesis and possible worlds. *Poetics Today* 9(3): 475–496.
Eco, Umberto (1976). *A Theory of Semiotics*. Bloomington: Indiana University Press.
– (1979). *The Role of the Reader*. Bloomington: Indiana University Press.
– (1984). *Semiotics and the Philosophy of Language*. London: MacMillan.
– (1990). *The Limits of Interpretation*. Bloomington: Indiana University Press.
– (1992). *Interpretation and Overinterpretation*. Cambridge: Cambridge University Press.
Gracq, Julien (1989). *Œuvres complètes I*. Paris: Gallimard.
Greimas, A. J. (1966). *Sémantique structurale*. Paris: Larousse.
Hamon, Philippe (1993). *Du descriptif*. Paris: Hachette.

Jacob, Christian (1995). Littérature et géographie en Grèce ancienne. In: *Descriptions et créations d'espaces dans la littérature*. E. Leonardy and Hubert Roland (eds.). 11–30. Louvain-la-Neuve: Collège Erasme and Éditions Nauwelaerts.
Johansen, Jørgen Dines (1993). *Dialogic Semiosis*. Bloomington: Indiana University Press.
Pavel, Thomas (1986). *Fictional Worlds*. Cambridge, MA: Harvard University Press.
Perec, Georges (1988). *Tentative d'épuisement d'un lieu parisien*. Paris: Christian Bourgois.
– (1989). Approches de quoi?. In: *L'infra-ordinaire*. 9–13. Paris: Seuil.
Prince, Gerald (1987). *A Dictionary of Narratology*. Lincoln, NE: University of Nebraska Press.
Ronen, Ruth (1994). *Possible Worlds in Literary Theory*. Cambridge: Cambridge University Press.
Ryan, Marie-Laure (1991). *Possible Worlds, Artificial Intelligence, and Narrative Theory*. Bloomington: Indiana University Press.
Sollers, Philippe (1990). *Drame*. Paris: Seuil.
Sternberg, Meir (1981). Ordering the unordered: Time, space, and descriptive coherence. *Yale French Studies* 61: 60–88.

H. K. Riikonen

The lure of etymology in the poetry and prose of Pentti Saarikoski

> *There is an ancient saying that knowledge of high things is hard to gain; and surely knowledge of names is no small matter.*
> (Plato, *Cratylus*: 384b)

I

According to Quintilian, etymology is the branch of knowledge that searches for the origins of words ("verborum originem inquirit"; *Institutionis oratoriae*: I.VI.28). Although Quintilian regards great learning ("multa eruditio"; ibid.: I.VI.31) as an important prerequisite for the etymologist, his brief definition does not give any idea of the great difficulties involved in the etymological and historical study of words. In the epilogue to his article on the word "pine" in the European linguistic atlas, Terho Itkonen enumerates several difficulties encountered by the etymologist, adding that most of them "seem to be almost beyond any checking" (1986: 151–152). Still, such difficulties have by no means deterred self-taught and self-made linguists, amateurs and dilettantes from indulging in far-reaching speculations and bold comparisons in the fields of etymology, comparative philology and historical linguistics. This is clearly (and amusingly) shown by Harry Halén and Tauno Tukkinen in their 1984 book *Elämän ja kuoleman kello* (*The Clock of Life and Death*) on the life of the Finnish dilettante etymologist par excellence, Sigurd Wettenhovi-Aspa (1870–1946). In the light of Halén's and Tukkinen's book, one cannot help thinking that the Finns, Hungarians, and Estonians have a special talent and inclination towards such speculative *Pseudowissenschaft*. In Finland the dilettante tradition reaches from C. A. Gottlund, Valter Juva, and Wettenhovi-Aspa to many less-known names (Halén and Tukkinen 1986: 199–213, 255–262, 306–325). As warning, Quintilian himself gives examples of how false judgements may lead to absurd results ("praviis ingeniis ad foedissima usque ludibria labuntur"; *Institutionis oratoriae*: I.VI.32), as exemplified by the Roman etymologists Gavius and Modestus (ibid.: I.VI.36).

The speculative line in linguistics has attracted even those who are better equipped with the methods of modern philology and linguistics, as in the case of many twentieth-century authors, poets and novelists. To give just one example, in his autobiography *Little Wilson and Big God*, Anthony Burgess does not conceal his pleasure in knowing that the Renaissance etymologists derived the name Antonius from the Greek word *anthos*, meaning "flower" (1987: 6–7). This etymological explanation of his Christian name holds a special attraction for Burgess, although he does not consider it valid in any scholarly sense: "I am stuck with a piece of bad philology," he says (ibid.). Like Burgess, Pentti Saarikoski (1937–1983), a leading twentieth-century Finnish poet and the translator of Homer's *Odyssey* and Joyce's *Ulysses*, was fascinated by what Burgess called "bad philology", philology meaning, in this connection, etymology and the explanation of words.

In what follows, I first give some examples of Saarikoski's approach to dictionaries and etymological explanations. It should of course be remembered that, along with Saarikoski, many other Finnish poets have drawn from the possibilities offered by etymology and word-play (see, e.g., Enwald's [1997] dissertation on the poetry of Mirkka Rekola [b. 1931]).

II

In his essays and his other prose works, which are mostly autobiographical, Saarikoski refers to a dozen dictionaries, including Liddell and Scott's famous *Greek-English Lexicon*, Moulton and Milligan's *Vocabulary of the Greek Testament* (which the poet used for his translation of the Gospel of St. Matthew), Webster's *Third New International Dictionary*, and a dictionary of Hebrew. He also comments on the remarkable Finnish-Swedish dictionary by Elias Lönnrot, compiler of the *Kalevala*, on the *Suomenkielen etymologinen sanakirja* (*Finnish Etymological Dictionary*), and on the *Nykysuomen sanakirja* (*Dictionary of Modern Finnish*). Saarikoski once said that he had always loved dictionaries as he had loved women, the loveliest among them being the *Lexicon Manuale Graeco-Latinum* by Cornelius Schrevelius, published in Dresden and Leipzig in 1707 (Saarikoski 1971: 32). Although this dictionary was of no direct use to him, he still loved it "because it was so beautiful, like an animal" (Saarikoski 1976: 42). Saarikoski's personal library also contained the *Suomen mustalaiskielen etymologinen sanakirja* (*Etymological Dictionary of the Finnish Gypsy Language*, 1972) compiled by Pertti Valtonen (see Riikonen 1996: 128). It was from this dictionary that he picked up for one of his poems the phrases *dives parjula* and *dives mekkala*, "the sun rises" and "the sun sets" (see Saarikoski 1996: 213, 293).

Saarikoski also gives some examples of the kind of information he obtains from dictionaries. As a translator, he found in dictionaries words which were outside his own experience, especially words connected with agriculture and hunting. Such (old) words held an attraction for him even if they were of no immediate use. In any case, he sometimes referred to such finds in his prose writings. One such word was *janhus*, which he mentions in his book *Euroopan reuna* (*Edge of Europe*, 1982) and which means "the hardest part in wood". He also refers to Lönnrot's explanation in Swedish (Saarikoski 1982: 37). (In his book on Finnish-Egyptian connections, Wettenhovi-Aspa translates the word "janhus" into German as "die härtesten Teile im Holz"; according to him, *janhus* had its equivalent in the Hindu language: *Jan*, meaning "Knochen"). The etymological dictionary was also important for Saarikoski because he wanted, as he said, to "hear the real echo of Finnish words".

In his prose works Saarikoski refers to many eccentric "semioticians", one might say. Among them are amateur linguists such as the engineer Siversen, who is interested in Latin; a certain Hedlund, who knows 40 languages and who is sometimes asked for advice by professors from the University of Helsinki; and Vicar Pettersson, whose hobby is archaeology. Saarikoski also describes an unfortunate poet-friend, who gave up writing poetry when he realized that his poems, when printed, did not preserve the carefully calculated relationships and measurements between the individual letters, lines, and stanzas of the manuscript. (Saarikoski 1982: 129; English trans., Saarikoski 1994: 31.)

In his poetry and prose Saarikoski himself assumes the role of ethnologist, ichthyologist, and mycologist. He also refers to more obscure sciences, such as "otokinetology", the study of human behaviour as revealed by the way one moves one's ears; Saarikoski remarks ironically that this is a field whose significance, for diplomatic and military purposes, has been well understood in the Soviet Union (1982: 49). We may also note that in translating Plato's *Phaedrus*, Saarikoski discovered so-called "oionohistics". According to Plato, oionohistics is "the rational investigation of futurity, whether with the help of birds or other signs"; in the same connection, Plato also gives some examples of curious etymology (*Phaedrus*: 244).

Saarikoski does not forget Wettenhovi-Aspa, whose most ingenious discovery – according to Saarikoski's ironic remark – was that the Finnish word *sirkka* (locust) is the same as *akris* in Greek, since the ancient Greeks read the Finnish word from right to left (Saarikoski 1980: 159). He even describes buying a book called *From Etruscan to Finnish*, by a dilettante philologist, although he wonders whether there is any reason to study "Etruscan, or Basque, Sanskrit, Greek, Navaho" (Saarikoski 1976: 9). The poet also recalls his own impractical and juvenile studies on language and etymology: "Recently I found between the leaves of my Hebrew dictionary a study written in Latin, where I tried to demonstrate that Finnish and Hebrew are related languages. When I wrote that study I was fifteen. At the same time I bought a grammar of Sanskrit. I noticed that the Finnish word *taivas* (sky) originates from the same root as the French 'dieu'. We were a civilized people and bearers of a long tradition; we were no Germans or Vikings" (Saarikoski 1976: 42). On the other hand, Saarikoski also did quite solid work on words and philology, the very first of his publications being a brief vocabulary for an elementary book on Italian. His most ambitious scholarly work consisted of the introduction and notes (over forty pages) to his translation of Xenophon's Socratic texts. He also had certain idiosyncratic ideas concerning small languages, such as Breton (see Saarikoski 1994), Lappish, Basque and Estonian, and their future. (Riikonen 1996: 129–131.)

Saarikoski does not confine himself to seeking words in books alone. He maintains that the spoken language is more important for the lyric poet than for the prose writer. While he was living in Sweden, where he spent the last seven years of his life, he often visited Finland, saying that he would go to the countryside "to listen to the language" (i.e., the language spoken by ordinary country people). These visits he used to call his "hunting expeditions", from which he returned home with his bag full of new words and expressions. At this later stage of his life, Helsinki and its urban slang were for him – the former translator of Salinger's *Catcher in the Rye*, Joyce's *Ulysses*, and the works of Henry Miller – merely an ancient monument, and the people there like those in some old rock paintings.

In his prose writings Saarikoski frequently comments on the etymology of the words *maaliskuu* (march), *joulu* (Christmas), and several place names. He is quite aware of the difficulties of etymological derivation. Words are like a whore's children, whose father is difficult to trace, says the poet (Saarikoski 1982: 15). He also recognizes that his etymologies are sometimes home-made and unreliable as such; he admits that in his fascination with his own etymological discoveries he is unable to be critical. In some cases he has to correct or reject his etymological explanations. In *Kirje vaimolleni* (*Letter to My Wife*) (1968: 60), the first-person narrator believes that the name of Fusciardas Café, which he visits in Dublin, is derived from the word for "fish" in Gaelic. Some twenty pages later, the narrator – who makes constant corrections and additions to his own narrative – has learned that the correct name of the café is Fuiscardas, and that it is the name of the Italian owner; now he also knows that the word for fish in Gaelic is "iasc" (Saarikoski 1968: 80).

There are etymologies in Saarikoski's poetry as well. They may be real etymologies, pseudo-etymologies, or *figurae etymologicae*. Of special interest for Saarikoski are words such as *uskoa* (believe), *käsi* (hand), and *käsittää* (understand), *runo* (poem) and *taivas* (sky). Here we need only recall the text called

"Runo ja jälkilause" ("Poem and afterword"), one of the poet's last writings published during his lifetime; here he once again returns to the word *taivas* (sky), enumerating its equivalents in the languages of Breton, French, and Prakrit (*deivasa, dieu, divasa*) (Saarikoski 1982b: 279–280).

III

Thus far I have limited myself to particular examples; taken out of context, these may seem mere jokes or even ridiculous oddities. The most crucial questions, however, still remain: why did Saarikoski refer so often to etymology, word history, and dictionaries, and in what relation do these etymologies stand to other elements in his poems and prose works?

As background we should keep in mind that Saarikoski's interest in these kinds of problems is by no means an isolated phenomenon in twentieth-century literature. Joyce made extensive use in *Ulysses* of Victor Bérard's etymological investigations into Homeric place names and their oriental roots. Proust, in *Combray*, the first part of *Remembrance of Things Past*, describes a vicar who is interested in the etymology of place names; the vicar's opinions and ideas are then criticized by the half-blind academician Brichot in *Cities of the Plain*. Nor was the lure of etymology avoided by the inhabitants of the Finnish islands in Volter Kilpi's (1874–1939) novel *Kirkolle* (*To the Church*, 1937), where two men, Herman and Heisala, quarrel about the etymology of place names and family names. Kilpi's novel also contains some genealogical speculations, which often are closely linked with dilettante etymology. And of course, Eco, in *The Name of the Rose*, gives examples of medieval etymologies, while in his scholarly writings he refers to etymological play in the works of Jorge Luis Borges. The Finnish writer Veijo Meri (b. 1928) has actually compiled an etymological dictionary, *Sanojen synty* (*The Birth of Words*, 1982), which has run to several editions, but which has of course been attacked by professional philologists.

In the light of these and many other examples, it is reasonable to maintain that etymologies have been used for different, sometimes contradictory literary, philosophical, or political purposes. In the following I rely on observations made by Derek Attridge in his interesting and many-sided essay "Language as history/history as language: Saussure and the romance of etymology" (1987).

Since the term "etymology" refers to a discourse on the true meaning of words, a truth about words (Gr. *etymon*), it implies the old notion that words have a certain "authentic" meaning, a notion which has been perpetuated by the educational system and by the status it confers on dictionaries as a cultural institution. This notion may seem historical, but in fact it is ahistorical in nature; it replaces, as Attridge notes, "the social and historical determination of meaning (operating upon the arbitrary sign) by a transcendent 'true' meaning." Etymology becomes an instrument of power. Thomas Aquinas, for instance, evidently appealed to etymological arguments whenever they favoured his own arguments and rejected them when they contradicted his thinking (see Attridge 1987: 211, who refers to William T. Noon's study of Joyce and Aquinas). And even St. Augustine, in arguing against the Manichæans, polemically derived the name of the founder of the sect, Mani, from *mania*, the Greek word for madness (Plato, too, was interested in the etymology of *mania*; see *Phaedrus*: 244b-c). In fact the entire European philosophical tradition, from Plato to Derrida, is replete with appeals to etymology.

The question is more complicated than this, however. We know that, given a lack of knowledge concerning the history of language and the rules of phonology, the search for etymologies easily leads to false and distorted conclusions. But etymological speculations and quasi-etymologies that rely merely on apparent similarities between words may have another function. Etymology then becomes a tool of rhetoric, and as such plays an important role. It comes very close to *calembour* or *paronomasia*, play with words. Referring to Jean Paulhan's book *Preuve par l'etymologie*, Attridge maintains:

> In both devices the same process occurs: two similar-sounding but distinct signifiers are brought together and the surface relationship between them invested with meaning through the inventiveness and rhetorical skill of the writer. If that meaning is in the form of a postulated connection between present and past, what we have is etymology; if it's in the form of a postulated connection with the present, the result is word-play (Attridge 1987: 193).

These questions were noted, for instance, by Saussure, in his discussion of folk-etymology and the so-called *coq-à-l'âne* discourse (cf. Attridge 1987: 197).

If we do not regard etymology merely as the quest for an authentic or true meaning and as a strict scholarly discipline, we find new possibilities in the use of that science, which show why it has always been so attractive. Very illuminating in this respect, as Attridge points out, is Ernest Weekley's book *The Romance of Words*, originally published at the beginning of the twentieth century. In describing the vicissitudes of some words, Weekley actually told little tales; he himself sometimes referred to his explanations as "short stories", while his book bears the title "Romance". The words described by him underwent a certain "Cinderella transformation"; they became something different from what they had been before (Attridge 1987: 189–191; 195). Weekley actually wrote several books of this kind, which were read up to the 1940s. As Colin MacCabe reminds us (1985: 116), in Great Britain the study of the historical change of words was then carried on mainly by literary critics such as William Empson (*The Structure of Complex Words*) and Raymond Williams (*Keywords*), rather than by linguists; the work of such writers as Williams, concerning ideological and political aspects in the development of cultural terminology, is well known.

The humanist approach to the development of words (and phrases) represented by Weekley has been fairly common in Europe ever since Erasmus's famous collection, *Adagia*. The Finnish equivalent of Weekley's popular books can be seen in the studies of W. O. Streng-Renkonen (1876–1959), who eventually became Professor of Romance Philology at the University of Turku. Renkonen, too, was a story-teller. In tracing the history of the word *pörssi* (stock-exchange), he begins with Queen Dido of Carthage and ends with the Finnish phrase *Matti kukkarossa*; literally, "Matti in the purse", "being broke" (Renkonen 1954: 148–149). Like fables, which so often carry a moral, Renkonen's "etymological stories" are sometimes flavoured with moralistic tendencies. In discussing the expression "the Sirens' song", he ends his story by warning the modern Ulysses of the perils of political opportunism (Streng-Renkonen 1938: 13). And Veijo Meri's etymological dictionary, *Sanojen synty*, includes many good stories about the wanderings of words in the course of history.

In the light of such material, we can conclude that etymology as fictitious storytelling has always attracted both writers and readers. Folk etymologies, for instance, owe their power to transform language to their success as stories – stories with a good plot – and as witty word-play, not to their scholarly accuracy or reliability. When writers and philosophers, from Plato's Cratylus to Nietzsche and Derrida, have used such etymologies and word play, they have in fact observed and acknowledged the impossibility of an objective science of language. We may add that Nietzsche, for example, approaches the matter through the nature of metaphor (see Allemann 1967: 105–109), but in this respect etymology is interesting as well. Thinkers like Nietzsche have emphasized the instability of language, but they have also shown that in a synchronic situation diachrony is also always present; they have demonstrated the constant openness of language to reinterpretation and changes. There are, of course, great differences in how openly they invite us to perform such reading and interpretation. But in any case the use of etymology fissures the synchronic surface of the text by introducing diachronic shadows and echoes; for instance, "the real echo of Finnish", as Pentti Saarikoski put it (1985: 95). The use of etymology opens the language to shifts of meaning, which can never be closed off. Attridge comes to the following conclusion:

> In thus employing etymology, writers are, in their different ways, exploiting its affinity with word-play – or, what amounts to the same thing, we are exploiting this affinity in thus reading etymological accounts. And the connection between etymology and word-play can be generalised to a connection between etymology and literature. Literature too can be read for or against absolutes, transcendence, closure, authentic and original meaning; and it too varies in the degree to which it invites a reading that opens rather than closes. But where etymology uses the tools of the tradition whose hierarchies it

> deconstructs – the tools of logic, empiricism, scientific method – and is thereby granted by our culture the right to be read in, and against, that tradition, the word-play of literature is all too easily partitioned off as another pathological development of the language to be kept under observation. This is one reason why the deconstructive etymological argument, and post-structuralist theory more generally, has an important role in the cultural and political arena, where the notions of "authentic meaning" and "true history", and the stories in which they are embedded, exercise a powerful ideological function, and where any challenge literature and its readers might mount against these notions is disabled by their prior marginalisation. (Attridge 1987: 204)

In other words, in the way etymology is employed in the works of modern authors Attridge finds a kind of justification for post-structuralism and deconstruction.

IV

After these historical and theoretical considerations, it is time to return to Saarikoski. In the light of Attridge's theoretical discussion, it is interesting to find that Saarikoski has a clear understanding of the fact that words have their own history and that they undergo change. He also emphasizes the difficulty of finding the "etymon", or the truth of a given word. As already mentioned, Saarikoski regards words as whore's children whose father is difficult to trace. Words have long histories, and these histories in themselves may be fascinating. In a newspaper article, Saarikoski, an "exile" to Sweden, wrote as follows: "When I write down a Finnish word, I hear an unbroken echo, which comes from the Caucasus. Every word is a sea, thronged with fish of different meanings" (quoted in Berner 1986: 59). In other words, he speaks of the fissure in the synchronic surface of the text and of the diachronic shifts and echoes, introduced by means of etymology. In a sense language is truly immortal. Saarikoski says, "The dead languages have loaned words to languages which are still living, and in this way languages are immortal, like people; as DNA-chains they live eternally, for after man as a species has disappeared, these chains will continue living in the kingdom of heaven, where there is no time" (Saarikoski 1982: 139). Such biological comparisons in describing the development of words and languages are fairly common in modern poetry. They appear for instance in the poetry of the Swedish writer Göran Sonnevi, whose poems Saarikoski translated into Finnish.

The etymologist often deals with old cultural phenomena, differing from those of today, and has to possess knowledge in such fields as ethnology, folk poetry, and mythology (cf. Itkonen 1966: 344). This kind of material is essential in Saarikoski's *Euroopan reuna*. This book – even more than his other works – can be said to be dominated by the constant observation of signs. But it is not only the search for and interpretation of signs which is present. It is also a search for earlier layers of language and its words. The linguistic sign, for Saarikoski, is not merely a synchronic phenomenon; it also includes a diachronic dimension. In the words of Roman Jakobson, it is a question of "dynamic synchrony" (Jakobson 1985: 6).

Like those dilettante "semioticians" whose Sisyphean labours Saarikoski briefly describes in his works, he himself sees signs everywhere. In this connection, I need only mention the alphabet. Even the shape of an individual letter holds its own significance for the poet. Saarikoski refers, for instance, to the shapes of Sanskrit and Singhalese letters; the latter have in their rotundity an erotic dimension (1980: 152).

We can say that Saarikoski's works, especially *Euroopan reuna*, are based on two main, often overlapping, factors: one is travel, the other consists of comments on stories and their nature. One paragraph in *Euroopan reuna* begins with ironic allusions to the *Odyssey* and the figure of Ulysses: "I have seen the world and people, learned languages; I have also learned how cats behave, how all this is; I do not say that I have found the truth, but at least for my part, when I know what I am doing" (Saarikoski 1982: 21). And he continues:

> It is nice to listen only to those people who tell stories. Of course I have heard all the stories before, but in the way of telling there is always something new. Telling is like sawing wood: the wood is the same pine, birch, or alder as yesterday, the saw is the same and the sawhorse the same, but the trace of the sawing is different every time; that is the nice thing in this otherwise so hard work. The reward is in being able to build and to make piles. (ibid.)

Languages and words are closely connected with stories, because words and tales wander, too. It is not by chance that in such connections Saarikoski frequently refers to such great wanderers as Ulysses, Ossian and Peer Gynt.

I have mentioned that etymology, especially when it involves establishing some "authentic" meaning, can be a form of exercising power. Saarikoski, too, is aware of the relationship between language and power. In his own writing – both poetry and prose – his goal was freedom, getting rid of various forms of power. It is no coincidence that he regarded St. Francis of Assisi's "Canto del sole" as an example of freedom and high aesthetic quality. As compared to St. Francis's poem, Goethe's "Über allen Gipfeln" was for Saarikoski mere poetic snobbery. If one writes unlike people's normal speech, it is teaching, and at its worst it is the exercise of power (Saarikoski 1982: 33).

Saarikoski's way of opposing all forms of power is closely connected with his use of etymology. He was ready to play with his derivations; at the same time, he was fully aware that they did not always correspond to the results of scholarly research. It was not his intention to offer strictly scientific explanations; what was more important for him was their crucial role in that constant journey into and play with both life and language which Saarikoski undertook in his works. Saarikoski's various but often ephemeral etymological remarks were part and parcel of that endless stream of fact and fiction, truth and semi-truth, historical and quasi-historical explanation which form his prose works. The attention paid to etymology in his work is also part of his poetic investigation of the limits and possibilities of language and communication.

Pentti Saarikoski began his career at the end of the 1950s as a radical and a reformer of poetic language, who broke with traditional and academic poetry as represented for instance by V. A. Koskenniemi. In the light of what I have said, we can maintain that Saarikoski's career as a poet and prose writer was characterized by his constant observation of signs, whether they be individual letters of the alphabet, words and their history, literature, or signs of nature, and by a constant reorientation by means of these signs in the chaos of the modern world. In Saarikoski's relation to words one also finds something of the attitude of the young Stephen Dedalus: "Words which he did not understand he said over and over to himself till he had learnt them by heart: and through them he had glimpses of the real world about them" (Joyce 1972: 62). This becomes even more obvious when we recall Saarikoski's transformations of the theme of the labyrinth. But this reorientation was also in many ways an ironic one. Saarikoski's references to etymology also perfectly illustrate Bakhtin's statement that "[p]oetry needs all of language, all of its aspects, and all of its elements; it does not neglect a single nuance of the linguistic word" (cited in Todorov 1984: 67).

In his book *Asiaa tai ei* (*True or Pretend*, 1980) Saarikoski maintains that there is hardly a better school for an author than to read without stopping *Dubliners*, *Ulysses*, and *Finnegans Wake*: "here you have student, master and doctor" (Saarikoski 1980: 22). As regards *Finnegans Wake*, Margot Norris argues that it is a book "about the quest for truth, the 'true' facts, the correct interpretation, the 'authentic' version, and ... it purposefully levels all such pretensions" (1976: 139). It was in this direction that Pentti Saarikoski was travelling in his absorption with words and their etymologies.

References

Allemann, Beda (1967). Metaphor and Antimetaphor. In: *Interpretation: The Poetry of Meaning*. Stanley Romaine Hopper and David L. Miller (eds.). 103–123. New York: Harcourt & World.

Attridge, Derek (1987). Language as history/history as language: Saussure and the romance of etymology. In: *Post-structuralism and the Question of History*. Derek Attridge, Geoff Bennington, and Robert Young (eds.). 183–211. Cambridge: Cambridge University Press.

Berner, Mia (1986). *PS. Merkintöjä suruvuodelta* [Notes from the Year of Sorrow]. Suomentaneet Liisa Ryömä ja Caj Westerberg. Helsinki: Tammi.

Burgess, Anthony (1987). *Little Wilson and Big God, Being the First Part of the Confessions of Anthony Burgess*. London: Heinemann.

Enwald, Liisa (1997). *Kaiken liikkeessä lepo. Monihahmotteisuus Mirkka Rekolan runoudessa* [There is Rest in All Motion. Ambiguity in the Poetry of Mirkka Rekola]. Helsinki: Suomalaisen Kirjallisuuden Seura.
Halén, Harry and Tukkinen, Tauno (1984). *Elämän ja kuoleman kello: Sigurd Wettenhovi-Aspan elämä ja teot* [*The Clock of Life and Death*]. Helsinki: Otava.
Itkonen, Erkki (1966). *Kieli ja sen tutkimus* [Language and its Study]. Helsinki: WSOY.
Itkonen, Terho (1986). Etymologiasta: On etymology. *Virittäjä* 90: 151–154.
Jakobson, Roman (1985). *Verbal Art, Verbal Sign, Verbal Time*. Krystyna Pomorska and Stephen Rudy (eds.). Oxford: Basil Blackwell.
Joyce, James (1972). *A Portrait of the Artist as a Young Man*. Harmondsworth: Penguin.
MacCabe, Colin (1985). *Theoretical Essays: Film, Linguistics, Literature*. Manchester: Manchester University Press.
Norris, Margot (1976). *The Decentered Universe of "Finnegans Wake"*. Baltimore: Johns Hopkins University Press.
Plato [1895]. *Cratylus*. In: *The Dialogues of Plato*. Vol. 1. Trans. B. Jowett. New York: Charles Scribner's Sons.
Quintilian [1970]. *Institutionis oratoriae*. M. Winterbottom (ed.). Oxford: Clarendon.
Renkonen, V. O. (1954). *Kulttuurin avainsanoja. Miten ne syntyvät ja kehittyvät* [Keywoards of Culture]. Helsinki: WSOY.
Riikonen, H. K. (1996). Katseita kotimaahan: Suomi, Karjala ja Virolahti Pentti Saarikosken Ruotsin-kauden tuotannossa. [Glancing Homeward: Pentti Saarikoski on Finland, Carelia, and Virolahti]. *Sananjalka* 38: 125–139.
Saarikoski, Pentti (1968). *Kirje vaimolleni* [*Letter to My Wife*]. Helsinki: WSOY.
– (1971). Suomentajan sana [Translator's Word]. *Weikko* 100: 32–33.
– (1976). *Ihmisen ääni*[*The Voice of Man*]. Porvoo: WSOY.
– (1980). *Asiaa tai ei* [*True or Pretend*]. Helsinki: Otava.
– (1982). *Euroopan reuna. Kineettinen kuva* [The Edge of Europe. A Kinetic Picture]. Helsinki: Otava.
– (1982b). Runo ja jälkilause [Poem and afterword]. *Parnasso* 5: 279–280.
– (1994). Breton without tears. In: *Euroopan reuna* [The Edge of Europe]. Trans. Anselm Hollo. Helsinki: Otava, 1982. *Books from Finland* 1: 26–32.
– (1996). *Tiarnia-sarja ja muut Ruotsin-kauden runot* [Tiarnia-Trilogy and Other Poems from the Swedish Period]. H.K. Riikonen (ed.). Helsinki: Otava.
Streng-Renkonen, W.O. (1938). *Siivekkäitä sanoja ja sivistyssanoja* [Winged Words and Foreign Words]. Helsinki: Otava.
Todorov, Tzvetan (1984). *Mikhail Bakhtin: The Dialogic Principle*. Trans. Wlad Godzich. (= Theory and History of Literature 13.) Minneapolis: University of Minnesota Press.

Sinikka Tuohimaa

Rebellious words: *Avant-garde* literature and theories, from Formalism to Post-structuralism

> *From my life I make a poem, from a poem a life,*
> *a poem is a way to live and the only way to die*
> *with ecstatic indifference:*
> *glide into infinity, drift*
> *at God's level for a special weightless moment,*
> *level with God's cold eyes,*
> *[...]*
> *a poem acknowledges one religion: curiosity*
> *wander through the habitats of Pisces, Scorpio*
> *and Capricorn,*
> *Borrowing from a bird desire and flight*
> *and floats down*
> *like a wing wrapped in the wind,*
> *swift freedom, like a bird.*
>   (Eeva-Liisa Manner)

Kjell Espmark says that art always carries its own definition within itself. A poem says, "This is poetry; this is how it looks". Similarly, the definition of Greek tragedy is inscribed in tragedy itself. Aristotle was only using this knowledge when he defined that genre in his poetics (Espmark 1982: 160). Espmark is writing about the difficulty in defining poetry – an object as hard to capture as a butterfly in flight. Poetry that follows strict norms is already dead, and so is a literary criticism that ends its definitions by saying, "This is a poem". We may console ourselves only with the thought that normative poetics gives poets the opportunity to rebel.

    Poetry is a fruit of tradition, of philosophies, of ideological, social and cultural ideas, as well as the personal history of the poet. And it is quite a complicated task to explicate the relationships between literature and its surroundings. The basic elements of poetry are author (as producer and sender), poetic work (as message), and reader (as receiver). These are surrounded by literary institutions and other social and cultural entities.

A glance at the development of literary theories shows that in early modern literary criticism viewed the author and her/his social and cultural environment as the key to interpretation. This biographical research tradition dominated from its beginning in the nineteenth to the first decades of this century, and such theories are still in use. But early in the twentieth century and later, theories also appeared that gave most attention to the literary work itself. Among them are Formalism, the New Criticism, and Structuralism. Since the 1970s, theories that concentrate on the reader have come to the fore.

In this paper I compare *avant-garde* literary ideas about poetic language to notions of poetic language as presented in semiotic literary theories. I particularly respond to some of the following questions: what is the ontology of verbal art? what is its function? what is the role of society and the individual author in poetry? and what is the origin of poetic language? My intent is to outline how ideas about verbal art have changed up to the time of postmodern art and post-structural theories. I assume that there are complex connections and mutual influences between art itself and theories of art. How these mutual processes work forms the focus of the present study.

The avant-garde in art

The term *avant-garde* was first used by Henry de Saint-Simon (1760–1825), a utopian sociologist and ancestor of communism. He changed this French term, originally related to things military (*avant garde* = vanguard, front line), to mean an art that has "arms" enough to put new ideas into circulation.

Avant-garde movements are most often understood as historical style-periods, such as Dadaism, Futurism, and Surrealism, which were all local movements within Modernism. From time to time, rebellious elements appear in art, such as nonsense syllables and sheer playing with sounds. This is seen in postmodern as well in some earlier avant-gardist styles. Below is an example from a writer who definitely was not viewed as part of the *avant-garde* in his day. This is the famous Finnish romantic poet J. L. Runeberg (1804–1877), who wrote a typically "dadaist" poem entitled "Höstsång"("Autumn song"):

Sum sum dilidang!
Brum brum dinglidang!
Hu hi plinglidang!
   Lululi dinglidang!

Runeberg claimed that his muse had provided him dictionaries of the language of nature, of goblins, babies, and animals. He regretted that he could not speak the language of fishes, but according to him the language of goblins was richer than all living and dead human languages combined (Kirstinä 1977: 168).

A conception of *avant-garde* art as something other than a style-period is presented by Calinescu, who defines it as an anti-style characterised by intellectual play, iconoclasm, non-seriousness, mystification, shamelessness, jokes and deliberately dull humour (Calinescu 1987: 119).

Avant-garde artists often take positions against both the norms of literature and literary institutions, which they see as representing old, hackneyed forms and procedures. *Avant-garde* artists often have connections with political parties. For example, some surrealists (Apollinaire), Russian Formalists (Majakovski), and the French Tel Quel Group, as well as many other French intellectuals, had close connections to the communist party; the Italian Futurists (Marinetti), in turn, had ties with Fascism (Mussolini). These artists saw political movements as means to achieve their aims. Other *avant-garde* artists have embraced anarchy, with its idealistic aim of complete liberty in social, judicial, and economical arenas. Anarchists believe the state and its institutions should be replaced with free organisations. For one example, the Finnish modernist poet Eeva-Liisa Manner claimed to be an anarchist. It is obvious to her readers that her attitude resulted from bitter disappointment with all human institutions and actions (wars, destruction of nature, and so on).

Some have wondered if *avant-garde* art is still possible today, when "normlessness" seems to be the norm in art and when artistic fashion changes as often as that of dress. Some researchers have talked about the death of the *avant-garde*. But according to Matei Calinescu, the death of the *avant-garde* cannot be pinpointed because it dies all the time, consciously and voluntarily (Calinescu 1987: 124). The idea of the demise of the *avant-garde* seems to belong to such arguments as the "death of the author" and the "death of the novel", which deliberately provoke careful reconsideration of traditional terms and concepts. Otherwise we should have to believe that the world has reached a point of stasis and that creativity and imagination have indeed finally passed away.

"A cuff on good taste"

The Russian Formalists, particularly the St. Petersburg group, had connections with Futurist artists. The most famous Russian Futurist poet was Vladimir Majakovski (1893–1930), whose book of Futuristic poetry was called *Cloud in Trousers* (1916). Russian Futurist writers wanted to create an art that slapped tradition in the face, that was "a cuff to general taste" (the name of their common pronouncement in the year 1912). They wanted to break with the language and forms of traditional poetry. The manifesto of the Russian Futurists appeared in 1912, reading as follows:

> A cuff on social taste. For those who read
> our New First Unexpected.
> Only we are the face of our Time. The horn of
> Time plays through us in works of art.
> The Past is dull. The Academe and Pushkin are
> even less understandable than hieroglyphs.
> Pushkin, Dostojevski, Tolstoi and others must
> be thrown over the side of the steamboat of Modern Times.

Majakovski argued that a new way to write poetry was needed. According to him, the principle of the unexpected does not belong only to political verse but to all poetry. In their second manifesto the Futurist artists claimed that richness of vocabulary is the right of the poet, and that when the word dies it gives birth to myth, and vice versa. The Futurists wrote that we are under the power of new subjects: "uselessness, senselessness, the secret of nothingness is our song. We degrade fame; we are familiar with feelings that did not exist before us. We are new people of a new life" (Peuranen 1979: 27).

The Futurists' manifesto mostly exhibits youthful rebellion, yet they did demand changes in language, metre, stanza arrangement, and they added new, non-poetic objects to poetry. Majakovski defines his ideas about the relationship between poetry and reality in writing that art is not a copy of nature but is more like an urge to abuse nature according to the reflections that nature evokes in an individual's consciousness.

The ideas about language developed by the Russian Formalists and the Futurists were partly a protest against the dominant positivist theories, which assumed causal relationships between the artist, his work, and the environment. According to the Formalists, literature should not be researched as a reflection of social reality, because it possesses its own, *linguistic* reality and therefore should be studied as a system of forms and linguistic constructs. The Formalists argued that literature is as formally abstract as music is, and thus they considered thoroughly matters of poetic rhythm, metre, alliteration, assonance, and other so-called "musical" constituents of poetry.

The Formalists resisted the traditional idea that the language of poetry is a somehow decorated language. According to them, poetic language forms an organic unity wherein signifier and signified are as inseparable as wine and glass in a wineglass, or as the two sides of a sheet of paper.

The push for a continuous renewal of poetic language comes from the Formalists' fear that language might lose its vividness and become mechanical. To avoid this situation, poetic language must constantly break with tradition and search for new forms. The Formalists regarded poetry as the transgression of norms.

To Formalists the analysis of a poem means the rigorous examination of the hierarchies among its different parts. Roman Jakobson argued that some features in a stanza always dominate over others. This is the basis of his theory of the "dominant". Also according to Jakobson, there are equivalencies between levels of meaning and levels of form (quality of sounds, melody, accent, etc.). This is called the *principle of equivalence.* Jakobson's method was picked up, among others, by Juri Tynjanov in his book, *The Problem of Verse Language* (1924).

According to Jakobson the *poetic function* appears in poetry in the insertion of the paradigmatic and metaphorical dimension into the syntagmatic dimension. By using sounds, rhythms, and figuration, poetic language widens the possibilities of language by diverting attention from referential meaning to formal qualities of language. The poetic function is not the only function of verbal art, but it is the dominating function in contrast to natural language (Jakobson 1960: 356).

Juri Lotman, semiotician of the Tartu school, continued the tradition of the Russian Formalists by analysing poetic language in his books *The Theory of Poetry* (1964), *The Structure of the Artistic Text* (1970), *The Structure of Poetry* (1972), and *The Poetic Text* (1981). According to Lotman, the world of art is a pattern of another world, and it correlates with that world in complex ways. Literature and other arts – colours, rhythms, melodies, geometrical figures, playing cards, science, religion, fashion, structure of society, different patterns of behaviour – form systems that shape secondary representational sign systems. Lotman writes:

> From the material of structural language, a system of signs that are conventional but so comprehensible as to be felt against the background of other, more specialised languages, there arises a secondary representational sign (which could very well correspond to the "image" of traditional literary theory).
>
> This secondary representational sign has the properties of iconic signs: it bears a direct resemblance to the object; it is graphic; it gives the impression of being less dependent on a code and therefore would seem to ensure greater truthfulness and greater intelligibility than conventional signs. This sign has inseparable aspects: its similarity to the object designated and its dissimilarity to the same object. One feature is always accompanied by the other. (Lotman 1972: 56)

The text of a poem is a strong and deeply dialectic mechanism for searching out the truth and for understanding and becoming oriented in the world. Lotman sees a connection between language, thinking, and the world. He argues that language is not only a vehicle of communication but a way to give structure to experience and to shape world-view. According to Lotman, semiotics urges us to decode the text according to its various levels: graphic, phonological, morphological, lexical, line, stanza, compositional, and the overall text.

In his book, *The Word and Verbal Art* (1977), semiotician Jan Mukarovski explored differences between the language of poetry and natural language. He emphasised that the poetic function makes a word of poetry different from a word of communicative language. In a poem, attention goes to the word-sign, whose relationship with context becomes primary. By contrast, in reportive communicative we focus on the object referred to by the word-sign. In a poem, the word effects a figurative impression even if it is used denotatively. A word in a poem refers to a meaning that is not explicitly expressed, and therefore it may refer to objects outside that narrow region covered by semantic context. In addition to its communicative function, the poetic text includes figurative and emotional elements which change according to the reader's experiences and impressions. In poetry a balance is struck between denotative and figurative meaning. Poetry can save and renovate; it both automatises and deautomatises (see Mukarovski 1977: 73–78). According to Mukarovski, art is a group experience that reaches the reader as a member of a collective; therefore, verbal art is a social phenomenon that is ordered according to how a society uses signs. Paradoxically, the work of art is part of a macro-structure (that of reality) and at the same time an autonomous system.

Russian formalist notions of language were continued and further developed in Anglo-American New Criticism. Although the latter has its own characteristics, both of these theories share in the critique against positivistic thinking and both support the autonomy of verbal art.

Art as its own world

The symbiosis between modern art and literary criticism shows up particularly in "imagism" and New Criticism. The great modernist poet T. S. Eliot was a central figure in both of these schools of thought. In 1912 Ezra Pound had established the imagist school, which demonstrated that poetry should use ordinary language. Poetry must find a new rhythm based on authentic musicality, not on the inevitable regularity of a metronome. The object of poetry should be free, and metaphor should have an autonomous position. According to this program, a poem should be precise and coherent and, most importantly, it should be an adventure. Imagist poets demanded cogency, saying that no word exists that doesn't add representation. Imagist poets admired metaphysical poetry and particularly that of John Donne. They wanted to continue the aims of the Symbolists, whose ideas about language affected the style called "high modernism". This was a compact, metaphorical style that sometimes led to hermetic expressions.

According to the New Criticism, verbal art is a hierarchically structured entity. The analysis of a text begins with the examination of its structure and inner tensions. The New Criticism, still the leading method in America, emphasises close reading and exact formal analysis of the text. By following thoroughly the instructions inscribed in the text, critics should arrive at the one and only possible interpretation.

The theory of autonomy developed by the New Critics is based on the idea that a work of art becomes separated from its creator after it is finished. As a symbol of this process (which he calls the *objective correlate*), Eliot adduces the birth of a child who becomes completely separated from the mother's body after the umbilical cord has been severed. In the same way, artistic work distances itself from the author. It is because of the New Critics that the author is no longer considered a key to the interpretation of poetry.

According to the New Criticism, poetry is its own independent world, a poetical universe. This is the declaration of the independence of poetry, which is no longer obliged to describe society, nature, or human beings. Poetry is a particular reality that cannot be described with any language other than poetic language. This means that poetry may represent things that have no existence outside poetry. Charles Morris gives the word "centaur" as an example of a *designatum* without *denotatum*, a word which does not have any referent in the real world. The word "centaur" creates its own referent.

Some representatives of the New Criticism, such as I. A. Richards and Cleanth Brooks, argued that poetry does not just mediate feelings, as had been assumed earlier. It also produces knowledge – a very special knowledge that is both cognitive and emotive. This kind of knowledge, which other languages cannot transmit, is produced by a synthesis of the concrete and the universal.

Eliot argues that there exists a timeless hierarchy between all the books ever written (this he calls "tradition"): that all European literature since Homer exists simultaneously and shapes a hierarchy together with the books of today. Because of this concept, the New Critics drew accusations of being ahistorical.

The term "New Criticism" appears again in the 1960s in France, in the form of the "nouveau critique", denoting early French Structuralism. In Paris, which was the centre of philosophical and scientific discussions after World War II, intellectual fashions changed rapidly. At first there was Existentialism, which was followed by Structuralism and Post-structuralism. Mirja Bolgar has described some reactions against representatives of the *nouveau critique*, who were viewed as snobs using pseudo-mathematical and linguistic theories and methods. The Structuralists were elsewhere criticised as players of the "Glass bead game" or other "language games". "The glass bead game" refers to Hermann Hesse's book of that title, which tells about a group of men living in the mountains, isolated and using their time for meditation and philosophical thinking. The comparison may have helped spark great interest in Structuralism, which also has concentrated on basic questions about existence and the essence of world, and itself has presented a certain kind of world-view. On this view, the world is seen as an organised unity in which every piece has its place. Structuralist researchers were working to demonstrate the elegant organisation of this world and all its parts. After World War II this theory was particularly attractive to a world in which everything seemed to be broken in pieces. Europe was in chaos, and people were willing to give structure to everything on the assumption that it would lead to organisation and harmony in their lives. And this is what Structuralists did: they searched for structure that was assumed to be hidden, just waiting to be found.

First came the works of Claude Lévi-Strauss, philosopher and anthropologist, who had met Roman Jakobson while they were both teaching in New York during the war. A result of their collaboration is their famous analysis of Baudelaire's poem, "Les chats". Structural analysis of literature was further developed by Tzvetan Todorov, Roland Barthes, and Umberto Eco. Narratological analyses, such as those of Greimas, were often variants of the method which Vladimir Propp developed for the study of folklore. Literary Structuralists described the work of art as an organic unity, in very much the same way as the Formalists and New Critics had done. Narratologists like Barthes and Todorov viewed the work of art has having different levels such as plot (*histoire*) and narration (*discours narratif*), terms which correspond to *fable* and *sujet* in Formalist theories of narrative.

In structural analysis the text is segmented into small parts which Lévi-Strauss calls *mythemes* and Barthes *functions*. These smaller parts are then rearranged according to various criteria, so as to bring out hitherto unseen meanings. Lévi-Strauss, for example, starts his famous analysis of the Oedipus myth from the organisation of the syntagmatic level and reorganises the text according to the paradigmatic level.

To make more concrete what a formalist-structural analysis of a poetic text entails, I shall analyse a poem by Eeva-Liisa Manner, a Finnish representative of high modernism. I use the original Finnish version of the poem, because I agree with Lévi-Strauss's view that poetry cannot be translated because its meaning is also dependent on the sounds. Sometimes it is necessary to translate poems, but only while keeping in mind that the translation will not be the "same" poem.

Aika ei mene joen yli
minun kaikki aikani on tällä puolen
Toisella talo tuhkassa ja sulanut kello:
muiston pysyvyys.
[Time doesn't cross the river
all my time is on this side
on the other a house in ashes and melted clock:
the persistence of memory.]
(Trans. Ritva Poom)

The structure of the poem above can be viewed such that the three first stanzas, which describe the situation, form the first part; the remaining part is the fourth stanza, which brings closure to part one. There exists another structuring possibility based on the binary oppositions of the poem. On the one hand there is "my time", and on the other, "another time". This point of view separates the second stanza from the third stanza, and the first and fourth stanzas together provide a symmetrical frame to the poem.

To bring out equivalencies between form and meaning, we can look at this map of the vowels and consonants in the poem:

```
ai-a ei -e-e -oe- y-i
-i-u- ai--i ai-a-i o- -ä--ä -uo-e-
-oi-e--a -a-o -u--a--a -a -u-a-u- -e--o
-ui--o- -y-y-yy-
--k- -- m-n- j--n -l-
m-n-n k--kk- --k-n- -n -ä--ä p--l-n
t--s-ll- t-l- t-hk-ss- j- s-l-n-t k-ll-
m--s-n p-s-v--s
```

There is a surprising numerical balance between the vowels and consonants in this poem, given that there is an equal number of each. The vowels usually provide "softness" while the consonants act as a supporting "skeleton". When there is a balance between them, it strengthens the impression of both emotional and cognitive elements of the poem. The third stanza distinguishes itself by its length and by the number of instances of the vowel /a/, which seems to open a space for what comes next. The colon supports the same effect of openness. Remarkable also are the multiple appearances of the vowel /y/, which connects to the words "nyyhkytys" (sobbing), "pyhyys" (holiness) and "hyvyys" (goodness). The word "pysyvyys", however, has its own world of sounds joining with the vowel /y/: the last letter /s/ forms a continuing sibilant tone that further strengthens the semantic meaning of the word "pysyvyys".

There are some grammatical anomalies in the third stanza, such as the absent word "puolella" after the word "Toisella" ("on the other side") and the missing predicate; this is a common poetic ellipsis. The initial /T/ attracts attention by giving power to the word "Toisella" ("Other") and thus signalling a deeper meaning: the river is not just a local borderline but is also a boundary of time, between past and present, as well as the limit between life and death. Although the poem speaks about past memories, the dominating tense here is the present, indicating the simultaneity of present and past.

The third stanza includes still other remarkable things, such as the colon followed by the strong metaphors of "a house in ashes" and a "melted clock". The symbol of the house is often used as a symbol of man and of the lyrical "I". But this house is burnt, suggesting that the lyrical "I" of the poem has gone through a destructive experience. The images of the "melted clock" and "the persistence of memory" refer to the gloomy and brooding Salvador Dali painting of a melted clock. These shadowy poetic images can be interpreted as breaking from chronological time in order to remain in the memory.

The poem "Time doesn't cross the river" also refers to another poem by Eeva-Liisa Manner, entitled "The persistence of time", which tells about the shooting of a horse on a bridge. The poem's lyrical "I" is shocked by this horrific sight, which is expressed at the end of the poem with the words, "I can never get away from this bridge".

The present poem is dominated by the binary oppositions my time / another time, present / past. (The search for binary oppositions in the poem, in structuralist analysis, is based on the idea that meanings are shaped through oppositions or similarities.) And the surrealistic image of the "melted clock" as a symbol of distracted time speaks to the level of unconsciousness, which includes implicitly its opposition: consciousness. Something has happened in the past which never disappears from the mind of lyrical "I". Eeva-Liisa Manner says that the memory about a horse shot on the bridge comes from reality. During wartime in Viipuri she had witnessed such a shooting, and this shocking experience was sedimented in her memory. This sort of biographical connection between the life of the poet and her poem does not belong to Formalist-Structural analysis, but knowing about it in this particular case adds to the world of this poem the horrifying spectre of the war.

Formalist-Structural theories and methods have given to literary criticism the precision of close reading. Before formalist-structural methods of reading, the analysis of poetry mostly consisted of impressionistic paraphrase. Still we must ask, Do we get a complete interpretation of poetry with the help of these methods, as many representatives of the New Criticism believe? In my view, no methods exist that could provide the full meaning of a poem and give it an ultimate interpretation.

An adventure of writing

In 1968 Philippe Sollers edited a book called *Theorie d'ensemble* in which some important researchers started their work. In the book were Jacques Derrida's article, "La différance" and Julia Kristeva's "Problèmes de la structuration du texte". Kristeva started to build her own theories of language in her books *Recherches pour un sémanalyse* (1969) and *La révolution du langage poétique* (1974). Roland Barthes began his work as a structuralist but later on, in the 1980s, developed new ideas the about language of poetry and criticism. His book *S/Z* (1970) has been cited as his point of change. These post-structural theorists derived new ideas about the ontology and interpretation of poetic language and its connections with social reality.

Young *avant-garde* writers and scholars gathered around the journal *Tel Quel*. In addition to Derrida and editor Sollers, the group included writers such as Michel Foucault, Jean Ricardou, and Marcelin Pleynet. Julia Kristeva, who had moved to Paris in 1966, later imported ideas from psychoanalysis into her theory of language. In the beginning this group voiced very radical ideas about the collective production of texts. When Mirja Bolgar interviewed Philippe Sollers in 1969 he did not want to be called an "author" but preferred the title "scriptor" (writer). Sollers said that the *Tel Quel* group were bent on creating a combined theory of language, science, and politics, which could be done in no way other than through the use of dialectical and historical materialism. According to Sollers, social revolutions often happen at the same time as rebellions in literature. He takes as example Mallarmé and Lautréamont who supported the commune of Paris. According to Sollers, the *Tel Quel* group sought to train a theoretical *avant-garde* that could accomplish a rebellion of forms: "We want to establish a dialectical union between social and theoretical *avant-garde*", he said (see Bolgar 1969: 196–198). Although writers and scholars of the *Tel Quel* group abandoned Marxism (and Sollers even argued afterwards that he had never been a Marxist), the idea of rebellion in language had a profound impact on Kristeva's and Barthes's theories of literary language. In this period there arose ideas of a social and linguistic revolution.

Writers associated with *Tel Quel* developed revolutionary ideas about language. For traditional genres they substituted the notion of a "text" that is produced in the process of writing. The text has many voices, and it is without centre and end. They conceived of literature as an adventure and an expedition into the depths of language. According to their notion of language, no mimetic relationships exist between text and reality. They wanted to construct a general theory of writing that had linguistic, semiotic, and psychoanalytic branches. This theory was to be developed together with the theory of production, power system, and social change (cf. Sollers 1970; Ihanus 1987: 128).

Philippe Sollers crystallised their notion of language by saying that the work of art exists only virtually. Its actualisation or its production depends on reading and on those moments when these operations of reading become activated (Bolgar 1976: 185). According to this view, the reader is an assumed author who "swims against the tide", in the same way as the author had done when writing the book.

Looking at the list of writers whose texts were published in *Tel Quel* shows us what sort of literature the group considered the most interesting. Among the authors were such *avant-garde* writers as Artaud, Bataille, Borges, Joyce, Mallarmé, Ponge, and Rousel. The *Tel Quel* group also read and published the articles of Russian Formalists, edited by Tzvetan Todorov. Many of them were interested in structuralist ideas but quite soon they started to criticise Structuralism as a "closed" theory.

How structuralist theories developed into post-structural ones is shown in the works of Roland Barthes. In his structuralist period of the 1950s and 1960s he aspired to systematic and precise analytic methodology. At the beginning of his career Barthes found the position of French literary criticism, based mostly on biography, to be quite depressing. Barthes thought that literary criticism could not exist without linguistics and that the literary text must be examined as one analyzes language, by studying syntax, word order, relationships between different parts, semantics, and associations. He argued that literature is not an imitation or mimesis of reality but rather semiosis or the play of signs. In these definitions Barthes seem to follow the Formalists.

Barthes saw Structuralism as a search for systems and patterns, a way of finding sense in human actions. According to him, the obligation of Structuralism is to uncover the structure that expresses the meaning of the text. We need not search for a message, because it does not exist. But we have to learn to know the inner organizational laws and how they fit together.

In his book *Le degré zéro de l'écriture* (1953), Barthes describes two different types of criticism. The first is sociological analysis as practised most often in newspapers, magazines, radio and television and which focuses on reportive communication between author and public. The other type of literary criticism concentrates on the formal structures of texts. The interpreter of literature performs a metacritique of other books. The critic's writing is comparable to that of the author in the sense that it, too, is a kind of art or literature. The first type of criticism is based on communication and the other type on creative writing. These two types of criticism can be correlated with the idea of two different kinds of texts. The first type of text Barthes calls "readable" (*lisible*) because it includes within itself its proper interpretation. Most traditional texts are written in this way. The other type of text is more open in meaning, and Barthes calls it "writeable" (*scriptible*) because it constrains the reader to become a writer so as to fill in the "missing" meanings. Barthes describes as follows the differences between the classical and the modern style:

> In classical speech, connections lead the word on, and at once carry it toward a meaning which is an ever-deferred project; in modern poetry, connections are only an extension of the word, it is the word which is "the dwelling place", it is rooted like a *fons et origo* in the prosody of functions, which are perceived but unreal. Here, connections only fascinate, and it is the Word which gratifies and fulfils like the sudden revelation of truth. To say that this truth is of a poetic order is merely to say that the Word in poetry can never be untrue, because it is a whole; it shines with an infinite freedom and

prepares to radiate toward innumerable uncertain and possible connections. (Barthes 1982: 57–58)

Both of these theories – of two types of criticism and of two different textual types – emphasise the role of the reader, as opposed to formalist and structural theories which emphasize the text in itself. The shift to focusing on the reader constitutes a remarkable change from those theories that have concentrated only on the work of art. Barthes changes the position of the critic/reader by emphasising her/his creative potentiality.

Barthes demands that the critic change her/his attitude toward language and writing since only by becoming a writer can one engage with the expressive process. The question of objectivity and subjectivity must be framed differently from positivistic theories. The idea that scientific language is a medium of thinking presupposes a neutral state of language that has several branches, such as literary or poetic language. Barthes argues against this presupposition, claiming that language is a diverse system and none of its codes are privileged. After reframing scientific language in terms of "writing", there remains one obligation: to occupy the region of pleasure (Barthes 1993: 73–74). The change in the role of critic that Barthes demands means a new kind of democracy. Earlier, during the hey-day of biographical theory, the author was located at the top of the hierarchy. Later, the critic had all the authority over the text. Now the reader prevailed.

When verbal art was defined by the New Critics and structuralists as a structured and hierarchical entity, it was at the same time described as closed and bound. In opposition to this view, some post-structural theorists began to define verbal art as an open form. In his book *Opera aperta* (1960), *The Open Work*, Umberto Eco defines open literature as a literature that is open to several different interpretations. Nevertheless, he still believes in a "correct" interpretation. According to Eco, closed texts (advertisements, detective novels, romances) allow only one interpretation that is directed to a specific reader and requires only minimal effort on the reader's part. After writing his novel *Il nome della rosa* (1980), Eco realised that his book had enjoyed enormous popularity and from very diverse types of readers. Eco analyses this popularity in his *Postille a "Il nome della rosa"* (1984) where he also presents some ideas about literature.

Eco defines poetic effect as the capacity that allows a text to be read in several ways without its becoming "worn out". The book is written for the reader and for her/his changing process. In the work of art, one dialogue takes place between text and readers (the writer is excluded) and another dialogue occurs between a specific book and all other books ever written. This is the notion of intertextuality, which claims that certain books are possible only by virtue of other books that have gone before (Eco 1985: 349–352).

Eco's ideas about the open text and intertextuality came close to the thinking of French post-structuralists. In fact, the concept of intertextuality was first framed by Julia Kristeva. According to her, the term intertextuality denotes the transposition of one sign-system into other. Kristeva warns against understanding intertextuality as the "study of sources", and she prefers the term "transposition" because it specifies that the passage from one signifying system to another demands a new articulation of the thetic-enunciative and denotative position. Thus the place of enunciation and denoted object are never single, complete, and identical to themselves, but are always plural, shattered, open to tabulation (Kristeva 1986: 111).

Language and power

Philippe Sollers, a central figure in the *Tel Quel* group and an avant-gardist author, has argued that genres and styles of literature are distinguished by the ways they either maintain or criticise power. Realistic literature is an example of a style that strives to reflect and repeat the reality accepted by a society. In Finnish literature the domination of the realistic style in literature supports social values and the *status quo*. In this situation, experimental books stand hardly any chance of being published. In contrast to the realistic style, *avant-garde* art takes a consciously antithetical attitude toward dominant norms, believing that by such opposition one can take distance from the tradition and thereby become open to fresh new views on writing.

Roland Barthes defined the Text in terms of its potential to act as a critique of power. His exemplary writers in this respect are Fourier, political utopianist and hedonist, the Marquis de Sade, chronicler of sadistic eroticism, and Loyola, founder of the Jesuits and writer of spiritual exercises. According to Barthes the Text is an ambiguous network of irony and radical instability which leads the reader to a state of indeterminacy where multiple, equally valid interpretations are possible. The Text, which can break institutions by confusing value systems, draws within itself other texts and voices from other writings (intertextuality). The different discourses meet in the Text and either support or contradict each other, resulting in irony or parody. This confusion of discourses is the basis for the Text's potential to trigger change.

According to Barthes, language is the basic equipment of power, because the dominant ideology is inscribed in language and everyone who uses language can only see the world through this ideology. In his inaugural lecture of the 1977 school term Barthes demonstrates that language is the place where power is inscribed: "We discover that the power is present in the most delicate mechanisms of social exchange: not only in the State, in classes, in groups, but even in fashion, public opinion, entertainment, sports, news, family and private relations, and even in the liberating impulses which attempt to counteract it" (Barthes 1982: 459). Barthes seems to share with Foucault the idea that power is everywhere. Power is not necessarily situated in some centre but it surrounds us and appears in all our relationships. If you try to destroy power "it will immediately revive and flourish again in the new states of affairs. The reason for this endurance is that power is the parasite of a trans-social organism, linked to the whole of man's history. This object in which power is inscribed, for all of human eternity, is language, or to be more precise, its necessary expression; language we speak and write" (Barthes 1982: 460).

Barthes defines power as a discourse that engenders blame, hence guilt, in its recipient. Barthes argues that when we use language we come under the oppression of the classification aspect of language. He refers to Jakobson who has shown that a speech system is defined less by what it permits us to say than what it compels us to say. Barthes worries that language "– the performance of the language system – is neither reactionary nor progressive; it is quite simply fascist; for Fascism does not prevent speech, it compels speech" (Barthes: 1982: 461). Because we cannot escape the confines of language the only possible way to use language is to cheat speech. "This salutary trickery, this evasion, this grand imposture that allows us to understand speech outside the bounds of power, in the splendour of a permanent the revolution of language, I for one call literature" (Barthes 1982: 462). Barthes advances the view that literature is the only form of language that allows the possibility for freedom in language. Literature can reproduce the diversity of sociolects, and it can envision and seek to elaborate a limit-language.

Literature is for Barthes something that produces knowledge and represents something. What does it represent? Usually literature is assumed to represent reality, the real. But Barthes argues that reality is not representable because there is no correlation between language and the real. But literature is categorically realist, in that it never has anything but the real as its object of desire; at the same time, it is just as stubbornly unrealistic, for it considers sane its desire to accomplish the impossible (Barthes 1982: 463–465).

In sum, Barthes presents language as something like a prison that incarcerates its users. But there is a means of escape which is literature, the world of freedom, in which some special types of Text can oppose the dominating power systems by creating confusion, irony, and parody.

The text of night

According to post-structural theorists, literature that questions power is usually written from a marginal position. But how can the voice of anyone get heard who writes outside power systems and whose books find few readers? Certain French theorists argue that texts which take positions against normative texts effect a confusion that can break the hold of power systems. In my view, literature that resists generally accepted ways of writing, literature that is written in silence and perhaps in isolation, may have the rebellious potential to change patterns of thought and world-view. Avant-gardist literature displays a timeless boldness that repeats itself again and again. In Finland we have several writers who were not understood in their day. For example, Edith Södergran was considered a "crazy" woman by critics, and Gunnar Björling had to pay to have his own books published. But even long after their death they remain avant-gardist poets who continuously question the norms of poetic language and its capacity to express strong feelings.

Julia Kristeva, drawing from psychoanalytic theory, has studied the process that brings heterogeneous elements into the writings of *avant-garde* writers. She argues that, in contrast to the conscious, socially determined language system, the unconscious produces material that transgresses and questions that system. The language produced in this way constitutes a sort of limit-language, a text of night. Philippe Sollers has written about this aspect of night: "We imagine ourselves to live in clear day, but the day is dead without the night. We grasp the day but it disappears from us to the extent that we lack the night, which we really are. Those texts that have rushed further into the chaos seem to be insanely dumb, senseless, empty, and they bring with them a presentiment of night, a time never seen, a state that was never remarked. The narrator of these texts can be anywhere; she/he does not tell about acting characters because her/his narration is an act; she/he acts in the narration. Her/his voice sounds unnatural, split and exaggerated, a farce without horror and jolly" (quoted in Ihanus 1987: 141). As examples of books of night may be mentioned works of Sade, Artaud, Beckett. and Joyce's *Finnegan's Wake*. These same writers happen to be classified as postmodern writers by most theorists of postmodernism. Juhani Ihanus has added to this list some examples from Finnish literature: Volter Kilpi's novel, *Alastalon salissa* [In the sitting-room of Alastalo], and Irmari Rantamala's *Harhama*. The list of Finnish books could be continued by Mariaana Jäntti's *Amorfiaana*, Arja Tiainen's *Mefisto*, Heidi Liehu's *Kirsikankukkia* [Cherry Flowers], and Hans Selo's *Diiva*. Djuna Barnes's *Night Forest* is also a good example of the book of night.

Kristeva's theories contain concepts that come very close to this idea of the text of night. One of them is her notion of "carnival" and the other is her ideas about *avant-garde* poetry. Throughout its entire history the carnival has remained a misunderstood and persecuted substratum of Western culture. It is most noticeable in folk games, medieval theatre, and such prose as anecdotes and fables. Kristeva views the carnival as a homology between the body, dream, linguistic structure, and structures of desire. In carnival, language parodies and relativizes itself, and in repudiating its proper role it provokes laughter but remains incapable of detaching itself from representation. Both representatively and anti-representatively the carnivalesque structure is at once anti-Christian and anti-rationalist. According to Kristeva all the most important polyphonic novels are inheritors of the Menippean carnivalesque structure; these include books by Rabelais, Cervantes, Swift, Sade, Balzac, Lautréamont, Dostojevski, Joyce, and Kafka. The carnival first exteriorizes the structure of reflective literary productivity and then it inevitably brings to light this structure's underlying unconscious: sexuality and death (Kristeva 1986: 48–50). It is not surprising that these two taboos of Western societies – sexuality and death – appear in the most contradictory discourses motivated by the unconscious.

In *La révolution du langage poétique*, Kristeva presents her notions of "the semiotic" and "the symbolic" of language, which refer to the unconscious and the conscious, respectively. The concept of "the semiotic" refers to the time when a child is connected with the mother's body and the two communicate non-verbally. When a child learns to speak she/he ascends to the world of the father's language. This is the world of "the symbolic", which is socially determined. By contrast, "the semiotic" has its source in body and instincts. "The semiotic" and "the symbolic" are simultaneously present in language. "The semiotic" brings to language those heterogeneous elements that one finds in the language of children, such as rhythm, imitation, and intonation. Later on, heterogeneity is expressed; for example, in the language of psychotics and in *glossolalia* or "speaking in tongues". This heterogeneity brings musicality and nonsense to language.

Heterogeneity also abounds in *avant-garde* literature, as seen in works by surrealists and dadaists (recall Runeberg's poem, above). Kristeva's examples are Joyce, Artaud, Mallarmé, and Lautréamont. She emphasises that although "the semiotic" is heterogeneous this type of language pushes through to something that is negative or overwhelming in relation to it. For Kristeva literature is a place where social orders are destroyed and renewed, and it therefore may offer escape from the angst of the time. (Kristeva 1993: 94–95)

In Kristeva's view the literary *avant-garde* presents to society a subject in process. The schizophrenia of *avant-garde* art produces a new moment of history that penetrates myths and symbolic systems and strives to reach beyond the limits of its own time. (For example, Artaud and Bataille unveil in their books the negative processes of the history of their day.) Kristeva began her career with a critique of Structuralism by arguing that it could not handle certain issues of interpretation because it had left the subject out of the equation. Kristeva herself has developed a phenomenological notion of the "speaking subject". The existence of a meaningful text presupposes a "speaking subject", which must at the same time be a "subject in process" (Kristeva 1993: 97–98).

It will be instructive to look at an example of a "text of night". I take Edith Södergran's poem, "Vierge moderne", published in the book *Dikter* (1916), which well illustrates a subject in process. At first the poem catches our attention by its unusually staccato and monotonous rhythm. (In *Dikter* Södergran has a couple of these "catalogue" poems, which seem to give the impression of an ultimate order.) Part of the rhythm of the poem is created by the mechanically repeated "I am" at the beginning of every stanza. The staccato rhythm and repetitions betoken a strong emotional power that threatens to explode the form. On the other hand, the rich metaphors at the end of every stanza form asymmetrical oppositions, the first part of which is built up of monotonous repetitions and the other part of a collection of polyphonic expressions.

The beginning of the poem presents the argument, "I am no woman. I am a neuter", and the rest of the poem is constructed of metaphors that answer the question, What is a modern virgin? The poem talks about sexual identity, which at the time of writing was a highly unusual theme, and thus to write about that subject was to break a taboo. In the poem the determinations of "what I am" implicitly include several so-called feminine and masculine qualities:

> I am no woman. I am a neuter.
> I am a child, a page and a bold decision.
> I am a laughing strip of a scarlet sun ...
> I am a net for all greedy fishes,
> I am a toast to all women's honour,
> I am a step toward accident and ruin,
> I am a leap into freedom and self ...
> I am the whispering of the blood in the man's ear
> I am a fever of the soul, the flesh's longing and denial
> I am an entrance sign to new paradise.
> I am a flame searching and quick
> I am water, deep but boldly up to the knees
> I am fire and water in honest union on free conditions ...

What "I am", to the contrary of being woman or being neuter, is expressed in this poem by a group of metaphors that describe a rich combination of qualities that betoken complex meanings. Motion is described as "a step", "a flame", "a water", and "strip of a scarlet sun". These are definitions of the subject of the poem which show that she is in a state of continuous change. Qualities ascribed to the subject also include paradoxes that further underline her changeability: "a flame searching and quick", "water deep, but boldly up to the knees", "the flesh's longing and denial". All these expressions escape singular definition.

The fourth and fifth stanzas present familiar Freudian sexual symbols: "I am a net for all greedy fishes" and "I am a toast to all women's honour". These metaphors ironise culturally determined womanhood and manhood by saying that a woman is "a toast" and men are "greedy fishes". Sexual images continue as metaphors of seduction: "I am the whispering of the blood in the man's ear" and "I am a fever of the soul, the flesh's longing and denial". The seducing images give to the subject of the poem partly masculine and feminine qualities. The poet as a woman of her times shows unprecedented courage and irony in her use of metaphors. This poem's ironising attitude shows it to be a rebellious text in the sense that Barthes and Kristeva give to the *avant-garde* text that questions norms and taboos.

Some of the metaphors have an abstract quality: "a step toward accident and ruin" and "a leap into freedom and self". The words "freedom" and "accident" include indeterminate qualities as do all the metaphors of this poem. The poem ends in an ultimate paradox – "I am a fire and water" – which flaunts even the laws of nature, and which closes the poem by arguing that the subject does not want to be defined; it wants to remain in process, searching and free.

Summary

All literary theories from Formalism to New Criticism, Structuralism, and Post-structuralism have emphasised the autonomy of the poetic text. The Formalists revised our view of poetry, conceiving it as an autonomous system of forms, an organic entity. According to New Criticism and Structuralism, verbal works of art are structured hierarchically. The autonomy of poetry in Formalism, New Criticism, and in some Structuralism means that literature should not be seen as a reflection of society or reality, although some semioticians, such as Mukarovski, have taken exception to this position by describing literature as a social and collective experience. Lucien Goldmann in his theory of genetic Structuralism tries to demonstrate a certain homology between the structures of literature and those of society. The relationship between society and literature is even more complex in post-structural theories, which view language itself as (re)inscribing power systems, and certain forms of *avant-garde* literature as having the potential to rebel against those systems.

Post-structural theories no longer consider the text as structured or hierarchical, but on the contrary have defined it as heterogeneous, fragmented, and open. Philosophers of postmodernism have declared that there remain no central or grand narrative themes but only small units and marginal narrations. Open texts may include the most heterogeneous material offering opportunities for a great number of variable interpretations. Post-structural theories consider the text as an intertextual network that refers only to other texts. Books talk about other books and every story narrates a story that is always already narrated.

The view that literature does not reflect or imitate reality is shared by all the theories under consideration. The New Critics viewed literature as its own independent world which does not describe society or nature but a place unique unto itself. The work of verbal art creates its own referent, which cannot be described by any means other than poetic ones. The post-structuralist Barthes argues that literature stubbornly refuses to represent anything. For him, literature that imitates reality, as realistic art tries to do, colludes in upholding traditional value and power systems. According to Lyotard, realism dominates where political parties dictate "correct" images and "correct" texts (Lyotard 1986: 149–150). Experimental *avant-garde* artists have often confronted political parties and others who dominate cultural institutions, while post-structural theorists and postmodern philosophers consider *avant-garde* art as an opportunity for freedom.

In spite of the fact that earlier theories of literature such as Formalism, Imagism, and Structuralism developed side by side with the *avant-garde*, it is Post-structuralism that holds a special place for *avant-garde* art in its theories of literature. *Avant-garde* art, though situated in the margins, carries within itself the potential for resistance and rebellion against language, claim Kristeva and Barthes.

Jean-François Lyotard, in his article "Sublime et avant garde", views the *avant-garde* as something that remains undetermined. According to him the *avant-garde* is not concerned with the question of what happens to the subject but rather asks, *Does* it happen? (Lyotard 1986: 173–175). Lyotard combines the *avant-garde* with the sublime, considering the mix to be pleasure joined with displeasure. It is something that evokes an unpleasant experience in the face of enormous things such as the desert, mountains, pyramids, or something powerful, such as a stormy ocean or the eruption of a volcano. The shocking experience of the sublime, too, includes incompleteness and ugliness. Lyotard refers to Paul Klee's remark that art does not imitate nature but it creates an other world, a limit-world (*Zwischenwelt*). Lyotard says it could be argued that art creates a limit-world where the dreadful and the formless have their own right to existence because they both can attain the status of the sublime (Lyotard 1986: 167–168). In this respect, Lyotard seems to combine some ideas about artistic work and *avant-garde* art that have been presented in formalist, structural and post-structural theories.

Contrary to the ahistorical approach of the New Criticism – whose theory of traditionalism views books present and past as existing simultaneously today – history receives a new position in post-structural theories that describe literature as a network of intertextual references to other texts, and text as a system of roots (Derrida).

All the theories considered above emphasize the importance of literary language, as is shown in their demand for precise analysis of phonological and grammatical features, rhythm, and metre. All the theories discussed here that preceded Post-structuralism sought to discover how the text is structured in terms of hierarchical levels, inner tensions, oppositions and equivalencies. All of these reading methods seem to prove up the unity, harmony, planning of poetry. These theories presume that the literary work has a limited number of interpretations that can be found by means of close-reading.

In contrast, post-structural theories do not consider the text a structured entity, but as a heterogeneous and indeterminate phenomenon for which there is no one "correct" meaning. The "roots" of the text may lead anywhere. Post-structural theorists do not believe the text can be studied objectively from the outside. Instead, the critic must recognize her/his position and subjectivity. In Barthes's theories, the critic is analogous to the author in her/his creativity. This means also that the critic loses authority over the author. This change of position is seen in those notions used by post-structuralists, deconstructionists, and reader-response critics alike: the "interpreter" has now become the "reader". The critic is no longer the one who knows the truth of a text but is instead another form of reader and writer.

In post-structural theories the border between text and criticism, author and critic has been blurred. Barthes has demanded that the critic descend from his lofty position and come down to the same level as author, reader, and writer. Does this mean that the language of criticism should come closer to the language of art, or vice versa? Should critical language follow the norms and rules of literature or break them as the avant-gardists do? Or does poetic language become more like scientific writing?

It seems likely that nobody wants the last choice to happen. We don't want to lose the beauty and the mysteries of poetic language – they cannot be replaced. Some post-structuralists, such as Barthes, have invented a language of criticism that comes close to the pleasure that they expect such language to have. Kristeva's language of criticism has also become more enjoyable, after the heaviness of her early writings. Both of these critics show how the *avant-garde* as an attitude may be transposed from avant-gardist art to criticism, thus completing the symbiosis of art and critical aesthetics.

References

Barthes, Roland (1982). *A Barthes Reader*. Susan Sontag (ed.). London: Jonathan Cape.
– (1993). *Tekijän kuolema tekstin syntymä*, Lea Rojola (ed.). Tampere: Vastapaino.
Bolgar, Mirja (1976). *Pariisin päiviä, kirjoja ja kirjailijoita*. Porvoo: WSOY.
Calinescu, Matei (1987). *Five Faces of Modernity. Modernism, Avant-garde, Decadence, Kitsch, Postmodernism*. Durham, NC: Duke University Press.
Eco, Umberto (1985). *Matka arkipäivän epätodellisuuteen*. Trans. Aira Buffa. Juva: WSOY.
Espmark, Kjell (1982). Runoudesta, *Parnasso* 3.
Fjord Jensen, Johan (1979). *Kirjallisuudentutkimus*. Trans. Sirkka Heiskanen-Mäkelä and Veli Ketvel. Jyväskylä: Gummerus.
Ihanus, Juhani (1987). *Kauneus ja kuvotus*. Helsinki: Gaudeamus.

Jakobson, Roman (1978). Linguistics and poetics. In: *Style in Language*. Thomas Sebeok (ed.). New York: Cambridge University Press.
Kirstinä, Väinö (1977). *Kirjarovioiden valot*. Helsinki: Tammi.
Kristeva, Julia (1986). *The Kristeva Reader*. Toril Moi (ed.). New York: Columbia University Press.
– (1993). *Puhuva subjekti: Tekstejä (1967–1993)*. Tampere: Gaudeamus.
Lehtonen, Maija (1984). Roland Barthes. *Parnasso* 7.
Lotman, Juri (1976). *Analysis of the Poetic Text*. Trans. and ed. M. Sosa and B. Harvey. Ann Arbor: University of Michigan Press.
Lyotard, Jean-François (1986). *Sublime et avant garde*. Finnish trans. by Jussi Kotkavirta and Esa Sironen. Jyväskylä: Tutkijaliitto.
Manner, Eeva-Liisa (1983) *From My Life I Make a Poem: Salt of Pleasure*. Trans. and ed. Aili Jarvenpa. St Paul, MI: New River Press.
– (1986). *Time: Fog Horses*. Trans. Ritva Poom. *Cross-cultural Review Chapbook* 18.
Mukarovski, Jan (1977). *The Word and Verbal Art : Selected essays*. (=Yale Russian and East European studies ; 13.) New Haven: Yale University Press.
Peuranen, Erkki (1979). *Neuvostorunoutta ja runoilijoita*. Juva: WSOY:
Sederholm, Helena (1994). *Olipa kerran avantgarde. Katkelma ja kokonaisuus. Postromanttisia kirjoituksia,* Keijo Virtanen (ed.). (= Jyväskylän kirjallisuuden laitoksen julkaisuja 7.) Jyväskylä: Yliopistopaino.
Sivenius, Pia (1984). *Avautua solmuun. Naisnäkökulma ja miehinen diskurssi*. Helsinki: Gaudeamus.
Tarasti, Eero (1996). *Esimerkkejä. Semiotiikan uusia teorioita ja sovellutuksia*. Tampere: Gaudeamus.

Pirjo Kukkonen

The Kanteletar as poetic text and discourse in the semiotics of culture

1. Text and discourse

The concepts of *text* and *discourse* are two of the most basic ones in semiotics. Yet there still exists a lack of consensus on how to interpret and apply them. Some central questions in this regard are, How can these concepts be defined? What is the relationship between text and discourse? How are texts and discourses constituted? And what are the relationships between texts made up of different sign systems? The etymology of text as "something woven" refers to a characteristic of an entity that can be circumscribed as a "coherent whole" (Nöth 1995: 332). In Latin and Greek the verb *texo, texui, texum* means "to weave"; the nominal *textus*, "woven fabric", "textile", "weave", "texture", is the result of an action. The verb *tektanomai* in Greek means "to weave together". The word *discursus* means something active, an action, "to run back and forth".

The aim of my presentation is twofold: to discuss the concepts of text and discourse, and, as illustration, to analyze the lyric song collection, *The Kanteletar*, as both a poetic text and a discourse that is semiotically woven into Finnish culture. I will also briefly discuss the translation of a poetic text, that is, how signs of one national culture can be transformed into the signs and representations of another. Central to the analysis of a cultural text, written or oral, is the concept of sign and its meaning. The discourses of oral Finnish folk poetry reflect the founding culture at the thematic level and in their central poetic structures – sounds, alliterations, repetitions, parallelisms, rhythms and rhymes – which became written texts in the middle of the nineteenth century.

Crucial to the collection is the union of mind and form. The form is the text, and the mind is the discourse, because it joins the language of the text with the natural world. A network of conceptual or symbolic relations forms the worldview represented in the poems. These consist of basic oppositions such as world/otherworld, living/dead, culture/nature, village/forest, and so on (cf. Tarkka 1990: 293).

As theoretical frameworks for my enterprise, I draw upon Mikhail Bakhtin's notion of the polyphonic text (1991); Roland Barthes's writings on text vs. discourse and written vs. oral (1990); and Yuri Lotman's views on the poetic text, text as culture and the semiotics of culture (1990).

A text-linguistic point of view stresses the interaction between syntax, semantics, and pragmatics, and it is what actually lies behind Charles Morris's semiotics (1971). When Basil Hatim and Ian Mason discuss the semiotic dimension, in their *Discourse and the Translator*, they define *text* as a set of mutually relevant communicative functions, structured in such a way as to achieve an overall rhetorical purpose (1990: 243). By *text linguistics* they mean that branch of linguistics which concerns itself with the analysis of spoken and written texts above the level of individual sentences. This involves, for example, the description of the way sentences link together to form coherent wholes. For them the term *discourse* refers to "modes of speaking and writing which involve participants in adopting a particular attitude towards areas of socio-cultural activity" (Hatim & Mason 1990: 240–242). The *mode* is the selected medium for language activity. It is essentially a choice between speech and writing, but such distinctions as monologue and dialogue are also seen as variations of mode. The *field* designates variation in language according to its usage in different professional and social discourses such as, for example, science and law (1990: 241). Hence, we may speak of the field of poetic discourse. The *tenor* is the relationship between addresser and addressee as reflected in their use of language; e.g., level of formality, relative distance, and so on (1990: 243).

The concept of discourse can be compared to the cultural codes referred to by Roland Barthes (1990: 18–20). These are conceptual systems that regulate how the denotative meaning of a textual element acquires extra, connotative meanings. This happens when culture is seen as dynamically imposing itself on the text. Thus, a culture or an ideology, for example, expresses itself through a variety of key terms that take us beyond the text to an established set of precepts (cf. Hatim & Mason 1990: 70–71).

Thematically, the concept of place, or *locus*, and especially that of road or way, manifests in different places, both concrete and abstract, in *The Kanteletar*, giving spirit to the lyrics as a sign of Finnish culture. The central concept concerning the spirit of place is what Mikhail Bakhtin calls *chronotope*, the concept of time and place in the novel (1991: 14–165). A road, castle, ballroom, country village, doorstep, and so on – all these exemplify the *chronotope* in its spatial idea of time, and temporal idea of space (we discuss this further, below). In the poems of *The Kanteletar* the starting point of the lyric singer is a place – the home and home village where his roots are.

Dialogism refers to interactions among a diversity of voices, a polyphony of points of view in texts, including the poems at hand. The thematic level of poetry is likewise determined by dialogism: *dia-logos* literally means "speaking across", that is, communication across existential or social borders (Tarkka 1994: 251). According to Bakhtin (1981: 13–40), dialogism is a feature of both literature and of discourse, but to him epic is monological, a form of discourse determined by one authoritative voice and closed meanings. Bakhtin nevertheless stresses the dialogic nature of folklore (1981: 31, 38) and thus oral epics (cf. Tarkka 1994: 296 n1).

The central issue is on one hand the concepts of text and discourse; and on the other, the theoretical and methodical implications of these concepts. So we must ask, What are the characteristic features of these two concepts, and how can folk poetry be seen as discourse or text? According to Roman Jakobson, oral expression (and, consequently, discourse) always comes first, and writing is but a derivative form of it. Hjelmslev, in contrast, uses the term *text* to designate the totality of a linguistic string, unlimited because of the system's productiveness (cf. Greimas & Courtés 1982: 340–341).

Greimas and Courtés give different meanings to the term discourse:

> In a first perspective, the concept of discourse can be defined with that of semiotic process. In this way the totality of the semiotic facts (relations, units, operations, etc.) located on the syntagmatic axis of language are viewed as belonging to the theory of discourse. When one has in mind the existence of two macrosemiotic systems – the "verbal world" manifested in the form of natural languages, and the "natural world" as the source of non-linguistic semiotic systems – the semiotic process appears as a set of discoursive practices: linguistic practices (verbal behaviour) and non-linguistic practices (signifying somatic behaviour manifested by the sensory orders). When linguistic practice alone are taken into consideration, one can say that discourse is the object of knowledge considered by discoursive linguistics. In this sense discourse is synonymous with text. [...] On the other hand – by extrapolation and as an hypothesis which seems to be fruitful – the terms discourse and text have also been used to designate certain non-linguistic semiotic processes (a ritual, a film, a comic strip) are then viewed as discourses or texts. The use of these terms postulates the existence of a syntagmatic organization undergirding these kinds of manifestations. (1982: 81–85)

In a somewhat different theoretical framework, discourse can be identified with utterance (that which is uttered). Discourse is thereby viewed as the result or operation of the concatenation of sentences. By contrast, discursive linguistics takes as its basic unit the discourse as a signifying whole. Consequently, sentences are only segments of the discourse-utterance. Of course, a discourse might at times be restricted to the dimensions of a sentence.

Linguistics lies at the origin of semiotic research (Greimas & Courtés 1982: 84), such that natural language is not merely defined as a semiotic system but is also viewed, explicitly or implicitly, as the model according to which other semiotic systems can and must be conceived. Natural language is a vast domain that is semantically coextensive with culture (ibid.). The term discourse nevertheless remains ambiguous. A semiotic domain can be called a discourse (for example, literary or philosophical discourse) because of its social connotations related to a given cultural context (cf. Lotman 1973 and 1990), which is independent from and prior to its syntactic or semantic analysis (Greimas & Courtés 1982: 84). The semiotics of culture regards "all human activity [as] concerned with the processing, exchange and storage of information," and culture as the "functional correlation of different sign systems" (Lotman in the *Encyclopedic Dictionary of Semiotics* 1986: 1087–1088).

Three distinct but complementary understandings of the *literary text* may be distinguished:
(1) as a text with a particular kind of internal construction;
(2) as a text that is multiply encoded;
(3) as a text that, in a given culture or community, is held to have cultural value.
All three of these definitions assume that the artistic text embodies a greater store of information than do other kinds of texts. Just as in Lotman's theory poetic language bears more complex meanings as a result of its greater conceptual "thickness" in comparison with ordinary language, so the literary text manifests a similar complexity of construction in comparison with the non-literary text. In poetry, the devices of metre, rhythm, rhyme, assonance, alliteration, as well as verse-line-stanza arrangements put formal elements into repetitions that force the other elements of language into relationships of juxtaposition. In prose, chapter divisions, or the recurring appearances of characters, for instance, can provide repetition, while the plot-line creates the relationship of juxtaposition. The understanding of the literary text as being multiply encoded is based on the notion of the text as the manifestation of a plurality of systems, codes, or structures. The text is regarded as a "semiotic space" in which various codes combine in a unique manner. Lotman's concept of code refers to semantic level, literary convention, level of consciousness or ideology. In his semiotics of culture, language holds a central position in the text, the place where different codes meet. The text has *energeia*; it manifests oppositions and conflicts. Old and new codes meet there, for the literary text has the dual function of both preserving old and generating new information (modeling). The literary text is held to have cultural value or function, because it imparts necessary or otherwise valued information to a given community. The literary text orders its material by an interplay of the paradigmatic and the syntagmatic axes. The process which hierarchises and evaluates texts within a given community is a culture's metalingual process (*Encyclopedic Dictionary of Semiotics* 1986: 1087–1088).

2. The poetic text in discourse

Art, aesthetics, and culture create harmony in life. Music and song create the harmony of Finnish culture as the repository of folk poetry. Elias Lönnrot (1802–1884) calls the full title of the collection that interests us, *Kanteletar taikka Suomen kansan Wanhoja Lauluja ja Wirsiä* (*The Kanteletar, Being Some Old Songs and Ballads of the Finnish People*). It is a compilation of lyrics and ballads, consisting of 652 poems based on Finnish oral tradition, first published in 1840 and edited by Elias Lönnrot. The collection is divided into three parts. Part I consists of general songs. Part II contains songs to be sung by a woman, those to be sung by a man, and songs and lullabies for children. Part III is comprised of ballads and legends. It is unquestionably a polyphonic totality, made up of songs to be sung by both men and women. *The Kanteletar* is a national sign and a representation of Finnish myths and mind, expressing the Romantic concept of folk culture as a repository of national identity, as Bosley states (1992). And we recall that central to Romanticism are the traces of man's history, tradition, and memory, his identity, roots, and longing (cf. Segerbank 1993: 11).

In his foreword to *The Kanteletar*, Lönnrot states that "the song and music are in a way another, more holy language with which one can express one's joy and delight, sorrow and cares, anxiety, one's happiness and contentment, one's hope and yearning, calmness, silence and other feelings better than with this usual, everyday language." Folk poetry gives us the mythical dimension, providing the spirit of place – *genius loci* – in the flow of time; it is the mythical contents of our memories and traditions. Music and song constitute the inner life of the poems. Metaphorically speaking, *The Kanteletar* is a place led to by many roads and having great indexical force. It has been translated into 35 languages and its music has inspired many composers, most notably Yrjö Kilpinen with his 64 *Kanteletarlauluja* (Op. 100) and Sibelius (the ballad whose tune he arranged for piano and the poems he set to song). In the mid nineteenth-century, Europe was already acquainted with many collections of folk poetry that owed their existence to the Romantic valuation of folk culture as a repository of national identity. Among these were J. G. Herder's *Stimmen der Völker in Liedern* (1778–1779), which first embodied the concept. *The Kanteletar*, based on oral tradition, represents poetry, the mother-tongue of the human race, as the Romantics claimed, the first language to be treated artistically (cf. Kuusi 1994: 93). Folk poetry was long the leading genre of literature, the novel appearing much later. "*Kalevala* language" (cf. Kuusi 1994: 41–55) is the language of poetry and myths, a language of its own, with its own special form and structure in which alliteration, parallelism and repetition are the most salient elements. They function as phonetic and poetic incantations that make the verses easy to memorize. *Kalevala* language was used for epics, lyrics, magic, weddings, and other festivities, often in Kalevala metre, which usually consists of eight syllables in trochaic tetrameter. The style is further built up by alliteration, parallelism, and repetition based on synonymy, analogy, or antithesis (cf. Kukkonen 1997a) . Word order is relatively free in Finnish, but *Kalevala* language imposes some restrictions; for instance, the noun and attribute have their own places, as do the shorter and longer words, which come at the beginning and end of a line, respectively. The verb and its particles are central to this language (Kuusi 1987: 184–197). The sounds and rhythms of the Finnish language constitute the special *genius loci* of these poems; as, for instance, in the song "Armahan kulku" (1:174), "The way of my beloved", from Part I (General Songs).[1]

Armahan kulku

Täst' on kulta kulkenunna.
Tästä armas astununna,
Valkia vaeltanunna;
Täss' on astunut aholla,
Tuoss on istunut kivellä.
Kivi on paljo kirkkahampi,
Paasi toistansa parempi,
Kangas kahta kaunihimpi,
lehto viittä leppiämpi,
Korpi kuutta kukkahampi,
Koko metsä mieluisampi,
Tuon on kultani kulusta,
Armahani astunnasta.
(*Kanteletar* 1840, I: 174)

1: 174 [Herding Song]

This way my treasure has walked
here my beloved has been
this way my dear one has stepped
and my white one has wandered
here she has stepped in the glade
there she has sat on a rock.
The rock is much brighter, the
boulder better than the next
the heath twice more fair
and the grove five times sweeter
and wild six times more flowery
all the forest more pleasant
because that treasure of mine
walked, that dear one of mine stepped.
(Bosley trans. 1992)

The original Finnish version of the poem contains many parallelisms and repetitions of verbs for "walk" (*kulkennunna, mennyt, astununna, vaeltanunna*) and repetitions for "more beautiful", (*kirkkahampi, parempi, kaunihimpi, leppiämpi, kukkahampi, mieluisampi*). A mood of pantheism is expressed when the beloved is compared to nature. The rhythm is built up by these repetitions and alliterations. In English, the lyric singer is a male describing his beloved. In Finnish, which lacks the grammatical gender, the pronoun *hän* means both "he" and "she", so the context does not tell us whether the singer is man or woman. The words *armas, mielitietty, valkia* and *kulta, kultani (-ni,* "my") are used with the meaning "beloved", which can be either female or male.

Lönnrot intended his collection as evidence of olden times and with it to show a by-gone style of life and mind, to portray everyday life and work, and to give a picture of the society which produced it. This included religious beliefs, and

Christian elements are common in the songs, reaching their fullest expression in "The ballad of the Virgin Mary" (III: 6).

The origins of *The Kanteletar* lie in the oral songs, poems and psalms of an agrarian, rural population, but the collection also reflects universal and central themes of humankind, such as walking along the road of life towards Tuonela or Manala, the regime of Death (Enäjärvi-Haavio 1935; Haavio 1935; Kaukonen 1989; Timonen 1993). On this road we meet with joys and sorrows, happiness and grief.

One proof of the indexical force of *The Kanteletar* on Finnish culture is the fact that it has inspired writers and composers to produce new iconic signs by which Finns can recall their national roots and identity. As Eero Tarasti has noted (1978; 1990; 1991), national culture creates iconic art, iconic symbols, which must have indexical force (cf. Peirce 1940) in order to continue to produce new iconicity; the signs of Finnishness are repeated in different manifestations of our national art. What Lotman calls the national semiosphere, which manifests the semiotics of a culture, can be studied not only through analysis of written and oral texts, but also of text as the culture it represents or produces. For such a purpose, *The Kantelatar* forms an excellent object of study.

3. Ontological aspects – Cognition and emotion

Three problematic concepts – *poetic*, *text*, and *discourse* – will be explored first, after which I shall discuss the poetic text of *The Kanteletar*. Literature, one of several cultural sign systems, is both a means of communication and part of a wider system of art in general. As Yuri Lotman says (1973; 1990), art is a means of communication by which sender and receiver make contact. The poetic features of Finnish folk poems, such as those in *The Kanteletar*, are expressed through language (*Kalevala language*), tempo, rhythm, and prosody, all of which are built up by the linguistic elements of words, syntax, and function of the structures as a whole (Kuusi 1994: 41–55). Charles Sanders Peirce's (1940) ontological categories can be used as a starting point for the analysis of a poetic text. When we read a poem as a text, we get a spontaneous feeling of *Firstness* from it. When we read the poem again, we begin to see different things in it by virtue of the cause-and-effect aspects that appear on the level of *Secondness*, the stage of antithesis. Lastly, when we understand, interpret, and draw conclusions about the poem, we have reached the level of *Thirdness*, the stage of synthesis.

As one example, we take the poem below, "Girl in love" (II: 31), which describes that emotion as the girl compares her feelings to a tree and a squirrel. The *Firstness* reading gives the atmosphere and rhythm of the poem. In *Secondness* and *Thirdness* we analyse, and form conclusions and syntheses:

The Kanteletar as poetic text and discourse in the semiotics of culture

31. Onpa tietty tietyssäni	Girl in love
Onpa tietty tietyssäni	There's a certain one I know
mesimarja mielessäni,	a honey-berry I like
Lempilintu liitossani,	a pet bird I'm attached to
Sinisorsa suojassani,	a wild duck I hold on to
Jok' on mieltynyt minuhun,	who is keen on me
Minä mieltynyt hänehen;.	and I'm keen on him.
Hänell' on ihanat silmät,	He has lovely eyes
Minulla syän suloinen.	he has not thrown me over
Ei hän heittänyt minua,	nor left me alone: he has
Eikä yksin jättänynnä;	taken me to be his own
Omaksens' on ottanunna,	called me his treasure
Kullaksensa kutsununna,	looked me out as his fair one
Kaunoksensa katsonunna,	chosen me as his white one.
Valkiaksensa valinnut.	I'll hang on to him
Niin minä hänessä riipun, jotta kiikun,	both hang on and swing
Niinkun lintu lehtipuussa,	like a bird in a green tree
Kuusen oksalla orava.	a squirrel on a spruce bough.
(*Kanteletar* 1840, II: 31)	(Bosley trans. 1992: 40–41)

What topics usually appear in lyric songs, especially in *The Kanteletar*? One finds themes of man's eternal yearning, his search for something, his sorrow, anxiety, love, marriage, the role of mother, the coldness of one's relatives, homelessness, eccentricity, the theme of being an outsider, an orphan in one's homeland, of being the object of evil and malicious gossip. The human being appears in different roles, as man, girl, and woman (especially a married one). The songs are to be sung at work or when walking in the thick forests, in the meadows and glades. Silence and nature are central themes in the collection. The silent Finn is described: long distances in the countryside deter communication with other human beings, so he talks to the trees and the birds. As part of nature, "the trees tell nobody", and are thus man's faithful friends. In Finnish mythology nature was holy and personified; man did not worship the trees themselves, but the spirit in them.

Though the lyric songs of Finnish folk poetry are characteristically rural, their contents show a quite sophisticated intellectual culture. Some of the songs have a joyful musicality; others display longing and passion (cf. Kukkonen 1997a). Painful love, with its utopian yearnings, its sorrow and disappointments, can turn into the seasoned wisdom of life. One's time in the childhood home is idealised; mother's love is praised; and deep feelings show forth in descriptions of Finnish melancholy, "the eternal yearning" (*iankaikkista ikävää*). As Lönnrot states (1840: xxxv), the leading theme of *The Kanteletar* is man's loneliness, solitude, and melancholy. In agrarian Finland, people lived in isolation, with long distances between them and the nearest neighbours – one reason for the Finnish national silence. We developed a specific grammar for this silence, as in Icelandic-saga culture. Silence became a subtle language that only other Finns could understand. Nature was, and still is, the place where the Finns find peace and redemption.

I have chosen to focus on the concept of "road", because the very idea of place implies a road to and from it. Hence, the road can be seen as a spatial metaphor in the life of a human being. Combining outer and inner aspects, the road acts as a bridge between man's concrete and abstract worlds. The semiotic aspects of the "road" in *The Kanteletar* appear in oppositions such as home/village, home/strange place, freedom/orphanhood, life/Tuonela (Death). Time is located in childhood/youth, youth/old age, here/there, before/now, now/future, past–present–future. Loneliness and melancholy are the leading themes. But music and song also have a mythical force that springs forth music/silence ("Why can't I sing?"), joy/sorrow, good luck/bad luck. The birds, especially the cuckoo, metaphorically express man's deepest feelings; birds belong to the mythical dimension, and they can take a man's soul with them to their home, *lintukoto*.

The road, the way, and the path are central themes in *The Kanteletar*; the road from x to y, then back or further on. It is a concrete pathway, a route (cf. Part II: 29), yet it receives abstract meanings. It is in fact difficult to make an explicit division into concrete and abstract roads, because the concrete one represents a mental stage and place, an existential state of man. The outer and the inner landscape are in dialogue.

The road is also a metaphor for man's continuous search for knowledge (cf. the heroic Väinämöinen in *Kalevala*), poetry, truth, beauty, and love. In Finnish the words *tieto*, "knowledge", and *tiede*, "science", are based on the expression *kulkea tietä pitkin*, "to go along a road". A *tietäjä*, "wise man", is literally a "knower" of secret lore, hence a magician, wizard, shaman (cf. Väinämöinen's song). In Greek, *meta hodos* means "along a road"; to choose a scientific method is to go along many roads.

The spirit of place is realised concretely in many songs and poems: the road, the home, the village, forest and trees, the sauna, Manala (Death's place), time, music and song. Man's mental place is reflected in almost every song through metaphors, where the concrete environment reflects the inner one. The mythical Pohjola – Nordic place of the North – and its magic spirit are described through nature. For example, Pekka Jalkanen, a researcher of Finnish popular music, says this about a well-known Finnish waltz, "Pohjolan yössä" ("In Pohjola's night"): "Pohjola represents the distant isle of Finnishness, an Elfland [Fairyland, a well-known Finnish tango Satumaa], a lucky place, Impivaara [allusion to Finland from Aleksis Kivi's novel] and the last place of safety. It is also the place for folk poetry and songs, the land of magic and magicians' drums, a land living on nature,

... and the magic light, the night that is not night but day" (1992: 7). The oppositions of light and shadow are an expressive metaphor for Finns. As is sung in *The Kanteletar* (I: 1), "music is made of sorrow, moulded from grief". The iconicity of *The Kanteletar* is reflected today, for instance, in the lyrics of Finnish popular music. It is especially evident in the role of nature in traditional Finnish tango lyrics written in the 1950s (cf. Kukkonen 1993; 1996; 1997b; Jalkanen 1992). They are truly folk songs of our time, as Matti Kuusi (1959) said about popular music songs and Schlager-songs.

In Finnish, many abstract meanings attach to the word *tie* ("road"): "Life is a road", "I am the way and the life" (biblical meaning), "The road stays in front of me" (to have difficulties). The road expresses the fact that we are on our way, in a concrete but also in an abstract sense, as Martin Heidegger states (1991: 103): "on the road we are on our home road". The meanings are at once abstract and concrete, forming so-called fuzzy categories rather than explicit ones (cf. Jackendoff 1985). The expression "Life is a road" shows how man organises his environment as a spatial metaphor. The road is concrete; life is abstract. Through metaphors in language we bridge the gulf between the concrete and the intellectual, non-material sides. Metaphor is ontological, expressing how we see phenomena, causal relations and so on; it is orientational, pointing out our direction; metaphors make a comprehensible whole of reality (Heikkinen 1993: 8–19; cf. Lakoff & Johnson 1980; Lakoff 1987; 1990). In Peirce's terminology, the spontaneous expression or feeling of a landscape is *Firstness* ("to see First"), past and present exist in *Secondness* ("to know"), and *Thirdness* ("to see, know and understand deeply") gives you a deep understanding of the outer and the inner landscape. The function of road can be interpreted in the same way. The road (*tie*, cf. *tao*) as a locus of time and place, as Bakhtin states, is an essential part of human life, both concrete and abstract. To choose a path or a road is to picture both oneself and the surrounding reality; the concrete landscape is interpreted through the mental landscape (cf. Nikanne 1990; 1992).

"Life is a road" that is formed by man's world-view, by space, time, values, ideology, one's very existence, the relations between natural and supernatural, by man himself, the different phases in life, happiness, life and death and life after death, society, nation, history, and the essential features of culture – aesthetic and ethical values – not just ontological ones (Pentikäinen 1994: 11). *The Kanteletar* values the mythical dimension in which man relies on a pantheistic view of life, and in which nature is the centre and home is where you have your roots. The road lies in front of man, the road to Tuonela and Manala (Death) is the object of yearning and longing, of *Sehnsucht*.

Spatiality is a primary category that is both an abstract and a concrete locus. The road begins in a place, goes somewhere, and back again, or further on.

Language joins together the concrete and abstract paths of man. Language, as well as music and song, are the essential *loci* of man, giving spirit to outer and inner places. Along a road, concrete or abstract, we often re-visit places located in different times, places where people before us have gone and left their signs and traces: the spirit of place – a tradition that allows us to recall the spatiality of time. The spirit of place and road in *The Kanteletar* manifests itself on many levels of time and place.

As Marcel Proust (1919) states, a smell or a taste can trigger massive works of memory. Hence, the spirit of place can not only be seen as a concrete place, but also as an abstract one in the human mind. Language, music and lyrics connect these two dimensions. The place of the human mind can be studied as reflections of the outer world, as is done in *The Kanteletar* with the aid of the *kantele*, a traditional zither-like instrument found in most eastern Baltic nations. In fact, in *Kanteletar* the feminine suffix *-tar* denotes in Finnish a resident spirit; thus the title of the collection can mean something like "zither-daughter", a kind of lyric muse. The *kantele* is the symbol of the hero who created the world, a myth, a tool of transformation, a more sophisticated version of the shaman's drum. It is a tool with which one can cross the gulf between culture and nature. In the enchantment of the music, the things that occupy man's everyday life – such as social values and status, permanency and temporality, good and evil, acceptability and non-acceptability, allowed and forbidden – all lose their meanings. *Kantele* makes possible the image of something holy, a place where the elements are not separated, a space and a place, primal chaos, where no different categories exist, and where culture with its values and meanings begins, according to the myths. Although *The Kalevala* (1835) describes the magical origin of the instrument and calls it "a joy for ever" ("ilo ikuinen"; 40: 234), the first song in *The Kanteletar* states that, "no, music was made from grief / moulded from sorrow" (I: 1). This is Lönnrot's own view of how art and poetry, the mythical aspects of life, are born. Hence, music, song and poetry are the essential elements of the spirit of *The Kanteletar*, which deals with the deepest dimensions of man (cf. Bosley 1992: Introduction).

The Kanteletar is in the Bakhtinian sense a "polyphonic" collection of men's and women's songs, songs for children, as well as narrative ballads. It is a collection that engages everyday life and feelings. In many oral cultures that make the distinction, epic poetry is for men, lyric for women. Bosley (1992: Introduction) asks if *The Kanteletar* is the feminine companion to the masculine *Kalevala*, and he answers to some extent, yes. But sexual roles in life – men did not look after children, women did not hunt – were not always reflected in art. Men would sing "women's" songs if they wanted to express tender feelings, and women used "men's" narrative style to sing of shocking events. The lack of grammatical gender in Finnish ("he" and "she" are the same word, *hän*) made this kind of singing possible.

Nature reflects the deepest dimensions of man: human knowledge and feelings, as well as our eternal longing for something; goodness, love, and truth, or the longing for Tuonela, the place of Death, where all sorrows disappear. The place Tuonela is a central theme in the following old Finnish lullaby:

178. Tuuti lasta Tuonelaan

II: 178 Lullabies

Tuuti, tuuti tummaistani,
Tummaisessa tuutusessa,
Tummaisella tuutijalla,
Tummaisen tuvan sisässä!
Tuuti, lasta tuonelahan,
Lasta lautojen sylihin,
Alla nurmen nukkumahan,
Maan alla makoamahan;
Tuonen lasten laulatella,
Manan neitojen piellä!
Tuonen tuutunen parempi,
Manan kätkyt kaunosampi,
Etevämmät Tuonen eukot,
Paremmat Manan miniät,
Tupa suuri Tuonelassa,
Manalla majat avarat.
 (*Kanteletar* 1840, II: 178)

Rock, rock my dark one
in a dark cradle —
a dark one rocking in a dark cabin!
Rock the child to Tuonela
the child to the planks' embrace
under turf to sleep
underground to lie
for Death's children to sing to
for the grave's maidens to keep!.
For Death's cradle is better
and the grave's cot is fairer
cleverer Death's dames, better
the grave's daughters-in-law, large
the cabin in Tuonela
and the grave has wide abodes.
 (Bosley trans. 1992: 64)

This theme returns in 1870 in the first Finnish novel, *Seitsemän veljestä* (*Seven Brothers*) by Aleksis Kivi, where one of the brothers' wives, "who had seen wondrous visions", says to her child: "... would you not want to sail away from here to the eternal haven of peace, while the white pennant of your childhood is still gleaming pure? On the shore of a misty, calm lake stands the dark manor of Tuonela; there in the heart of a dim grove, in the womb of a dark thicket, a cradle is ready for a child, with white sheets and coverlets... ." Kivi then has the mother sing a lullaby in the same spirit, the "Sydämeni laulu", "Song of my heart" (set to music by Sibelius as Op. 18 No. 6):

Sydämeni laulu

Song of my heart

Tuonen lehto, öinen lehto!
Siell' on hieno hietakehto,
Sinnepä lapseni saatan.
Siell' on lapsen lysti olla,
Tuonen herran vainiolla

Grove of Death, grove of night's land!
There's a cradle of fine sand,
There I will bring my baby.
There 'tis merry for a child,
With Death's lord upon his field,

Kaitsea Tuonelan karjaa.	Tending the herd of Deathland.
Siell' on lapsen lysti olla,	There 'tis merry for a child,
Illan tullen tuuditella	When day closes to be lulled,
Helmassa Tuonelan immen.	Folded by death's maiden.
Onpa kullan lysti olla,	Merry for a darling child,
Kultakehdoss' kellahdella,	In a golden cradle sprawled,
Kuulella kehräjälintuu.	Listening to the nightjar.
Tuonen viita, rauhan viita!	Thicket of Death, place of peace!
Kaukana on vaino, riita,	There pursuit and quarrel cease,
Kaukana kavala maailma.	far from the world's betrayals.
(Kivi 1944: 454)	(Bosley trans. 1992: 45)

The theme of Tuonela is prevalent in Finnish lullabies. A mother wished her baby to be in another, better world, the otherworld of Tuonela, and the available language for this was that of death (cf. Bosley 1992: Introduction). The lullabies illustrate the focal point and very beginning of human relations: mother and child. More problematic is the type of lullaby in which the mother wishes her child to be carried off to the otherworld or to be buried in the church graveyard. In these lullabies, the child's death is seen as something to be desired and the grave as paradise. Positive death-wish lullabies of this kind seem to occur mainly in Baltic-Finnish and north Russian traditions. These probably reflect earlier beliefs in the unity of life and death, are connected with ancient ancestor worship, and recall a time when babies were believed to have come from the other world. From this point of view, a baby's death was nothing more than a premature return home. Yet another theory seeks to explain the death-wish lullabies in terms of the physical and psychological hardship of women's daily existence in the north, and interprets the child death-wish metaphorically as a veiled protest at the harshness of the mother's life (Timonen 1993: 344).

The poems exhibit a conscious striving to become one with nature, freed of feelings, knowledge or thought – that is, to become a plant, flower, berry, tree, water, or to vanish into the sky or the earth. The sense of unity with nature functions as a metaphor for human loneliness and alienation: the kinless performer turns to nature for solace. At the same time, nature represents a living partner with which the self of the songs can communicate. With its trees, plants, flowers, creatures and heavenly bodies, nature evolves into a huge living, thinking, caring, responsive surrogate world into which the self of the songs can endlessly spread. In this way, plaints provide not only a medium to convey sorrow or grief but also a cultural means of transcending one's lot in life. When exterior phenomena are mentioned, it is to symbolise something interior: the speaker's own heart, soul, suffering, longing or joy (Timonen 1993: 339, 346).

4. Poetic translation

Semiotics and translation studies both deal with communication, and both are concerned with the use, interpretation, and manipulation of messages or texts, that is, of signs (Gorlée 1994: 11). Following Roman Jakobson's (1971) three "modes of translation" – intralingual, interlingual, and intersemiotic – *The Kanteletar* goes through all these processes. Oral folk poetry becomes a written collection of lyric songs in the middle of the nineteenth century. The collection is translated into various other languages (interlingual translation). And, especially from the beginning of the twentieth century, poems from the collection become musical compositions (intersemiotic translation) (cf. Kaukonen 1989: 135–138). The lexical and semiotic network is quite peculiar the collection, such that the modern reader has to translate the words into contemporary Finnish concepts (intralingual translation). *The Kanteletar* has inspired many composers, hence, the collection has undergone intersemiotic translation. The written text, in discourse, has received another artistic form – music and song – according to its various interpretations by different composers. The collection has an iconic function, and an indexical force, because it always produces new Finnish interpretations of the poetic text (cf. Tarasti 1990).

An interesting question is, If *The Kanteletar* is the goal of these different processes, is it a text or a discourse? Is the text the result, the stable element, a representation of phonological, morphological, and syntactic form and semantic content? The text becomes active and gets receives discursive function when the reader begins his/her dialogue with the voices in it. In Bakhtin's words, "I am me, I am other." The text is a hermetic unit, a result; the discourse is the unit where the dialogue begins, the polyphony with words and structures, rhythms, meanings, and so on. A reading experience is dialogic and consists not only of the text but also of the different writers, readers, and contexts – past, present, and future. The word is always born in a dialogue and forms a concept of the object in a dialogic way. In Bakhtin's view, we live in a dialogic relationship with our language. In a new tongue, in a new culture, with new readers, it receives new life and new meanings. Bakhtin points out (1981: 286): "Everything that the poet sees, understands and thinks, he does through the eyes of a given language, in its inner forms" (cf. Oittinen 1993: 74–76). Language is an essential part of every situation.

The concept of text can be viewed as very limited, for instance as co-text or context of the linguistic environment, or on a larger scale, as the social and cultural environment. Historical linguistic contexts are always, so to say, written in the wind; historical arguments are hypotheses, the explicit analysis of which is often difficult. In folk poetry, oral tradition takes the "truth" or the "myth" through history. Place and time are joined together, with place implicating the concept of time. This is Bakhtin's concept of the *chronotope*, or "time-place".

In my study of different Swedish translations and interpretations of *The Kanteletar* (1839–1989), the poetic text is the whole collection, including the linguistic contexts (cf. *Visor och ballader ur Kanteletar* 1989). In sociology, for instance, the text can be seen as a larger whole, with the sociological environment considered equivalent with Yuri Lotman's notion of text (1990), combined with Greimas's (1966; 1970; 1990) model of semes, lexemes, actants and modalities. Greimas talks about semiological networks representing different symbolisms, i.e., various semiotic discourses of culture such as aesthetics, myth, history, politics, law, film, architecture, and advertisements. As Eero Tarasti has noted (1990: 77–78), the Greimassian and Lotmanian models can be combined. Lotman's cultural semiotics involves culture as the highest level, then discourse, then text, then lexeme, and the first level is seme. According to Lotman, the analysis of a seme is already an analysis of cultural semiosis.

The starting point of all this is a linguistic semiotics still mainly based upon Saussure and, to some degree, Charles Morris (1938; 1971), the behavioural psychologist inspired by Peirce's triadic thought. As Gorlée states (1994: 12), Peirce's impact on the work of semiotic linguistics has mostly remained indirect. Morris's conception of semiotics consists of the syntax, semantics, and pragmatics of the sign (Morris 1971: 21–27 and 301–303; see also, Levinson 1989; Miller & Johnson-Laird 1976). The relation between signs themselves is *syntactic*; the relation between signs and what they denote is *semantic*; and the relation between signs and sign users is *pragmatic*. The text can be seen as performance or *parole*; text linguistics considers it to be the product of a three-dimensional – syntactic, semantic, pragmatic – interactive process (Gorlée 1994: 13).

In the analysis of folk poetry, these three levels are important: form, meaning, and function. The grammatical (phonological), morphological, and syntactical structures give the style and rhythm. The semantic level is that of cognition and culture level, since words generate culture. The pragmatic level deals with the poem as speech and rhythm. On this level we have to interpret the text's linguistic features and structures, as well as the experiences, attitudes, feelings, and construction of the lyric subject. We must, as Viikari says (1987: 55), "read what is written in the sound", that is to say, written *aloud*. The pragmatic information also concerns the poem as a complete speech-act, though it is very difficult to analyse paralinguistic signals such as voice nuances, tempo, intonations, and so on. On this pragmatic level we handle the poem as the discourse of the lyric self or singer. As Viikari claims (1987: 54), the language of a poem must always be thought of as if it were being spoken. Jakobson states that the poem is a discourse of double sender, receiver, and reference (1975: 371). Together these levels generate the semiotic component. They give the reader or researcher the ultimate, "inner hearing" as J. L. Runeberg called it, the "inner singing" which August Ahlqvist considered to be the starting point for the poem (Viikari 1987: 69).

The concept of discourse has many meanings depending on the point of departure for the particular study, be it sociological, aesthetic, pragmatic, or whatever. In linguistics, discourse can be seen as oral discourse, as speech, as reading, as talk, small-talk, and so on. Discourse is a pragmatic whole comprising who says something, to whom, why, when, and where. Pragmatics deals with the use and function of language, and in written discourse, too, the pragmatic aim is central. The message of the linguistic text makes demands on the sender, channel, receiver, indeed, the whole communication situation. And the study of a poem should engage it as form, meaning, pragmatics, and semiotics (of culture).

For Greimas (1966), discourse is based on Saussure's concepts of *langue* and *parole*. *Langue* is the collective, normative system that is actualized in the individual *parole*. *Discourse* refers to the meaning of the communication act and its manifestation. Though the speaker has some freedom in creating discourse, this freedom is highly constrained (Tarasti 1990: 69–70). It is instructive to compare Greimas's and Morris's models of discourse. Morris (1971) takes as his starting point its outer (i.e., pragmatic) aspect, whereas Greimas (1966; 1970; 1990) argues that the semantic universe is a closed system that can be divided into hierarchical levels (text, metatext, meta-metatext), but its action and structure can only be understood from itself. In later work, Greimas tried to classify discourses according to pragmatic arguments. He takes the view that holistic mythical communication comes first, when archaic societies combine codes of poetry, music, and gestures together. More developed societies turn those activities into the different and independent discourses of poetry, music, and dance. Also, they no longer are part of the realm of the sacred, but take on playful or aesthetic functions. Finally, they are no longer collective phenomena; rather, their production and use reflect individual styles (Tarasti 1990: 71).

Hence, the soul of the poem is reflected in the linguistic text by phonological, morphological, syntactic, and semantic features. The message, use, and function of the poem are communicated only through cultural codes. The *genius loci* of the present poems is constituted by pragmatic (non-linguistic), linguistic, and extra-linguistic knowledge of Finnish history and traditions of folk poetry. In the text, structure and meaning are in dialogue. In the discourse, the dialogue takes place among aesthetic and historical aims and meanings, acts and results.

Singers traditionally learned *Kalevala* language (cf. Kuusi 1985: 184–197) – prosody, melodies, themes, texts, and uses – as it existed in the their home region, gradually developing a personal style and repertoire that suited the tastes and performance contexts of the community (DuBois 1994: 138). As Hymes puts it (1985: 15), "repetitions of particles, for example, prove to be not the limitations of a primitive mind, but the signs of an implicit structure, a structure which gives shape and point". The verses are often organised according to certain rhetorical patterns (cf. DuBois 1994: 140).

5. Dialogic discourse

As mentioned above, the central concept concerning the spirit of place is Mikhail Bakhtin's notion of the *chronotope* (time-place). The different places that give spirit to *The Kanteletar* center around man in Nature, in the forest, speaking to the trees and birds. In Finnish mythology the forest, the domain of the forest-lord Tapio (cf. Sibelius's *Tapiola*), trees, and birds have a central meaning; as metaphors they represent the inner states of man. Linguist Ray Jackendoff states in his book *Semantics and Cognition* that semantic or conceptual structures can be organised according to ideas of locale and space: "time is location, being possessed is a location, properties are locations, events are locations" (1985: 140–141). Hence, place-and-space is an essential category that is both concrete and abstract; even knowledge, feelings, and mental properties are located somewhere, representing a locus in the mind (cf. also, Jackendoff 1987; 1990; 1992; and Tabakowska 1993).

6. Conclusion

I have discussed the different levels of the poem: text, discourse, as well its aesthetic, cultural, and ontological levels (i.e., the mind behind the forms of folk poetry discussed here). Finnish folk poetry deals with people's everyday life, their work and acts, their mental and emotional states. A place-view of language takes into account that the text is also a location. Cognition, culture, discourse – all these are locations. And the text is filled with various culturally-bound linguistic features, such that its every word generates culture. In order to analyse and understand this, we keep up a continuous dialogue within this thing called discourse.

The question for us is, Can the folk poem in itself, as a structural semiotic entity, live its own life as a poetic text? or is the discourse always where the reader has his/her dialogue with different persons, times, and especially cultural elements? Lotman uses the term *semiosphere* (1990: 123, 125), defining it as "the semiotic space necessary for the existence and functioning of [verbal and non-verbal] languages, not the sum total of different languages; in a sense the semiosphere has a prior existence and is in constant interaction with languages. The semiosphere is the result and the condition for the development of culture". Hence a poetic, including a folk-poetic, text is always in a dialogue with its discourse, that is, with its stylistic, cultural, and ontological environment. Text is a result; discourse is an activity. In it we deal with the *chronotope*: place implicates time, time implicates place, the spatial and the temporal carry on a dialogue with past, present, and future in the cultural and socio-semiotic text.

Note

1. Keith Bosley, who translated *The Kanteletar* into English, does not give a title to the song, "Armahan kulku", but only the title "Herding Song" to three of that type in the collection, all of which appear in Part I.

References

Bachtin, Michail (1991). *Det dialogiska ordet* [*The Dialogic Word*]. Swedish trans. by Johan Öberg. Uddevalla: Anthropos.
Bakhtin, Mikhail (1987/1963). *Problems of Dostoevsky's Poetics*. Trans. and ed. Caryl Emerson. Minneapolis: University of Minnesota Press.
– (1981). *The Dialogic Imagination: Four Essays*. Ed. Michael Holquist (ed.). Trans. Caryl Emerson and Michael Holquist. Austin: University of Texas Press.
Barthes, Roland (1990/1973). *S/Z*. Trans. Richard Miller. Oxford: Basil Blackwell.
Broms, Henri (1994). *Paikan henki* [*The Spirit of Place*]. Helsinki: Arator Oy.
DuBois, Thomas (1994). An ethnopoetic approach to Finnish folk poetry: Arhippa Perttunen's *Nativity*. In: *Songs beyond the Kalevala: Transformations of Oral Poetry*. Ed. Anna-Leena Siikala & Sinikka Vakimo (eds.). Studia Fennica Folkloristica 2. 138–179. Helsinki: Finnish Literature Society.
Encyclopedic Dictionary of Semiotics 1986. Tome 1–2. Thomas A. Sebeok (general ed.). (= Approaches to Semiotics 73.) Berlin, New York, Amsterdam: Mouton de Gruyter.
Enäjärvi-Haavio, Elsa (1935). *Lyyrilliset laulut. Suomalaisen muinaisrunouden maailma* [*Lyric Songs: The World of Ancient Finnish Poetry*]. Porvoo, Helsinki: WSOY.
Gorlée, Dinda L. (1994). *Semiotics and the Problem of Translation: With Special Reference to the Semiotics of Charles S. Peirce*. Diss. Amsterdam: Rodopi.
The Great Bear: A Thematic Anthology of Oral Poetry in the Finno-Ugarian Languages (1993). Lauri Honko, Senni Timonen and Michael Branch. Poems translated by Keith Bosley. (= Finnish Literature Society Editions 533.) Helsinki: Suomalaisen Kirjallisuuden Seura, Finnish Literature Society.
Greimas, A. J. (1966). *Sémantique structurale: Recherche de méthode*. Paris: Larousse.
– (1970). *Du sens: Essais sémiotiques*. Paris: Seuil.
– (1990). *The Social Sciences: A Semiotic View*. Minneapolis: University of Minnesota Press.
Greimas, A. J. and Courtés, J. (1982/1979). *Semiotics and Language: An Analytical Dictionary*. Bloomington: Indiana University Press.
Greimas, A. J. and Fontanille, J. (1991). *Sémiotique des passions*. Paris: Seuil.
Guenat, Satu (1994). Puulajien perusolemuksista kansanperinteessä [Basic features of trees in folk tradition]. In: *Kalevalaseuran vuosikirja* 73. Pekka Laaksonen and Sirkka-Liisa Mettomäki (eds.). 120–133. Helsinki: Suomalaisen Kirjallisuuden Seura [Finnish Literature Society].

Haavio, Martti (1935). *Suomalaisen muinaisrunouden maailma* [*The World of Ancient Finnish Poetry*]. Porvoo, Helsinki: WSOY.
Hatim, Basil and Mason, Ian (1990). *Discourse and the Translator.* (= Language in Social Life Series.) London and New York: Longman.
Heidegger, Martin (1991). *Silleen jättäminen* [*Gelaßenheit*]. Finnish trans. Reijo Kupiainen. Tampere: Tampereen yliopisto.
Heikkinen, Mervi (1993). Tie spatiaalisena metaforana [The road as a spatial metaphor]. *Alue ja Ympäristö* 1: 8–19.
Herder, Johann Gottfried (1778–1779). *Stimmen der Völker in Liedern.* Halle: n.p.
Hymes, Dell (1985). Some subtleties of measured verse. J. Hesch (ed.). In: *Proceedings of the Niagara Linguistic Society*, 15th Spring Conference. Buffalo.
Hägglund, Tor-Björn (1994). Luonnon ja mielen metsä [The forest of nature and mind]. In: *Kalevalaseuran vuosikirja* 73. Pekka Laaksonen and Sirkka-Liisa Mettomäki (eds.). 151–163. Helsinki: Suomalaisen Kirjallisuuden Seura.
Jackendoff, Ray (1985/1983). *Semantics and Cognition.* Cambridge, MA; London: MIT Press.
– (1987). *Consciousness and the Computational Mind.* Cambridge, MA: MIT Press.
– (1990). *Semantic Structures.* Cambridge, MA: MIT Press.
– (1992). *Languages of Mind.* Cambridge, MA: MIT Press.
Jakobson, Roman (1971/1959). On linguistic aspects of translation. In: *On Translation.* Brower, Reuben A. (ed.). (= Harvard Studies in Comparative Literature 23.) 232–239. Cambridge, MA: Harvard University Press.
– (1960). Roman Jakobson, closing statement: Linguistics and poetics. In: *Style in Language.* Thomas A. Sebeok (ed.). 350–357. New York: Wiley.
Jalkanen, Pekka (1992). *Pohjolan yössä* [*In Pohjola's Night*]. Suomalaisia kevyen musiikin säveltäjiä Georg Malmsténista Liisa Akimofiin. Jyväskylä: Luovan säveltaiteen edistämissäätiö/Suomalaisen musiikin tiedotuskeskus, Kirjastopalvelu Oy (Helsinki).
The Kalevala (1989/1835). An Epic Poem after Oral Tradition by Elias Lönnrot. Translated from the Finnish with an Introduction and Notes by Keith Bosley and a Foreword by Albert B. Lord. Oxford: Oxford University Press.
Kanteletar elikkä Suomen Kansan vanhoja lauluja ja virsiä (1925/1840). Alkulause Elias Lönnrot 1840. Suomalaisen Kirjallisuuden Seuran toimituksia 3 osa. Kahdeksas painos. Helsinki: Suomalaisen Kirjallisuuden Seura.
The Kanteletar (1992). Lyrics and Ballads after Oral Tradition by Elias Lönnrot. Selected and translated from the Finnish with an Introduction and Notes by Keith Bosley. Oxford, UK and New York: Oxford University Press.
Kaukonen, Väinö (1989). *Lönnrot ja Kanteletar* [*Lönnrot and Kanteletar*]. Helsinki: Suomalaisen Kirjallisuuden Seura.
Kivi, Aleksis (1929/1870). *Seven Brothers.* Trans. Alex Matson. New York: Coward-McCann.
– (1944/1870). *Seitsemän veljestä* [*Seven Brothers*]. In: *Selected Writings*, vol. 1. 13–457. Helsinki: Suomalaisen Kirjallisuuden Seura.
– (1994). *Odes.* Selected and tran(s. Keith Bosley. [= Finnish Literary Society editions 611]. Helsinki: Finnish Literature Society.
Kukkonen, Pirjo (1993). *Kielen silkki: Hiljaisuus ja rakkaus kielen ja kirjallisuuden kuvastimessa* [*The Silk of Language: Silence and Love in the Mirror of Language and Literature*]. Helsinki: Helsinki University Press.

The Kanteletar as poetic text and discourse in the semiotics of culture

– (1996). *Tango Nostalgia: The Language of Love and Longing. Finnish Culture in Tango Lyrics Discourses – A Contrastive Semiotic and Cultural Approach to the Tango*. Helsinki: Helsinki University Press.
– (1997a). Jos mun tuttuni tulisi – Om min älskling nu sig tedde [If the one I know came now]. In: *Ord och visor tillägnade Kurt Zilliacus 21.7.1997*. Marianne Blomqvist et al (eds.). 140–145. Meddelanden från Institutionen för nordiska språk och nordisk litteratur vid Helsingfors universitet, B:18. Helsingfors.
– (1997b). *Ilon ja surun sointu: Folkloresta poploreen* [The Sound of Joy and Sorrow: From Folklore to Poplore]. Helsinki: Helsinki University Press.
Kuusi, Matti (1959). Kansanperinteen metamorfoosi [The metamorphosis of folklore]. In: *Suomalainen Suomi*, 395–399. Helsinki. (Virkaanastujaisesitelmä.)
– (1985). Kalevalakielestä [On Kalevala language]. In: *Perisuomalaista ja kansainvälistä* [Original Finnish and International Finnish]. 184–197. Helsinki: Finnish Literature Society. – (1994a). *Mind and Form in Folklore*. Helsinki: Finnish Literature Society.
– (1994b). Questions of Kalevala metre. In: *Songs beyond the Kalevala: Transformations of Oral Poetry*. Anna-Leena Siikala and Sinikka Vakimo (eds.). (= Studia Fennica Folkloristica 2.) 41–55. Helsinki: Finnish Literature Society.
Lakoff, George (1987). *Women, Fire and Dangerous Things: What Categories Reveal about the Mind*. Chicago: University of Chicago Press.
– (1990). The invariance hypothesis: Is abstract reason based on image-schemas? *Cognitive Linguistics* 1(1): 39–74.
Lakoff, George and Johnson, Mark (1980). *Metaphors We Live By*. Chicago: University of Chicago Press.
Levinson, Stephen C. ([1983] 1989). *Pragmatics*. Cambridge: Cambridge University Press.
Lotman, Yuri (1973). *Die Struktur des künstlerischen Textes*. Frankfurt am Main: Suhrkamp Verlag.
– (1990). *Universe of the Mind: A Semiotic Theory of Culture*. Trans. Ann Shukman. Introduction by Umberto Eco. Bloomington and Indianapolis, In: Indiana University Press.
Miller, George and Johnson-Laird, P. N. (1976). *Language and Perception*. Cambridge, MA: Harvard University Press.
Morris, Charles (1938). *Foundations of the Theory of Signs*. Chicago: University of Chicago Press.
– (1971). *Writings on the General Theory of Signs*. The Hague: Mouton.
Nikanne, Urpo (1990). *Zones and Tiers: A Study of Thematic Structure*. Diss. (= Studia Fennica Linguistica 35.) Helsinki: Finnish Literature Society.
– (1992). Metaforien mukana [Along with metaphors]. In: *Metafora. Ikkuna kieleen, mieleen ja kulttuuriin*. Lauri Harvilahti, Jyrki Kalliokoski, Urpo Nikanne and Tiina Onikki (eds.). 60–78. Helsinki: Finnish Literature Society.
Nöth, Winfrid [1990] 1995. *Handbook of Semiotics*. Bloomington and Indianapolis: Indiana University Press.
Oittinen, Riitta (1993). *I Am Me, I Am Other. On the Dialogics of Translating for Children*. Diss. Tampere: Tampere University Press.
Peirce, Charles Sanders (1940). *The Philosophy of Peirce*. New York: Harcourt, Brace and Company.

Pentikäinen, Juha (1994). Metsä suomalaisen maailmankuvassa. [The forest in the Finn's world-view]. In: *Kalevalaseuran vuosikirja* 73. Pekka Laaksonen and Sirkka-Liisa Mettomäki (eds.). 7–23. Helsinki: Finnish Literature Society.
Proust, Marcel (1919). *À la recherche du temps perdu. Du côté de chez Swann*. Tome 1. Paris: Editions Gallimard.
Segerbank, Catharina (1993). *Dödstanken i svensk romantik* [*The Idea of Death in Swedish Romanticism*]. Diss. (= Bibliotheca Historico-Eccesiastica Lundensis 31.) Lund: Lund University Press.
Tabakowska, Elzbieta (1993). *Cognitive Linguistics and Poetics of Translation*. (= Language in Performance 9.) Tübingen: Gunter Narr Verlag.
Tarasti, Eero (1978). *Myth and Music: A Semiotic Approach to the Aesthetics of Myth in Music, Especially That of Wagner, Sibelius and Stravinsky*. Diss. (= Acta Musicologica Fennica 11.) Helsinki: Suomen musiikkitieteellinen seura.
– (1990). *Johdatusta semiotiikkaan: Esseitä taiteen ja kulttuurin merkkijärjestelmistä* [*An Introduction to Semiotics: Essays on the Sign Systems of Art and Culture*]. Helsinki: Gaudeamus.
– (1991). *Romantiikan uni ja hurmio*. [*The Dream and Ecstasy of Romanticism*]. Porvoo, Helsinki, Juva: WSOY.
Tarkka, Lotte (1994). Other worlds: Symbolism, dialogue and gender in Karelian oral poetry. In: *Songs beyond the Kalevala. Transformations of Oral Poetry*. Anna-Leena Siikala and Sinikka Vakimo (eds.) (= Studia Fennica Folkloristica 2). 250–298. Helsinki: Finnish Literature Society.
Timonen, Senni (1993). Love. In: *The Great Bear: A Thematic Anthology of Oral Poetry in the Finno-Ugrian Languages*. Lauri Honko, Senni Timonen and Michael Branch (eds.). Poems translated by Keith Bosley. 287–298. Helsinki: Finnish Literature Society.
Viikari, Auli (1987). *Ääneen kirjoitettu: Vapautuvien mittojen varhaisvaiheet suomenkielisessä lyriikassa* [*Written Aloud: The Beginnings of Free Verse in Finnish Lyric Poetry*]. Diss. Helsinki: Finnish Literature Society.
Virtanen, Leea (1994). "Suomen kansa on aina vihannut metsiään" ["Finns have always hated their forests"]. In: *Kalevalaseuran vuosikirja* 73. Pekka Laaksonen and Sirkka-Liisa Mettomäki (eds.). 134–140. Helsinki: Finnish Literature Society.
Visor och ballader ur Kanteletar [Songs and ballades from the *Kanteletar*] (1989). Swedish trans. Marita Lindquist, Ole Torvalds and Thomas Warburton. Thomas Warburton (ed.). Juva: Schildts.

Immo Pekkarinen

The poetic legacy of the eighties: In the home of human voices and touches

In the collection of his poems entitled *Zoo* (1979), Arto Melleri (b. 1953) describes the poetic and political legacy of the Seventies. The aspirations of the previous generation have exhausted their sources and lost their legitimacy, as well as the capability to inspire future generations:

Ainoa perintö aikakaudelta
mailleenmenonsa lapsille:
tanssikengät. (NSV: 140)
[The only legacy of the epoch
to the children of its decline:
dancing shoes.] (In this article, all translations of the poems are mine. – I. P.)

The Seventies in Finland were a decade that bored followers of the intellectual scene to the verge of sleep. The speaker of the poem "counts lambs" – the conformist representatives of an overly politicized cultural scene, who had made a lot of noise but left little of substance. What is more, these lambs thought they were following the "Good Shepherd", counting themselves among the saved. Instead, it seems that they were misled by the cloven-hoofed Devil himself. According to Melleri, the welfare state of Finland, with its "pastoral power" (to use a Foucauldian term) of surveillance over people, is in danger of turning into a state of serious societal malformation if not outright dystopia.

And yet the alternative – submission to the economical forces of the free market – has little better to offer. According to the poem at hand, developments in culture have led to mechanization, for example, in the production and distribution of music: "The coloured lights / are congealed blood / music is dying / inside a glass box" ["Värivalot hyytynyttä verta, / musiikki tekee kuolemaa / lasikaapin sisällä"] (NSV: 140). Live bands, which in Melleri's early youth still played at dance halls around the country, are in danger of being swept aside by the wave of "dead", programmed disco music. The "enlivening" of this music with fantastic lighting only emphasizes the absence of the human factor.

To Melleri, this perspective of a world dehumanized by the new electronic media had dawned early on. In an early poem – "The Ferris wheel", published in the collected poems in 1989 – he comments on the arrival of the age of television to the still agricultural and conservatively religious, western part of Central Finland:

> pillastunut uutisfilmi
> laukkaa lisää kuvia huoneeseen
> Vaiteliaina
> maailmanpyörän liian nopeassa liikkeessä
> istuvat taatto, iso, emo,
> renki, piika, sisko, veikko,
> ja Hankkijan maatalouskonekonsulentti! (NSV: 21)
> [The runaway newsreel
> gallops ever new images into the room.
> Silent
> in a movement too fast of the Ferris wheel
> sit grandpapa, daddy, mama,
> the hand, the maid, brother, sister,
> and Hankkija's agricultural agent!]

The archaic forms (*taatto, iso, emo*), used of close relatives, emphasize the abyss that has opened between world events and the still static way of life in the countryside. The reference to a horse that "scratches the ground with hoofs in the stable" ["hepo tallissa / maata kuopii"] is also set in contrast with the "galloping newsreel". The "agricultural agent" has hitherto been the herald of the modern age. His presence allowed for negotiations and the drawing up of contracts. But with the "Ferris wheel" of world events gone wild, one does not negotiate: it takes people up and down, arbitrarily and at will. The Ferris wheel also refers to the world of the circus, where life is more or less an irresponsible game played behind masks and representations, whereas country life traditionally consists of heavy toil in the fields and cow-barns.

In *Zoo*, Melleri returns to the image of the "galloping newsreel" of his earlier poem. Only this time it is not a starting gallop but a final, apocalyptic hoofbeat:

> Kuutamolla
> kun peilit kirkuvat
> kylmää valoa, hopeista kirousta
> uutisfilmi pillastuu, laukkaa
> ruudun pimeäksi (NSV: 143)
> [At moonlight
> when mirrors scream
> cold light, silvery curse
> the runaway newsreel gallops
> the screen blank]

One of Melleri's constant targets has been the mirror-like or photographic image of realist representation, which was favoured even by some poets in the Seventies. Radio and TV do not escape the poet's disdain for passive representations, which resemble "the gossips of old grooms traveling / ... from one washroom to the other" ["Valokuva ja langaton lennätin / ovat valehdelleet ennemmän / kuin ... pesutuvasta toiseen / akkojen hameissa höyryävät juorut"] (NSV: 94). The "screaming mirrors" show forth and endlessly multiply these representations, and as such are a menace, a "silvery curse".

According to Melleri, these representations, with us since the birth of the realist novel (he refers in the poem to Dickens) and photography, are rooted in the dreams of the classical age and the Enlightenment – the representational age *par excellence*, if we are to believe Foucault. Film and television are embodiments and extensions of these dreams. In the modern world the romantic ideal of living presence is displaced by a fascination with developing ever newer and better means to mediate and multiply representations. The connecting of people into the "field of electric experience" ["Me ollaan keskellä / sähköisen kokemisen kenttää"] (NSV: 16) rips them violently from their traditional life-worlds. Although the real and concrete surroundings lay in ruins, "the light reflected by Hollywood / turned the tinsel trinkets of her earrings / into platinum" ["Hollywoodin taittama valo / teki platinaa hänen korviensa / peltihelyistä"] (NSV: 143).

From this perspective, the increase of mass media and other electronic equipment does not bring an aestheticizing of the world, as has been suggested. Quite the contrary: the "aura" of an aesthetic presence becomes totally lost, and we live in the world of simulacra. The means of producing and mediating these simulacra are the technological and microelectronic achievements of our age (transistors, TV sets, etc.), but they totally lack aesthetic value in themselves. This is revealed to Melleri, when some disturbance in transmission occurs, as when the TV screen goes blank for a moment. Or when, as a consequence of some larger – even apocalyptic – catastrophe, "an urn full of / transistors burned black" ["Uurnantäysi / mustuneita transistoreja"] (NSV: 144) remains to indicate the nature of our civilization. This urn is certainly far removed from the classic Grecian vessel to which Keats devoted his ode.

Anne Hänninen: The snow-woman

To Melleri, the distaste for representations never takes the form of distaste for poetry itself as a form of representation. The poet's absolutely singular, "tortured handwriting" ["Linnunrata hohtaa kiusatun käsialan lävitse"] (NSV: 330) places him outside the world of technology and makes it possible for him to decipher the universe not only as an object of scientific research, but in all the miraculousness of its existence. In Anne Hänninen's (b. 1958) poetry the status of representation is, however, more radically questioned.

The opening poem of Hänninen's first collection, *Yön tina sulaa aamuun* (1978) (*The Tin of the Night Melts into the Morning*), can be taken as an introduction to her problematics:

> Katalasti kaasi talvi jään silmiini,
> tyhjensi suuhuni lumisaavin.
> Olen luminainen kuolleessa lehdossa,
> luminainen tiheänmustan taivaan alla.
> Kasvaa nielustani
> jääenkeli harteilla maailman vilu. (YT: 7)
> [Wickedly the winter threw ice into my eyes,
> emptied a tub full of snow into my mouth.
> I am a snow-woman in a dead grove,
> snow-woman beneath the thick blackness of the sky
> From my mouth there grows an angel of ice,
> the coldness of the world on its shoulders.]

In the Seventies, some poets still took part in the political process, by either intra- or extrapoetic means. They were thus working within the *polis*, in the sphere of rational decision making. But poetry, seen as bearing the coldness of the deceitful world, finds itself in the position of scapegoat, expelled outside the city limits. Laying bare the irrationality and contingency – the tragic conditions – of human life, poetry has no place in the modern world, which believes optimistically in the endless advance of knowledge and the ability to govern phenomena.

For the speaker of Hänninen's poem, however, the role of scapegoat afforded to poetry dawns only retrospectively and is, in the end, of a secondary nature: if the speaker had not encountered the deceitfulness of the world, if her eyes had not been filled with ice and her mouth with snow, she would not have given birth to poetry. She would have participated in the life of the community as an "ordinary" woman, and perhaps also giving birth to real children, instead of the "dead children" – "angels of ice" – of poetry.

The underlying polarity of Hänninen's poetry is formed from the opposition between Life – understood as the possibility of full presence – and the results of artistic production, which are seen as dead representations. These representations are often described in terms of the imagery of winter: "angel of ice", "opaque ice", etc. The incompatibility of Life and art makes, in the end, the speaker of her poem cast herself into purgatory, where all oppositons melt into a "sea of fire"(this brings to mind also the burning of scapegoats outside the city limits, so as to purge the city of whatever menaced it; see Derrida 1981: 133). But this attempt to purge oneself leads inevitably to a total aesthetization and poetification of the world:

oppositions are annihilated through figurative use of language, which spreads like fire along the structures of the poems. And figurative language does not escape the order of representation, except in a world-view in which the distinction between the literal and the nonliteral, or *mythos* and *logos*, has not yet been decided. In the end, Hänninen never comes to question the primacy of a *logos* – for example, in the form of a subject present to itself – that would make this distinction.

There remains, after all, in Hänninen the faint hope of making contact with the presence of Life in and through her poetry, despite a constant threat of deadly "crystallization" into representations (this threat was present already in the name of her collection: the solid "tin of the night"). The "angel of ice" – not actually living or dead – of her opening poem is still connected to the breath of the "snow-woman", and thus resembles living speech. Later the "opaque ice" of one of her poems, born in the purgatorial fires, is said to be "dazzling, colourful, melted, / free, exploding, boundless" ["Jäinen himmeys on häikäisevä värikäs sula / vapaa räjähtelevä rajaton"] (TT 1982: 29).

In the collection *Ikuisuudenavara* (1986) [*The Spaciousness of Eternity*], Hänninen gives a more detailed account of the aspirations and achievements of her poetry:

> Minä jätin jonkun jäljen kai:
> villin uneksivan polun
> talven rajalle
> lehtiä leijaavia punaisia
> tulenoranssin syksyn: toukokuu sielultaan!
> Jätin kai huudon
> korkean ja loputtoman!? (IA: 63)

> [I hope I left some traces:
> a wild and dreamy path
> on the border of the winter
> leaves falling red
> of an autumn, burning orange: I, with a soul like May!
> I hope I left a scream
> high and endless!?]

Although she had "a soul like May", full of springtime and life, she was able to produce only "dead leaves" of poetry as witnesses to a once-burning existence. These sad leaves, as well as the traces on death's border, remind us primarily of the absence of the speaker, who can no longer participate in the sweetness of Life. Yet in contrast to these signs of absence, the speaker hopes also to have left behind "a scream / high and endless".

This scream, as a symbol of Hänninen's poetry, sets the *telos* and the standards for its inner hierarchy. Any poetry that cannot detach itself from the order of representation, that uses "dead" and ready-made material and refers outside itself

– to the point of vanishing in front of the object referred to – ranks low in the hierarchy. Conversely, a poem ranks higher the more it resembles "a scream", referring to nothing but the presence of the subject to herself, assuring her of her pure and immediate Life.

The poem in question, however, does not itself rank highly in the hierarchy that it sets up. We may consider it among Hänninen's best poems, to judge by its economy and capacity for revelation. But when it refers to Hänninen's poetry, represents it, and thus gives an illusion of including in itself the essential truth of her work, it locks itself outside of the announced ideal of avoiding representation and reference. To speak of a scream is never to utter a scream (see Gasché 1986: 217–218).

Hänninen's poetry thus forms a series of supplements, which resembles the supplementary structures in Rousseau's writings, as analyzed by Jacques Derrida. First, poetry comes to replace life, in which the poet has become unable to participate directly. Second, a "metapoem" comes to supplement poetry: it replaces Hänninen's poetry, when it announces the speaker to have attained the ideal of full presence in and through her verse. At the same time, it is an addition on the outer fringe of her poetry, which informs us of a possible failure in this aspiration and replaces it with a wish: "I hope I left a scream" (see Derrida 1974: 144–145). It presents an idealized picture of her poetry, forms to us its truth, but in itself is absolutely excluded from the ideal picture it draws.

This, in turn, reminds us that we should perhaps read her poetry also according to criteria other than those explicitly announced in this idealization. Hänninen's poetic procedures, which lead toward the postulation of a transcendental "spaciousness of eternity" (where the infiniteness of time and space merge), resemble Husserl's phenomenological reduction, in which consciousness is present to itself only in the element of voice (Derrida 1973: 75–79). Hänninen's phonocentrism, however, more likely results from an affinity with the Expressionist tradition rather than from studies in phenomenology.

Tiina Kaila: a journey beyond visions

Anne Hänninen's poetry started by denouncing the possibility of living according to a rational order, which ignores the fundamentally tragic conditions of human existence. She advanced toward grasping a transcendental "spaciousness of eternity". In this respect, her poetry is subject-centered, even if it also investigates the possibility of freeing oneself from the bounds of the deceitful world and thus to offer itself as an example of doing so.

In Tiina Kaila's (b. 1951) poetry the primacy of the subject is contested, and the possibility of a great Order, as the goal for humanity, is tried and denounced. But this repudiation of a rational order takes place on grounds quite different from those of Hänninen or Melleri. For Kaila is, from the beginning, a Heideggerian existentialist.

Kaila's first collection, *Keskustelu hämärässä* (*A Discussion in Twilight*), starts with an introduction in which the speaker finds herself in the middle of everyday events, the ultimate purposes of which are unclear to her (p. 7). She resorts to seeking an answer from a man called "Kafka", who lives alone in the countryside. One interpretation of the real Kafka has been that he sometimes gives us a glimpse of humanity's existential "erring". Man is found to be in the middle of a "Prozess", the meaning and goals of which it is impossible for him to decipher.

The speaker of Kaila's poem, too, is amidst the "processes of the world" ["maailman prosessit ovat päämäärättömät, vailla mieltä"] (KH: 10). She does not oppose these processes in themselves. Rather, she protests against the seemingly meaningless pain that they are bound to cause:

> Pyörät syytävät
> sivutuotteenaan tuskaa
> maailman ylle,
> pilviharson alle. (KH: 21)
>
> [The wheels exert
> pain, as a by-product,
> over the world,
> beneath the veil of clouds.]

In her opinion, it would be possible for mankind to establish an Order, from which the causes of pain are finally removed forever.

For her companion, Kafka, this presumption is a naïve fantasy possible only in the realm of fiction ["Kafka ryhtyy syyttämään minua / runollisuudesta"] (KH: 22). The pain inflicted by the world's processes is not a by-product, but a fundamental part of them: only pain detaches man from "insisting" on the sphere of the already-known and thus makes him aware of his "existence" (see Heidegger 1968: 344). These processes are ultimately "for the sake of being" ["prosessit ovat olemisen tähden"] (KH: 18). Thus, they are necessary and unavoidable.

In the course of the discussion the speaker finds that the limits of her subjectivity begin to dissolve. She realizes that "my body" – as a symbol of a delimited subject – has been "torn apart / from top to toe", and "[w]arm blood runs along my arms / my elbows have stuck to the table" ["ruumiini on revennyt / ylhäältä alas asti. / Lämmin veri valuu käsivarsia myöten / ja kyynärpäät ovat tarttuneet pöytään"] (KH: 32). From the beginning "Kafka" has been of the opinion that the subject's "limits are fully hypothetical / maybe even illusory" ["rajat ovat täysin oletetut / ehkä jopa kuvitellut"] (KH: 15). For him, consciousness is in the world like "a water molecule in water": if these molecules were removed, one after the other, the water – and thus the world – would obviously vanish. "Consciousness", then, cannot be separated from the "world", as traditional metaphysical philosophy has always presupposed. Heidegger (and "Kafka") replace both consciousness and world with the unity and fact of *Dasein*.

The poem ends, rather pessimistically, with a silence, in which "nothing moves, not even water" ["Täällä ei liiku mikään, / ei vesi, / ei pilvet"] (KH: 33). Something new may be revealed and something be forgotten, as witnessed by the morning paper. But ultimately nothing new enters the sphere of existence. The speaker resides within, and is at one with, the closed totality of beings and their inevitable and mysterious being.

In her subsequent poetry, Kaila repeatedly and insistently develops the thematics called forth by these existentialist presuppositions. She surveys the possibility of poetry in an age and philosophical scene that in principle allows for no poetic fantasies whatsoever. Everything is revealed only in the light of its irreversible existence:

Ei ole missään hämyjä
...
ei varjoja, ei koloja jonne
sijoittaisi siipensä,
asettelisi henkiä asumaan,
rakentaisi ulospääsyteiksi
oviaukon näköisiä kuvia. (TT: 49)

[Nowhere are there shades
...
or shadows, or holes, where
one could place one's wings,
imagine spirits living,
build, as exits,
images, that look like doors.]

The "existentialist awe" investigated in her 1983 collection, *Kala on meren kuva (The Fish is the Image of the Sea)*, shows no way out of this impasse. In the poem "Meren poikki kulkee veneen varjo" ("Across the sea travels the shadow of a boat"], such awe does reveal a doorway leading outside the universe of actualities revealed by the sciences, "the fragile tender rampant sediments of brains" ["ja huuhtoutuu pois tämä maailma: / aivojen hatara lempeä rehottava sakka"] (KMK: 42). The speaker of the poem seeks a "primal scene, beyond visions". According to Heidegger, "it is just where few actualities are known or where they are known hardly at all by science or only very roughly, that the manifest character of what-is-in-totality can operate far more essentially than where ... the technical control of things seems limitless in its scope" (1968: 339). So, the speaker heads in her "shadow-boat" toward the limits of existence, where the "rampant sediments of brains" do not prevent her from seeing clearly.

But the possibility of "nothing", which turns out to haunt everything that exists, finally reveals all the more clearly the "kingdom ruled by Materia", which in its ambitiousness and grandiosity even forms life and endows man with consciousness. This consciousness tries to deny the supreme status of matter, by resorting to religion or idealistic philosophy, by dividing the world into "subject" and "object", or by immersing itself in all kinds of egocentrism. In her collection of 1986, *Valon nälkä* (*Hunger for Light*), Kaila writes ironically of this desire to escape:

> Me emme ole ainetta,
> josta meidät on tehty,
> vaan aina jotain muuta,
> niinkuin henkeä tai eetteriä
> huuman virtoja, älyn kipinöitä,
> muttei ainetta koskaan
>
> ...
>
> Meidän ilmestyksellisyytemme
> pikästyttää meitä
> kun se on alati läsnä (VN: 44)
>
> [We are not matter,
> which we are made of,
> but always something else,
> like spirit or ether,
> streams of rapture, sparkles of wit,
> but matter, never
>
> ...
>
> The miracle of our existence
> bores us,
> when it is always present]

In these existentialist revelations, no task remains for the poet but to supplement and artificially to set things in contrast, so as to make it easier to outline "the happening of the world"; or, to build imaginary worlds, which, however, are admittedly secondary and childish; or, to utter statements of frustration, in an age deserted by gods and alien to poetry; or, finally, in an incantation triggered by inspiration, to praise the existence of existents, thereby expressing gratitude for the "gift of Being". For example, upon returning from her journey to the "House of awe" ("Kauhun talo"; p. 44), she praises the familiar and restricted ground from which she started: "There is / my house! / Yellow! / Turned to gold in the dawn! / From the floor to the ceiling / it dazzled" ["Siinä on / minun taloni! / Keltainen! / Aurigonnousussa tullut kullaksi! / Lattiasta kattoon / se häikäisi"] (KMK: 51).

It is only in her latest collection of poems, *Valon nälkä*, that the essential difference between beings and their being – as well as that between being and the possibility of non-being – is in practice, if not thematically, displaced by the difference between signs in themselves, and signs referring to other signs. Only this play of reference between signs can liberate language from a merely revelatory task, where the sign must always submit to referring to a signified (see Heidegger 1968: 329). And it is only within such play that poetry can once again emerge without implying a sense of "bad faith".

Kaila does not refer directly to Heidegger or other existentialists; however, when she writes, in the opening poem to *Valon nälkä*, of matter, which "passed the threshold to existence, / creating itself" ["Aine ylitti olemattomuuden kynnyksen, / niin se loi itsensä"] (VN: 7), she leaves us no doubt of her preoccupation with existentialist thematics.

Satu Salminiitty: the wounds of the sun

Kaila's poetry led to an impasse, where the subject's assimilation with the actualities of the world formed a state of stand-still, a feeling of being imprisoned within a finite universe of existents:

> mutta toisinpaikoin on jo niin paljon valoa,
> että on mahdotonta pyristellä eteenpäin,
> huitoa käsillä,
> käännellä kasvoja piiloon,
> vältellä auringon piiskaniskuja. (TT: 26)

> [but at places there is already so much light,
> that it is impossible to strive forwards,
> to fling one's arms about,
> to hide one's face,
> to avoid the lashes of the whip of the sun.]

In this world, which has "the form of a head", everything – even the fact of being – is thematized, subjected to the "laws of the head" ["Näin pään muotoisessa maailmassa / on pään lait ja pään mukainen logiikka"] (TT: 38).

Satu Salminiitty's (b. 1958) poetry forms an exception to both the preference for total thematization, as well as its reverse, a total repudiation of thematization in aesthetic rapture. Her poetry places ethical relationships at its center. The distaste for a subject-centered conception of the world shows up clearly in a poem from the 1986 collection, *Elämän huoneet* (*The Rooms of Life*), which can be thought of as a key to her aspirations:

> kun ei voi olla eilistä vanhempi
> eikä nuorempi
> huomista

on nostettava itsen miekka
ja lyötävä keskipäivään
    sellainen vako
että se universaalisen kivun tähden aukenee oveksi

keskipäivään se on lyötävä
haava minän aurinkoon. (EH: 63)

[since one cannot be older than yesterday
or younger
than tomorrow
one has to raise the sword of the self
and strike into the midday
    a furrow, such
as, for the sake of a universal pain, turns into a door

Into the midday it has to be struck,
a wound into the sun of the I.]

The speaker of the poem is a finite being, who is not the master of herself. She must respond to the exigencies of the situation: she "has to raise the sword" and "strike" a wound. She thus is in a state of obedience: she "has to". According to Jean-François Lyotard, writing on Levinas, "the simplest prescription, instructively empty but pragmatically affirmative, at one stroke situates the one to whom it is addressed outside the universe of knowledge" (Lyotard 1989: 308).

The "sword", within the sphere of the self, belongs to an inherited order, and thus forms an impure element, which the "sun of the I" – seeing and thematizing everything – does not totally control. It can thus be likened to language, "the sword of the word", which, in addition to revealing actualities, can also function performatively, establishing and founding things. The poem, as a furrow or a door opened up by the power of words, serves as a means to make contacts and alliances, rather than glorifying the writer's grand and unique ego.

The word "ethics" refers originally to a "traditional way of acting, talking, and behaving", as Rodolphe Gasché reminds us (1994: 174). In a motto to one of her own poems (PA: 62), Salminiitty quotes William Butler Yeats's "A prayer for my daughter": "How but in custom and ceremony / Are innocence and beauty born?" (Yeats 1954: 181). This emphasis on ethics and tradition should not, however, be interpreted as serving the cause of conservatism – especially an aesthetic conservatism – as some critics have done. Salminiitty has been seen as epigonic of the politically conservative Finnish modernism of the Fifties (Koivisto: 232). The ethical relationship, however, never was one of the main concerns of these modernists, who tended, rather, toward a hermetic aestheticism. And Salminiitty also explicitly refuses "to weigh the beautiful with the scales of the familiar", thus making it impossible to see her emphasis on tradition as epigonism ("mitä omaansa voi nimetä ... kauneus sittenkin punnitaan tuttuuden vaa'alla."; EH: 14).

For Salminiitty, the "tradition of hope" detaches man again and again from his dwelling place, propels him towards the unknown, and "replaces with new life / the minds, sprinkled into the tunes of the night" ["(toivo) korvaa uudella elämällä / yön säveleen pirskotut mielet"] (EH: 14). Man is lulled by these familiar melodies into the rhythm of myths, which to Levinas form the sphere of artistic expression. But, for Levinas, a modern artist could also detach himself from the grip of even his own myths, by interpreting them in his art. (Levinas 1986b: 133, 143)

According to Salminiitty, one modern myth is the belief in humankind's ability, as a species, to transcend her finite being:

Unessa hän on
...
yhtä haavoittumaton
kuin itse haavan nimi (ROV: 52–53)

[In her dream she is
...
as unwounded
as the name of the wound itself]

Man would thus have an essence that rises above the all-corrupting powers of nature, to which all the archaeological evidence refers as "the testament of dust, / the flours of bones, the ashes of forests". But humanity is capable of this transcendence only "in her dream", in the illusion of an all- and self-thematizing subject. From this dream, human consciousness has not yet been awakened by the catastrophic work of the Infinite and by the face of the Other. When awakened, man must see himself in his relationship to nature as an open wound, rather than as being capable of transcending the circumstances at hand.

Salminiitty herself has no illusions of being able to thematize her life and fulfill her intentions. On the contrary, the real blessings of life befall only those whose dreams – and with this, whose intentions – life has broken. When fulfilled, these dreams would keep the subject forever in the sphere of the known, within the solipsistic ego, under the royal rule of the unwounded "sun of the I":

Särkyneen sydämen ihme
kannattaa jalkojasi,
...
Viimein unelmasi lunastaa sinut. (PK: 80)

[The miracle of the broken heart
carries your feet
...
Finally your dream redeems you.]

Only broken dreams can redeem man, save humanity from itself. And when "the King hides his face / every day", we are left with the endless task of encountering the faces of the others, "within the home / of human voices and touches / caressed by breath" ["joka päivällä on oma kuvansa / hetkien kahlehtima onni ... sen on pysyttävä ihmisäänien / ja kosketuksen kodissa / hengityksen hyväilemänä / kuningas kätkee kasvonsa, / joka päivä"] (EH: 71–72). Salminiitty's enigmatic King is thus certainly not Materia, admiring himself in the mirror of consciousness, as was the case in Kaila's poem. It is rather the ethical imperative of endless obligation in front of the of face of the Other, which, as a desolate "quarry of the I", is subjected to the all-corrupting processes of time.

Salminiitty seems to have no contact, direct or indirect, to Levinas's philosophy, although her unorthodox religiousness resembles that of Levinas. The emphasis on the ethical relationship, in her case, seems to derive partly from the erosion of collective value systems. She does not, however, want to resort to the sterility of a "private heaven, / which would crown / 'the enlightened' " (PA: 59), as the existentialists were prone to do. Nor does she believe in the revelatory task of poetry, which would place the poet in a special position, and afford the poem the status of "the home of Being", revealing in its fragility the possibility of non-being. Her poetry forms rather "The rooms of life", which smell of "boredom, salt, night, / hunger, work, / belching enjoyment", and where "happiness is a quest, / who invites herself" ["onni on itsensä / kutsuma vieras / miltä elämän huoneet tuoksuvat? / kyllästymiseltä suolalta yöltä / nälältä työltä / röyhtäilevältä nautinnolta"] (EH: 37).

Against totalisation

In Hänninen's poetry the play between signs and sign systems takes the form of a supplementary comments upon her own poetry. Kaila ends up the same way, commenting on her own text as well as those of others. In these processes, to use Derrida's words, "one truth about another, one truth on (top of) another, one above or below the other, each step more or less true than truth", form the infinite "stairway or escalade of truth" (quoted in Gasché 1994: 129).

But, instead of as this infinite and desperate accumulation of truths, "the fragile handwriting of man" can also be seen as Salminiitty views it: "a suffering light, against the naked afternoon" ["Sillä sinä olet nähnyt / kärsivän valon, alastonta iltapäivää vasten / ihmisen hauraan käsialan"] (ROV: 69). Only writing's "wounds" – or its "face", as the face of the Other – can carry it beyond the tautological, the order of truth, which is governed by intentions and calculations. In the words of Paul Célan, "the poem speaks! It is mindful of its dates, but it speaks" (quoted in Derrida 1992: 381). And, according to Derrida, it speaks, first of all, "in its own name, without ever compromising with the absolute singularity

... of the other, and to the other" (Derrida 1992: 381–382). It is only because it is impossible to reduce writing to an ideal essence or to the intentions of the writer, that "man's handwriting", with all its faults and wounds, becomes unique and singular. And by definition, only a unique and singular being can be saved or redeemed, given a "new life".

The Finnish poets introduced here, of the generation of the Eighties, thus seek a world beyond systems, be they socialist or capitalist in nature, where economical imperatives and technological innovations do not sweep aside all aesthetic and ethical values, a world that still has room for concepts like "sacrifice", "holiness", "grace" and "redemption".

References

Derrida, Jacques (1973). *Speech and Phenomena: And Other Essays on Husserl's Theory of Signs*. Trans. David B. Allison. Evanston, IL: Northwestern University Press.
– (1974). *Of Grammatology*. Trans. Gayatri Chakravorty Spivak. Baltimore and London: Johns Hopkins University Press.
– (1981). Plato's pharmacy. In: *Dissemination*. Trans. Barbara Johnson. London: Athlone.
– (1992). From shibboleth: For Paul Célan. In: *Acts of Literature*. Trans. Joshua Wilner. New York and London: Routledge.
Gasché, Rodolphe (1986). *The Tain of the Mirror: Derrida and the Philosophy of Reflection*. London: Harvard University Press.
– (1994). *Inventions of Difference: On Jacques Derrida*. Cambridge, MA: Harvard University Press.
Heidegger, Martin (1968). On the essence of truth. Trans. R.F.G. Hull and Alan Crick. In: *Existence and Being*. 3rd ed. London: Vision.
Hänninen, Anne (1978). *Yön tina sulaa aamuun* (= YT) [*The Tin of the Night Melts into the Morning*]. Porvoo: WSOY.
– (1982). *Tulitemppeli* (= TT) [*The Temple of Fire*]. Porvoo: WSOY.
– (1986). *Ikuisuudenavara* (= IA) [*The Spaciousness of Eternity*]. Porvoo: WSOY.
Kaila, Tiina (1975). *Keskustelu hämärässä* (= KH) [*A Discussion in Twilight*]. Keuruu: Otava.
– (1983). *Kala on meren kuva* (= KMK) [*The Fish Is the Image of the Sea*]. Keuruu: Otava.
– (1986). *Valon nälkä* (= VN) [*Hunger for Light*]. Porvoo: WSOY.
Koivisto, Risto (1988). Avaruus [Space]. *Parnasso* 4: 232–239.
Levinas, Emmanuel (1996a). God and philosophy. Trans. Richard Cohen and Alphonso Lingis. In: *The Levinas Reader*. Sean Hand (ed.). Cambridge: Cambridge University Press, pp.167–189.
– (1996b). Reality and its shadow. Trans. Alphonso Lingis. In: *The Levinas Reader*. Sean Hand (ed.). Cambridge: Cambridge University Press, pp. 130–143.
Lyotard, Jean-François (1989). Levinas' logic. Trans. Ian McLeod. In: *The Lyotard Reader*. Andrew Benjamin (ed.) Oxford: Basil Blackwell, pp. 275–313.
Melleri, Arto (1979). *Zoo*. Keuruu: Otava.

– (1989). *Nuoruus, siivekästä ja veristä: Runot 1972–1989* (= NSV) [Youth, with Wings and Blood]. Keuruu: Otava.
Salminiitty, Satu (1983). *Paratiisiaavistus* (= PA) [A Premonition of Paradise]. Porvoo: WSOY.
– (1986). *Elämän huoneet* (= EH) [*The Rooms of Life*]. WSOY: Porvoo: WSOY.
– (1989). *Raottuvien ovien valo* (= ROV) [The Light of Opening Doors]. Porvoo: WSOY.
– (1991). *Palava Kirja* (= PK) [A Burning Book]. Porvoo: WSOY.
Yeats, W. B. (1954). *Selected Poems*. London: MacMillan.

Erja Hannula

Signs between

Introduction

A more conventional title for this article would be: A Multidisciplinary Approach to Punctuation. My category of "multidisciplinary" is quite broad and includes not only linguistics, translation theory, and applied semiotics, but also graphic design, and above all, typography. In the present essay I draw on all these to explore the form and meaning of punctuation in printed texts.

Rules of traditional grammar are not at issue here because much literature on the subject already exists, and also because to a writer or to a translator, even a solid knowledge of *where* to put the punctuation marks is not always enough. She or he also has to know *what* the punctuation marks are, *how* they must be placed, and *what impact* punctuation has on the text.

I start with the general idea of punctuation then proceed to a definition of text punctuation proposed by the French linguist Nina Catach. Secondly, I ask to what extent punctuation marks are universal and if they have to be translated at all. Thirdly, I consider the relation between punctuation, readability, and communication. Finally, I discuss the future of punctuation in this age of rapidly advancing technology, and also ask who has the responsibility for punctuation.

The semiotic term *sign* is used here in the Saussurian sense, such that it is formed by a *signifier* (*signifiant*) and a *signified* (*signifié*). In other cases the content of the word *sign* is shown by its context.

Typography is the combination of techniques and devices that enables the reproduction of texts in print, electronic media, and so on. It is also the way, style and form (font choice, text layout, etc.) by which reproduction is accomplished. A *typographer* is a practitioner of typography. Before the typographer there was the typesetter in a printing house, and typography nearly a synonym for printing.

A general idea of punctuation and punctuation marks

The conventional understanding of punctuation is a narrow one – punctuation is said to represent certain signs used in speech. For instance, Osmo Ikola, in his *Handbook of Contemporary Finnish* (1992: 185–186), writes on punctuation and its function that punctuation marks are "helping sings", the meaning of which is to clarify the text. Punctuation marks help make up for the lack in written language of gestures, expressions, emphasis, tone of voice, and other clarifiers of the spoken word.[1]

When Ikola says explicitly that punctuation marks correspond to certain speech-act phenomena, he is actually following Aristotle's idea about writing as the symbol of speech. But you can also have a different view of the relationship between spoken and written language. For instance, the well-known Finnish actor and director Asko Sarkola once said, during a discussion at the University of Art and Design in Helsinki, that the full stops in a script are actually disturbing, because they lead the actors to suppose that one must leave off speaking whenever one appears.

Just as there is a general idea of punctuation, there is also one of punctuation marks. But which signs does one actually consider as punctuation marks? This is a simple question, but hard to answer. Claude Tournier (1980: 34) has collected a revealing table showing the differences in the definitions of punctuation marks amongst French linguists and grammarians during the 50 years from 1930 to 1980. I have added some contemporary as well as some Finnish and English views. There seems to be mutual agreement on the existence of six punctuation marks only (see Table 1).

Punctuation defined by Nina Catach

In her general definition of punctuation Nina Catach (1996: 7) also says that such marks are "helping signs", as Ikola stated, but her description of their function is much broader. For her, punctuation is

> a system that strengthens the writing, formed of syntactic signs whose function is to organise the relations and the proportions of the parts of speech and the pauses in speech and in writing. Thus these signs take part in all syntactic functions, grammatical, intonational and semantic.

In addition to her general definition, Catach gives two more precise definitions. First, punctuation proper (*la ponctuation proprement dite*) (1996: 9; author's italics):

> The ensemble of organisational and presentational visual signs which accompany the written text, *interior* to the text and *common* to the manuscript and the printed matter; the punctuation contains several classes of discrete graphic signs forming a system, completing or supplying alphabetic information.

In this definition punctuation marks no longer serve only as "helping signs" but constitute an independent visual unity that completes the written text. At this point Catach reminds us that the use of word spaces, capital letters, and division into paragraphs are also part of punctuation.

	.	,	;	:	!	?	( )	« »	[ ]	...	—	-	al	*
GALICHET	+	+	+	+	+	+	+	+						
Petit ROBERT FISCHER et HACQUARD *Code typographique*	+	+	+	+	+	+	+	+	+	+	+			
SENSINE, LE GAL ORTHO-VERT, BLED HARTMANN et DUTREUILH	+	+	+	+	+	+	+	+		+	+			
DAMOURETTE, AMEN	+	+	+	+	+	+	+	+	+	+	+	+		
GALIZOT	+	+	+	+	+	+	+	+		+	+		+	
JAVET et MATTHEY	+	+	+	+	+	+								
LEDUC	+	+	+	+	+	+	+	+	+	+	+		+	
THIMONNIER DIDIER et BANVARD	+	+	+	+	+	+	+	+		+				
LECERF	+	+	+	+	+	+		+		+	+			
GREVISSE	+	+	+	+	+	+	+	+	+	+	+		+	+

	.	,	;	:	!	?	( )	« »	[ ]	...	—	-	al	*	'
Nouveau petit ROBERT 1994	+	+	+	+	+	+	+	+	+	+	+				
CATACH 1996	++	+	+	+	+	+	+	+	+	+	+	+			+
RAEKALLIO-TEPPO 1974	+	+	+	+	+	+	+	+	+	+	+	+			+
IKOLA 1980	+	+	+	+	+	+	+	+		+	+				+
Finnish standard 1993	+	+	+	+							+				
WEBSTER'S II 1988	+	+	+	+	+	+	+	+	+	+	+				+

al = alinéa = new paragraph

Table 1.

Her other definition seems to be a logical continuum to her development. Her concept of text punctuation (*la ponctuation du texte*) goes far beyond the general idea of punctuation, since Catch also includes page design as part of punctuation (1996: 8–9; author's italics):

> The ensemble of organisational and presentational visual techniques of a book [or any printed matter] which go from *white spaces within words* to *white spaces on pages*, using all processes *interior* and *exterior to the text*, making possible its arrangement and its appreciation.

Compared to previous definitions the essential difference here is that elements exterior to the text are also accepted as part of punctuation. Thus the manner or style of presentation becomes a part of the signification of written language. This is how I want to see punctuation considered.

The decision to adopt a certain definition of punctuation – narrow or broad – also determines what layers of the text are perceived. Only when the definition of punctuation is understood broadly, as Catch does, can all the significations of a particular text be understood.

But is Catch's definition of text punctuation unique? Do other scholars hold the same opinion as hers? There is at least one whose view approaches that of Catch, and he is Geoffrey Nunberg. He does not, however, consider layout as part of punctuation (Nunberg 1990: 17; my italics):

> The term "punctuation" is generally used to refer to a category defined in partially graphic terms: a set of non-alphanumeric characters that are used to provide information about structural relations among elements of a text, including commas, semicolons, colons, periods, parentheses, quotation marks and so forth. From the point of view of function, however, punctuation must be considered *together with* a variety of other graphical features of the text, including font- and face-alternations, capitalisation, indentation and spacing, all of which can be used to the same sorts of purposes.

Nunberg still states that punctuation marks proper should be separated from the (other) graphical features that affect text reception, but that they should all be viewed as a totality.

White spaces

What interests me especially is the unprinted surface of the paper, *the white spots and white places*, which at first seem to have no meaning, because they are empty, because in them there is no *signifier* or expression, in the case of printed text no image, nor do they have a *signified*, or content.

As long as metal typesetting was the primary technique in printing, the *things* that created the white spaces – which I call *invisible signs* – were concrete. They were differently sized metal pieces, lower than those of the printing letters which left an imprint – a *visible sign* – on the paper. In printers' jargon the metal pieces that produce the *invisible signs* are called *blank material*, in Finnish *sokeisto*, something that you don't see. It seems to me that typesetters considered them, because of their concrete nature, at least as typographic signs or maybe even as punctuation marks.

When arranging the text on the book page the typographer used the blank as a device of expression and style, by adding or subtracting empty spaces. These invisible signs as *signifiers* produce different *signifieds* in relation to the *visible signs* (prints on the page) and thus different semiotic signs and significations.

Today there is an invisible punctuation "hidden" in computer programs. One could refer to these marks as "helping signs" or "guiding signs" for the writer or typographer. Using the command *Display all hidden characters*, we see on the screen a contemporary visual presentation of the metal typesetting blank material which is internal to the text. There are different word spaces, paragraph divisions and indentations; they are all signs that do not belong to the punctuation marks proper, and they are not traditionally considered as part of punctuation.

Are punctuation marks universal?

It can be said that the general contours of languages are universal, and the same goes for punctuation marks as syntactical language units. But even though the basic meaning of punctuation marks is the same, their *signifier*, or the *perceptible side of the sign* (compare with Joly 1994: 14), is not always uniform.

A question mark? Kysymysmerkkikö?

¿Signo de interrogación? Un point d'interrogation_?

The *signifier* of the question mark is the same in English and Finnish. Spanish uses the same graphic sign but doubles it, with the first one inverted before the question; thus the *signifier* is formed by two separated graphic signs. At first sight, the French *signifier* does not seem different from the English one, but there is a word space (a no-break space) between the last word and the question mark. Thus the French *signifier* is comprised of a white space and a graphic sign – as are French quotation marks (this is also the case with the exclamation point, colon, and semicolon). Compare the following:

"quotation marks" "comillas" "lainausmerkit" «_guillemets_»

Despite the different *signifiers* of these quotation marks, their *signified* is the same. (Though we cannot go into it here, the quotation marks do have different *signifieds* depending on the context.)

Do punctuation marks have to be translated?

The attitude of translators towards punctuation marks is often less constrained than their approach to other elements of text, maybe because such marks seem so obvious – which they are not, as we have already seen. The question *to translate* or *not to translate* them comes up in unexpected situations.

As we have also seen, many languages feature small but important variations in the realization of punctuation marks. More attention should be paid to the graphic forms of punctuation, that is, to the *signifier* side of the sign. For instance, for a Frenchman reading a text translated into his native language, the reception of the message is disturbed if it contains punctuation marks that are not composed according to French typographic norms. The reader himself seldom understands why his reading seems awkward, he only *experiences* the strangeness. Let us look at two examples relevant to the use of blank space.

First, in general texts: What attitude should one take towards phone numbers? Do they have to be translated? If a French phone number is to appear in a Finnish text, which convention does the translator follow? Do we have to use the Finnish norm to replace the French arrangement, or should we simply adopt the French way to set it (Perrousseaux 1996: 78)? The fact that the practice varies a lot in French (*01.12.34.56.78 instead of 01 12 34 56 78) does not facilitate the decision-making.

The way one composes the figures affects their pronunciation. In France, phone numbers are written and pronounced in two-digit groups. Typographically, these groups are separated by word spaces: 01 12 34 56 78 (area code + eight numbers) and pronounced as units: "zero one, twelve, thirty four, fifty six, seventy eight". In Finnish the numbers are enumerated one by one: "zero-one, one-two-three-four, five-six-seven-eight", but grouped according to length: (01) 1234 5678 (area code + eight numbers), (01) 123 4567 (seven numbers), (01) 123 456 (six numbers).

Secondly, in fiction: During a 1997 international and multidisciplinary colloquium called *À qui appartient la ponctuation?* (To whom does punctuation belong?) in Liège, Nadine Dejong compared some passages of Manuel Puig's novel *El beso de la mujer araña* to the French translation of it, *Le baiser de la femme-araignée*, by Albert Bensoussan. The example that I have chosen poses a question of text punctuation rather than of punctuation in the usual sense (see Figure 1).

CAPÍTULO CATORCE

DIRECTOR: Sí, señorita, deme con su jefe, por favor... Gracias... ¡Qué tal! ¿Qué se cuenta por ahí? Por aquí poca novedad. Sí, por eso mismo lo llamaba. Dentro de unos minutos lo vuelvo a ver. No sé si usted recuerda que le había dado a Molina una semana más de tiempo. Incluso hicimos que Arregui pensase que a Molina lo cambiamos de celda de un día para otro, por ser candidato a libertad condicional. Exacto, fue idea del propio Molina, sí. Caramba... Sí, el tiempo es lo que apremia. Claro, si quieren este dato antes de lanzar la contraofensiva, lo comprendo, claro. Sí, dentro de unos minutos lo veo, pero por esto es que lo llamo a usted antes. Digamos, en caso de que no me tenga nada... absolutamente nada que declarar, en caso de que no haya el menor progreso, ¿qué voy a hacer con Molina? Usted cree... ¿Dentro de cuántos días? ¿Mañana mismo? ¿Por qué mañana? Sí, claro que no hay tiempo que perder. Sí, comprendo, hoy no, así Arregui tiene tiempo de planear algo. Perfecto, si le da un mensaje, el mismo Molina nos conducirá a la célula. La dificultad está en que no note la vigilancia. Pero mire... hay algo raro en Molina, hay algo que me dice, no sé cómo explicarme, hay algo que me dice... que Molina no está actuando limpio conmigo... que me oculta algo. ¿Usted cree que Molina se haya puesto del lado de ellos? Sí, por miedo a las represalias de la gente de Arregui, también puede ser. Sí, también Arregui puede habérselo trabajado, vaya a

249

14

DIRECTEUR : Oui, mademoiselle, passez-moi votre chef, s'il vous plaît... Merci... Comment allez-vous ? Qu'est-ce qu'on raconte chez vous ?... Ici pas grand-chose de neuf... Oui, c'est justement pour cela que je vous appelais... Je le revois dans quelques minutes... Je ne sais si vous vous rappelez que j'avais donné à Molina une semaine de plus. Nous avons même fait en sorte qu'Arregui pense que nous allions changer Molina de cellule un jour ou l'autre, du fait qu'il est question de libération conditionnelle... Exact, ce fut une idée de Molina lui-même, oui... Sapristi... Oui, c'est le temps qui nous presse... Bien sûr, si vous voulez cette information avant de lancer la contre-offensive, je vous comprends, bien sûr... Oui, dans quelques minutes je le vois, mais c'est pour ça que je vous appelle avant. Disons, au cas où il n'aurait rien... absolument rien à déclarer, au cas où il n'y aurait pas le moindre progrès, qu'est-ce que je fais de Molina ?... Vous croyez ?... Dans combien de jours ? Demain même... Pourquoi demain ?... Oui, c'est sûr, il n'y a pas de temps à perdre... Oui, je comprends, aujourd'hui non, comme ça Arregui aura le temps de préparer quelque chose... Parfait ; s'il lui donne un message, Molina lui-même nous conduira à l'organisation... La difficulté, c'est qu'il ne se sente pas surveillé... Mais écoutez... il y a quelque chose de bizarre chez Molina, quelque chose qui me dit, je ne sais comment l'expliquer, il y a quelque chose qui me dit... que Molina ne joue pas franc-jeu avec moi... qu'il me cache quelque chose... Croyez-vous que Molina ait pu se mettre de leur côté ?... Oui, par peur des représailles des gens d'Arregui,

231

Figure 1.

What do the *white spaces* represent in the lines of the Spanish text? During a telephone conversation, they represent the speech at the other end of the line that the reader does not "hear" – thus they represent silence. In the French translation, these silences have been removed (replaced by ellipses), and the original narration along with the visual impression have been radically changed. (According to my knowledge, this decision was made by the publisher, not by the translator.)

Signs between

Punctuation, readability, and communication

Why should we follow the norms of punctuation? There are at least two good reasons. The first reason is to maximize understanding, as poor punctuation is likely to distort the writer's message. Yet it is sometimes meaningful to depart from traditional conventions in order to gain more power of expression. This leads to the second reason: exceptions to the rule are significant only if the majority of writers respect grammatical and typographic norms. Thus, for instance, students and academic writers enable the exceptional expression of creative writers, if they compose all their own texts according to rules. It could be said that fiction writers, poets, and copywriters live like parasites on those who respect the norms.

Readability of the text can be assured by following the norms, and thus also the legibility of the message becomes possible. But readability does not automatically mean the same as maximal communication or maximal signification in the content.

To identify the author or the title of the following lines is not an easy task, even to a Francophone or a Frenchman:

> *Il pleut des voix de femmes comme si elles étaient mortes même dans le souvenir*
> *c'est vous aussi qu'il pleut merveilleuses rencontres de ma vie ô gouttelettes*
> *et ces nuages cabrés se prennent à hennir tout un univers de villes auriculaires*
> *écoute s'il pleut tandis que le regret et le dédain pleurent une ancienne musique*
> *écoute tomber les liens qui te retiennent en haut et en bas*

The lines are a poem by Guillaume Apollinaire called *Il pleut* (*It is raining*) arranged in normal linear typography. In its originally published form (Spencer 1990: 82), which follows carefully the manuscript, the poem demonstrates clearly the importance of presentation (Figure 2). To many, just a glimpse would have been enough for them to identify this famous *calligramme* of Apollinaire. The use, or actually absence, of the proper punctuation marks here is nothing special in poetry. What is exceptional is the punctuation in its broad sense. In the layout each letter is itself a raindrop, and the "dripping" of letters downward from the top of the page resembles our visual image of rain.

Because of this arrangement, the reception of the message is so effective that the form of this typographic poem is imprinted or engraved (note the vocabulary of printing!) in our memory even though we might not memorise any of its individual lines.

When thinking about the signification of written language it would be interesting to study how the typographer is situated in a communication scheme. The situation might resemble that of a musical world where the composer (writer) is the creator of the piece of music (text) and a musician (typographer) the professional that interprets it.

Erja Hannula

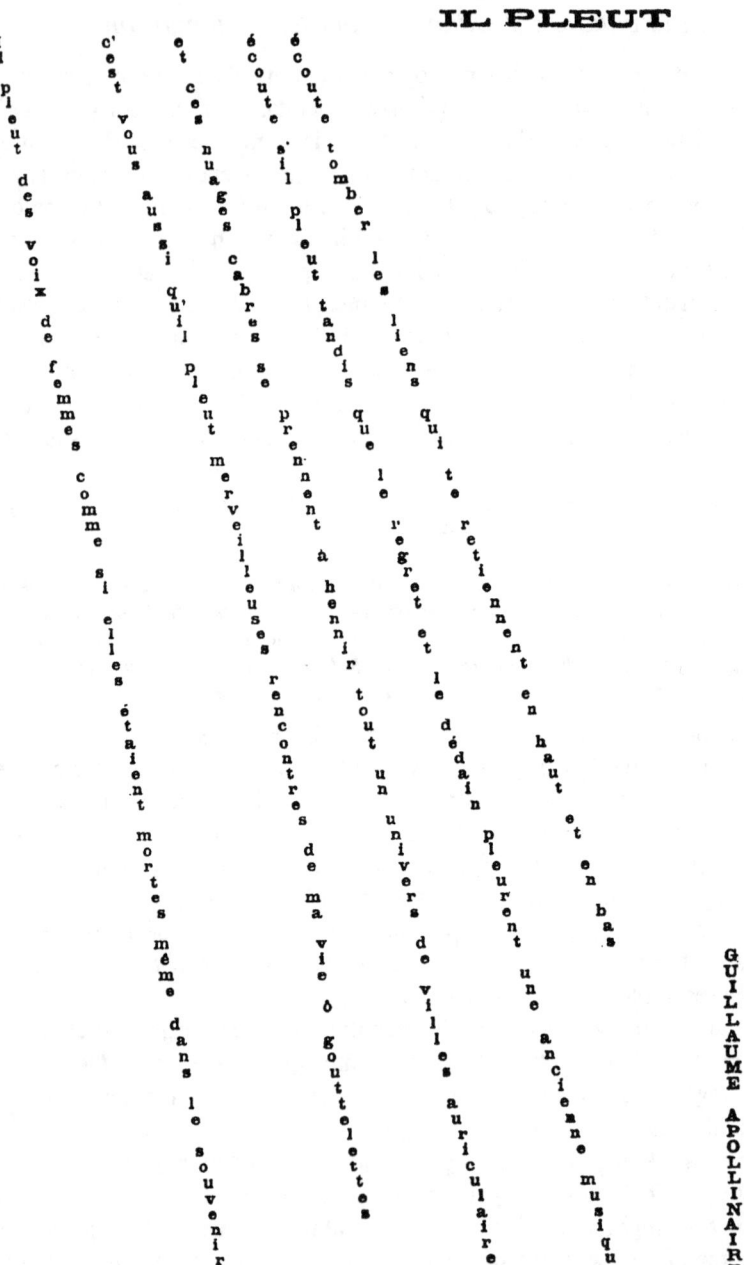

Figure 2.

Picture or punctuation?

Of course, to accept this broad conception of punctuation raises new questions, such as in the case of *Il pleut*, "Is this punctuation or graphic design?" and "Is this picture or punctuation?"

Raymond Gid has continued Apollinaire's work by creating an interpretation of *Il pleut*, setting it with a new typeface for Jérôme Peignot's book, *Typoésie* (1993: 155; see Figure 3). Here we are no longer talking about a written and punctuated text but about illustrating with single symbols. Gid's interpretation of the poem should be seen in the context of cultural texts, such that analytic approaches to it would come from the area of visual semiotics. In every single letter there is the whole idea of Apollinaire's calligramme, since every individual character describes the rain with vertical lines. I do not share Peignot's view (1993: 154), however, that because of the characters chosen from a rainy alphabet the poem "rains more", because it seems to me that, in this case, the act of repeating the *signifier* of the one and only *signified* does not add but instead diminishes the signification.

Advancing technology and the future of punctuation

Most of us have lived in the typewriter age, which I call the *Dark Ages of Written Language*, and especially that of punctuation. The typewriter had (or has) an extremely limited choice of characters, punctuation marks and graphic signs, and the keyboard did not allow the free – and correct – choice of punctuation marks. Many of the errors that we still encounter almost daily are due to typewriter practice. For instance, the wrong use of the inch mark < " > as quotation marks < " " >, hyphen < - > as a dash < – >, and so on. I speak of the *Dark Typewriter Ages of Written Language* even though the future might reveal positive aspects of this particular era – as has happened to the *Dark Middle Ages*.

Happily for literal expression, the printers' wide variety of punctuation marks survived the typewriter period. Now the computer age offers freedom of choice to every writer by bringing within our reach the professional typesetter's whole range of punctuation marks and graphic elements.

With advancing technology, word-processing programs have become many-sided. They may include dictionaries in different languages, along with rules for orthography, grammar, and typography – and often all this with personalization capabilities. Also, desktop publishing is becoming a skill learnt at school – just as penmanship used to be. And easy-to-use programs exist for typeface design. For hundreds of years, to produce any printed text demanded the skills of a large number of professionals. Today in its extreme form, the printing process includes only the writer, his text in his own layout in digital form, and a "printing machine"

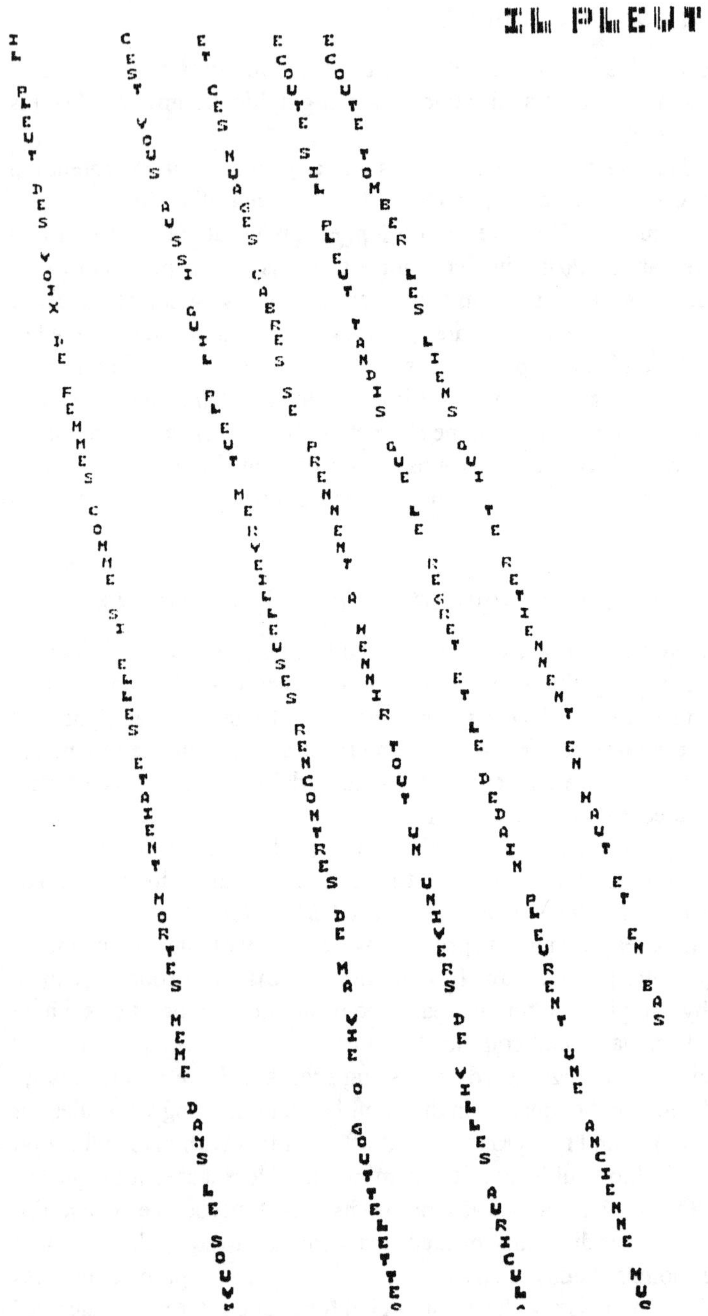

Erja Hannula

IL PLEUT

IL PLEUT DES VOIX DE FEMMES COMME SI ELLES ÉTAIENT MORTES MÊME DANS LE SOUVE

C'EST VOUS AUSSI QU'IL PLEUT MERVEILLEUSES RENCONTRES DE MA VIE O GOUTTELETTES

ET CES NUAGES CABRÉS SE PRENNENT A HENNIR TOUT UN UNIVERS DE VILLES AURICUL

ÉCOUTE S'IL PLEUT TANDIS QUE LE REGRET ET LE DÉDAIN PLEURENT UNE ANCIENNE MU

ÉCOUTE TOMBER LES LIENS QUI TE RETIENNENT EN HAUT ET EN BAS

Figure 3.

much like a normal copying machine; the system is called *Print on demand*.

Not only are advances in technology pushing us toward the mastery of punctuation in printed matters. Also, the growing cooperation among countries, on a European and international scale, means that we can expect in different fields more and more need for us to master multilingual publications. How can we respond to these demands?

We need an expanding dialogue and cooperation between all parties concerned. I would like to see scholars and professionals from different fields gathered in a roundtable meeting, including linguists, grammarians, communication experts, semioticians and the like, along with professionals such as writers, translators, graphic designers, typographers, font designers, software programmers, teachers, and so on.

Today punctuation belongs to everybody. But, in my view a multidisciplinary and multiprofessional community should take the responsibility for giving everybody the information and facilities for the appropriate use of punctuation in the future.

Note

1. In this article, all translations from Finnish and French are mine.

References

Catach, Nina (1996). *La ponctuation*. (=Que sais-je? 2818.) Paris: Presses Universitaires de France.
Ikola, Osmo (1992). *Nykysuomen käsikirja*. Jyväskylä: Weilin+Göös.
Joly, Martine (1994). *L'image et les signes*. Paris: Nathan.
Langue Française 45 (1980). La ponctuation.
Le nouveau Petit Robert (1994). Paris: Dictionnaires Le Robert.
Nunberg, Geoffrey (1990). *The Linguistics of Punctuation*. CSLI lecture notes 18. Stanford, CA: Center for the Study of Language and Information.
Peignot, Jérôme (1993). *Typoésie*. Paris: Imprimerie nationale.
Perrousseaux, Yves (1996). *Manuel de typographie française élémentaire*. Paris: Atelier Perrousseaux.
Puig, Manuel (1992). *El beso de la mujer araña*. Barcelone: Seix Barral.
– (1996). *Le baiser de la femme-araignée*. Trans. by Albert Bensoussan. (=Collection Points 286.) Paris: Seuil.
Raekallio-Teppo, Vuokko (1974). *Välimerkit*. Tapiola: Weilin+Göös.
Spencer, Herbert (ed.) (1990), *The Liberated Page*. London: Lund Humphries.
Tournier, Claude (1980). Histoire des idées sur la ponctuation, des débuts de l'imprimerie à nos jours. *Langue Française* 45: 29–40.

GASTRONOMY

Eero Tarasti

On culinemes, gastrophemes, and other signs of cooking

Food and gastronomy as objects of semiotic inquiry

Nearly all the great semioticians have discussed food and cooking – indeed, they could scarcely have overlooked such a fascinating and central human activity. Using a phonetic model, Claude Lévi-Strauss elaborated his famous culinary triangle of raw/cooked/rotten (and Umberto Eco has punningly bemoaned the fact that, due to his gourmandise, he can no longer squeeze himself into Levi Straus jeans). Roland Barthes examined the syntagms and paradigms of the menu as a manifestation of modern French mythology, and A. J. Greimas investigated the recipe for *la soupe au pistou* as a "narrative program". Even in the cultural semiotics of Lotman food makes an appearance, when the author examines ancient Slavic texts and considers what pie decorations have to say about an entire culture. It thus appears that food and gastronomy are eminently open to semiotic study. But if semiotics is communication plus signification, then how does food communicate and function as a sign?

The answer is not so simple. For first of all, gastronomy examines only one species of food, namely, the kind of excellent cuisine that pleases gourmets. Brillat-Savarin, author of *Physiologie du goût* (1826), succeeded in defining that special human agent – the gourmet – who alone can receive the message of good food. In other respects, too, Brillat-Savarin's classical text emphasizes the receiver's part in the communication of food. Altogether, *gourmandise* – a term which Brillat-Savarin suggests should not be translated but left in the French – appears as a *marked* phenomenon in the linguistic sense. As a kind of foregrounded type, it stands out from most of humanity, which eats only to live and not to enjoy.

Does, then, food as a sign exist only for the receiver? If so, then food as communication would clearly represent a message directed towards that recipient, though not in Jakobson's conative sense. In the latter case, one would attempt to use food to influence the conduct of the receiver. Yet some would say that the opposite takes place: the reception of the food sign is completed in the act of the food being enjoyed. Thus, in this scenario, food communication would be focused on the receiver and at the same time be non-conative.

The role of the sender – the cook – crystallizes in the recipe, the verbal rules for food preparation. Recipes vary in character and length. Often they present in an extremely condensed form the paradigmatic elements (ingredients), and then as laconically prescribe that the food preparation take place in a certain temporal order. Televised cooking programs little alter this procedure, though all the phases of cooking may be shown visually, step by step. In the end, it seems as if food as a sign could be summarized into a series of commands for action, a procedure which nearest illustrates the operational definition in logic: the definition of a cake is its recipe.

Yet it would seem rather strange and contrary to most semiotic practices if food as a sign could be reduced to this mode of existence. Naturally the experienced gastronome can from the mere recipe quite easily imagine how the food would look and taste if prepared according to the directions. He can mentally reconstruct the food object without actually producing it. Conversely, working from a prepared dish or from a picture of it, he can analyze and reconstruct the recipe without ever touching the food.

This process is amazingly analogous to that of musical communication. The musical specialist can, by merely leafing through the score, conceptualize how the piece would sound when played. Composition contests are based on this kind of judgement. Confronted with new pieces that have not yet been performed, the judge must evaluate them by sight, or by the "inner ear". Correspondingly, when a specialist has heard a piece, he can sometimes at least partly reconstruct its score. As the extreme case there was Mozart, who could notate an entire piece of music after hearing it only once. These two cases, however, illustrate the outer limits of musical communication. Generally, it is hard to imagine music without its physical support, the musical sign, the sounding form.

But what remains between the recipe and the experience of enjoyment? There is of course the food itself as object, as a ready-made physical product. But this object cannot fully function as a sign until it is tasted, sipped, eaten – in a word, enjoyed. As the consequence of this experience, however, the corporeal food-sign vanishes; the physical basis of the communication act is annihilated. What remains is only a memory image of the sign – which can be quite powerful and generate, as in the case of Proust, a whole series of the most poetic associations. For one who travels a lot, a gastro-cognitive map of the world gradually takes shape alongside that of geography. Countries and towns find their positions on the map according to what kind of food has been enjoyed in each place. In this extreme form, dishes can also serve as signs for people – as their "doubles", as Proust used to say. For once we have tasted the bravura of someone's culinary skills, this becomes his or her "sign", and it is inevitably evoked even when we enjoy that food or dish elsewhere or even only when we think of it.

The undeniable, sad truth is that the semiotic sign of food is at its inception doomed to destruction, and that this species of signs does not have the same stability as, say, those of painting, literature, or architecture. Gastronomy should thus be equated with the performing arts of music, theatre, dance, and the like, whose signs are always bound with time that is understood not only as fleeting and fragile moments but as the very physical basis on which they subsist. All the performing arts also have the same essential problem; namely, they can either succeed or fail. The notation of sign production does not guarantee success, which depends instead on the whole situation of communication in which the sign is produced, transmitted and received. As is the case with all performing arts, in food preparation, too, the slightest disturbance can prevent the product from functioning as a sign.

For Greimas, food had the semiotic status of a "value object", that is to say, an object in which values have been invested. In the construction of such objects, the essential point for Greimas is the achievement of values, their discovery and manipulation: "The objects themselves are of no interest. They are worth constructing, creating, producing only to the extent that they form the place for the manifestation of values" [*les objets ne l'intéressent – et leur construction ne mérite d'être entreprise – que dans la mesure où ils constituent des lieux d'investissement des valeurs*]. (Greimas 1979: 157)

This same view applies also to music, in the idea that the music is not the same as the tones, but only manifests itself by means of them. But can we adopt such a radically "spiritual" view here? For what could food be as mere value, without the material object carrying it? Everything spiritual which is connected to food seems to be an *a posteriori* phenomenon. It seems difficult to isolate the food sign with any kind of phenomenological reduction, since it is always bound to its context, its multiple connections in the chain of communication and process of signification.

It is generally thought that those interested in food are incurable hedonists, and that those who care about table and other manners are stiff formalists. And a philosopher might at this stage make recourse to Kant's *Metaphysics of Manners*, only to be surprised that the latter's categorical imperative – "Do to others what you wish them to do to you" – crops up in one of the central passages in Brillat-Savarin's *Physiologie du goût*!

Two historical perspectives

It will be instructive to compare the views of two world-famous French gourmets and chefs, Brillat-Savarin and Eduard Nignon. The first of these was a well-known doctor whose starting point in his previously cited book on taste was the "medical" observation of food and eating. The charm of the book comes from the fact that it reads as if it were objectively precise description, while it is in fact highly subjective and evaluative. Running completely contrary to Greimas's view, Brillat-Savarin takes the position that values, all spiritual things, all of culture and society stem from human physiological necessity, from the need to satisfy and sustain the senses. Such satisfaction ennobles one, making one happy, tolerant and benevolent toward others. Ultimately, all of society depends on *gourmandise*. In the chapter entitled "The Advantages of *Gourmandise*", Brillat-Savarin states the following: "[Gourmandise] is the impulse which moves living foods from one country to the other; it is a judge which determines the prices of food; it is the hope which arouses competition; it is a profession which creates life and causes the perpetual circulation of monetary resources" (op. cit.: 135). On this view, one could say that Lévi-Strauss's theory of three levels of society – the exchange of messages, things, and women – rests upon a fourth, deeper level. And that level is the exchange of foods.

All great historical events, even conspiracies and political coups, have been decided upon, prepared, and carried out during feasts (op. cit.: 57). Brillat-Savarin views all the arts and all spiritual things as being based on sensations; they are continuations and refinements of the senses: "The visual sense created painting, sculpture and dramatic arts; the auditory sense, music; the olfactory sense, the use and cultivation of perfumes; the taste sense, the production of alimentary goods, their selection and elaboration; the tactile sense was included in all the arts; and the physical sense of love yielded coquetries and other phenomena."

When we turn to another scion of French gastronomy, Eduard Nignon, the viewpoint changes. In his book, *Éloges de la cuisine française*, he contrarily states that food reflects higher, non-sensual values. Nignon (1865–1934) was one of the illustrious chefs at the imperial court of Russia. At the parties of the millionaire Ivan Morozoff he concocted spectacular meals such as an aquarium of Chinese fish that sprayed champagne, and a bear sculpted from ice that proffered caviar at the same time as a lamp in the animal's stomach made its eyes twinkle. Around 1915 Nignon moved from the court of Czar Nikolai to the Hotel Metropol in Moscow, where he prepared fantastic meals for diners in the famous hall with a fountain in the center. Eventually, though, Nignon was forced to return to Paris, when during the Bolshevik Revolution his cooks went on strike. There he became the proprietor of the Restaurant Larue and at last realized his dream of operating his own establishment. His clientele consisted of the leading artists of France, from Marcel Proust to Alfred Capus and Anatole France. Nignon had a sublime conception of the art of cooking, as the opening of his book illustrates:

> What is art, in general, but the lively, harmonious, subtle expression of all that the human brain can conceive about the great, the beautiful and sublime? Every work of art is determined by the intellectual and moral environment of which it is the offspring. The products of the Culinary Art are not an exception to this rule.... " (Nignon 1995: 21)

Nignon goes on to note that culinary art does not depend on the external brilliance of its products. The same artistic mastery can show forth in a simple *pot de feu* soup just as it does in Imperial chicken, the Queen's smoked salmon, or the Royal Deer Steak, since everything depends on the *savoir-faire* of the performer. The mind of a great cook unites great knowledge, long practice, and a poet's soul that is sensitive to all nuances of the Good and the Beautiful. The art of cooking presupposes strict obedience to the rules, but not as blind dogmatism. Nignon encapsulates his doctrine in the slogan, *Routine est crime en cuisine*. He encourages younger cooks to seek Beauty and Truth (op. cit.: 23), and exclaims:

> "Carry and develop in yourselves the profound love for the Culinary Art, generator of Force and Life. May your creations be healthy and may they reveal extreme care in the slightest details. Do not walk mechanically on paths already trod. Study, meditate, search always, be creators!" (p. 45) "One is born a poet or musician; one can also be born a cook." (p. 43)

The great teacher of Nignon was Careme. And Nignon also mentions Brillat-Savarin, when admitting that the invention of a new dish can be compared to the discovery of a new star. Still, Nignon's basic attitude toward cooking artistry clearly differs from that of Brillat-Savarin.

Semiotic questions about food

Let us leave our two famous chefs, and return to some basic questions in the semiotics of gastronomy: what is a gastronomic sign? How does food function as a sign? The problem can be approached from two directions. One may engage the food sign, or rather the entire gustatory "text", by taking into account its overall functioning and context and every aspect of the food experience. Or one may scrutinize the smallest significant units of food, as in linguistics we speak about phonemes and morphemes, semes and phemes. Taking the latter approach one might call the minimal unit of food a *gastreme*. Or if we conceive of every sign as divided into signifiers and signified, then we might speak about *gastrophemes* and *gastrosemes*. The gastropheme would refer to the physical qualities, and gastroseme to the meaning of the food. Such a distinction immediately poses questions. Can, for instance, the taste sensation be a gastropheme and a taste experience a gastroseme? Or are the ingredients of a recipe gastrophemes, which in various combinations would produce gastrosemes?

To begin answering these questions, we can turn to a history of gastronomy by the Finnish scholar Jussi Talvi. He speaks about the first "taste experience" of mankind as taking place in 1765, when a Monsieur Boulanger invented a strong bouillon for the poor people of Paris (see Talvi 1989: 213). From this event comes the word *restaurant*, which literally means both a food that revitalizes and restores, and the place where it can be enjoyed. Talvi says: "Such a soup may have provided the first deliberate taste experiences of man." Should then the gastreme be defined as a deliberate, intentional taste experience? Following from this, it would appear that gastropheme/seme come nearest to the signs of poetry and not to those of everyday communication. And yet, since the terms "seme" and "pheme" imply a certain generality, we should perhaps reserve the terms "gastropheme/seme" for referring to the "poetic" function of the cooking art, and use terms such as "culineme" (or "culinopheme/culinoseme") to describe generalized cooking in all its forms.

Lévi-Strauss elaborated his famous theory of culinary triangles, raw/cooked/rotten, which serve as three distinctive features in the world's cooking systems. For instance, in the Finnish dairy-products culture, milk = raw, cheese = cooked, and rotten = soured milk, yogurt, and the like. In the category of "cooked", Lévi-Strauss distinguishes several modes of production which provide foods with their particular meanings. In this way one might try to analyze the gastrophemes/semes that do not depend on subjective experience, and on this basis determine the distinctive features of various food cultures. To food we could easily apply the commutation test proposed by Roland Barthes: one switches the places of the supposed gastrophemes (for instance, two materials) and then observes whether this change produces a difference on the level of gastrosemes, or taste experience (just as in French we can change the consonants /p/ and /b/ and get two different words *pas* and *bas)*. Omit the apricot jam from a Sacher torte, or replace it with orange jam, and the item is no longer a Sacher torte.

When we move from reflections on the smallest units of meaning to food in its global signification, we find that the latter meaning comes not so much from the food itself as from the broader context(s) in which it appears. Food is a part of man's life-world, or *Umwelt*, his/her whole life praxis, which provides food and the enjoyment of it with significations. This is particularly true in societies which still live either entirely or partly in a so-called ethnosemiotic state, which is characterised by a certain cyclicity, the adaptation of life to the alternation of seasons, religious occasions, feasts, and so on. In such a state, the meaning of food is not so much determined by its inner qualities, gastrophemes and semes, but by what Greimas called *isotopies* and what Lotman termed *semiospheres*. These terms refer to the semiotic continuum that enables the life of its constituent, individual signs. The existence of this continuum is clearly proved by the so-called traditional food cultures, which the gastronomes do not often appreciate:

> The history of gastronomy without exception shows that the so-called average person has created none of those delicious foods which we can enjoy even today. People have created traditional foods, but a major part of them are, however, the foods of times of starvation... they cannot be polished to become something more refined. (Talvi 1989: 201)

Yet there are numerous descriptions of gastronomically delicious foods, created "anonymously", which reflect the entire living world. In Gogol's short story, *The Old-World Landowners*, Afanasi Ivanovitch and Pulheria Ivanovna spend quiet lives in their village house which is bubbling over with abundance. Although the servants steal as much as they can, nothing is missing from the table of Afanasi and Pulheria. In fact, the two protagonists do hardly anything, and their repeated dialogues go something like this: How is it, Pulheria Ivanovna, should we not taste something? What would you like to eat now, Afanasi Ivanovitch? Perhaps pies with fat or puppet pies or perhaps salted mushrooms? Strangely, in the description of their food habits the order of the dishes seems not to follow any pre-established narrative program, which in this case would be a menu. As Roland Barthes has shown, the menu has its paradigm, the store of possible dishes, and its syntagm, the linear course of their enjoyment. Yet it seems that in Gogol's story there is only one paradigm for Afanasi and Pulheria: the inexhaustible food store from which they impulsively choose things. This reflects an ethnosemiotically articulated culture, in which food symbolizes a certain stable, static, sleepy, but at the same time undeniably poetic life style. The narrator describes such an isotopy, or semiosphere, of food in the following way:

> ... always when my wagons approach the verandah of such a house, my heart is taken by a wonderfully sweet and quiet state ... the faces of those old people always have such mildness, they reflect such hospitality and puremindedness, that one deliberately abandons, even if for only a while, all unscrupulous wishes and unnoticeably shifts to their silent, close-to-nature life...

Gogol's novel also describes the abrupt mutation of a society from an ethnosemiotic to a sociosemiotic state in which organic solidarity no longer prevails, but everything becomes mechanized and isolated. Most modern cookbooks, which only give prescriptive advice for preparation without reporting on the origin of the dish, present food as detached, as its own more or less artificial product. Such food can be offered to anyone, and enjoyed anywhere and at any time.

When a recipe book does describe the origin of the food and its context of usage, it better attains to the original ethnosemiotic state. Some cookbooks almost presuppose that the reader's competence is sufficient to cover the life style which is reflected in the dishes. For instance, Mary Emma Showalter's *Mennonite Community Cookbook* (1986) is such a book. Although the recipes in it are very scanty, they are fascinating because by following them the reader imagines himself as reconstructing part of an almost extinct life-style – the world which the movie *Witness* showed to millions of spectators around the world. One encounters here the art of cooking as an oral culture, which the author attempts to reach by literal means:

> Since a cookbook of the favorite recipes of Mennonite families had never been published, I now began to sense that the handwritten recipe books were responsible. I asked wherever I went and was astonished to learn how many of them had been destroyed in recent years. The daughters of today were guilty of pushing them aside in favor of the new, just as I had done one day. It is true that many of our mothers were still using the old favorite recipes, but were doing so by memory. When I found them, the little notebooks were usually at the bottom of a stack of modern cookbooks and were kept only for memory's sake. Through the years many had become so worn and soiled that in places they were no longer legible. (Showalter 1986: ix)

To the same category belongs the cookbook by Duchess Olga Obolenski, published under the title *Herkkuja ruhtinattaren keittiöstä* (*Delicacies from the Kitchen of a Duchess*). The recipes are quite ascetic, and at the end of the book there are facsimile printings from the Finnish-language version (from the first edition in 1931). Still, the recipes are made appealing by the fact that they reflect a certain life-style at the manor of Rantalinna, near Imatra. By preparing, for instance, "The old cake from Riga" according to the book, we can imagine ourselves to participate in that earlier way of living.

Cooking as a generative course

Thus far, I have approached my object from two angles: from its smallest units of signification and from its broader social contexts. Can these two approaches be brought together so as to elaborate a unified methodology for examining food? This poses quite a challenge to semiotics, but it is surely possible to do.

Cooking can easily be paralleled to a generative course. In the same way as generative grammar presents the rules for the production of language, we could consider a recipe as a collection of rules for "producing" or "generating" food. Yet there are many kinds of generative grammars. A. J. Greimas, among others, has applied his own theories to a recipe from Provence for *la soupe au pistou*. The preparation of food is made explicit with a particular "narrative program" in which the sender-cook attempts to conjoin his receiver-guest to the value object, *la soupe au pistou*.

In my own work, I have applied Greimas's theories in a somewhat different way, especially to music (and as was stated above, noteworthy similarities exist between the generation of music and food). In doing so, I have distinguished four levels which from the isotopies, go to the spatial, temporal and actorial categories, and further to the modalities, ultimately reaching the surface level of phemes and semes (see Diagram 1).

The isotopies of food have already been discussed above. They indicate that whole world of *Dasein* with all its significations, which forms the background and starting-point of culinary activity and which determines its *raison d'être*. The isotopy of food can be ceremonial, for instance, as in the category of a "formal dinner", to use Emily Post's vocabulary (such a meal is often illustrated by dinner scenes in English upper-class castles in the novels of Wodehouse and in their film realizations). Or the food isotopy can be ritual, such as the eucharist in Wagner's *Parsifal*. It can be biological-medical, as occurs when one dines in a restaurant containing live food (housed by aquariums, cages, and the like). It can be social, as dinner is envisioned in *Minnen från mitt liv, hemma och ut* (1931), the memoirs of the Finnish sculptor and gourmet, Ville Vallgren (whom we shall return to later). The food isotopy can be economic: a business lunch during negotiations; it can be political: say, in the encounter of two heads of different states (for instance, the rector of Paris University V, Pierre Villard, has investigated the history of a dinner set that was used only at royal meals). The isotopy can be erotic: *Dejeuner sur l'herbe* in Manet's painting or in Renoir's film. There can be an endless amount of isotopies, any of which can constitute the starting-point for all cooking and culinarism. They provide the whole semiosis of food with sense.

On the next level, food is approached via three categories: spatial, temporal, and actorial. Some basic questions regarding spatiality are these: Where is the food eaten? How is the food related to a certain place? If such a thing as a "spirit of place" exists, how does it appear as a food sign? True gastrosemioticians are recognized by the fact that they do not remember places by their names, events, atmospheres, or smells, but by what they eat and where they eat it.

Conversely, certain foods perform their gastronomic markedness function only if they are enjoyed in a certain place. Due to a kind of intertextual infiltration, the "semes" of a location penetrate, so to say, to the place of the gastrosemes; they connect on the level of experience to the network of semes which in our minds characterise that place. An entirely different type of map emerges on the basis of these gastrosemes, which experience scatters in often unexpected places. A guest may arrive in New York for the first time in the morning and, after the long flight, stagger to a coffee shop. With his coffee, he is probably offered pancakes, whipped butter, and bacon. In such a way the new arrival is initiated into American-ness via a taste experience that unites the sweet and the salty – two rather opposed phemes – in the same meal. Or when the gastrotourist arrives at Rio de Janeiro or Sao Paulo, the thick juices of caju, goiaba, abacaxi and the like

On culinemes, gastrophemes, and other signs of cooking

ISOTOPY

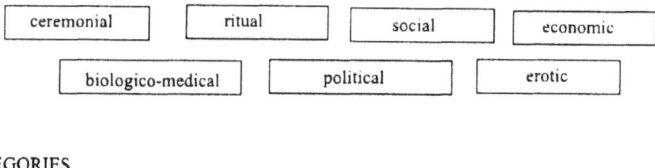

CATEGORIES

    spatial   temporal   actorial

    (where?)   (when?)   (who?)

MODALITIES

For which human needs, or modality of being or doing, the food is prepared; on which modality the food is assumed to have its impact

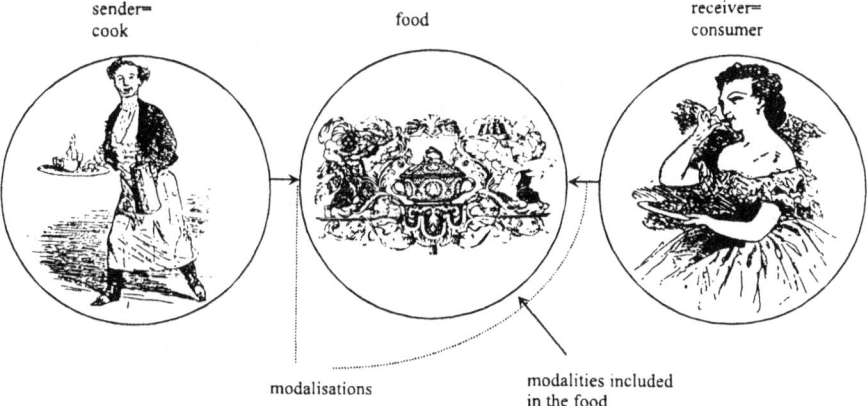

modalities of food
to know: to fulfill curiosity, the food must be innovative
to want: "will to food", energy
can: the technical skills of food preparation, virtuosity
must: the norms regulating communication by food
to believe: the persuasiveness of the food, "truth"

PHEMES/SEMES

Food as such; the smallest significant units of the food (gastrophemes and gastrosemes)

Diagram 1. The generation of food (Eero Tarasti after A. J. Greimas).

may give him his first conception of the tropics, which he perhaps glimpsed from the window of the airplane. In Mexico one is invited to taste a certain black mushroom which belonged to the diet of the Aztecs, thus at once being transported to a distant culture. When one has seen Pablo Neruda's house at Isla Negra in the Pacific, one may drive to San Antonio to taste the soup made of fish with unbelievably coloured shells, which experience is mixed in the mind with the sea-evoking poetry of Neruda and the contours of the Andes. And many a semiotician has paid a visit to the Tudor Room on the Bloomington campus of Indiana University, or has taken morning coffee at the Up-Town Café with Thomas A. Sebeok. The list could be continued endlessly.

Cooking, as any performing art, is also a temporal activity. Precise timing on the microlevel is one of the most essential aspects of the "generation" of a meal. The principle of the *quandité* of time, as one French philosopher calls it, is most important in gastrosemiosis. Some dishes require several days' or even weeks' patience; in others a delay of one minute can be fateful. For instance, Nordic rye bread cannot be prepared hastily; and if French chocolate cake remains in the oven one minute too long, it is no longer French chocolate cake. Some dishes are connected with cyclic periodisation, or what could be called the ethnosemiotic calendar. (Finnish life, for one, still strongly follows such seasons and their particular foods.)

As to the last Greimassian category, that of actoriality, it is quite apparent that cooking cannot take place without actors. For who else has the competence or *savoir-faire* to prepare food, judge it, and "perform" it? Eduard Nignon defines such competence and performance in his *Éloges* (cited above) and sees it as based on three principles: experience, theory, and reasoning (1995: 43). Marcel Proust invented the notion of a "*Sonata pathétique* of cooking". To him cooking, musical performance, and receiving guests were cases of the same category, whose perfection in each case was a certain simplicity, moderation, and charm (Proust in his preface to John Ruskin's essay, *Of Kings' Treasures*).

The three categories of place, time, and actors together constitute the situation in which the semiosis of food is realized. In addition to these basic principles, all the other species of signs – icons, indices, and symbols – obtain in the semiosis of food.

The next level of generation concerns the modalities of cooking. Modalities are the ways by which participants in communication colour and "humanize" their messages and sign objects. Modalities are thus the most dynamic part of the semiotic process and hence the most difficult to fix as categories and concepts. The one who prepares the food and the one who enjoys it both "modalize" the food. In addition, some modalities are already included in the food object itself. For one, the modality of "knowing" already appears in the requirement that food satisfy our curiosity, in the sense that it must be a new taste experience. We do not willingly serve the same food to our guests on two consecutive occasions, just as at a concert of new music one normally does not perform a previously heard piece (unless it is a masterwork which the audience insists on hearing).

Then there is the modality of "will", in Schopenhauer's sense. Culinary activity is based upon the *Wille zum Essen*, a kind of meta-will. Though the cultural differences are great in this area, the ingestion of every meal follows an energetic process which makes one eat its various segments in the "right" order, such as the alternation of sweet and salty dishes (in Italy, for instance, the ice creams and sorbets as mid-deserts may cool the overheated modality of will before the next meat dish arrives).

The modality of capability, or "can", appears in the technical realization of the food, its virtuosity and performance. As Ruskin said: only the one who has measured the resistance of the material can judge the modality of "power" (can).

We come next to the modality of "must", which in this case refers to all the norms that govern culinary communication. These norms can stem from many different isotopies (nutritional, medical, social, and so on), but they can also originate from the next level of generation. Finally, the modality of "belief" refers to food as the manifestation of a certain symbolic value, food as conveying a certain persuasiveness. When all the other modalities are in harmony with time, location, and actor, we experience the food to be in its proper "place", thereby manifesting the category of truth. But of course it is also possible to cheat or to "lie" with food by substituting the wrong ingredients, altering a recipe, serving a dish in improper order, and so on.

As the last level of generation we have the phemes and semes of the food, its smallest units, already pondered above. This level concerns the food as "such", that is, as combinations of phemes and semes.

The generative model just sketched proposes various rules and levels of cooking. The model is Greimas-inspired, but it does not seek to produce a strictly formal analyses on the order of his own study of a provençale recipe. Rather, my theory can be taken as a mnemonic and heuristic model of gastrosemiotic analysis. It fixes our attention on all essential aspects of food, and also helps us to judge whether a menu or recipe is lacking some crucial aspect of meaning. My model is not generative in the prescriptive sense, such that by it one could produce, say, skillful, authentic, convincing, surprising, or even "correct" dishes. Rather, it is descriptive, insofar as with its help one can model any processes related to cooking and elucidate them with a particular metalanguage that has already proved itself in connection with other verbal and non-verbal sign systems. In this way, cooking is elevated from its often underestimated status as one of the "lesser arts" among human texts and sign activities. Furthermore, my model is evaluative, since it tries to analyze the goodness or badness of the product, and to answer why certain combinations of gastrophemes and semes are successful and others are not.

An application: cooking in Paris according to Ville Vallgren, Finnish sculptor and gourmet

Here I shall test the applicability of my theory by analyzing one well-known cookbook, written by the Finnish sculptor and gourmet Ville Vallgren, entitled *The Food Catechesis of Old Man Ville*. Vallgren's descriptions of food are rare in the literature, in the sense that he moves on all levels of generation. The bohemian life of Paris forms the background for his recipes, a life in which he participated from 1877–1921. He lived in artistic neighborhoods in Montmartre with such well-known Finnish and Swedish artists as Gunnar Berndtson, Stigell, Aukusti Uotila, Otto Wallenius, Carl Larsson, Ernst Josephson and Axel Munthe. They often held merry afternoon feasts to celebrate expositions in their favourite restaurants Jesus Syrak, Clarisse of Café Neapolitaine. In the mornings Vallgren would often be awakened by his roommate, Pelle Eskträm, who had already bought brioches and prepared coffee. Ekström would ask the rising Vallgren, "Behagar Ers Höghet morgonkaffe?" (Would your Excellency like to take morning coffee?).

In his memoirs and in passing comments in his food catechesis, Vallgren writes about his Parisian friends; for instance, how Émile Zola disapproved of the way the Russians were treating the Finns (at that time Finland was still an autonomous part of Russia). Vallgren notes ironically that the real reason for Zola's indignation was that he received no royalties from any of his novels that were printed in Russia. Paul Verlaine was once saved by Vallgren when he left the Café Procope drunk, since he never enjoyed other than a ham sandwich and a beer. After Verlaine had recited the poem *Il pleure dans mon cœur*, Vallgren took him home to Rue Monsieur le Prince, and soon thereafter Verlaine died. In sum, Vallgren's circle of acquaintances consisted of all kinds, from creative originals to shiftless idlers. (When reading his stories one notices how little things have changed. For his Paris is not so far from that of the contemporary Finnish movie producers, the Kaurismäki brothers).

I shall now analyze in more detail one day and its meals from a week in Paris, as described at the beginning of Vallgren's food catechesis. The week was supposed to serve as a model of how meals could be planned with reason and alternation, although at the end Vallgren came to the following conclusion (Vallgren 1994: 53):

> Now we have eaten one whole week and lived, feasting heartily, well, and expensively. We cannot continue this way any longer, although it is good to do so sometimes; but

if we should go on living in this reckless way, the bark of our stomach would soon capsize on the waves of our life. So, we must be moderate and save our health capital and not spend it all, along with any interest ... a good, simple food and drink (wine, of course) will guide us in our daily work to happy days at the age of 100 years.

The spatial, temporal, and actorial situations appear quite clearly in Vallgren's text: the place is Paris; the time, one week from May 31, 1920; and the actors are Ville and his artist colleagues. The "we" form of the story refers not only to this community but also to the readership, in which Vallgren includes his "us". The chapter is entitled "The cooking worries of Wednesday". The narrator notes that, having eaten too heavily on Tuesday, today he might eat somewhat lighter. So he decides to prepare scrambled eggs and adds the following remark – which recurs throughout the book: "Everyone knows how good scrambled eggs are prepared in Paris." The narrator thus refers to an oral tradition that certainly exists, but which cannot be defined explicitly.

The eggs require white wine (a Bordeaux Graves) rather than red, says Vallgren, who always chooses the drinks. He has a clear conception of the compatibilities and incompatibilities of certain gastrophemes and -semes. "[W]e can eat kidneys or calf liver. I would rather eat kidneys", says Vallgren. The recipe for kidneys follows: butter is browned in a pan into which the kidneys are placed after they have been doused with hot water and vinaigrette. Then come chopped mushrooms and onions, and finally red wine or Madeira. (Vallgren often uses wine in food, which Careme, according to Nignon, completely rejected.) Then Vallgren announces: "Now it is ready. With it you can eat cooked potatoes or stewed beans or carrots". Vallgren's text is very "deictic", in the sense that his cooking always takes place at certain places and times to which the reader is pointed. If we wish to have rice, Vallgren advises that "we stir well two cups of rice in cold water and with them pieces of ham and small round spring onions". In three hours the food is ready to be enjoyed with either red or white Bordeaux. Then follows good Roquefort cheese, "since it fits well after the mild rice". This method of putting dishes in series could be called the "inner indexicality" of the meal. One dish, so to say, "invites" the next by a forward-proceeding, indexical reference. It is also essential that the dishes are not blended, but are eaten one after the other, in the syntagmatic order. Finally, one takes "big beautiful cultivated strawberries with sugar, together with a creamy and healthy fresh cheese called *petit suisse*. Add some swigs of Chateau d'Yquem and we are satisfied", Vallgren announces.

One notes that in Vallgren's text every food sign is sanctioned according to descriptions of the euphoric or dysphoric modalisation of the receiver. Moreover, all the described recipes are extremely easy to prepare, thus requiring or exhibiting a very small degree of the modality of "can".

As the text continues the depiction of food ceases, and Vallgren declares that he will leave by car for a dinner tour in the countryside, to the "charming Meudon, which is on the shore of the Seine". When the company arrives at a famous restaurant, the *Pêche miraculeuse*, they immediately order eel ragout, since the expert knows that that dish takes a long time to prepare. From the verandah, the group can see the River Seine, its "water calm in the evening sunshine". This makes Ville remember a meal he had in the same place on May 17, when the national day of Norway was celebrated. He similarly recalls *vernissage* dinners of the nineteenth century, with many celebrities, ranging from Edelfelt to Strindberg, sitting at a table placed on the green meadow, and their "speeches and song as one big choir". In his memoirs Vallgren tells how "all" Paris was astonished when they sang the "Suomis sång" (a well-known choral tune written by Fredrik Pacius) in the restaurant Clarisse:

> *När Suomis sång gick av stapeln, blev det stort jubel, succen var storartad, vi måste sjunga den fyra gånger. Alla voro förvånade och undrade huru vi hade kunnat åstadkomma någonting så vackert.*
>
> [When the song of Finland was sounding, jubilation broke out; so well was it received that we had to sing it four times. Everyone was amazed and wondered how we had been able to produce something so beautiful.]

The essential thing to note here is that food and eating are not detached phenomena. Rather, they call forth other artistic performances and associations.

Then the dinner is described in detail, beginning with the main course of fish, which is followed by grilled chicken. The burgundy wine taken with the dishes puts the company in a rollicking mood and loosens their tongues to the point of speechmaking. Vallgren quotes his own ode to Paris and the River Seine, in which he describes the latter as wriggling like an eel – an iconic sign that connects the food and its environment: "It offers its poetry as a balm to the man who understands the Parisian atmosphere of life, where nature, food and wine, this Trinity provides man with a sentimental but passing moment. Amen". Now they take asparagus and drink champagne, dropping sweet strawberries in their glasses. Finally come the cheese and fruits, and thereafter coffee with cognac. "Then we drive by car through the forest of Boulogne, each to his home".

Only now does Ville tell us about the preparation of the eel ragout, which in his excitement he almost forgot to do. This means that our gastrosemiotician is not always thinking about cooking, but that he wants to enjoy it immediately. The eel is described as one "actor" of the story:

> The eel, this ugly snake fish, is of course peeled, but it is still alive; it is chopped into pieces, but the damned thing still lives. Ach! How cruel! Now it is put in the pan but it still lives. Only when we stuff its stomach with the pieces of calf kidneys and calf liver does it become frightened and die.

It is noteworthy that the ingredients appear in this narration as anthropomorphized actors. They are not mere semiotic objects, but characterized as having the same modal properties as the sending and receiving actors. The food lives in union with its isotopy. Nothing is formalistic or mechanical, neither the description of procedures nor that of the meal, which has not been reified into a rote recipe.

Conclusion

The theories of Barthes and Greimas have led me to the narrative of Vallgren. In his story the generation of food does not take place straightforwardly but via many twists and turns. Undeniably, the main protagonist of the Wednesday story becomes the eel. And the story itself wriggles, iconically following the lead of this archi-actor. Vallgren transmits his enthusiasm to the reader, and the meal inspires its receivers to other action as well. At the feast the food is omnipresent, but at the same time it provides a marvelous, material isotopy to something quite spiritual, an artistic celebration of Paris in the spring. In this model *tout se tient*, everything depends on everything. The story and the model show how food belongs to the intertextual network, in which it can, in the words of Lévi-Strauss, function as a sign of something quite different.

References

Barthes, Roland (1985). *L'aventure sémiologique.* Paris: Seuil.
Brillat-Savarin, J. A. (1826/1988). *Physiologie du goût.* In Finnish: *Maun fysiologia. Suuri ranskalainen gastronomian klassikko.* Jyväskylä: Koko kansan kirjakerho.
Eco, Umberto (1995). *How to Travel with a Salmon & Other Essays.* San Diego, New York: Harcourt Brace & Company.
Gogol, Nikolai (1985/1835). *The Complete Tales of Nikolai Gogol.* Vol. 2. Ed. Leonard J. Kent. Chicago: University of Chicago Press.
Greimas, A. J. (1979). La soupe au pistou ou la construction d'un objet de valeur. In: *Du sens II: Essais sémiotiques.* Paris: Seuil. 157–169.
Leach, Edmund (1970). *Lévi-Strauss.* Helsinki: Tammi.
Lévi-Strauss, Claude (1964). *Le cru et le cuit: Mythologiques I.* Paris: Librairie Plon.
Naudin, Jean-Bernard, Anne Borrel, and Alain Senderens (1992). *Zu Gast bei Marcel Proust. Der grosse Romancier als Gourmet.* München: Wilhelm Heyne Verlag.
Nignon, Eduard (1995). *Éloges de la cuisine française.* Liguge: Inter-Livres.
Obolenski, Ruhtinatar Olga (1991/1931). *Herkkuja ruhtinattaren keittiöstä* [*Delicacies from the Kitchen of a Duchess*]. Reprinted as *Nuoren emännän herkkuleivosopas.* Porvoo: WSOY.
Post, Emily (1945). *Etiquette: The Blue Book of Social Usage.* New York: Funk & Wagnalls.
Showalter, Mary Emma (1986). *Mennonite Community Cookbook.* Scottsdale, Pennsylvania; Kitchener, Ontario: Herald Press.
Talvi, Jussi (1989). *Gastronomia historia* [*History of Gastronomy*]. Helsinki: Otava.

Tarasti, Eero (1991). Sur l'authenticité et l'inauthenticité des arts. *Degrés* no. 68, numéro spécial sur sémiologie et pratiques esthétiques. Sémiotiques finlandaises, pp. a–a26.
Vallgren, Ville (1920). *Guldranden*. Helsingfors: Holger Schildts Förlagsaktiebolag.
– (1931). *Minnen från mitt liv hemma och ute.* Helsingfors: Mercators Tryckerie Aktiebolag.
– (1994) Pariisin Villen ruokasaarna. [*The Food Catechesis of Old Man Ville*]. Finnish trans. by Kyllikki Villa. Helsinki: Taide. Originally published in Swedish as *Wille-gubbens matkatekes*. Helsingfors: Schildt, 1921.

Contributors

HENRY BACON, Helsinki, docent of film studies
KRISTIAN BANKOV, Sofia, assistant professor of semiotics
THORSTEN BOTZ-BORNSTEIN, Paris, doctor of philosophy
HENRI BROMS, Helsinki, docent of Persian literature
MATTHIEU GUILLOT, Paris, doctor of aesthetics
ERJA HANNULA, Helsinki, coordinator of semiotics studies program
TUOMO JÄMSÄ, Savonlinna, associate professor of pedagogy
NIILO KAUPPI, Helsinki, docent of sociology
HEIKKI KIRJAVAINEN, Helsinki, professor of theology
PIRJO KUKKONEN, Kouvola, associate professor of translation
HANNU LAUERMA, Turku, doctor of medicine
HEIKKI MAJAVA, Imatra, psychiatrist
ILKKA NIINILUOTO, Helsinki, professor of philosophy
MAARJA PÄRL LÕHMUS, Tartu, journalist
IMMO PEKKARINEN, Helsinki, doctoral student of literature
ERKKI PEKKILÄ, Helsinki, associate professor of ethnomusicology
PAULI PYLKKÖ, Helsinki, doctor of philosophy
ANTI RANDVIIR, Tartu, coordinator of semiotic studies program
HANNU RIIKONEN, Helsinki, professor of literature
KARI SALOSAARI, Helsinki, docent of theater studies
THOMAS A. SEBEOK, Bloomington, professor emeritus
VIKTOR SHIBANOV, Izhevsk, Udmurtia, writer
ANNE SIVUOJA-GUNARATNAM, Helsinki, assistant of musicology
EERO TARASTI, Helsinki, professor of musicology
SINIKKA TUOHIMAA, Oulu, professor of literature
HARRI VEIVO, Bruxelles, doctoral student of literature
VILMOS VOIGT, Budapest, professor

www.ingramcontent.com/pod-product-compliance
Lightning Source LLC
Chambersburg PA
CBHW050427240426
43661CB00055B/2302